Readers of *The Ram in a Thicket* write:

This book is a life changer. It allows folks like me to feel included and loved by a religion that saved my life and probably my buddies' lives in combat.

♦

This is the best breakthrough discussion on Christian Science I have ever seen—the world has need of your views. There is so much pain, judgment and divisiveness in communities and in families because of dogmatic approaches, and your words will be the bridge to reconciliation between others and in the hearts of each individual.

♦

Your writing just made my heart sing!

♦

The tone is as persuasive as the substance. You codify what so many of us have felt instinctively and have experienced.

♦

"Ram" encompasses a broad scope of reasoning. It probably speaks to many people because we all have different reasons for doing what we do. And, most of us do not want to repeat mistakes, such as bad religious policy, whether unwritten or written.

Rather than dictating a course of action, *The Ram in a Thicket* invites readers into an honest conversation and provides factual and intuitive food for thought.

I love your statement—'The healing Christ is the surprise guest by the Christian Scientist's hospital bedside.' This stresses the all-inclusive power of Love and healing. Like Abraham I was in a dire situation. The "ram in a thicket" appeared each time, and this has been for me clear proof of God's loving care and presence under any circumstance.

♦

First, let me say how valuable, even vital, I think your book is for anyone who has practiced, is practicing, or will practice Christian Science. The historical perspective your book explores is thought-provoking and eye-opening.

♦

This will bring freedom, relief, and peace of mind to many. I love your book. Very freeing. Thanks for putting into concrete terms these questions and case studies.

♦

A topic ripe for this age that needs thoughtful discourse and prayer. I respect this so much.

This is more than a book that you "can't put down." It's a book that you can't stop thinking about.

◆

I cried when I read it. You captured my story so well that I felt I was reliving it, only this time with great joy and gratitude.

◆

What you are writing about is what my wife and I talk about privately, but you have been willing to bring the discussion out into the open.

◆

I loved the quotes, examples, analogies. Even though I've been a student of Christian Science for nearly 70 years, I still found many concepts that were new that I needed to learn and much food for thought.

◆

Many, perhaps most Christian Scientists, will see themselves in this book. If not "through a glass, darkly," then in life-excerpts that had been puzzling. Imbibing this book left me with a sense of utter relief.

I actually read your book while at a medical clinic with my husband. I shared some things with him when I could, and he plans to read it as well. It was like a weight was being lifted off my shoulders.

◆

Maintains a balance of exposing errors of the past while maintaining a forward-looking positive perspective; I felt more buoyed than overwhelmed or discouraged.

◆

Your book is thoroughly thought out and researched. So marked with humane care.

◆

Reading your book is like having a really great discussion with a colleague!

THE RAM IN A THICKET
Rebirth and Reform in the Practice of Christian Science

FIRST EDITION
Copyright©2021 by George Wadleigh
All rights reserved. No part of this publication may be reproduced, stored in a retrieval system or transmitted, in any form or by any means–electronic, mechanical, photocopying, recording or otherwise–without prior written permission from the Author except for the inclusion of brief quotations in a review.

Inquiries should be addressed to:
GeorgeWadleigh@TheRamInAThicket.com
www.TheRamInAThicket.com

For information about this title or to order books and /or electronic media, contact:
Fairway Press, 5450 N. Dixie Hwy., Lima, Ohio 45807.
Email csr@csspub.com | Call (419) 227-1818 or (800) 241-4056.
(The Publisher, Fairway Press and its parent company CSS Publishing Company are not affiliated with the Christian Science Church).
Printed in the United States of America.

♦

Library of Congress Control Number: Cataloging–in–Publication Data

Names: Wadleigh, George, 1949- author. Title: The ram in a thicket : rebirth and reform in the practice of Christian Science / George Wadleigh. Description: Lima: Fairway Press, 2021. | Includes bibliographical references and index. | Identifiers: LCCN 2021013910 | ISBN 9781736760208 (paperback) | ISBN 9781736760215 (ebook) Subjects: LCSH: Health--Religious aspects--Christian Science. | Medicine--Religious aspects--Christian Science. | Christian Science. Classification: LCC BX6950 .W24 2021 | DDC 261.5/61--dc23
LC record available at https://lccn.loc.gov/2021013910

First Printing, 2021
ISBN-13: 978-1-7367602-0-8 (Paperback)
ISBN-13: 978-1-7367602-1-5 (ebook)

ACKNOWLEDGMENTS

I will always be grateful for the many contributions that have made this book possible. Research resources and staff at the Mary Baker Eddy Library in Boston, the Boston Public Library, and the New York Public Library provided me with invaluable materials. The countless hours and effort that friends have poured into *The Ram in a Thicket* will always be remembered by this author, though those gifts will be hard to ever repay. Those who have shared stories that were close to their hearts, but known by very few, were willing to give to this book what one person's writing could never accomplish.

While it is generally unwise to write a "book by committee," over one hundred friends and those associated with Christian Science have weighed in on and supplied much of the contents here, and the constructive comments and suggestions of many have helped shape these pages. Any credit for narratives and ideas that have come my way belongs to those valued contributors, and any blame for not accurately presenting experiences or ideas in this book rests solely with the author.

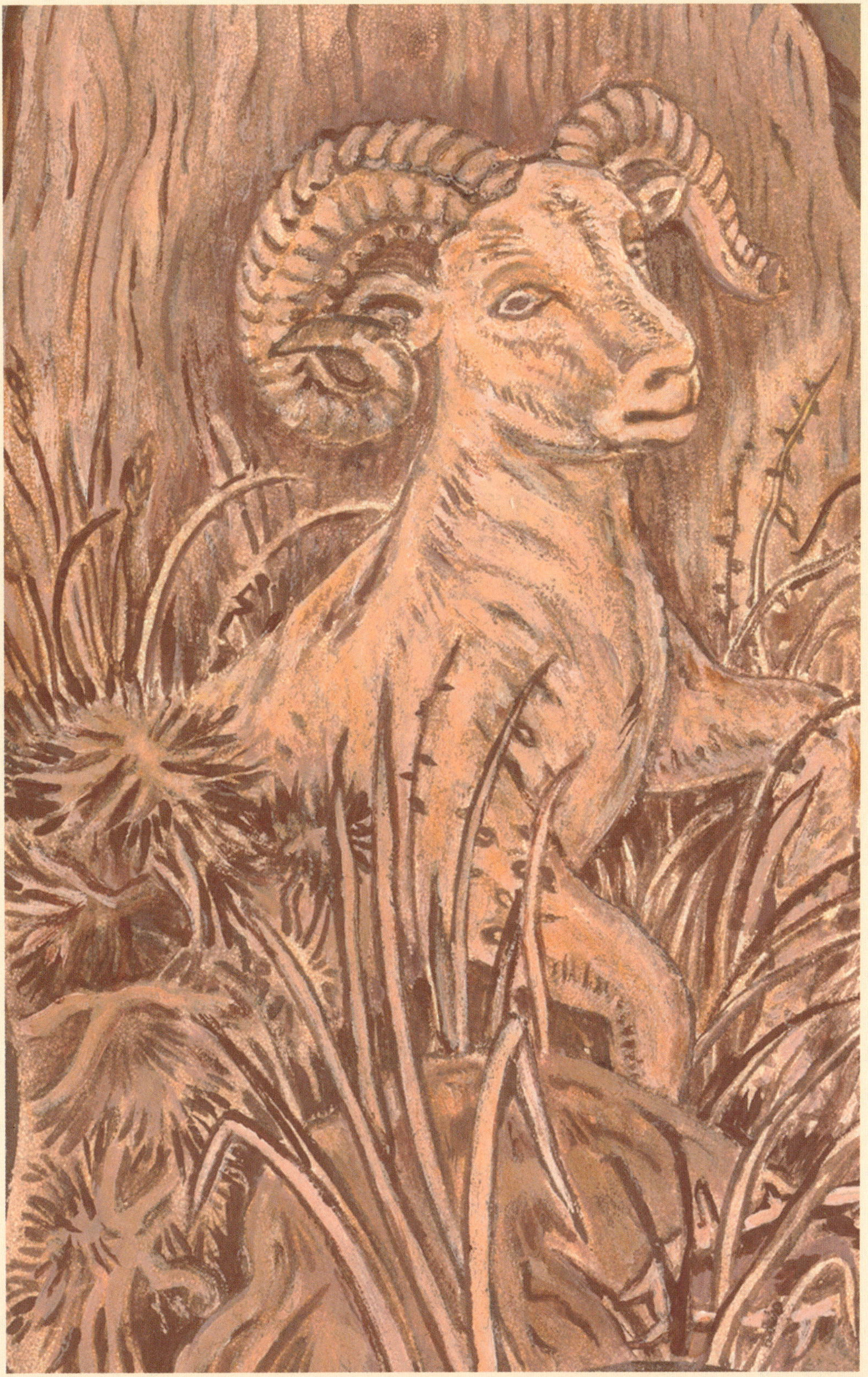

THE
RAM
IN A
THICKET

Rebirth and Reform
in the Practice of Christian Science

George Wadleigh

Fairway Press
Lima, Ohio

TO
M.D.W.

Contents

i	Preface
1	Introduction
3	**CHAPTER 1** **Prayer in a foreign land** —when Christian Scientists consider medical treatment
33	**CHAPTER 2** **Dogma** —hijacking travelers on the way of holiness
39	**CHAPTER 3** **"Radical"** —what happens when a word changes meaning and teaches fear instead of faith
65	**CHAPTER 4** **Billboards of sorrow and glory** —dealing with protracted physical problems
81	**REBUILDING TOGETHER**
83	**CHAPTER 5** **"First restore friendship…"** —reconciling differences in building unity
105	**CHAPTER 6** **Sitting at the end of the pew** —community and individualism and why spiritual life requires teamwork
125	**CHAPTER 7** **Peter's distraction** —evolving needs and church forms

141 **CHAPTER 8**
"As wide as the love of God"
—caring for others

147 **CHAPTER 9**
Guilt, blame, responsibility, blessed assurance

163 **CHAPTER 10**
Longevity, vision, life celebrations,
and comforting those who mourn

185 **CHAPTER 11**
Shutting the door on progress
—Christian Scientists' views of class,
race, gender, and identity

219 **CHAPTER 12**
Waking Eutychus
—youth leadership and mission work

233 **CHAPTER 13**
Earth helping the woman

251 **CHAPTER 14**
The Great Inclusion
—modesty in religion

263 **AN EXPLANATION**

265 **CHAPTER 15**
Isaac on the altar…and the ram in a thicket

275 **PROSPERING IN A SCIENTIFIC AGE**

277 **CHAPTER 16**
Time, place, and receptivity
—how our times and location
relate to spiritual healing

287 **CHAPTER 17**
The 1902 "Change of Front"
—an unknown compromise

299 **CHAPTER 18**
Getting Isaac off the altar

309 **CHAPTER 19**
The law and Saul's armor

329 **CHAPTER 20**
Listening to our ardent opponents

335 **CHAPTER 21**
Angel of mercy
—the work of Cathryn Keith

343 **CHAPTER 22**
The lesson of the grass
—the how and why of concessions

365 **CHAPTER 23**
Living with questions about prayer and medicine

387 **CHAPTER 24**
Accountability and standards for spiritual healing

419 **CHAPTER 25**
Satisfying Thomas
—how do Christian Scientists view diagnosis?

447 **CHAPTER 26**
Considering the lilies…
—the Spindrift research and prayer-testing

475 **CHAPTER 27**
When the coroner gave a testimony
—light at the darkest hour

487 **CHAPTER 28**
"The drums of dawn"
—the demand for rebirth and evolution in religious practice

495 **CHAPTER 29**
If…the future

505 Epilogue

507 Appendix

511 Selected Bibliography

521 Index

529 About the Author and Illustrator

Key

BIBLES

AMP	Amplified Bible	**MOF**	James Moffatt
ASV	American Standard Version	**NASB**	New American Standard Bible
CEB	Common English Bible	**NEB**	New English Bible
CEV	Contemporary English Version	**NIRV**	New International Reader's Version
CPV	Cotton Patch Version of Luke and Acts	**NIV**	New International Version
ERV	Easy-to-Read Version	**NKJV**	New King James Version
ESV	English Standard Version	**NLT**	New Living Translation
GNT	Good News Translation	**NLV**	New Life Version
ISV	International Standard Version	**NMB**	New Matthew Bible
JSB	Jewish Study Bible	**NRSV**	New Revised Standard Version
KJV	King James Version	**Phillips**	New Testament in Modern English—J.B. Phillips
KJ21	21st Century King James Version	**RSV**	Revised Standard Version
KJV2000	King James 2000 Bible	**TLB**	The Living Bible
MES	The Message	**TPT**	The Passion Translation

*All Bible passages not specificied are from the KJV.

WORKS BY MARY BAKER EDDY

S&H	*Science and Health with Key to the Scriptures*	**Ret.**	*Retrospection and Introspection*
Mis.	*Miscellaneous Writings*	**No.**	*No & Yes*
My.	*First Church of Christ, Scientist, and Miscellany*	**Hea.**	*Christian Healing*
		Un.	*Unity of Good*

EXPLANATION OF TERMS

Christian Scientists frequently refer to themselves informally as "Scientists" as Mormons refer to themselves in their own company as "Saints." Similarly, "Science," when capitalized, is church short-form for Christian Science. "Practitioner" most often refers to a Christian Science practitioner rather than a medical one. *Monitor*, *Journal*, and *Sentinel* are all used occasionally as short-form for their full names *Christian Science Monitor*, *Christian Science Journal* (also *C.S. Journal*), *Christian Science Sentinel* (also *C.S. Sentinel*).

"Mother Church," "Boston," and "Church headquarters" are used synonymously in referring to the Christian Science international center in Boston, Massachusetts. "Church," when capitalized, refers to the Christian Science organization, whereas "church," when not capitalized, may refer to our church or any other denomination. We have omitted the capitalization of the article "the" customarily used by Christian Scientists when referring to the Mother Church because other Christian churches such as the Catholic and African Methodist Episcopal Church also have "mother churches." The founder of Christian Science, Mary Baker Eddy, is regularly referred to as "Mrs. Eddy" because that familiar usage is common among Christian Scientists.

Preface

"And now the rest of the story...." [1]

THE RAM IN A THICKET is about mercy and honesty in religious practice. It is not a treatise on the theology of Christian Science. It brings to light the often-downplayed humane dimension in the practice and teachings of Christian Science, as well as pointing out dogma[2] which has for decades subordinated and concealed that humane dimension. Christian compassion, embodied in the life of Jesus, is the vital part of all Christian living, and is evident in the basic teachings of Christian Science and much of its practice.

In the following pages, the reader will discover important historical information that few church members are aware of. This book attempts to gather out stones from the path of faith without putting other stumbling blocks in their place.

The Old Testament prophet Gideon posed the problematic question: **"If the Lord is with us, ...where are all the miracles our ancestors have told us about?"** (Judges 6:13 *The Living Bible*) Gideon's question found an answer in his age by a refreshing of old signs and deeds, and Gideon himself helped lead a resurgence of faith among his people.

Prophets who succeeded Gideon needed to point out obstacles to

---

1. The signature line used by radio broadcaster Paul Harvey (1918-2009).
2. The term "dogma" has a diversity of meanings in the Christian world. *Webster's Dictionary* (1828), a text referred to by the founder of the Christian Science Church, defines dogma as "a settled opinion." Elsewhere we find this definition: **"a point of view or tenet put forth as authoritative without adequate grounds"** *Merriam-Webster* (2019). This author works from these definitions, which are quite distinct from definitions attached to that word, which other faiths subscribe to, and that equate *dogma* with divinely revealed truth.

the progress of Israel. Isaiah, Jeremiah, Micah, and other prophets made clear to their audience why things were the way they were, both from a human and spiritual standpoint. Nobody understands today without understanding yesterday.

If we don't point out "elephants in the room," that is, the significant undiscussed and unresolved problems at hand, how are we going to begin to usher those elephants out the door, or at least tame them? Progress must **begin with self-knowledge.**

The following chapters consider a variety of areas of controversy within the world of Christian Scientists and offer possible forward steps that Christian Scientists may consider and act upon. The primary focus of this work centers on the interaction between Christian Scientists and the field of medicine, because of the importance of that relationship. While these pages offer a critical assessment of current and past problems in the practice of Christian Science, they put forward positive potential solutions to those problems, and do not ignore the negative aspects of today's conventional medical practice. The chapters are both direct and hopeful. The reader is invited to take seriously the ideas and suggestions in these pages for their intended corrective value. The aim of this book is improvement of the practice of Christian Science, while pointing to promise for the future.

The Ram in a Thicket is not an exhaustive description of important matters. The author hopes to encourage a discussion but not put a capstone on that discussion. There's a herd of issues in the room, so let's get after them.

Introduction

A perfect storm creates the reason for this writing.

Problem 1
- the steady rise in global health-care costs
- the financial constraints on the world economy from the cost of conventional medicine
- an increasing shortage of primary-care doctors in the United States[1]
- the growing ineffectiveness of antibiotics to deal with resistant strains of disease
- most urgently of all—the world's present crisis of dealing with a pandemic and the possibility of future pandemics

Problem 2
- A small religious movement is staring at a discouraging picture of disappearing congregations and demoralization.

What does a seemingly insignificant religious crisis have to do with an apparently far greater crisis in the supply of the world's health care? Problem 1 seems so much more significant than Problem 2, as well as unrelated to it.

In this accident of history, the religious sect, Christian Scientists, have a choice to make: to either transform their practice in a way that

---

1. The Association of American Medical Colleges has projected that the United States, by the year 2032, will lack between 21,100 and 55,200 primary care physicians (AAMC press release 4-23-2019).

can help meet the demands of this present era, or be relegated to the back pages of religious history. Others can ultimately take up the mantle of expansive and unprejudiced spiritual healing. If either Problem 1 or Problem 2 occurred in isolation without the other, there might be no demand for serious change in the way organized religion and modern medicine interact. But the two problems have coincided in our time.

Much of what has been stated about Christian Science by its adherents in the past hundred years is reliable and useful, even when the writers' language has too often made the ideas difficult to access and nearly impenetrable for outsiders to the faith. Furthermore, the words of the Christian Scientists have too frequently failed to tell the full story of their Christian faith. The fog of religious dogma, making inroads on the practice of Christian Science, as dogma has done to other churches, and the subsequent mispractice of religion, have turned many away from even considering spiritual practice as relevant to a modern age, or as a societal factor that could remotely bless medical practice.

This book aims to clarify some of what has been said or done by those in the Christian Science faith that has been inaccurate or is unhelpful today, and it will point out how a practical and merciful application of religious teaching may help students of that teaching as well as aid society at large.

CHAPTER 1

Prayer in a foreign land
—when Christian Scientists consider medical treatment

How shall we sing the Lord's song in a strange land?

Psalm 137

Where can I go from your Spirit? Or where can I flee from your presence?

Psalm 139 International Version

EVERYONE THIS AUTHOR knows would like to be healthy without seeing a doctor. Doctors would as well.[1] Whether the recovery of bodily normalcy without a doctor's attention is called self-healing, outlasting self-limiting conditions, or spiritual healing, there is near-universal preference for healing without the cost and physical intrusion involved in medical care. But what happens when that healing does not occur for those who have sought it through alternative means, and those people feel impelled to turn to doctors for help?

Christian Scientists are supposed to be the people who "don't believe in doctors." Church members will tell you of spiritual healing experiences of their own or those of friends where no medical intervention was necessary. This chapter deals with the occasions, less often shared in Christian Science circles, where a church member actually ends up going to a hospital, or at least seriously considers that possibility. In later chapters we'll ask if the practice of Christian Science can survive in an age that has become far more

---

1. Thomas, *Youngest Science*, 220-232.

medically oriented than a century ago.[2] Can Christian Scientists coexist with, even cooperate in some ways and instances with, orthodox medical practice and still maintain their integrity in a fashion that benefits both the Christian Scientists and the physicians?

Let's first look at how Christian Scientists have fared in medical settings. The following experiences illustrate some of the struggles, disappointments, failures, and successes of Christian Scientists when they have confronted the possibility of medical involvement or by some circumstance have ended up in a hospital. If anyone has heard Christian Scientists speak proudly of not ingesting so much as an aspirin for decades, you could conclude that **going to a hospital should be a Christian Scientist's worst nightmare.** But we'll notice in the following stories an interesting combination of quandaries and solutions, sometimes showing up in the same hospital visit.

The thinking and circumstances that lead Christian Scientists to consider medical involvement vary greatly and are touched upon throughout this book. We will see individual lives in flux. The author has tried to present a variety of thought-processes, motivations, and different views from those he has interviewed, the totality of which shows similar themes but also a tapestry of individuality.

Michael's story

My family story includes interesting interactions between the medical and the spiritual. My grandmother was an RN. When later she started studying Christian Science, she soon discovered that she had seen her Christian Science teacher before.[3] Her teacher had been visiting patients and praying for them in the hospital where she had worked as a nurse. This was in

---

2. Getzen, Thomas E., "The Growth of Health Spending in the U.S.: 1776 to 2026." Getzen notes the proportion of U.S. GDP (Gross Domestic Product) devoted to health care rose from approximately 2.5% in 1900 to 18% in 2019.
3. A Christian Science teacher, as distinguished from a Sunday school teacher, is a practitioner who gives students of the faith "primary class instruction." This class consists of an intensive twelve-day course in the nuts and bolts of both the church's theology and the basics of spiritual healing. The initial class is followed up with study assignments, annual conferences, and other contact between the teachers and their students.

the 1930s. Perhaps it was less controversial then for a Christian Science practitioner to visit patients in hospitals.

I became serious about Christian Science because I had very severe migraine headaches. My parents took me to a doctor who worked with me for over a year, giving me multiple tests. The doctor said there was no hope for me with the migraines. My folks were not Christian Scientists at that time, but my dad would take my siblings and me to the Christian Science Sunday school and wait for us.

One day, (this would have been in the mid-1970s), my doctor asked my parents to leave the examining room so he could speak with me privately. Keep in mind that we lived in a very small town (pop. 2,000) where everyone knew your business. The doctor said to me, 'I know you go to the Christian Science church in town.' I said, 'Yes, sir.' He said, 'You know you can be healed by going there. Have you ever thought of that?' I said, 'No.' Because I had always gone to Sunday school just to talk about God. I hadn't thought about the power of God. But the doctor had thought about it.

That's when I started reading *Science and Health*,[4] and I found the migraines were of decreasing duration. I had a Sunday school teacher at that time who was very focused on healing, and we would talk about that subject for more than a few weeks at a stretch. By the time I was eighteen, I had a final healing of the migraine headaches.

Michael's hospital experience

About fifteen years ago in the spring, I was not doing well and was experiencing intense abdominal pain. My colleagues at work began to notice the tone of my skin was changing, and I became bedridden. Because the pain was so difficult, I could not pray for myself, so I called a Christian Science practitioner.[5] As we prayed together, the Love that I called God had new meaning for me. I began to understand that Love was promises kept. The ideas and prayers of the practitioner improved my physical condition, but I continued to be bedridden with a fever and ongoing pain. These symp-

---

4. The primary writing about Christian Science, first published by Mary Baker Eddy in 1875.
5. A Christian Science practitioner is someone engaged in the prayerful healing ministry of that faith.

toms, together with my absolute spiritual focus, were also beginning to scare my family and friends.

I now realize that even as I was learning a great deal about God as Love, I was also believing in a religious ideology that could have been fatal to me—that I would 'rather die than be treated in a hospital.' My Christian Science teacher said those words to me one evening, years before this particular trial of mine occurred. His thought lurked in the back of my mind. I later realized that I had taken what he told me out of context, and I certainly had not examined it in the light of either the Bible or Mrs. Eddy's writings. So I was making the dangerous mistake of taking the word of another church member as gospel instead of thinking about the 'common sense and common humanity' which Mrs. Eddy cites as prerequisites to 'evoke healing from the outstretched arm of righteousness' (S&H 365). But at that moment I wanted to have healing without medicine, without doctors, without a hospital.

I have a distinct memory of a dear friend from church coming to our house one morning to stand with my wife in urging me to go to the hospital. Rather than resisting them both, I realized that my love for my family and my love for Christian Science meant more to me than anything else. I remember the worried look on the faces of my two young children that morning. I remember feeling determined that these two precious kids must never grow up believing that Christian Science had killed their father. I loved my family more than that. I loved my church more than that. So I was prepared to abandon my Christian Science prayers for medical treatment. I dismissed the practitioner who had been praying for me, since I believed that medicine and Christian Science could not in any way combine. You did one, or you did the other. I believed that a trip to the hospital meant that I would be alone without my faith and without the God I had come to know as Love.

As my family drove me to the hospital that morning, I remembered that a doctor had once told me that a patient who could walk into a hospital had a high probability of walking out alive. So whether or not this was just that doctor's opinion or a medical dictum, I made the best attempt I could to walk through the hospital doors, but my efforts only resulted in me collapsing in an emergency room chair.

Before long the hospital's chief of thoracic surgery was at my bedside with a file of X-rays and medical test results. I thought he would begin medical treatment immediately, but he had another question:

- *'I see from your admittance papers that you are a Christian Scientist.'*
- *'Yes. But can you go forward with your treatments? I trust you will do what is needed.'*
- *'That's not my concern right now. I will help you, but I want to know more about Christian Science.'*

Sweet Jesus! Here I was experiencing the most intense physical pain I had ever felt, and this man wanted to know more about Christian Science. Yet his story and his reason for asking that question were so compelling that I forgot about my pain for a moment as he spoke.

The doctor told me about his next-door neighbor who refused to acknowledge him. He explained to me how this neighbor would call her children in from playing in the yard when the doctor drove up his driveway. He once overheard the neighbor tell her children to 'never speak to or look at that doctor ever again.' One day when the neighbor's son was outside playing, he fell and appeared to break his arm. The surgeon knew his mother was not going to get the arm set, so he fashioned a sling to support the child's arm. He knocked on the neighbor's door, offered the sling, and any other support he could give. Before he could finish speaking, the door was slammed in his face. [Author's note: The behavior expressed by the neighbor has absolutely no doctrinal basis in the writings of Christian Science, nor does, of course, her attitude. But Michael's doctor didn't know that. Have other Christian Scientists acted or spoken like this towards their medical brethren? We would only hope not.]

The doctor continued, 'After that, I could not believe that any Christian religion could be truly represented by people like that. So I bought a copy of Science and Health. *I've read the book twice so far, and Mary Baker Eddy has a lot of nice things to say about doctors. So I need to know what you think. Is Christian Science like my neighbor or like what I read in the book?'*

At this point in the doctor's story, tears were welling up in his eyes. I could see he really needed me to tell him the truth as a Christian Scientist, and I did.

'Yes, Mrs. Eddy had a lot of nice things to say about doctors.'

The surgeon was relieved. He told me that my liver had a dangerous virus. He would perform surgery the next morning, but he could not guarantee the result. He would need my prayers to keep me alive. Later that afternoon my practitioner contacted me in the hospital. She assured me that the power of God was very much with me right where I was, and that power would never leave me, no matter what place or circumstance I was in. She told me that my love for my family and my church was my reason for being in the hospital, and this love would only bring truth closer to me than ever before. She reminded me that taking any Christian Scientist's words for gospel was not what anyone expected of me. She assured me that she would pray for me right then, and that I should rouse my thought and pray for myself as well. At that moment, I realized that both my doctor and my church needed me to pray, and I soon began to see the effects of this new view of prayer.

As I began to continue praying in my hospital bed, I saw that the painkillers [morphine] *that the nurses were administering had no effect on my pain.* [Author's note: See Chapter 23 on the relation of prayer and medicine]. *Finally, one of the nurses told me the surgeon had said another shot would only kill me; I needed to overcome the pain myself without any morphine.* So I prayed that evening for the pain to subside, and it did.

Michael's surgery happened the next day, and it was successful. Doctors found that the damage caused by the virus had remained confined to his liver.

That afternoon I was sitting, standing, and walking around my hospital room. I took my first meal in weeks that evening after losing over forty pounds from my ordeal. A radiologist who assisted with the operation came to my room, saw me, stood speechless, and then said, 'Pardon me, but I have never had the experience of operating on someone in the morning and then seeing them completely recovered in the afternoon. I am shocked.'

In spite of my improved condition, the doctors' concern over the virus kept me in the hospital for a few more days. After a series of tests, it was determined that indeed all was well. My surgeon put it best when, in summing everything up, he said, 'Whatever has happened here, there is certainly enough credit to spread around.'

Michael's reflections on his experience

There were two 'doctor referrals' in what I've described of my life's story, first when the physician recommended prayer help for me in my teenage years, and then more recently when the surgeon asked me to help his work and my survival through prayer. Some doctors are willing to step over the bridge, the understanding gap between us Christian Scientists and the physicians.

Where was the doctor's neighbor or where was I, up until the time I went in for surgery? Are we Christian Scientists willing to step over that bridge from our side and help close the gap? Many doctors are seeing this stuff. How come so many of us can't? How come so many of us have been anti-doctor? Christian Science is not antithetical to what is best in medicine, and vice versa. We are all healers learning what real healing is all about. We need to support each other as God gives us the light to understand what that support may be in any particular case.

After my hospital experience, I spoke with my teacher's wife. She asked me, 'Did my husband tell you in your class instruction, or in any association meeting, or in a church lecture about his preference 'to die rather than to go to a hospital'? I said, 'No.' He had said it only in a private conversation with me. 'Good,' she replied, 'because that is not Christian Science. That is fundamentalism.'

So we are not about a priesthood or tradition or ritualism or fundamentalist beliefs or sayings. We should all be scientists trying to figure out how to work out our problems, and to really understand what we're needing to see. The answer that came to me is powerful, as Moses discovered [Exodus 4] when he handled the snake and watched it become a staff. The spiritual authority that Moses saw behind that experience led his people forward. What I've been learning through my experience is very profound, to the point where people are calling me for prayer help, and I've been able to help others.

What the doctor gave me that I treasure beyond his surgical work was his realization: 'I need you (Michael) to pray.' This ongoing theme of in-

teresting interactions with medical folks runs through my life, even when I have resisted it.

Prayer in hospitals, and what is gained

There are so many cases like mine where people like me want to be healed by God but may end up in the hospital for a variety of reasons. Deep down we know that we're going to be healed by God, as we see it, regardless of the medical treatment we receive. We may have arrived at the conclusion that, 'I'll just have to do this alone with God, with no help or encouragement from my fellow Christian Scientists.' That's just wrong. And I want to say in my case I had been wrong. The practitioner who had been praying with me before I went into the hospital wanted to continue to pray with me after I was admitted. I said, 'I've got to dismiss you.' She said, 'But, Michael, I can do this.' I said, 'No.' Now that was where my thinking was at that point. She wasn't refusing to help me. My thought gradually got untangled.

We can work and discover for ourselves and perhaps share with others that you can go to a hospital and be shot up with all kinds of pain-killers and have people cut into you, and you can come out a stronger Christian Scientist than ever before because you did that for unselfish reasons. You did it out of love for God, but also out of your love for your church, and your love for your family and friends.

"*The very circumstance, which your suffering sense deems wrathful and afflictive, Love can make an angel entertained unawares*" *(Science and Health, 574).*

Being guided

Most Christians in a medical setting naturally pray that their doctor will be guided to do the right thing. Non-believers hope for the same thing. Since your average Christian Scientist's experience might have included little or no time under a doctor's care, he or she often doesn't know what to think about in regard to surgery. One church member who went through surgery wrote: *I asked myself, is the surgical team being guided by intelligence or non-intelligence? By love or by a lack of love? I found the obvious answer to those questions both helpful and comforting.*

Prayer during surgery

Another Christian Scientist had this to say:
Several years ago, I had surgery to remove cancer. The doctors were hesitant to proceed because of my weight, but they went ahead. My Christian Science practitioner told me to give a message to the head surgeon: 'It is God's hands doing the surgery.'[6]

I told the surgeon that, and he gave me a hug. The team wasn't positive about the outcome. Three days later I saw the surgeon, and he told me: 'Tell your friend he was right. It was like someone was clearing a path for us.' I've had yearly check-ups since that time and have developed a friendship with the surgeon. Today he looks at me and says, 'Yeah, it was God.'

In discussing surgery in *Science and Health*, Mrs. Eddy wrote:
Until the advancing age admits the efficacy and supremacy of Mind, it is better for Christian Scientists to leave surgery and the adjustment of broken bones and dislocations to the fingers of a surgeon, while the mental healer confines himself chiefly to mental reconstruction and to the prevention of inflammation.

S&H 401

These words from the Christian Science textbook have never appeared in our church's Lesson-Sermons in the past half-century to the author's knowledge, and the above passage rarely shows up elsewhere in church-wide discussions or in the church magazines. This helps explain why there is so little clarity on the subject of surgery among Christian Scientists.

The consequent absence of this passage about surgery from the average Christian Scientist's attention creates a void and leaves room for dogma to take the place of actual church teaching. The displacing dogma encourages many Christian Science practitioners to tell their

---

6. This counsel from the practitioner might appear atypical for a Christian Scientist, but it evidently resulted from the practitioner's inspiration.

patients that if and when they engage a surgeon, the practitioner must stop praying for that patient.

But don't Mrs. Eddy's words about surgery suggest that a practitioner may indeed be prayerfully engaged for their patient while surgery is going on? *While* means "during" and "at the same time" (Webster's *American Dictionary of the English Language, 1828*). The Christian Science practitioner may be prayerfully treating something that is not being aided by the surgical procedure, and so the practitioner is not competing with the doctor's work. The passage above about surgery suggests that the mental healer can be productive and not just "sitting on the sidelines" when their patient is in the middle of surgery.

A surgeon, while he is working, may not be able to doctor his patient's fear, his own fears, or handle by his surgical skill any number of possible bodily functions or malfunctions, such as inflammation or infection, that could occur during or after an operation. So here is opportunity for constructive prayerful action that is too often overlooked. Certainly, this subject calls out for further exploration and examination by Christian Scientists.

In regard to the subject of prayer and surgery, it's interesting to read the following account from a friend of the author that describes a practitioner whose healing career began in the early 1900s. (Margaret Matters took practitioner training in 1911, and her work in healing extended until her passing in 1964. She authored two well-known hymns in the *Christian Science Hymnal*.)

Margaret Glenn Matters was more complex than people believe, but that's probably true of everyone. She was known as very 'orthodox' in many ways; she stood up for what she felt was correct (so she would have seemed dogmatic to those who didn't agree with her). She was practical in ways that might have seemed incompatible with her image.

There was a case which she took involving the son of one of her students. This boy's face had been ripped open by a fishing line in a boating accident, and the local M.D. had butchered the surgery with a really bad sewing job, distorting the child's face. The mother took her son to Mrs. Matters. She evaluated the situation, including obviously the mental state of the mother and the child and what they were ready to accept. She then told the mother that she had among her acquaintances a plastic surgeon and could make that contact if that was their choice.

They did choose that way, and Mrs. Matters prayerfully supported the corrective surgery through the whole day it took. Afterwards, the surgeon said it was almost a holy experience for him. He obviously respected Mrs. Matters from prior contact and was willing to work with her. He felt as if God was guiding his hand in an operation that was so challenging that it seemed beyond even his expertise to effect a total restoration, with no trace of what had happened.

When I saw the son decades later as an adult, there was absolutely no trace of the accident or the surgery. The whole circumstance strengthened both the mother and the son in their faith and understanding and showed that Christian Scientists don't neglect such cases by saying there had to be 'radical reliance' with absolutely no surgical intervention. Yet Mrs. Matters definitely taught 'radical reliance.'[7] The question would be though, could Mrs. Matters have handled the case entirely metaphysically without any medical involvement, given the thought and experience of the mother and son? She took this on perhaps as a situation where it was not 'humanly possible' to reverse all the effects of the mishandled surgery without further corrective plastic surgery. It was an opportunity to reinforce the faith of mother, son, and her surgeon friend.

For some, this practice would have been viewed as inconsistent with Mrs. Matters' teaching. Today, I think, there would be far greater acceptance of this solution among Christian Scientists, and less tendency to condemn those who made this choice (whether the teacher, practitioner, or patient).[8]

What Christian Scientists can do for their hospitalized church friends

- Be there for them and with them.
- Don't worry about what to say. Your actual presence speaks volumes.
- If you're a church friend or the family's practitioner, be happy to join your friends at the hospital, or go with them, especially if it's

---

7. See examination of this teaching in Chapter 3.
8. For more on this subject see Chapter 23.

a new experience for them. The emergency room is a lot warmer place with supportive friends there.

- Before the visit, digest the first few pages in "Christian Science Practice" (*Science and Health*, 362–367) about the crucial need for a compassionate, humane attitude. These pages constitute a Christian Science version of the Hippocratic Oath.

> **The Lord is in this place; and I knew it not.**
> [the words of Jacob in the wilderness as he fled from Esau]
> Genesis 28:16

- "First learn to bind up the broken-hearted" as in the above-cited pages).
- In whatever way you can, point out to your friends in the hospital, if they are tempted to feel guilty, that there is no basis for their feeling that way. They are the loved of God, and Love comes nearer when and where we are hurting, and Love doesn't stop at the hospital door. The Bible is full of heroes whose faith faltered at times, and whether anyone goes or doesn't go to a hospital should never be the test of their faith in God.
- Remind your friends that Mrs. Eddy took morphine on several occasions to relieve the severe pain from kidney stones, but that didn't stop her prayerful work, her prayer for her church, or her spiritual advancement.

When a "miracle man" and a spiritual "failure" live in the same body

After over a year of persistent prayer accompanied by discouraging bodily debility, a lifelong Christian Scientist decided he had to go to a hospital. A church friend drove him there. The doctors diagnosed him with cancer against his spinal column. They warned him of his slight chances of survival, and then the surgical board narrowly approved (by a vote of 6–5) proceeding with surgery. In this man's words:

> *I don't remember much of my hospital conversation with the doctors. I do know that the head surgeon said that the cancer had tentacles like an octopus. And, much to the doctor's amazement, and that of the other*

surgeons and nurses, the thing came out of me in one pull and in one piece 'as if it wanted no part of me.' The doctor called it a 'miracle.' I was the 'miracle man.' The odds of success for the surgery were very poor. Sadly, I thought of it as a failure on my part as a Christian Scientist.

Why the miracle of the cancer coming out as it did, I'm unsure. The surgeon's statement that 'the cancer came out as if it wanted no part of you' is spooky. He had never seen such a thing. I can't testify that it was a healing through Christian Science because it all goes counter to what I was taught. It is very interesting though!

So the doctor calls the outcome a "miracle," but the church member feels he has betrayed his faith because his recovery did not take place in a medicine-free setting. Was his year of prayer for nothing? Evidently not, but it took a medical intervention to reveal that fact. This is the unpredictable medicalized zone, infused with God's presence, where Christian Scientists have been reluctant to tread. It is the place where varying perceptions coincide and collide. There is some heat and plenty of light.

Fully supported and calming the fear

Heather had stomach cramps, nausea, and vomiting. She began praying with a practitioner, but the pain continued for four days. Family members encouraged her to go to the hospital, and Heather agreed she would.

Heather's mom:
The practitioner was supportive of us doing what we felt was needed. Once the issue of going to the hospital came up, we [Heather's mom and dad] *let Heather know we supported her. I had this sense that maybe now the fear was broken, and we could move on. Since it was late Friday night, and many doctors would be off-duty, I asked Heather if it would be okay to wait until morning. She said that was fine. We called the practitioner back and got some ideas to work with, which Heather really liked. She was more relaxed. She slept well. I was really confident all would be well in the morning. Sure enough, Heather woke up the next day and bounded out of bed so happy at how good she felt.*

In reflecting on this incident, I believe the turning point came when Heather felt supported in her choice without judgment. It helped dissipate the fear so she could be absolutely receptive to the prayer that had happened before the crisis and during it.

There may be a placebo effect going on when anyone believes that help is "on the way," and the body is relieved by this prospect of help. Would it be useful and honest for Christian Scientists to point out when a placebo effect may be at play in their healing experiences?

Patty's daughter: "deprived" of medicine

My daughter felt deprived of medicine. Her dad is not a Christian Scientist. When she was feeling very ill one day, we took her to the Emergency Room. Out of the whole deal all she did was take an aspirin, and she vomited that up. Shortly after that she was fine. She had to discover for herself that medicine is no panacea. But we as parents learned that fighting the desire to go to the doctor was not necessarily the answer.

Testimony from a Christian Science nurse… more placebo effect

I nursed for a family whose child was running a fever. They released the practitioner when the condition remained unchanged, and they called another practitioner. Finally, when the fever persisted, they called a pediatrician, went for an appointment, and on the way to the hospital, the child's fever broke.

In this situation, a Christian Scientist might say simply, "The problem was the parents' fear." But shouldn't we remember that Jesus did not forego using an occasional placebo-like treatment in his healing ministry when the situation warranted it? Mud and saliva on a blind man's eyes, the laying on of hands in various instances, home visits sometimes. The only recorded instances we have of Jesus pointing to anyone's lack of faith involved his disciples. When Jesus' disciple Peter fell down in his attempt to walk on water, Jesus said, "Oh you of little faith, why did you doubt?" (Matthew 14:31 NKJV) He met people where they were, and brought light and life to them, instead of attempting to drag struggling mortals where they were not ready to go.

Failed prayer and the magic aspirin

Another placebo story—a newer student of Christian Science was praying about his headache, but the headache persisted, so the Christian Scientist took an aspirin. He was shocked to see that the headache went away immediately as soon as the aspirin passed his lips, and before the pill could be digested. (Aspirin generally takes at least thirty minutes to start working in the body.) When he was asked if the aspirin incident had affected his faith or not, the Christian Scientist said that he recognized better the mental cause and effect relationship between illness and medicine. A friend commented later to him that a belief in the aspirin as instant relief had removed the headache and not any pharmacological effect.

Dr. Doom and quieting "devils' talk"

Today there are hospitals that have replaced crucifixes on some of their walls with comforting, empowering passages from the Psalms. The Catholic hospital in the author's hometown has done this. So when you see a hospital called St. John's Mercy, you may find signs of that mercy quite visible without ever having to speak with a chaplain. It's not uncommon to encounter doctors who encourage the spiritual as well as physical progress of their patients. But for whatever reasons, there are some physicians who could use some tutoring in bedside manners. These doctors make a practice of giving unqualifiedly blunt prognoses of worst-case scenarios to those entrusted to their care.

A Christian Scientist was hospitalized and was given dire predictions, with no hint of any positive possibilities, for their health outcome by "Dr. Doom," their physician. A sympathetic nurse waited for the doctor to exit the room, and she watched as he walked down the hall. When she returned to the patient's bedside, she said in a strong stage whisper, "Don't listen to all that stuff the doctor told you. It's just devils' talk." She encouraged her patient in his prayers and trust in the Almighty's healing power. Her encouragement helped the Christian Scientist walk through that valley of fear.

Dealing with medical entanglement

What if a Christian Scientist encounters not just one "Dr. Doom" but an overall prognosis, based on medical tests, and projected plans of on-going medical treatment that look like they will continue forever or will end in the patient's certain demise? This problem does not just apply alone to Christian Scientists but to everyone in our society. A century ago and less, doctors would have been willing to cease treatment for any number of ailments and remand patients to self-care at home.

Today, even if patients are dismissed from a hospital, a prolonged train of everything from physical therapists to hospice workers can follow them home. This protocol is well-meaning and intended to be therapeutic, but it can be very entangling, especially for a Christian Scientist who is used to simple forms of self-care together with their prayerful treatment.

As we have stated earlier, we live, especially in Western nations, in a culture that is super-saturated with medical information. The author visited a hospital that posted every thirty days a notice called "disease awareness month." The administration must have realized that patients needed more awareness since there were two diseases that everyone needed to be aware of during that month. What does a Christian Scientist do when snared in ongoing cycles of medical tests and treatment?

More than placebo healing—light in the ICU

From a practitioner friend: *In 2014, after several years as a full-time practitioner listed in our church magazines, I awoke in severe discomfort and went to the hospital where I was diagnosed with acute heart failure and rushed to the coronary ICU where I lay for three days and nights, given meds every few hours, attached to a heart monitor, and with IVs drip-*

ping in both arms. At night, the only light was a computer screen. On the third night, I began to wonder if I should give up hope. After all, it seemed I had no more choices left in life, I felt so alone, and it appeared God was not there. (In my Christian Science practice, I had told several patients I could pray for them 'until they walked through the hospital door.')

I dozed off with these sad thoughts, but later was awakened by a brilliant light. The light was so bright that the ICU appeared really beautiful. I looked around and said 'wow!' and then heard these words clearly. I AM HERE NOW, AND I KNOW YOU. Suddenly I felt very happy! I knew it was God, who cared enough to remind me of His presence in a way I could understand. What more could anyone ask for? I wrote the words on a card before the light faded, to prove I was not dreaming.

Ten days later I was sent home with instructions to 'enjoy life and let your heart heal.' I didn't know until later that the doctors only expected me to live another few months to maybe a year. At home I first needed a wheelchair, then a walker, then a cane; in a few months I could move almost normally again. When I returned three months later for an echocardiogram, the cardiologist was astonished. 'When you came to us, you had the worst heart I'd ever seen that was still beating,' he admitted. 'But look at it now. The clot is gone. Your heart is healthy.' He laughed and told me not to buy any lottery tickets, because 'you've used up all your luck.' I told him about the voice I heard in the ICU. He said to always heed that voice. 'It restored your hope,' he said.

When I had come home at first from the hospital, church members were very supportive. One member brought twenty delicious prepared suppers. Another sent flowers. Two others accompanied my wife and me back to the hospital for follow-up visits, and helped my wife push my wheelchair. Even a busy member with three small children offered to help! A few months later, the Wednesday church readings were about 'light' and I told of seeing a bright light in the ICU. One member emailed me afterward, 'There wasn't a dry eye in the house, including mine. We're all behind you.'

Was this man's recovery hindered in any way by his going to the ICU? Do you think the unhesitating, embracing love of the church congregation had anything to do with his healing? He had sensed God's unconditional presence and love in the ICU, and then he must have felt that continuing blessed assurance when he came home. He felt it, and his doctor saw the outcome.

Under medical supervision for a higher calling

A young Christian Scientist was taken by his mother for regular check-ups over a period of several months with a local physician because of a persistent heart murmur. After the healing of that condition which the doctor acknowledged, the boy's mom concluded: "We actually were in that doctor's clinic to answer a call to be disciples rather than feeling we were out of our element, or that we just wanted to get out of there as soon as possible."

Prayer and medical verdicts for Christians

You don't have to be a Christian Scientist to run into faith conflicts in the hospital.

While most Christians see no problem with prayer in medical settings combined with conventional medical treatment, there can still be clashes between those believers of various faith-backgrounds engaged in persistent prayer and their skeptical medical caregivers. In a 1996 *Guideposts* article Linda Shublak testified about her prayer-battle in the resuscitation of her husband from what was diagnosed as his "brain-dead" state.

David Shublak had been hit by a car while jogging. During the time when David was on life-support and showing no encouraging signs of normal brain activity, Linda visited his hospital room, sang hymns, and read Scripture to him. "A neurosurgeon stopped me in the hall... 'Get a grip on reality,' she told me. 'Stop talking about miracles!' For someone usually so awed by authority, I wasn't the slightest bit intimidated. 'Our God is a mighty healer,' I replied simply."

A week after the initial accident, Linda Shublak wrote in her diary: "Buzzers and beeps resound in my husband's room—signs of life to all who hear that Jesus Christ is the healer!" David recovered from his vegetative state and returned to active military duty.[9]

What too few of us want to admit

Grace for the fearful believer or Christian Scientist, whose prayers have frozen up, may take the form of medical help. Grace for the physician who has failed to heal his patient with conventional medicine may take the form of prayer that heals that patient.

Pronounced spiritual healings—*inside* hospitals

In a special issue of the *Christian Science Journal* in 1991 appeared an article describing the healing of Brian Emerson who was crushed in a construction accident in California. Brian had so many broken bones (thirty-three) that the attending physicians hardly knew where to begin helping him. His wife called a practitioner who prayed diligently for him, and sixteen days later Brian walked out of the hospital. Should Brian's practitioner have hesitated to pray for a hospitalized patient? Could his healing have happened anywhere but in a hospital in our medicalized age?

Lastly, what did not appear in the printed testimony of Brian's recovery is a fascinating point—Brian's practitioner during this healing experience was a woman who was quadriplegic, paralyzed from the neck down. Though that practitioner was not healed as Brian was, her disability did not keep her from being able to capably pray for Brian. Let this woman's example be an encouragement to anyone who thinks they can't pray for somebody because they're not "good enough," or they haven't had enough healing experiences of their own.

---

9. Shublak, "Covered with the Word," *Guideposts*, 28.

Location vs. Motivation

"It's not where they're located; it's what they're thinking about."
A Christian Science teacher

Is there an uncomfortable parallel between the prohibitions against healing "work" on the Sabbath in Jesus' time, and the belief, far too common among Christian Scientists, that real, spiritual healing can never happen in a medical setting?

The "gold standard" and other healing

In medical practice the "gold standard,"[10] or "best practice," is the optimum treatment in quality and quantity. It is what is considered generally in the field to include the most favorable conditions and treatment conducive to a patient's recovery. A Christian Scientist's "gold standard" healing might likely consist of total, whole-hearted reliance upon God with no medicine given—a healing effected in the company of supportive believers. This chapter points out that the **exceptions to the "gold standard" of healing in Christian Science are quite capable of accomplishing healing.**

From a Biblical perspective, Jesus' "gold standard" in spiritual healing might be exemplified in the regeneration of the Roman centurion's servant (Matthew 8). The centurion had such faith that he felt no need for Jesus to personally visit his servant. Jesus' spiritual command was sufficient.

But in many other circumstances, Jesus healed people whose lack of "gold standard" receptivity might have made them unpromising candidates for Christian recovery. Even the man whom Jesus pointed to as an epitome of great faith, the Roman centurion, would have fallen far short of the ideal in the eyes of some of Jesus' followers, especially Simon (not Peter), the anti-Roman Zealot.

Jesus healed those with half-faith and those with superstitious faith.

---

10. Segen (ed.) *The Dictionary of Modern Medicine*. "Any standardized, clinical assessment, method, procedure, intervention or measurement of known validity and reliability which is generally taken to be the best available, against which new tests of results and protocols are compared."

He was not above using placebos (John 9:6). In one case he needed to pray twice to heal a blind man. He appeared to grudgingly go along with the local tradition (not a Christian one) of demonology or animism which included the conviction that in order for demons to authentically exit from someone, those demons had to go somewhere else, and could not just disappear into thin air (Mark 5 and Luke 8). All this was less than "gold standard."

So it is only dogma, ingrained prejudice, and custom which have established benchmarks for healing by Christian Scientists which are more exclusive than in Mrs. Eddy's era, let alone those standards for healing in Jesus' time. Christian Science dogma, not doctrine, has traditionally excluded medical involvement in any way as a helpful factor. If a healing doesn't fit into our metaphysical glass slipper, we reject it or discount it as "not a Christian Science healing." This is said as we look down our noses at disparaged but improved and rejuvenated mortals.

Mrs. Eddy and the "gold standard"

Science and Health includes healings which Mrs. Eddy witnessed before she had fully formulated in her own mind what she called a science of healing Christianity. In one instance, she took on a patient suffering from edema, formerly called *dropsy*. The poor woman "looked like a barrel" (*S&H* 156). She had been unsuccessfully treated by a doctor, but Mrs. Eddy began her work by first giving the woman homeopathic doses of the same medicine previously administered to the patient by her doctor. Then as the patient began to improve, she tried unmedicated pills, or placebos, and kept doing that until the woman recovered entirely. *Science and Health* cites many mental factors, in the cause of or recovery from illness, which lie beyond the fence of today's common Christian Science practices (for example, Sir Humphrey Davy's use of a thermometer having a healing impact; the Oxford students' experiment on a prisoner; the aforesaid woman with edema—see *S&H* pages 152, 379, and 156).

Did Mrs. Eddy ever belittle a healing as sub-par because it happened under less than perfect circumstances? She even allowed for the spiritual treatment of those who were under a doctor's care...under specific conditions. "If the patient is in peril," (*Mis.* 89) "it is humane, and not unchristian, to do him all the good you can…" She is clearly not talking here about bringing flowers or get-well cards to the bedside but says this in answer to the question about giving prayerful help while a patient remains under medical supervision. Mrs. Eddy warns in this instance that the attempted healing aid may likely be met with resistance or spite, *but she in no way discourages the attempt from being made.*

"In peril" suggests times when conventional medical treatment is not helping a patient. Why wouldn't patients want a new offer of help at a juncture when their conventional treatment did not appear to be working, and why shouldn't a Christian Scientist be willing and happy to meet a friend's need at such a time? This type of situation has been generally overlooked by Christian Scientists in relation to their patients, and that is to our detriment. We will delve more into this subject in Chapter 23. (Also see chapters on "Lesson of the Grass" and "Radical.")

"Never let your patient die"

From the recollection of one of Mrs. Eddy's students:

In talking at another time in regard to healing, she [Mrs. Eddy] said, ***"Give your patient the best treatment you can, then leave the case to God. Never keep a patient in your thought."***

"If a case does not respond quickly, should I advise another practitioner?" I asked.
"No," she said, "that would instantly suggest fear. If the patient desires a change, let him make it."

"If [Christian] *Science is not bringing out a case, what then?" I said.*
"Never let your patient die," was her reply.[11]

---

11. Baker, 48. Confirming the recollection of Anna White Baker are the notes of Mary Armstrong of her primary class instruction (1887) with Mrs. Eddy which indicate that there were dire emergencies where Mrs. Eddy expected her students to be open to medical help when the Christian Scientists' prayers had not proved to be adequate to the situation. See McNeil, Vol. III, 1356–1357.

What does this conversation suggest? That Christian Scientists pray so concertedly that no one ever dies under their prayerful treatment? Or that there are some emergencies when medical treatment should take place in order to save the life of the patient?

Wrinkles in the stereotype and cautions

The healing of Mrs. Eddy (though she was Mary Baker Glover Patterson at that time in her life), often seen by Christian Scientists as the "falling apple" of the discovery of Christian Science, occurred when Mrs. Eddy was still under a doctor's care. Mrs. Patterson was initially given morphine and then possibly arnica, as a form of pain relief and bruise reduction—all administered by the homeopath Dr. Alvin Cushing after her accident and shortly before her initial recovery.[12] This fact does not fit the stereotype of how Christian Scientists have idealized Mrs. Eddy's recovery in 1866 as free of any medical services. Treatment with arnica may not possess a rapid resuscitating power to revive someone who has been seriously injured; however, the presence of the homeopathic doctor's attentions concurrent with the vigorous prayer which Mrs. Patterson was engaged in at that time is usually not mentioned when Mrs. Patterson's recovery is discussed by Christian Scientists.

Caution!

The purpose of this writing is not to fully explore the norm or mean of Christian Science healing practice, or to belittle the "gold standard" of spiritual healing. But we cannot exclude from our fellowship and church-wide discussion what has often skirted the edges of the norm. This book does not dispute the great usefulness of a "gold standard" of healing as much as it challenges its exclusivity. Critics may be tempted to assume that this author recommends against a whole-hearted spiritual approach to healing. That is far from the truth. The reason that anomalies or outliers of healing by Christian Scientists, those that do

---

12. Peel, *Years of Discovery*, 196. See also, McNeil, *A Story Untold*, Vol. I, 189–205.

not conform to the traditional norm, must be examined is that indifference to these unusual healings has resulted not in clearer metaphysics, but in a one-note symphony, if such could be possible. To a Christian Scientist, God and Christ are united and yet multiform in essence and expression. Therefore, any monotone expression of an expansive idea turns away multitudes from a healing teaching and is an incomplete and dishonest depiction of spiritual healing in its entirety.

As Paul expanded the Christian tent…

Just as the Apostle Paul expanded the vision of the Christian world from a narrow, geographically confined and culturally swaddled point of origin, so the world of the Christian Scientists of the twenty-first century can be opened to include the widening needs of humanity. The author contends that an excluding prejudice, similar to that which kept the non-Jewish world separate from Christian teachings in the Christian movement's earliest years, has repeated itself in the years immediately following the passing of the founder of Christian Science. This excluding prejudice has based its credentials on passages isolated from other qualifying or counter-balancing statements while all the time claiming to be the full gospel of the teaching of spiritual healing. It is high time to point out the "rest of the story."

Legitimizing honest effort

"Several years ago, I had an awakening: Individuals, no matter who they are, are doing the best they can."

A Christian Scientist college professor

Let's think about this observation. The man who said the foregoing has been battle-tested by serious family health-issues and feels stronger spiritually for the battle. But he can look out and see others in this supportive manner. Is he being too forgiving? Both Moses and Jesus would have had all their followers be prophets and healers, whereas their more cold-hearted followers sought punishment and exclusion for those whose practice was a little different in a slight dimension from their "brand" (Numbers 11:26-29 and Mark 9:38-40).

Mrs. Eddy worked hard to embrace and reconcile with renegade students. She wrote: "Who is afraid of being too generous has lost the power of being magnanimous" (*My.* 165).

> *magnanimous:* **great of mind, lit. of great spirit, elevated in soul or in sentiment, brave, not selfish** (Webster's 1828)

Fearing slippery slopes of tolerance

Do Christians or Christian Scientists fear that by being too tolerant of their fellows' weaknesses (as they see them), that tolerance will "give away the store"? Christian Scientists refer to it as a "slippery slope," especially when discussing medical interludes in the lives of their fellow church members.[13] Or they say that once the camel of unconventional approach gets his nose in the tent, watch out! Or "the horse is almost out of the barn." Perhaps directly because of our intolerance and hardness of heart, the horse isn't just out of the barn, he's two miles down the road. And as for the camel…he walked into the tent, and then left it for a tent where he could actually stand up.

Yes, there are times when Christian Scientists and anyone in Western society and elsewhere can become tied up in apparently endless tests and hospital stays that do not lead to a restoration of health. Those can indeed become "slippery slopes." Those times may become not so much a downward slide of losing one's spiritual belief-system, but, more so, they can lead to a loss of hope in the prospects of life itself. A major point of this book is that **Christian Scientists have not in the past hundred years been unqualifiedly supportive of their spiritual brothers and sisters enough,** so that when our church members have sought out medical help, too few from their church have been there to comfort and pray for them.

---

13. Eustace, 658. Herbert Eustace, a former member of the Church's Board of Trustees in the early 1900s, makes this argument against "slippery slopes": "(A)re we going to… argue for the expediency of first one little concession and then another; thus gradually drifting little by little away from Spirit to matter?" The author suggests that, while Eustace's question has some merit, instances cited here indicate that slippery slopes can slide in more than one direction.

The most common slippery slope our church members have encountered has been one that too frequently has ended in social isolation caused by a lack of both Christian compassion and awareness of all that Christian Science stands for. There is a better way, and in these pages we will give many examples of how Christian Scientists can raise the standard of their Christian performance and truly be there for their fellows when they most need help.

We will give examples of where innumerable people who have slid down the slippery slope of medical interludes in their lives, have scooted deep into the valley of despair and complication, and then gained enough spiritual momentum to climb the hill on the other side, the better for their journey.

"God will still guide them"

The judgments that some Christian Scientists have levied on their fellow worshippers fail to take into account both the steady eternality of God's mercy and five little words in *Science and Health:* **"God will still guide them"** (*S&H* 444:9). These words appear in the passage where Mrs. Eddy addresses the need of those Christian Scientists whom their fellow church members have failed to heal. Far too often church writings cited in this book have spoken down at Christian Scientists who have secretly sought out surgery. Other Christian Scientists, dogged by persistent illness, have become convinced by church dogma or by their fellow members that they didn't possess enough spiritual moxie in order for them to recover their health.[14] Aren't the self-righteous ignoring two crucial points, namely: (1) our church members seeking material means for healing have often first sought spiritual help, yet for any number of reasons they have found that help was not sufficient to heal them. (2) All that said, God is still a very present help for the unhealed and provides steady direction and encouragement for those seeking healing, regardless of any temporary prayer failures.

Yes, *Science and Health* says whole-hearted reliance upon God is

---

14. Rosten, Leo (ed.) *Religions in America,* 77. See Q & A from Committee on Publication.

needed for healing. No, *Science and Health* does not say that the unsuccessful prayer warrior will be dropped into a pit of metaphysical hell from which he must atone or slide forever downward. **"God will still guide them into the right use of temporary and eternal means."** This statement has seemed a little too promising and slack to some who contend that Mrs. Eddy must not have intended "temporary" to mean "material." Church officials have even gone to the extent of insisting that these "temporary means" could only have narrowly applied to crutches and eyeglasses.[15] If that's what the author of *Science and Health* meant, then why didn't she write "God will guide them into the right use of crutches and eyeglasses?" Elsewhere in that book Mrs. Eddy was very specific about means of pain relief (464). Throughout *Science and Health* material means are classified as temporal or temporary. If, as individuals, we wish to interpret which explicit material means are allowable for Christian Scientists to employ and which are not, we may happily do that, but are we free to impose that personal interpretation on all our brothers and sisters?

"Not departures from Science…"

The thought of God's continuing, merciful guidance for the Christian Scientist even in a medical setting is reinforced in an article Mrs. Eddy wrote around 1901.[16] In this article she addresses the predicament of a Christian Scientist who opts for an anesthetic when undergoing a surgical operation. She argues for the appropriateness of doing this, for two reasons: (1) if the anesthetic was not administered, then the *physician's concern* over the potential suffering of their Christian Science patient would hinder the prayerful work of the Christian Scientist, and (2) allowing for use of the drug is similar to what Jesus said about his being baptized by John: "Suffer it [the concession of allowing John to baptize him] to be so now, for thus it becometh us to fulfil all righteous-

---

15. Private letter from the Clerk of the Mother Church to Robert Swank, C.S.,1984.
16. A10407 courtesy Mary Baker Eddy Library. Privately printed by Gilbert Carpenter, Jr. in 1934, this manuscript was not published in Mrs. Eddy's lifetime. It was later included in the compendium, *In My True Light and Life,* 634, 635.

ness." That is, "*Allow* these things to happen now...," and not for the patient to suffer on!

Mrs. Eddy continues in this article to explain the metaphysical logic behind taking temporary means such as pain relief:

> *Truth is the absolute, intermediate and ultimate of all things. To attempt the absolute demonstration of Truth in its intermediate stage is to delay its ultimatum in the minds of men. Hence the impracticability of under taking to prove the entire power of the infinite to finite thought, and before your own thought has grasped all that is practical and demonstrated what you know is true of the divine Principle which governs.*[17]

Can we walk before we crawl? Some infants do. Most of us learn to crawl before we walk. Repeated, frustrated attempts to walk prematurely might discourage or delay those first steps. Christian Scientists since Mrs. Eddy's time have too often reversed the logic of her statement here and called that reversal proper Christian Science. They have argued that to not attempt the "absolute demonstration of Truth in its intermediate stage" is to be an inadequate, or even disobedient, Christian Scientist who forfeits spiritual progress and healing. We have lumped together all conditions and peoples regardless of a patient's particular readiness or receptivity or the relative severity of a circumstance and said, "You can all jump into the deep end of the pool and swim, and don't tell us you can't." In doing this, we have lost many would-be students of our faith practice.

Intermediate steps belittled

Though the writings of Mary Baker Eddy do not dismiss the need for intermediate or transitional stages, such as the use of a painkiller, in an individual's upward path, her followers have too often done just that.

---

17. Ibid, 634-635; the logic and symbolism used here by Mrs. Eddy parallel a discussion between Adam Dickey and herself, found on p. 46 of *Memoirs of Mary Baker Eddy,* wherein she uses the analogy of taking too big a step and falling, rather than taking smaller steps and maintaining one's progress.

Followers of all faiths tend to be more immaturely zealous than those who have been the spiritual pioneers. Jesus' students wanted the Master to call down heavenly disaster on some hapless Samaritans who had not welcomed him to their village (Luke 9:54).

Genuine spiritual pioneers have often learned life the hard way and so have grown to be more sympathetic to the human condition than those who have only taken for granted the pioneers' words or traipsed along on a trail blazed by those going before them. Those followers, not having learned first-hand the humility, patience, and compassion that their spiritual forefathers and mothers learned, too often have tended to fashion a religious practice that lacked the magnanimous spirit of a leader or founder, and they have merely established a series of rules as a map to spiritual progress. No wonder then that the humane or transitional aids for Christian Scientists found in Mrs. Eddy's writings have too frequently been neglected by successive generations of Christian Scientists, and abstract ideals have too often exceeded their Christian practice.

The Lord is in this place as well

So we arrive at the ethical question: **"How can Christian Scientists help each other to progress spiritually and draw close to God, no matter whether their regimen is drug-free or doctor-dictated?"** It's a big question that will be touched upon in succeeding chapters.

This chapter has given some examples of how Christian Scientists have managed to not only progress spiritually under less than ideal circumstances, but how they have found renewed and continuing physical healing, whether medical means were employed or not. Some of the foregoing accounts can easily be classified as placebo-like recoveries. Others may seem miraculous to us and not easily attributable to any treatment by physicians or accomplished through aid from the human mind. The invisible Christ is here in this gray area between the medical and the metaphysical—the Christian Science "no-man's zone."

The healing Christ is the unexpected guest by the Christian Scientist's hospital bedside. The Bible patriarch Jacob exclaimed in amazement, "The Lord is in this place; and I knew it not" (Gen. 28:16), as he found the comfort of angels in the wilderness. Abraham, Jacob's ancestor, fighting with his conscience on Mt. Moriah, uttered the words "Jehovah-jireh" ["God will provide"], and a ram in a thicket appeared to the patriarch. So the fearful, guilt-ridden Christian Scientist, feeling betrayed or betraying, still finds the abiding, powerful Christ present in surprising places.

Let's explore some of the core reasons why Christian Scientists over the years have come to feel so removed from, and in too many cases very fearful of, a conventional medical setting. If the reader finds some of the thinking and actions of church members in this past chapter confusing, those confusing and self-contradictory elements are likely dogma and not primal elements and pathways of faith. We'll now take a brief view of dogma and how it operates. Then in the following chapters we'll explore how the weeds of dogma can be and have been replaced by lively thought and teaching both in the Christian Science faith and that of other religious traditions.

CHAPTER 2

Dogma
—hijacking travelers on the way of holiness

Their fear toward me is taught by the precept of men.
Isaiah 29:13

They have forsaken me, the fountain of living water, and dug out cisterns for themselves, cracked cisterns that can hold no water.
Jeremiah 2:13 NRSV

Dogma: a settled opinion, a doctrinal notion.[1] Webster's 1828

A point of view or tenet put forth as authoritative **without** adequate grounds. Merriam-Webster 2019

DOGMA IS THE SUBTLE **distortion of inspired teaching**. It's not the actual truth of a spiritual teaching. Dogma is the conscious or unconscious attempt of the human mind to limit and misrepresent truth and things of the Spirit. Dogma is the dangerous "leaven" in religious teaching which Jesus warned his disciples about.[2] Dogma is not just a major problem in religious practice. It is also the fruit of what uninspired mentality constantly does. The human ego tends to evade or change the subject, **substitute the trivial** for the essential, twist inspired thought out of shape, and find fault with others.

---

1. For those who may have skipped the Preface, here we repeat the note regarding the meaning of dogma used in this book: *Dogma* has a diversity of meanings in the Christian world. Webster's (1828) defines dogma as "a settled opinion," and the recent Merriam-Webster's definition is similar. The author works from the basis of these definitions that are quite distinct from the more positive meanings given that word by other faiths that equate *dogma* with divinely revealed truth.
2. Matthew 16:6.

A culture rife with dogma doesn't spring up overnight. It develops over time. It's as common in religious practice as weeds are in gardens. Sometimes dogma is only dust, and not that harmful. Often it acts like rust and changes the chemistry and meaning of what it mingles with.

How does dogma happen? In the party game "telephone" the first person in a circle whispers a phrase to the person next to them, who whispers the phrase to the person next to them, and so on around a circle. What is amusing in the game is how often the initial phrase becomes distorted by the simple act of the phrase being repeated, not always understandingly or accurately, around the circle.

In religious dogma, whether it is created by intentionality or by lax person-to-person communication, whatever its origin or the way it has arrived, dogma can distort an original spiritual message. And when it leads to abuses, it leads multitudes to stay away from religion altogether.

The dogmatic use of doctrine as a weapon

A friend of the author was visiting a Christian Science church in California for its midweek testimony meeting. He had arrived early before the church service had started, found himself praying about a physical pain, and was quickly relieved of that pain as he waited for the service to begin. Later, during the testimony section of the service, my friend stood up and gave thanks for being healed that evening. All was going well here, right? Yes…until the dogma police showed up.

There is a by-law in the Christian Science *Church Manual* entitled "Prayer in Church." Exactly what prompted this by-law is not entirely clear, but it appears to encourage church attendees to keep their thoughts and prayers broad and inclusive, to not be centered on their own problems, but to remember other church members, including "the congregations," during the service. Dogma police never let the overall innocent intent of a spiritual saying, rule, or by-law get in the way of a good smackdown.

No sooner had my friend shared his thanks and sat down but a local member stood up and said, "Mary Baker Eddy wrote in the by-laws of the

Christian Science Church that prayers in churches shall be 'offered for the congregations collectively and exclusively'" (*Church Manual* p. 42, Section 5). The woman was no doubt suggesting that my friend had violated the *Manual* provision by praying for himself and not "the congregations."

An essential purpose of any religious gathering is to comfort, shelter, and support its participants through the troubles in their lives. **The petty flaunting of church rules** clashes with that purpose and is the "letter" which Paul said killed the spirit.

Some call the hypercritical use of dogma the degraded "culture" of a church, but isn't that too kind a word? The culture or spirit of a church, be it healthy or not, develops over the years depending on how that congregation deals with dogma. A church by-law, whose original purpose may have been to expand thinking and the affections, was, in the above instance, turned on its head by the desire to lord over others with self-righteousness.

Dogmatic bullying in Bible times

The Apostle Paul rebuked the imposition of dogma in his letter to the Galatian church. He addressed Christians who had gone before him to Galatia and who had insisted that new converts get circumcised if they wanted to be true to the Christian faith. This was Paul's take on that topic: "They want you circumcised **so that they may be able to boast about your submission to their ruling**" (Galatians 6:14 J.B. Phillips). Paul saw insistence about church rules having less to do with concern over the spiritual advancement of fellow believers, or about protecting a religious teaching, than it had to do with the desire to control fellow believers.

The Golden Rule winning over indifference

Mrs. Eddy cautioned that, while Christian Scientists should pray universally and steadily, they should not mentally minister to others indiscriminately or for self-serving reasons. Her specific teaching on this subject can be found in *Miscellaneous Writings* (282-285). But even as she discussed in this article what she meant by "mind your own business," she presented a number of exceptions to her cautionary statement. Those exceptions included: emergencies (such as accidents on the highway with no help present), and cases where prayerful treatment is sought by friends of a person who is unaware of any request for prayerful help. Mrs. Eddy calls this latter action a "sometimes wise" thing to do. Specifically, this article warned against prayerfully treating a stranger in hopes of receiving money for doing that, or "where there [was] no necessity for it," or in cases where a spoken word would be sufficient to meet the need of the moment.

Here's the problem: Christian Scientists have circulated a dogma that church members should never pray for someone if that person does not ask for it. Period. **What started as a caution with broad qualifications has been reduced over time to a prohibition with very unchristian side effects.**[3] The following incident illustrates how a Christian Scientist followed the Golden Rule when confronted with another person's pain or injury. This church member didn't "walk by on the other side" of a stranger's pain and justify their indifference with dogma:

This friend of the author was eating in a small restaurant near Springfield, Illinois. There were only a few tables, and my friend and his wife sat within earshot of a couple at another table. A waitress hobbled out of the kitchen to take the order of the other couple who immediately noticed the woman's impaired condition. The man told the waitress, "Honey, you need to go home and soak that foot in Epsom salts." "No," his wife interjected. "After work you should just put your foot up, and stay completely off of it." My friend, over-hearing this batch of advice, muttered under his breath, to himself and his wife, "What she really can do is forget all that stuff and 'rise in the strength of Spirit'" (*S&H* 393:12).

A few minutes later, after taking all the orders and disappearing into the kitchen, the waitress re-emerged. Only this time she was walking normally. The other couple asked somewhat incredulously, "What happened to your foot?" The waitress answered, "I don't know, but it feels

---

3. In a *Sentinel* article from June 21, 1947, a well-known Christian Science teacher makes helpful points on this issue ("Some Thoughts on 'Obtrusive Mental Healing'") but omits all the exceptions mentioned above. Also see Aug. 2010 *CSJ*, "Questions and Answers," for an illustration of the continuing influence of this dogma.

fine now." Was this just a case of spontaneous remission? If not, what happened here was not mental interference, not seeking money, not butting in, or minding somebody else's business. The waitress obviously had a need that was not being met, and the Christian Scientist knew it. My friend uttered a short verbal prayer of protest that apparently blessed that waitress.

There's a statement in the prose writings of Mrs. Eddy: "The spiritual power of a scientific, right thought, without a direct effort, an audible or even a mental argument, has oftentimes healed inveterate diseases" (*Rud.* 9:21). My friend saw the power of that action in this instance at the restaurant.[4]

Here's an example of how dogma can turn upside down the most Christian of actions:

In the early 1960s a couple who were Christian Science practitioners drove out West for a vacation. Along the way Mr. J felt impelled to take an unfamiliar route. On that stretch of road, the couple encountered a car collision with injuries. Mr. J asked for his wife's supportive prayers, left his car, and walked over to the scene of the accident. He asked those who had already stopped if he could help in any way. No emergency technicians or ambulance had arrived. A body with a sheet over it lay alongside the road. "She's a goner," Mr. J. was told by a man who was helping another one of the injured victims. So that was Mr. J's patient! He knelt down by the body of this woman and prayed for her for over fifteen minutes. Finally emergency vehicles arrived, including an ambulance, and the EMTs asked Mr. J and the others to leave. But by that time the woman who had the sheet over her, the "goner," had revived. So Mr. J left the accident scene.

Over ten years later Mr. J shared this incident at a testimony meeting in the Mother Church in Boston. He probably never suspected dogma police would be on duty that day. Immediately after the church meeting Mr. J was accosted by a church member who stated emphatically, **"You had no right to treat that woman without her permission."**

---

4. It could justifiably be suggested that my friend's prayer here approximated a mental argument, but to him it was a firm mental protest of spiritual truth.

Let's look past the absence of charity, logic, or intelligence behind the intrusive comment and note primarily the dogma or questionable teaching that fueled the words. The Golden Rule had been trumped by the strained interpretation of a church article.[5]

It might be apparent to the reader that most of the healing experiences mentioned in these first two chapters, and throughout this book, have not seen the light of day until printed here. Why is that? In many cases because of dogma. It is the tendency of most religions to present life as black and white and to avoid shades of gray.

A friend writes, **"We** [Christian Scientists] **have not figured how to account for healings with 'mixed modes' of religious and medical thought.** Christian Science has had a tremendous effect on thinkers and healers not ready to sign-on with an institutionalized church."

Articles in our church magazines rarely point out the ways in which church dogma has served to squelch even inspiring testimonies for petty reasons. So Christian Scientists require both a direct correction of our more dangerous dogma and a reborn spirit to take its place. The Holy Presence cannot be confined to the broken bottles of traditions that have never blessed God's children.

In our next chapter we'll see an elaboration of how dangerous dogma can become. The skewed interpretation of just a few words in a church text can affect the lives of many over an extended period of time. More crucial than merely getting rid of, or altering, offending elements of dogma is the reinvigoration of thought and spirit which rebirth requires.

---

5. There are testimonies in the back of Mrs. Eddy's *Miscellaneous Writings* (401–460), including one incident where some Christian Scientists quietly, firmly prayed without invitation for a visiting preacher. The good results of that prayer and the minister's reinvigoration support the importance of not necessarily waiting for a prayer request when the need is obvious. (See Eddy, *Mis.* 421.)

CHAPTER 3

"Radical"
—what happens when a word changes meaning
and teaches fear instead of faith

*Only through **radical reliance** on Truth can scientific healing power be realized.*　　　　　　　　　　　　　　　　　　　Science and Health, 167

NO ONE WORD has caused more damage for and to Christian Scientists than the *improper* use of the word "radical." If an inspired sense of "radical reliance" upon God has healed "its ten thousands," surely a distorted, fear-laden sense of the same phrase has "slain its thousands" (I Samuel 18:7).

A Christian Scientist may protest, "I was healed by 'radical reliance' on God!" That could well be true. But we answer: "Did your healing experience rest on an extreme reliance or upon a basic, natural leaning on the Almighty? Because that is a crucial distinction."

Christians who feel close to the God that is Love, and are not intimidated by their condition, are living joyfully in the Spirit and are healed by and in their closeness to their Maker and Redeemer.

So how does "radical" harm? **Most people in the Western world think "radical" means "extreme."** Because of confusion in the meaning of this one word, fear enters the sick room. Many Christian Scientists have not grasped that fact.[1]

---

1. This misunderstanding about a word's meaning is known as an *etymological fallacy*, whereby an earlier meaning of a word and its current meaning are confused.

A little background…

Some words undergo a "semantic change" or shift in their meaning over time. *Radical* has experienced a semantic change that can be characterized as "pejorative." In the mid-nineteenth century *radical* meant **"original, fundamental, native, natural, primitive, uncompounded."**[2] In the twentieth century along came the Bolsheviks, the Communists, the resurgent Ku Klux Klan, the Nazis, Al Qaeda and many others known for violent behavior. As each of these movements was classified in books and in the media as "radical," that word gradually **came to possess the connotation "extreme, drastic, excessive, fanatic,"** and so on.

"New Tactics Rein in Radicals" —appeared as a headline referring to armed American militia members and white separatists. (*Christian Science Monitor* March 30, 1998)

While older definitions of *radical* with more benign meanings are still in the current Webster's dictionary, with "extreme"[3] only as a latter definition, thesauruses give meanings to that word that are predominantly synonymous with "extreme."

As far back as the mid-1800s "radical" possessed the "extreme" definition when it was applied to political activities,[4] but otherwise during the nineteenth century "radical" conveyed a **positive, unfrightening meaning**. Mrs. Eddy wrote during the late 1800s and on one occasion used the "extreme" meaning of the word "radical," when she referred to a "red-tongued assassin of radical worth" (*Mis.* 226:29). All her other eight published uses of "radical," when examined in the context of their surrounding words, imply the meanings **"consistent, wholehearted, or fundamental"** (e.g. *S&H* 167:30). None of these eight usages suggests "extreme." How is this provable?

---

2. Webster's *American Dictionary* (1828). An abridged version of this dictionary is entitled *Student's Reference* Dictionary.
3. For those interested, there are a number of other words from *Science and Health* whose common meanings have changed since that book's final edition. See the inserted table on the next page.
4. Clark, *English Society, 1660-1832,* 8. "A word in very bad odour" when used in the political context.

If we try inserting the word "extreme" in any of Mrs. Eddy's eight usages of "radical," the sentence doesn't make sense. For example: "...Christ's way is the only one by which mortals are radically [fundamentally, not extremely] saved from sin and sickness" (S&H 458:29).

\multicolumn{4}{c}{Shifts in Word Meaning Since 1900}			
Word	Citation	Student's Reference Dictionary*	Merriam-Webster Online
apparently	..."the understanding came to me gradually and apparently (S&H 109:23)	"Openly; evidently; as the goodness of God is apparently manifest in his works..."	"Appear[ing] to be true based on what is known..."
awful	"An awful guide in smoke and flame" (S&H 566:18)	"fills with profound reverence"	"Extremely disagreeable or objectionable"
fabulous	"...discords have only a fabulous existence." (S&H 231:17-18)	"feigned,...devised; fictitious..."	"wonderful, marvelous"
fashion	"At present mortals progress slowly.... they are slaves to fashion..." (S&H 68:2)	"...the state of anything with regard to its external appearance..."	"the prevailing style...during a particular time"
include	"man is not included in non-intelligence" (S&H 120:3); "The body does not include soul" (S&H 318:32)	"to confine within..."	"to take in or comprise as part of a whole..."
mundane	"mundane formations..." (S&H, 209:25)	"belonging to the world..."	Mundane has retained its older meaning, with the additional nuance of "commonplace"
superstition	"Long prayers, superstition, and creeds clip the strong pinions of love...." (S&H 4:30)	"excessive exactness or rigor in religious opinions or practice"	"a belief or practice resulting from ignorance, fear of the unknown, trust in magic or chance...."

*abridged version of Noah Webster's 1828 dictionary, which Mrs. Eddy was known to have used

Other words which have changed meaning: Mrs. Eddy's use of the word *"superstition,"* which today generally applies to a belief in omens and supernatural phenomena, varies in *Science and Health*. In several instances her usage follows the predominant meaning of a century ago—"excessive exactness or rigor in religious opinions or practices," such as what Jesus criticized in the practices of the Pharisees. "Infidelity" today commonly refers to marital unfaithfulness, but a century ago its primary meanings were "want of faith or belief" and "disbelief of the inspiration of the Scriptures, or the divine origin of Christianity" (e.g. *S&H* 494:5).[5]

The wrong in "extreme"

Mrs. Eddy writes: **"Extremists frantically affirm and doggedly deny what is what"** (*Mis.* 374:23). In a nutshell this passage describes the *fear* and *stubborn will* that summarizes most of the harmful distortion wrought by misapplication of the phrase "radical reliance." The mental qualities of *frantic affirmation* and *dogged denial* not only possess no power to heal, but they war against the healing power of the Infinite.

Frantic affirmation

If we're frantic, we're too afraid to think, let alone to think clearly. **If we teach "frantic affirmation," we are teaching fear.** If, on the other hand, we affirm something to be all-powerful, there is no need to be frantic at all. Christians who are praying frantically are unconsciously feeling a sense of imminent danger and uttering words in prayer that deep down they don't believe, but only wish that they believed. **Prayer becomes a psychological default setting or nervous habit.** This prayer whirls around in a thought-cycle that aims not heavenward but spirals

---

5. Webster's *American Dictionary*, 95. The definition of "believe" states that that word "in popular use and familiar discourse...often expresses an opinion in a vague manner, without a very exact estimate of evidence, noting a mere preponderance of opinion, and is nearly equivalent to *think* or *suppose*." *Science and Health* cites the Greek meanings associated with "believe" in the New Testament as conveying a meaning that implies stability or firmness of understanding, rather than to vaguely think something. "Constancy, reliance, assurance" are all words synonymous with "believe" in its New Testament usage which convey a stronger image than the popular connotation of "believe" today.

downward and wonders, "What would happen if I stopped praying or my prayer utterly failed?" So even if that downward spiral might be considered a prayer, it is a "prayer to an unknown god."

Dogged denial

If we're dogged, we have substituted **willful determination** for divine guidance. Lively joy in the Lord is gone. Without the influx of the Holy Spirit, mere persistence possesses no buoyant, spiritual element. It is a sailboat without a sail. We've heard a hapless parent in the grocery store listlessly chiding a child for some misbehavior that is sure to be repeated because there is no conviction or consistency behind the parent's request.

The understanding that weans thought away from both frantic affirmation and dogged denial is built on the assurance that divine Love is really there for us, and that Christ is present at every one of life's extremities. A situation can seem extreme, but our words and actions in response to that predicament don't have to be.

> **"In our daily activities there's a right way and a wrong way to be vehement. To the extent we allow personal willfulness to outline our mental position, it's the wrong way...."** February 1978 *C.S. Journal* "Vehemence in the Truth" Isabel Bates

How did "radical reliance" achieve its status for Christian Scientists?

What we might call the "doctrine of radical reliance" was forcefully articulated in a 1957 *Journal* article entitled "The Christian Science Standard of Healing."[6] The writers of the editorial quoted from *Science and Health*: "Only through radical reliance on Truth can scientific healing power be realized" (167). This article essentially christened the phrase "radical reliance" as "the standard of Christian Science healing," and it went on to state that "this unequivocal statement (*S&H* 167:30-31) is not modified ["limited" or "changed"—Webster] by any other statement in the textbook...."

---

6. November 1957 *C. S. Journal*. This editorial was later reprinted in a popular church pamphlet called "Radical Reliance in Healing."

Contextomy, or quoting out of context

The writers here unwittingly committed something called **"contextomy,"**[7] a mistake with potentially grave consequences. In all ages **phrases and words have been torn from the wholeness of their context** and have been lifted to a privileged position that has distorted entire teachings. Jesus himself was the target of the devil's *contextomy*.

> **A whole forest can be set ablaze by a tiny spark of fire.** James 3:5
> J.B. Phillips

Did the Psalm that promised angelic deliverance when we "dash our foot against a stone" suggest that anyone should jump from a temple's spire to prove God's power to save? Jesus was not enticed by that lure because he knew what other psalms and proverbs said regarding such appeals to ego. (See Ps. 91 and Matt. 4:6.) The purpose behind taking inspired passages out of context is very important.

Other examples of "contextomy"

St. Augustine interpreted Jesus' parable of those invited to attend "a great supper" (Luke 14:23) in a way that indirectly would cause much bodily and mental injury to unorthodox Christians in centuries to come. Augustine argued that the phrase, later translated in the King James Version **"compel them to come in," justified forcing the Donatists, a Christian faction, back into the Church.**[8] In a later era, torturers for the Inquisition used Augustine's interpretation to justify their cruel treatment of the unfortunate unconverted who didn't wish to "attend the supper" of the Church.

Centuries after Augustine, slaveholders in the United States justified forced servitude by regularly reading to their human property Paul's mandate: "Slaves, obey your earthly masters...." (Eph. 6:5 NEB). A former slave was so incensed by this plantation practice that one of the first things she did after her emancipation was to take a pair of scissors and cut out from her Bible every one of the letters attributed to Paul.

The potential danger in the abuse called *contextomy* requires a more

---
7. Contextomy is called an *informal fallacy* in the field of logic.
8. Laymon, *Interpreter's Bible*, Volume 8, 1952 edition, 258.

precise antidote than a pair of scissors. Here is one: Peter Henniker-Heaton's healing of near-total paralysis is well known among Christian Scientists.[9] His recovery certainly required wholehearted dependence upon God, yet years after he was restored to health, Henniker-Heaton told a co-worker at the Christian Science church headquarters in Boston in reference to the phrase "radical reliance": "**Every sentence in** *Science and Health* **must be read in the context of everything else she** [Mrs. Eddy] **wrote."**

Couldn't we say the same thing about the Bible or any inspirational text? **Read everything in context**. Reading in that way doesn't push the reader into moral relativism or suggest that the reader regularly downplay teachings he or she doesn't like, in favor of more pleasing ones. It means that we **respect the entirety of a teaching**.

The demand for wholehearted reliance upon God for healing appears in the same book that encourages the reader: "Emerge gently from matter into Spirit" (*S&H* 485:14). Was Mrs. Eddy writing from opposite ends of the same pen? This author believes that she articulated spiritual completeness and support for all forward-moving states of faith, just as Christ preached and lived. Furthermore, every religious teaching, if held to a standard of absolute internal consistency, would likely not pass that test.

Instances of the establishment of "radical reliance"

Example 1

"Radical reliance and the church member" *C.S. Sentinel* editorial, April 11, 1983

The editorial writer states that Mother Church members who resort to material means for healing are not disciplined "by Church action." That assertion is inaccurate. Veteran Christian Scientists with broad experience in different Christian Science churches and at church headquarters know of members dropped from a variety of church positions after seeking medical help of some kind. This practice continues today in some branch churches.

---

9. Christian Science Publishing Society, *A Century of Christian Science Healing*, 156-158.

Is forced demotion not the equivalent of discipline?[10]

The *Sentinel* editorial cited here suggests that practitioners who have medical aid will be wise enough to "withdraw from the *Journal* until...readiness for public practice has been spiritually strengthened and reestablished" (624).

Mrs. Eddy writes nothing about any demotion policy for those Christian Scientists who have gone to doctors, nor does she set any precedent for this kind of punitive downgrading. When Mrs. Eddy in her last decade resorted on several occasions to taking morphine to relieve extreme pain, she made no special provision for her own demotion from her post of spiritual watchfulness and the editing of her writings. So why should latter-day Christian Scientists invent a church standard that excludes from active prayer-duty those who have some physical problem that requires temporary material help?

George Kinter, a practitioner who served as Mrs. Eddy's secretary at her Pleasant View home, fell down in the night (ca. 1904) and cut his nose on a writing desk. Dr. Ezekiel Morrill was called for, and he stitched up Kinter's wound. From the journal of a fellow worker at Pleasant View: "Mr. Joseph Mann, who was with Mr. Kinter at the time, told us that when the physician finished his work, Mr. Kinter smiled and remarked, 'You are a pretty good seamstress.'"

The only aftermath of this matter was a comment by Mrs. Eddy after she had been informed of the accident the next morning. Mrs. Eddy "told her maid, who repeated it to me [Mrs. Weygandt] that Mr. Kinter's [prayer] watch had been heavenly that night."[11]

Herein is a noticeable tone at the Pleasant View household comparable to what cowboys might feel like when they're thrown off a horse, only to be encouraged to dust themselves off, and climb right back into their saddle for the long ride.

---

10. Dummelow, *Bible Commentary*, 678. Rabbi ben Hazar in ancient Israel was excommunicated from his synagogue because of his undervaluing of the ceremonial washing of hands. In case the reader believes that Christian Scientists are the only religionists to preach extreme positions, others have preceded us.
11. Weygandt, "Reminiscences," 63, courtesy Mary Baker Eddy Library.

Again, should Christian Scientists of today demand from their fellow church members what the founder of their church did not? Christian Scientists have done so, and far too often, and have done this with self-righteousness that neither Jesus nor Mrs. Eddy ever preached or embodied. What is even more regrettable is that those reprimanded and discouraged members who have left our church fellowship have frequently blamed themselves for not being better examples of faith.

Example 2
An Enlarged View of Radical Reliance" (C.S. Journal, Vol. 92, 1974):

"Jesus relied radically on Truth in every case of physical, as well as mental, temptation."

If Jesus was consistently radical, as in "extreme," then why did he do the following? He employed placebos (putting mud on a blind man's eyes—John 9). He healed people of professed weaker faith (Mark 9:23, 24) and slightly superstitious faith (Luke 8: 44–48). He did not rebuke his disciples for fleeing in fear when he was arrested and then crucified, but he did chastise them for not believing the women who witnessed his rising from the dead (Mark 16:14). He then encouraged his followers to go ahead and "feed my sheep" instead of declaring them unworthy specimens of discipleship.

Where does Mrs. Eddy write that Jesus was radical as in "extreme"? She, in fact, suggests the opposite of "extreme" in the following passage that refers to Jesus' cautionary advice regarding how his disciples should equip themselves as they ventured out on evangelical journeys (Luke 22:35–37).

"[T]*hat his divine wisdom should temper human affairs, is plainly set forth in the Scriptures."*

My. 215:32

Jesus withdrew himself from danger in some cases and exercised precaution in others.[12] He withdrew from the Pharisees who planned

---

12. Verhoeven, 110. Christian scholar (ca. 250 CE) Origen wrote that Jesus acted as he did "so as not to expose Himself to danger rashly, or unseasonably, or without good grounds." *Contra Celsum*

to kill him (Mark 3:7). Jesus' parents had fled to Egypt (Matt. 2:14, 15) in fear of Herod. The Master delayed going to a feast in Jerusalem when his enemies were lying in wait for him (John 7:3, 6-10). Jesus advocated paying taxes to Caesar. His conduct was not extreme or fanatical, but it was wise and grounded in the fundamentals of Mosaic teaching, if not upon the Pharisaical interpretations and elaborations of Mosaic Law. If Jesus was radical, as in "revolutionary," we need to make clear what kind of radicalism we are talking about, or we should use a more accurate word.

When does "radical (extreme) reliance" heal?

Radical reliance heals when it is deeply rooted. The word "radical" comes from the Latin word for "root." Roots spread out like an underground tree growing downwards, sinking deep into the surrounding soil. Roots grow deeper and stronger over time forming an unseen superstructure of natural advancement. The greater the tree, the more expansive and lively is the root system.

So the breadth of divine healing does not rest on one root only—that of committed faith. What are some of the compound spiritual qualities that Mrs. Eddy points to as nurturing healing?

- "Absolute faith that all things are possible to God." But she didn't stop there. (S&H 1)
- "A spiritual *understanding* of (God)…." (Ibid.)
- "…*an unselfed love*"…and farther down the same page….
- "*watching*"and "*working*"
- "*self-immolation*" …and on further pages….
- "*reason*" (logic), "*revelation*," "*demonstration*" (S&H 109)
- "*humility*" (S&H 8)

This is by no means a complete list, but it shows the broadly rooted or grounded range of qualities, all of which can produce healing. "Reliance" on God is just one of these.

Radical reliance heals when it is based on vision, self-knowledge, and experience, and therefore is "fully persuaded" (Rom. 14:5). Loren Janes, the long-time Hollywood stuntman, was a Christian Scientist who possessed a very persuaded trust in the power of Truth to heal. Janes survived countless death-defying stunt jobs, but one of his least-known brushes with death came at a time when he was bitten by a bamboo pit viper, while he and his fellow actors were filming *The Sand Pebbles* in a remote area near Hong Kong. Janes refused to have his arm amputated and not only recovered but was back on the set in the next few days.[13]

"Prayer and fasting" might be the Gospel equivalent of "radical reliance" that heals. This prayer and fasting is not so much forsaking of human nourishment as it is a consistent, heart-felt downgrading of what our bodily senses are yelling, and doing this with the vision and strength that flows from faith, spiritual understanding, and experience.

Had David recklessly sought to beat the toughest guy in the valley (Goliath), his **bravado** could easily have killed him. David's courage was powered not by sheer will and bluster but by trust in a holy cause and a confidence inspired from earlier victories (I Samuel 17:36). God's protective presence had given him the strength to defeat a threatening lion and bear. Goliath was just another threat in different packaging.

The context of General Grant's bold "proposal"

From the Battle of the Wilderness, Ulysses Grant famously wrote in a dispatch to Washington, *"I propose to fight it out on this line, if it takes all summer"* (May 11, 1864).[14] Was General Grant being a willful extremist by saying this? In examining the context of Grant's words, we can catch their significance. A major turning point in the Civil War had been Grant's victory at Vicksburg in May of 1863. Two frontal assaults did not take down the Confederate stronghold. It was a series of feints and diversions that allowed Union troops to proceed past Vicksburg's batteries. Grant and his men then crossed the Mississippi and were able to seize the city of Jackson, the source of supplies for Vicksburg. After Jackson had been taken, the success of besieging Vicksburg was inevitable.

Grant's determined words, cited above, followed this morale-boost-

---

13. Testimony shared by Loren Janes at the Adult Summer Sessions at Principia College (Elsah, Illinois).
14. Eddy, *Science and Health*, 492:18. See Eddy's quote.

ing victory in Mississippi by a year. Between the triumph at Vicksburg and the inconclusive Battle of the Wilderness came Union victories at Gettysburg, Port Hudson, and Chattanooga. So it was no idle boast on Grant's part that he would outlast the enemy. He could foresee the end of the war, which was less than a year away. Historian Bruce Catton attributed Grant's success not "to a matter of piling up overwhelming resources and trusting that something would break under the sheer weight of men and muscle," but instead to "a business of finesse, of daring decisions and fast movement, of mental alertness and the ability to see and use an opening before it closed."[15]

An ideal sense of "radical reliance" requires **vision, self-knowledge, and trust** in God, again often based on prior experience. Moses was encouraged to free his fellow Hebrews not just by his belief that the Almighty had told him to do that, but by at least two remarkable signs from God. At the divine command Moses overcame the vision of a fearsome snake, and he faced down the terrifying sight of a leprous hand (Exodus 4).

A practitioner once told the author, **"Radical reliance doesn't begin when you have a serious problem."** Healing occasions under stressful circumstances emerge naturally and often stand on the shoulders of previous healing occasions and those of our friends and family.

When does "radical" harm?

…when it's uncertain. The America theologian Reinhold Niebuhr wrote: **"Frantic orthodoxy is never rooted in faith but in doubt. It is when we are not sure that we are doubly sure."**[16] This doubt is not the creative kind of skepticism that seeks answers or that questions a course of action. It's the more dangerous kind—doubt well-concealed by self-conscious fear of being found less than faithful. The philosopher George Santayana corroborates this thought: **"Fanaticism consists in redoubling your efforts when you have forgotten your aim."**[17]

---

15. Catton, *U. S. Grant and the American Military Tradition*, 104.
16. *Weidhorn, An Anatomy of Skepticism*, 88.
17. Santayana, *The Life of Reason: The Phases of Human Progress.* Vol. 1, *Reason in Common Sense*, Chapter 30.

What appears to be extreme conviction, or what might be termed radicalism or reckless conviction, is often thinly veiled confusion and internal conflict.

> "The reckless will be unsure of himself...."
> Habakkuk 2:4 NEB

If Christian Science is the "sober, second thought of advancing humanity,"[18] then we should encourage among ourselves the approach that waits on the Lord and doesn't rush into the heat of unknown battles. An engineering professor advises his students: "Stop, think; don't do something stupid." There's a creative window in this "stop and think" approach. At that momentary pause, angels show the wisest way.

...when it's overactive. Large fluctuations in the action of the human body are a sign of disease not health. This is one reason why doctors seek to "stabilize" a patient before resorting to any treatment or surgery. The overaction of excited consciousness is not helpful to the body but harmful.

> "Paul's uncertain sense of right yielded to a spiritual sense, which is always right...." *Science and Health*, 326

The redoubled effort that Santayana cautions against in the above quotation is overcompensation for a lack of foundation and an absence of clear thinking.

We see overactive behavior in epigones—lesser followers of great philosophers or students of great teachers, who mask their lack of originality and substance by attempts to be outstanding in some minor way. Some religious fundamentalists do this by randomly emphasizing certain isolated sayings or writings to the exclusion of tempering or countervailing scripture.

Truly great athletes know their capacities and play "within themselves." That is, they have mastered skills that enable them to make difficult maneuvers appear simple, even commonplace. A lot of hard work, repetition of simple actions, and many hours of practice are required for those athletes to reach a point of mastery.

Mrs. Eddy advocated shorter, measured steps in faith rather than giant leaps. She once posed the question to her secretary Adam Dickey, *"Mr. Dickey...did you ever take such a long step that you fell to the ground?...Would it not have been better if you had taken two steps*

---

18. Eddy, *No and Yes*, 19.

and retained your equilibrium?"[19] Mrs. Eddy once corrected the "abstractions" of a *Sentinel* editor [20] who had written that one could not heal a disease without first realizing the nothingness of all matter, including the body. In her correction, she referred to the passage in *Science and Health*: "An **improved belief is one step out of error, and aids in taking the next step....**" (*S&H* 296).

...when it's unrestrained zeal. Mrs. Eddy calls this "zeal without knowledge," a co-partner of overaction (*Mis.* 284). When the very word "radical" **appeals to our emotions like a primal battle cry**, we have been lured away from our native Christian spirit. How can one little word make us feel that we're being very bold and fundamental in our faith practice, like Peter brandishing a sword in defense of his teacher? Jesus told Peter that the zealot's way is not our way. That directive applies to us today.

...when we lack self-awareness. *Self-knowledge* tells us when we are working either beyond or within our own capacities. The apostle Stephen was courageous, but he also appeared lacking "audience awareness." Didn't he need the "wisdom of serpents," when, seeing the bitter hatred of his hearers, that sight failed to restrain him from a greater intensity of expression. As a result he was instantly killed by an irate mob, and at his death commenced "a great persecution of the church" (Acts 8:1; Acts 11:19). What if instead, Stephen had broached a defense of Christ and then concluded his speech when he could see the implacable anger facing him? He might have escaped with his life to preach another day to a more receptive audience. A lack of self-knowledge or awareness of one's surroundings has shipwrecked many a faith effort.

> "...zealots...like Peter, sleep when the Watcher bids them watch, and when the hour of trial comes would cut off somebody's ears."
> *Mis.* 335:23

---

19. Dickey, *Memoirs*, 46. See also, Eddy, *Miscellaneous Writings*, 359: 24-26. "Science is demonstrated by degrees..."
20. Eddy, *Miscellany*, 217. The editorial had appeared October 12, 1899.

Was Stephen's boldness more right than wrong? It is difficult to sort it all out from our safe distance across the ages, but Jesus himself resisted the temptation to preach aggressively against his opponents even as he was urged to do so by his enemies (Luke 11:53).

> "The kingdom of heaven has suffered violence, and the violent take it by force."
> Matthew 11:12

...when it's great fear wearing a mask of courage. Mrs. Eddy describes consumptive patients (S&H 375:26) whose great courage covered a fear so huge that it couldn't be faced head-on. This kind of courage is not healthy, because it attempts to conceal and not destroy fear. The church magazines of Mrs. Eddy's era warned Christian Scientists regarding ***bravado*** that Webster (1828) defines as "pretended courage or feigned defiant confidence."[21]

...when it's based on bad information. If we are tempted to portray Mrs. Eddy as a woman who never ever quit, we should first remember the frequent misquotation of Winston Churchill's words on this topic. This is what Sir Winston actually said:

> *"Never give in, never give in, never, never, never, never—in nothing, great or small, large or petty—never give in **except to convictions of honor and good sense.**"* (A very large caveat there at the end of Sir Winston's address to Harrow School 10-29-1941)

Yes, Mrs. Eddy made compromises and concessions (see Chapters 17 and 22), since **wise leaders know that they may well lose battles on the path to winning a war.** Christian Science is not a metaphysical game of "chicken" to determine who possesses enough super-faith to overthrow the world. It is a step-by-step process of spiritual advancement that is not helped or supported by holding out illusive ideals to its aspirants. Bad information can lead to mindless loss.

...when it's self-consciously so. Authentic courage arises appropriate to the moment of necessity and is not ginned up by loyalty to slogans or goaded into leaping off unknown temple pinnacles. When you believe you're being radical (as in "extreme"), you're being self-consciously so. You are faith-acting, performing for the church, rehearsing

---

21. Skinner, *C. S. Sentinel*, May 28, 1904.

for a future testimony meeting, or for the world crowd, and not for God or because of God. Often the most courageous individuals, when asked about their brave actions (if they have survived them) will say, "I was only doing what I had to do. My conscience and honest conviction would not have allowed me to do otherwise."[22]

...when it's mere avoidance of all things medical. There is no special virtue in never visiting a doctor. But many Christian Scientists measure being a **good church member** by that benchmark. Avoiding something doesn't mean we are positively committed to something else. It just means we have avoided something. The inertia of inaction then becomes self-perpetuating. Again, just because we're not going to see a doctor doesn't mean that we are necessarily happily praying for ourselves and turning steadily to the Great Physician for our reliable help. We just haven't gone to a doctor.

The irony here is that by the studious avoidance of all things medical, Christian Scientists can end up worrying more about their physical well-being than the average person. Psychology illustrates this by the "law" of attraction to opposites. This phenomenon is called "ironic process theory."

If a friend tells you that whatever you do, ***"Don't think about a large, white bear!"***[23] you will unconsciously think about a large, white bear. If the Christian Scientist says, **"Whatever I do, I can't think about going to a doctor,"** that very possibility will tend to dominate thought.

A church spokesman wrote in 1902: "...I am sure that those who launch out and depend upon God as the only means of healing the sick will never have cause to regret it, provided they **do this understandingly. To attempt to discard material remedies without having an intelligent understanding of God, and how to apply the divine power to one's troubles, is not wise. There is a vast difference between depending upon Christian Science and depending upon nothing."**[24]

...when it's a brave contest that harms those closest to us. Earlier references to the role of context apply here. When Christian Scientists

---

22. J. B. Phillips, Luke 17:10. "We have only done what we ought to do."
23. Mark Twain tells the story of a little boy who was told to stand in a corner and not to think about a white elephant.
24. Farlow, *C. S. Sentinel*, 10-2-1902.

take a strong stand for what they firmly believe, do they ask themselves: **"How does this 'stand for truth' connect with those around me, especially my immediate family and friends?"**

If we want to follow the "Golden Rule" (Matthew 7:12) that Jesus taught, we must take into account how living our ideals will affect the lives of those close to us. What might be socially acceptable actions in a wilderness or while alone on a desert island may be breaking the law when done in heavily populated areas. Very few of us in the modern age live unto ourselves, in a vacuum. The vast majority of modern lives are inextricably intertwined with the lives of others.

The fruits of mistaken radicalism

There are a number of obvious sad results from the misapplication of "radical reliance."

Needless suffering Testimony of a practitioner: "I encountered a forty-year-old woman who at age twelve had a three-inch pin become lodged in her foot. The pin had never been removed. Her mother, who was a practitioner, had said **'it didn't happen.'** The pin was finally taken out by a physician, partly at my encouragement. This is nothing short of **abuse, based on ignorance, heartlessness, and a serious misconstrual of the teachings of Christian Science.**"

Mrs. Eddy wrote that her "**prime object…had been to prevent suffering, not to produce it**" (S&H 457:10). If the mistaken practice, or, more accurately, malpractice, of Christian Science causes needless suffering as in the case of this woman, should we not be very anxious to point out this type of mistake and strongly warn others why and how not to follow suit? Quackery means "pretending to cure" something. When we say a disease "isn't real" or "did not happen," and we fail to back up those statements by healing the disease, we are nothing short of a fraud or metaphysical quack. Instead of saying that this kind of abuse doesn't happen in our name, let us take specific measures to ensure that it does not and will not happen in the name of Christ. (See recommendations at the end of this chapter).

Needless death The ex-husband of a Christian Scientist commented about his former spouse's death at a relatively young age: "What good did that [her death] accomplish? Did more people believe in God because she died?" Her children believe less, though her former husband still goes to church.

Contrast this unfortunate experience with this testimony by a young woman whose health was failing and who submitted to a life-saving medical procedure: "I didn't want to make the people I love afraid of Christian Science." This woman came to understand that surgery was not forbidden to Christian Scientists. Her recovery from her illness has been succeeded by a number of opportunities to heal others through prayer.

Cleaning our own house first

It is obvious that orthodox medicine is not fail-safe. Over one hundred thousand people die each year from improperly administered medical treatment in hospitals, and a recent study calculates that number to be closer to a quarter million.[25] But that number of failures is no excuse for failures or abuse in the practice of Christian Science. A portion of those medical failures can be corrected by reforms such as shortening the hours of hospital interns, tightening standards for the approval by the Food and Drug Administration of drugs, and improving the transcription standards of prescriptions. The medical faculty have these issues and many others to work out and remain very humble about, but the shortcomings and failures in conventional medical practice do not in any way justify the failures by Christian Scientists in their caregiving.

If we Christian Scientists are unwilling to examine the causes of needless death among our people, why should we believe it appropriate to speak out against abuses in the practice of conventional medicine? (Chapter 24 includes fuller coverage of this subject.)

Mistaken teaching resulting in a culture of fear A Christian Science teacher who taught many other teachers, some of whom are still

---

25. Sternberg, "Medical Errors Are Third Leading Cause of Death in the U.S," *U. S. News*, 5-3-2016.

active today, is quoted as telling his students that "*materia medica* [a Christian Science term for orthodox medical theory] is the anti-Christ and its hospitals an invention of the devil." He remarked (to his students): 'I might be persuaded to go to a tavern or a bawdy house, but never to a hospital."[26]

These statements, if authentic, are a clear violation of the spirit of a church by-law that prohibits "uncharitable" or "impertinent" published references to religion and medicine (Article VIII, Sect. 26). Arthur Corey also noted that another prominent teacher told his students that it was "better to die for lack of an operation than to live in consequence of one."[27]

Might it not have been helpful for both these Christian Science teachers to have read carefully what Mrs. Eddy wrote about surgery and other "temporary means" before they emitted pronouncements such as these? The author of *Science and Health* makes clear that Christian Scientists should never "condemn rashly" the medical faculty or others who are endeavoring to do good for humanity (*S&H* 444). Another Christian Science church member had a family motto of sorts which could send shivers down the spine of even the spiritually stout-hearted: "Deny the pain, or give up the cause!" Imagine the flickering wicks of earnest faith that were doused by that battle-cry.

These types of sayings violate the standard rules for Christian Science teachers and presumably for other church members that personal opinions not form any basis for the actions of Christian Scientists (*Church Manual* 84:18-20). What began as a casual remark has ultimately echoed down through generations of Christian Scientists. Then the very phrase "radical reliance" has become employed as a **scare tactic**, a kind of veiled threat that says, "We will love you as long as you continue to rely on God *radically*" (as in "extremely"). Conditional love is not the grace of Christ. We thrive under Love's unconditional grace. Love dies under the withering gaze of pharisaism.

---

26. Corey, *Behind the Scenes*, 155.
27. Ibid.

Dogma about "going medical"

A church official once told the author, "We have a saying in our church office, that once you 'go medical' you never come back." The dogma articulated here that has circulated for years finds unhappy parallels in early Christian prophecies against fellow-believers whose faith lapsed in the face of lethal persecution.

During the third century attacks on Christians by the Roman Empire, Bishop Cyprian, who ironically had himself fled from persecution, wrote regarding those whose faith faltered: "How many are daily possessed by unclean spirits? How many are driven out of their minds and racked by a frenzy of fury and madness."[28] Don't these words sound as if the bishop's imagination was overheated about those whom he judged so freely?

Though not as specific as Cyprian's pox upon the weak-in-faith and definitely milder in tone is a latter-day judgment by Christian Scientists from a notable teacher who wrote in the 1952 *Journal*: "[Jesus] knew that yielding to material means and methods invariably is at the expense of spiritual understanding and growth."[29] Now compare this statement with one from *Science and Health*: "You weaken or destroy your power [to heal] when you resort to any except spiritual means."[30] When read in context this latter passage addresses specifically Christian Science healers who use some form of electricity or "manipulation" *on their patients,* but does not appear to address patients themselves.

Many of the testifiers in the "Fruitage" section of *Science and Health* had tried every medical avenue available before they came to Christian Science. Their approach was unradical in the extreme. But somehow successive generations of Christian Scientists have pushed the dogma that medical contact of any form threatens church members.

The difference between those who had testified to healings in Mrs. Eddy's day and those of today is that the former testifiers did not believe that their experiences with conventional medicine had tainted their spir-

---

28. Fox, *Pagans and Christians*, 144.
29. "The Consistency That Is in Christ," *C. S. Journal, January, 1952.*
30. Eddy, *Science & Health,* 181:12–13.

itual being. Their experiences with medicine just had not healed them.

Partly because of the foregoing and other widely circulated anti-medical sayings of Christian Scientists, the public assumes that we "don't believe in doctors." Indeed, the previous paragraphs point out how Christian Scientists have been led to believe that weakness of faith or "belief in doctors" leads to regrettable consequences for the body and soul of the church member. The Christian apologist author Peter Williams wrote in 1990: "Christian Science…has rigorously forbidden its followers to employ conventional medical techniques in seeking healing."[31]

All our formal church protests and disclaimers notwithstanding, that we do not force any of our members to avoid anything of a medical nature, the anti-doctor message has gone out to the public. The lightly veiled threat to church members regarding what medical interventions might do to their spiritual well-being still resonates with far too many Christian Scientists. Both the message to the public and the message to church members will continue to preach a lie, as long as both messages are not thoroughly and publicly corrected.

We Christian Scientists are principally responsible for the common conception that we "don't believe in doctors." **The world gets what we do and really mean, regardless of what we say that we do.**

Grounded in faith or fear?

Now if a sincere Christian Scientist stays away from doctors and hospitals not because he relies on God, loves God, and believes in prayer, but more so because he is afraid to be seen "going medical," which he believes to be a sin, is he grounded in faith or fear? Mrs. Eddy wrote that a man who refrains from sin "*only through fear of the consequences* [the author's italics] is neither a temperate man nor a reliable religionist" (S&H 322:22). If Christian Scientists want a flock that mainly refrains from conventional medicine (seen as "sin" here in this context) for fear of what taking that step might do to one's church standing, haven't we created an unreliable fold.

---

31. Williams, *America's Religions*, 335.

A demoralized congregation

A Christian Science nurse remarked to me that she believed there was "no strong conviction" in many Christian Scientists she had observed. She felt that many older Christian Scientists opt for conventional medical care rather than go to a Christian Science nursing facility. Did some of these "unradical" Christian Scientists see too many of their fellows relying "radically" (as in "extremely") upon God for healing, but then see them meeting a tragic or premature demise?

Extreme positions invite extreme reactions, and they create a climate of fear. Elijah's slaughter of the prophets of Baal was followed by the victorious prophet falling into fatalistic depression (I Kings 19). Why should we believe it odd that the extreme position of "radical reliance" could become "a custom more honored in the breach than the observance?"[32]

Dogmatism biting the dogmatic

A church member shared the following:

"My ex-mother-in-law had a stroke and was hospitalized. We contacted a practitioner in the Southwest for her, but that practitioner said she would never set foot in a hospital or doctor's office [to visit and pray for anyone]. Not long after, that same practitioner had a stroke and passed on before my mother-in-law."

> **"Let him that thinketh he standeth take heed lest he fall."**
> I Corinthians. 10:12

How "radical" can cause fear even when it succeeds

What did Mrs. Eddy mean by urging students to "keep their demonstrations modest"? (*Mis.* 171:30) Aren't those words similar to her caution against "a miracle that frightens people"? (*My.* 216:12) **Jesus turned down the devilish temptation to perform the spectacular** for the cause of God. The spiritually spectacular often causes the outside observer to think or say: "That's amazing, but I could never do that!" or

---

32. *Hamlet*, Act I, iv, 14.

"How could that possibly have happened?" Just when Christian Scientists think they may be impressing someone in describing an astounding healing, those church members may be mystifying that friend rather than drawing him or her to Christ.

The foundations of Christian Science, its primal building blocks, are the basic, day-to-day indications of God's power and presence that do not need to be amazing in order to be divine. Of course, the failure of an awe-inspiring but unsuccessful attempt at healing advertises like nothing else as an argument against Christian Science, and it creates ripples of prejudice that travel out, misinforming generations against a solid idea.

What's to be done with the "radical" in reliance?

Recommendations:
- The church needs to make crystal clear that **"radical" reliance upon God for healing is in no way extreme but "natural, original, fundamental, uncompounded,** etc." Christian Scientists are not asked to be martyrs of their faith or to take giant leaps of faith, but to "advance from the rudiments laid down" (S&H 462:15).
- Words such as "wholehearted," "consistent," "basic," even "revolutionary," may convey the clear meaning that "radical" meant one hundred years ago, and those words can be used today to clarify what we believe in and what we do not.
- Fear, peer pressure, guilt, and internal compulsion are mental elements that have never belonged in the sick room. They constitute a dangerous form of "mixing" the means of mortal mentality with divine means and motives.
- We need to do to *radical* what the prophet Jeremiah did to the word *burden*—**call for its clarification or disuse**.

Jeremiah's critics had mocked him because every time he opened his mouth he doled out more "burdens of the Lord," heavy in his listeners' ears and on their shoulders. **"The burden of the Lord shall ye mention no more,"** was the prophet's concession to the resistant ears of his hearers (Jer. 23:36). "Burden" had outlasted its usefulness.[33] The problem with "radical" is that its meaning can slide all over the linguistic map.[34] This inconsistency of interpretation confuses the reader who is seeking healing. **Let us discourage the use of the word "radical" in our church publications at this time out of motherly care for our own people and out of consideration for a confused public. The purpose of our faith is neither to confuse, to create fear, nor to endanger.**

- **A very public apology** should be made to those harmed by the false sense of "radical" which has caused damage to many over the years. Words cannot bring back lives, but they can **plant a new foundation for the responsible practice and clear articulation of Christian Science.**

The October 1997 *Christian Science Journal* explained one reason for our church changing the term "Org," as a shortened term for Christian Science Organization, to "CSO": **"Sometimes a family becomes so used to one of its own phrases that the members may not realize it sounds strange or has different connotations to their neighbors and friends."**[35] This is an excellent description of the problem with *radical* in "radical reliance," and one of the reasons for our re-examination of that word.

Questions for thought and discussion

- How does our church best communicate in its publications a change as significant as is suggested here?
- In any institution, even small changes should be subject to appraisal after the change is initiated. Christian Scientists should be careful that recommending caution over a phrase that has been subject to dogmatic abuse should not justify a new wave of counter-dogma that would be harmful in an opposite direction. The pendulum of the

---

33. Dummelow, *Commentary*, 470. **"The misused phrase 'burden of the Lord' is to be used no more. Some other expression is to take its place."**
34. From Nicolson, *God's Secretaries,* 121: In 1630, a British preacher Rev. Giles Widdowes spoke of the label **"Puritan"** as **"ambiguous and so it is fallacious."**
35. Another possible reason for the change of the term "Org" is the common usage of that abbreviation by L. Ron Hubbard (of Scientology), which may have subtly added to the public's confusion of Christian Science with Scientology.

human mind swings in extremes (*Mis.* 353:3). So how can the change suggested here happen without encouraging an opposite extreme of relying on medical attention in any and all human circumstances?

A different approach

The following is a little hint of how Christian Scientists and others can approach dire circumstances without being extreme. What follows is just about baseball, but it's an example of what the author has found to be effective as one of the alternative approaches to what has been discussed in this chapter.

In 2004, the Boston Red Sox baseball team won the first baseball championship for their city in eighty-six years. But before they claimed their trophy, the Red Sox had fought back, winning four games in a row against great odds. They had lost the first three games of a best-of-seven-games series against the New York Yankees, a team that had been humbling them for eight decades. Making matters especially dark was the crushing Yankees' victory in Game Three, 19-8. That's more of a football score.

The Red Sox manager Terry Francona realized that while no American baseball team had ever before come back from a 3-0 deficit in a seven-game series and won, still the manager knew his team and its potential. This was his approach:

"You can feel sorry for yourself and pack it in, or you can give it a shot," said Francona. *"Whatever they* [our team] *believed, I believed. Totally. Four in a row is awful daunting, but we just decided to* **play pitch to pitch, out to out, inning to inning**. *It wasn't like we had to dig deep. It was about* **being the same…the idea is to be consistent.**" [36]

You can call this what you will—steady believing, keeping your heart and head in the game, being consistent, living in the "now," working patiently. **Triumphs in life don't usually come in a sudden rush of effort. Success in life more commonly comes from many small things**

---

36. Francona, *Francona,* 113.

done step-by-step, done with persistence, and done well, with all this effort often buttressed by high goals, a desire to do good, and other divine supports. If a baseball team facing overwhelmingly negative odds can succeed by taking modest steps, individuals can do this as well. Healing is not a baseball game, but it does involve thinking straight-forwardly, listening as keenly as we can to divine guidance, knowing and proving that divine Love is seriously "a very present help in trouble."

CHAPTER 4

Billboards of sorrow and glory
—dealing with protracted physical problems

Spiritual intuitions...tell us when 'the night is far spent, the day is at hand'...
S&H 174:12

My strength is made perfect in weakness...for when I am weak, then am I strong.
Paul writing to the church at Corinth (II Cor. 12:9,10)

AFTER THE SERVICE today, my son said, "Now I remember why I don't invite my friends to church." What was he talking about? In the church we were visiting was a woman with a disfiguring growth on her face that was probably correctable through surgery.

This is not a subject with easy answers. Billboards along the highway are advertisements that distract you while you are driving to a desired destination. The billboards we're addressing here are distractions from the spiritual purpose of a church. These distractions broadcast sorrow when they advertise the apparent failure of spiritual healing. If a healing eventually takes place, these billboards can also advertise victories. But even those victories come with a price. In attempting to perform a Herculean task, a high proof of what we believe, and then, whether failing or succeeding over time, **we become poster children not for spiritual healing but against it.** We walk around, wounded warriors, with our badges of courage that astound the world and dismay our brothers and sisters.

We aspire to be good servants. We imagine how wonderful our testimony will be, and how the skeptics of spiritual healing will be impressed when healing occurs. How do I know about billboards? I have been one. For two years, I was nearly completely blind with cataracts.

Cataracts have been healed spiritually by other Christian Scientists, but they are also correctable through surgery, as happened in my case.

In the early Christian era, the Apostle Paul was a billboard. He apologized to the Galatian Christians, "…[Y]**ou resisted the temptation to show scorn or disgust at the state of my poor body; you welcomed me as if I were an angel of God, as you might have welcomed Christ Jesus himself**" (Galatians 4:13, 14 NEB). Paul might have felt self-conscious about his unhealed appearance, but he didn't live in an age that boasted readily available material quick fixes for health problems.

> I was a reproach among all mine enemies, but especially among my neighbors, and a fear to mine acquaintance.
> Psalms 31:11

Paul was healing and being healed on his journeys, though he was sometimes a repelling example of his own preaching…and yet, maybe a true example. He was bearing the cross of Jesus who died in the most **"open shame"** (Hebrews 6:6) of anyone. Who would have wanted to identify with a man who died like the lowest of criminals? Before any of us worry about what others think of our condition, we have to remember Jesus, who didn't care what anyone thought of his ignominious death, because his heavenly mission and destination were far more important to him than the conditions of his death. And his mission was ultimately triumphant.

A special shame

Christian Scientists in the early twenty-first century bear a special shame when they suffer **conditions that their neighbors are convinced can be treated successfully with medical means.**[1] The Gospel of Matthew (Matthew 16:21) indicates that Jesus knew he had to pass through the shame of the crucifixion. Paul, despite his occasional ill-health, was buoyed up by his mission and by the grateful support of those to whom he ministered. The Christian Scientist with a visibly unhealed situation often prays while feeling uncertain and alone with God.

---

1. The author has spoken separately with both Christian Science nurses and a medical doctor who have described "Third World" diseased conditions of Christian Scientists rarely seen in developed nations.

What's to be done? The following is one approach: A worker at the Mother Church in Boston had endured years of paralysis during World War II before he was healed. Ironically, given his prior prolonged invalidism, he commented to a friend, "If someone has a facial growth, it's not fair to others to parade it around. They should have it surgically removed." This worker wasn't known for judging others, but he felt strongly on this point, and he likened "billboard" Christian Scientists to those who are cautioned in the *Church Manual* from giving gory or graphic testimonies (*Manual* 47:18-20). **But is the unhealed individual's determination not to go to a doctor an isolated personal predicament?**

What are reasons shared by many Christian Scientists for why we strive for spiritual healing over a period of years? **None of us starts out wanting to advertise for the opposite of healing.** We don't seek to be a gazing-stock (Hebrews 10:33). We don't go out of our way to be looked at with pity or censure. It is our problem, and we are doing what we can to heal it.

What we "billboards" may not have noticed has also been overlooked by most in the Christian Science Church. This particular gray area of prolonged healing has too often been shrugged off in our public presentations or pushed under the rug. The following are some of the dogmas underpinning the "billboard" problem.

Perfectionism

In the midst of imperfection, perfection is seen and acknowledged only by degrees. The ages must slowly work up to perfection.
Science and Health, 233

Voltaire is paraphrased as saying, **"The perfect is the enemy of the good."**[2] What did Voltaire mean by that? While Jesus is quoted in the Sermon on the Mount, "Be ye therefore perfect, even as your Father in heaven is perfect," the Master was speaking about perfect, forgiving love, and not about a check-list perfectionism that the Pharisees strove to follow in their desire to follow every letter of the religious law. Therefore, we might paraphrase Matthew 5:48: "Be therefore

---

2. Voltaire's actual words were: "The best is the enemy of the good."

extraordinarily loving, even as your heavenly Father is infinite Love itself." *Perfection* for the Christian Scientist is spiritual wholeness, while *perfectionism* is the humanly willful attempt to mold our lives into conformity with models that may be quite different from what the Almighty has in store for us.

| Matt. 5:48: **"Be ye therefore perfect…"** "the Hebrew word (tamin, or *teleios* in Greek) **does not imply** perfection in a pedantic sense (def. pedantic: overemphasis of rules or minor details **as in 'absolutely flawless')**… The Lucan '**merciful**' is more suitable to the context…"[3] |

Jesus gave us a parable of the shrewd manager (Luke 16:1) in which a man's imperfect efforts to fulfill his delayed tasks are commended. Dummelow comments on this parable, "The [rich man] **praised not the morality of** [his manager's] **transaction, but its far-sighted prudence** (760)." Jesus also said that the children of this world can be wiser in their own way than the "children of light" (Luke 16:8).

So do we seek to be perfect or just do the very best job under the circumstances? Questions for the Christian Scientist: "How perfect does our physical and spiritual condition have to be, in order to let our spiritual light shine? **In our striving to be perfect, do we end up with a far-from-perfect result?** Is perfect healing doable under all conditions? At what point is any compromise with the world required by Christian Scientists to better carry on with their lives and with their spiritual work?"

"There are sinners in all societies, and it is vain to look for perfection in churches or associations."[4]

Reluctance to accept surgery

Surgery (also discussed in Chapter 1) requires a large discussion simply because it has been studiously avoided in church publications for nearly a century. Articles are not written about it. Testimonies in which Christian Scientists have surgery of any kind are not generally acceptable in our church magazines. It has been observed by many of our critics that Christian Scientists think little of having wisdom teeth extracted but

---

3. Black, *Peake's Commentary on the Bible*, 777.
4, Eddy, *No and Yes*, 41:12–13.

not other kinds of surgery. So what is the difference between the intrusiveness of some forms of dental surgery and other non-dental forms of surgery that are not typically looked on with approval by church members? The justification for dental surgery is that it is merely "mechanical," though we are hard-pressed to find passages in Mrs. Eddy's writings that back up that justification. In a real sense, all surgery is mechanical. What is also not cited in our church discussion is what Mary Baker Eddy wrote and said regarding surgery and dentistry.

An event in Mrs. Eddy's household We cited in the previous chapter an incident when George Kinter, a member of Mrs. Eddy's staff in her New Hampshire home, fell down one night and injured his face. A doctor was brought in who stitched up Mr. Kinter, and the doctor's good stitchery was complimented by his patient. No one was chastised over the incident.

Again what Mrs. Eddy wrote about surgery "Until the advancing age admits the efficacy and supremacy of Mind, it is better for Christian Scientists to leave surgery and the adjustment of broken bones to the fingers of a surgeon, while the mental healer confines himself chiefly to mental reconstruction and to the prevention of inflammation" (S&H 401:27). She also said in an interview: **"The work done by the surgeon is the last healing that will be vouchsafed** [def. 'permitted to be done without danger'] **to us, or rather attained by us, as we near a state of spiritual perfection. At present I am conservative about advice on surgical cases"** (*My.* 345:21). Why does Mrs. Eddy use the term "better," when Christian Scientists generally would not think of it that way? Does "conservative" mean "cautionary"?

Mrs. Eddy acknowledged the occasions of successful mental surgery by her students, but she clearly made allowance for the concession to conventional surgical methods "until the advancing age admits the efficacy and supremacy of Mind" (S&H 401). When would that age be, and has it arrived already?

Some Christians Scientists have believed that the "advancing age" is upon us. Herbert Eustace, a former member of the Christian Science Church's Board of Trustees, argued in 1934 that the "bonds of belief in human thought have been so loosed by the leaven of *Science and Health* that it has reached the point of being ready for anything."[5] The father of a friend of mine believed that "the 'advancing age' for him was now." His case was that of a badly broken ankle that a bone specialist predicted had only 10% probability of becoming normally functional again. The ankle was instead rapidly healed without physical surgery. (See November 1970, *C.S. Journal.*) Do testimonies such as this one indicate that the "advancing age" is here for the general usage of Christian Scientists and others? Or is this kind of evidence of spiritual healing wonderful but also "ahead" of a period when it is more consistently found to be replicable? (We continue this discussion about the "advancing age" in Chapter 16 "Time, Place, and Receptivity.")

Mrs. Eddy wrote in the *Journal* in regard to a tooth she had removed by a dentist, **"Long ago I instructed Christian Scientists not to interfere with methods of surgery, but if they should call a surgeon, to submit to his methods without discussion"** (Jan. 1901 *CSJ* 593).

Mrs. Eddy's reasoning about this compromise

What may be more pertinent to the Christian Scientist about the subject of surgery than the nature of the physical injury or the surgical process itself, is the **metaphysical and practical reasoning which Mrs. Eddy turned to in discussing this subject** in an article once known as "Repaid Pages" but not published formally by the Church until 2002.[6] **Three points of reasoning stand out in this article:**

- **By foregoing an anesthetic in surgery,** a Christian Scientist adds to his healing "workload" because he **is then confronting the serious fears of the doctor or dentist.**
- Jesus' words, **"Suffer this to be so now"** and his parable that **cautioned about going to "war with ten thousand against twenty thousand"** (Luke 14:31) are part of Mrs. Eddy's reasoning in exercising caution in regards to surgery.
- Most surprising of all might be her following statement: *"I have*

---

5. Eustace, *Christian Science*, 664.
6. A10407, courtesy of Mary Baker Eddy Library and Eddy, *My True Light and Life*, 634-635.

taken these preliminary steps [in regard to the employment of anesthetics in surgery on a Christian Scientist]...*and these steps are **not departures from Science, they are the effects of what he** [Jesus] **enjoined upon his disciples, 'Be ye therefore wise as serpents and harmless as doves'**...Truth is the absolute, intermediate, and ultimate of all things. To attempt the absolute demonstration of Truth in its intermediate stage is to delay its ultimatum in the minds of men. Hence the impracticability of undertaking to prove the entire power of the infinite to finite thought, and before your own thought has grasped all that is practical and demonstrated what you know is true of the divine Principle which governs."*

Her comment is related to both the use of ether in dental surgery and the use of an anesthetic in the case of the amputation of a limb or "a surgical operation of less severity," in both hypothetical cases involving a Christian Scientist.

Do these words here not suggest that **by grasping at more than we can spiritually and humanly prove, we may actually delay or hinder our progress**? One reason this point is not raised among Christian Scientists is that church members have been taught the polar opposite for decades. The prevailing church message has been that if a Christian Scientist turns to medical means, he or she will forfeit spiritual good in the present and future. The passages that encourage this line of thought in *Science and Health*[7] are never juxtaposed with the ones condoning surgery. Why?

Does Christian Science forbid a resort to medicine?

The short answer to this question is "no." There is the aforementioned statement in the Christian Science textbook that indicates that surgery in our age is "better" than not having it. There are other statements allowing for the use of hypodermic injections in the case of debilitating pain (*S&H* 464), as well as condoning the "right use of temporal and

---

7. Eddy, *S&H*, 445:10-13. For example: "Teach the dangerous possibility of dwarfing the spiritual understanding and demonstration of Truth by sin, or by recourse to material means for healing" (*S&H* 445:10-13).

eternal means" when a Christian Scientist has failed to receive healing through prayer (*S&H* 444). These citations and others notwithstanding, Christian Scientists since Mrs. Eddy's time have made pronouncements that have condemned their fellow church members for going to doctors for help. (See examples of these statements in Chapter 3.) Possibly one of the most forthright church articles condemning the use of medical means occurred in the early 1950s in a statement from the Christian Science Board of Directors as follows:

"The Christian Science religion requires its adherents to reach progressively and rapidly that state of spiritual understanding which **forbids their use of material means for healing***. Adherents of Christian Science regard medication and medical examination of all sorts as methods of indoctrination..."* [8]

Notice that this carefully worded statement of policy doesn't bluntly state that either Christian Science or the church organization forbids its members from going to doctors. The statement takes the church off the hook, but instead it deflects the onus and guilt onto church members who are "required" to "rapidly" reach a state of spiritual understanding which naturally would keep them from going to doctors.

With this kind of statement circulating widely among members, **is it any wonder that Christian Scientists themselves and the public at large have been convinced that Christian Science prohibited its members from going to doctors?**

There is a long-accepted assumption among church members that any Christian Scientist undergoing a procedure like surgery has implicitly departed from the faith practice and needs to progress in their spiritual understanding before returning to normative Christian Science, regardless of what Mrs. Eddy wrote on this subject. In the book *Religions in America*, the official Christian Science Church position, as of 1963, is stated thus:

---

8. *C. S. Sentinel*, July 12, 1952, 1225. Reprinted in four other *Sentinels* between 1951-1953.

> "If the Christian Scientist has not reached the degree of spiritual understanding which is needed for healing by spiritual means and resorts to some other means, he obviously cannot be said to be employing fully the method of Christian Science. He does not undergo condemnation for this; nor does he assume any burden of guilt. He is always free to improve his spiritual understanding and employ it exclusively, thus restoring his status as a Christian Scientist."[9]

These words are misleading in at least three different ways:

- Mrs. Eddy never stated or implied that it was the singular burden of a patient to heal themselves, but she placed primary responsibility of healing or failing to heal on the mental healer.[10] Her textbook makes no mention of a Christian Scientist who cannot heal themselves being in need of restoring his or her church status.
- Is the "method of Christian Science" summarized and outlined in *Science and Health*? If so, we must repeat—*Science and Health* includes a portrayal of surgery as a "better" alternative for the Christian Scientist than abstention from it (*S&H* 401:28).
- How can a church spokesperson write that no condemnation or guilt redounds to the church member when the statement above from *Religions in America* wags an accusatory finger at Christian Scientists who dare go to a doctor? As a result of statements like the above, the author is aware of numbers of church members who have been demoted from one position or another in the aftermath of a surgery or hospitalization.

---

9. Rosten, This book has been revised as *Religions of America*. The 1975 version maintained approximately the same wording as the 1963 version with the exception of noting that *Science and Health* allows for surgeons to "set a bone." That revised statement of policy is a misleading reduction of the actual words from the church textbook—"surgery *and* the adjustment of broken bones and dislocations...."

10. Von Fettweis, *Christian Healer* (Amplified Version), 151. Also see *Mis*. 41:29–31.

Moderating our church's approach, but without an explanation

Fifty years and more after the above policy statements were issued, the Christian Science Church has softened the wording of its public views about medicine but without any clear admission that church policy or views have been altered or have evolved.[11] Therefore you still find Christian Scientists carrying around old dogmas because those dogmas have never been publicly corrected. It is healthy for churches to evolve and grow, but it is less healthy when those churches do not openly acknowledge that change has taken place nor explain the reasons for that change.

Did the surgery of 1900 approximate what is done surgically today?

Yes, but to a limited degree. Surgery with lasers and other innovations has become quicker, more exact, more far-reaching in scope, and often more painless. But surgery in 1900 was being attempted for far more than the setting of bones. After the development of anesthetics in 1846 surgeons saw broader possibilities in their field. By 1882 surgery for gallbladder and cancer had been performed in the United States. By the late 1890s brain surgery had been accomplished at Massachusetts General Hospital, and in 1893 a doctor replaced the total shoulder joint of his patient. Mrs. Eddy surely would have been aware when she wrote about surgery in the church textbook, that the word "surgery" applied to far more than the adjustment of bones during her time, given that she continued editing her textbook into the early years of the twentieth century.

We look forward to a fuller discussion of these points and an analysis of the practical experiences of Christian Scientists regarding this field of inquiry.

---

11. "Christian Science Church Seeks Truce with Modern Medicine," *NY Times, 3-23-2010.*

Where the needs of a church confront a member's desire for healing

It has been pointed out by different religious commentators that Christian Scientists have culturally put more emphasis on an individual's connection with God than on the individual's tie with the larger Body of Christ or church as a whole.[12] So in seeking a spiritual healing, most Christian Scientists tend to think first about how their healing impacts themselves, and give less thought to how their healing, or absence of healing, impacts their church. Paul reasoned along these lines, **"You say, 'I have the right to do anything.' But not everything builds us** [the larger Christian community] **up"** (I Cor. 10:23 *New International Readers' Version*).

In Paul's letter to the Christians at Rome, he wrote: "That no man put a stumbling block or an occasion to fall in his brother's way" (Romans 14:13). In the case of prolonged healings where there is uncertainty about how to handle the situation, a Christian Scientist could take Paul's words in two ways:

- Would going to a doctor or a surgeon cause a stumbling block for my fellow Christian Scientists? Would it hurt the morale of my church?
- Or would the discomfort caused by a prolonged problem in the midst of church members be more of a stumbling block and a morale weakener for the church than if the member had sought medical help?

Let's look at **a few examples** of how Christian Scientists have handled long-term, visible problems.

Example 1
A well-known Christian Science practitioner in the 1960s was asked to consider being an editor for the church magazines and flew to the national headquarters in Boston. When he got there, the church officials were surprised to see that the practitioner had a very visible goiter on his throat. He was then asked not to give a public talk or take the editorial

---

12. See Chapter 6.

position. The goiter was healed through prayer several years later.

This case raises a couple of questions: Why did the practitioner not forewarn the church officials? Did he think that they wouldn't be bothered by his condition? To what degree should Christian Scientists shelter themselves from visible exposure while appearing in public with a disfiguring condition? Or shouldn't that matter?

Example 2
Robert Peel, author of a three-part biography of Mrs. Eddy, was so willing to "bear his cross" publicly that on the photo jacket of his book *Christian Science and its Encounter with American Culture*, a wen, a kind of growth above his eye, is clearly visible.

Example 3
A practitioner whom the author knew had a growth on her eyelid. She sought spiritual help for this problem from practitioners and teachers without success. One practitioner suggested surgery. After over ten years of prayers it was healed. Medically speaking, could this be considered normal for cysts or a growth of this kind or not?

Example 4
A branch church member in the Midwest had a visible growth on his head. It got larger during his adult life. A relative and a friend from his town finally pressured him about the problem, so he prayed seriously with a practitioner for about three months. A few months after that prayerful effort the growth emptied and drained. The church member then had a physician remove the remainder of skin and cyst from where the growth emptied, and his head was stitched up. Reactions to this varied. One friend said, "I know you were praying about it, and I was so glad it was removed." Another friend asked, "Why did you wait so long?" He answered, "I don't know. I really wanted to get spiritual growth. I guess I was ready [for healing]. I grew a lot from it all. But I don't think I can write a testimony because the doctor removed the cyst that caused the growth and the sac of skin after it emptied. In my church testimony I said I wasn't trying to be willful about it all, but was just working for spiritual growth."

Example 5
Harold Hobson, who worked as a drama critic for the *Monitor* from the 1940s to the 1960s always hobbled because of a broken ankle that had never been set. Mr. Hobson had been raised in the church before his accident, but he eventually rejected Christian Science as an adult, while apparently harboring no bitterness towards it.

Example 6
A well-known Christian Science teacher defended his use of radiation treatments for cancer late in life, saying, "It's better to be a live Christian Scientist than a dead one."

Example 7
A Christian Scientist "billboard" wrote about his experience this way: "My family knew the joy of God's healing power, but they also knew the deep pain and embarrassment of tending to a wounded warrior who refused to be helped by a surgeon. How did that picture change? I chose to exchange my mountain climb for the sake of my family. Their burden of putting up with me in my unhealed condition hurt me far more than my physical problem and lack of physical healing. Today, several years later after successful surgery, I am still committed to the power of God to heal, but I am willing to be humbled."

Example 8
And from the viewpoint of a family member of a "billboard": "Strength and courage were so visible at that time in your life. When I remember getting mad at you for not getting surgery sooner, I kick myself, because that was a time of building. I would never take those years of struggle back."

Note
There are any number of healings of prolonged physical conditions cited in the Christian Science magazines over the decades, but hardly ever a mention of the frustration of a healing effort.

| Let every man be fully persuaded in his own mind... Romans 14:5 |

If we have erred in this chapter by mainly pointing to examples where medical intervention of some kind was required, it is only to present the "rest of the story" and counter-weigh an imbalance in our historical church discussion. Just as Christian Scientists are willing to note the failures and shortcomings of orthodox medical practice, so we should be honest, humble, and willing to examine and learn from our own shortcomings and failures.

Hanging on a rope down a well

There once was a man who accidentally fell down a well but was able to grab onto a rope that dangled down the well, and he held onto this lifeline with all his might.

| **"He drew me out of many waters."** Ps. 18:16

After a long while in this condition, he had forgotten whether the rope was there to help him get out of the well or to keep him from falling to the bottom. Finally, a friend happened by. The friend peered down into the darkness and quietly informed the man that inches below his feet was dry concrete. He urged his friend to let go of the rope, rest his arms for a little while, and then allow the friend to pull him out of the well.

There are times when we must let go of our way of working things out. Maybe too much will has been impelling our actions. The friend in this story is the Christ. The bottom of the well is the fact of everlasting Life and infinite Love or grace. As we "work out our salvation," hanging onto our hope and prayer, or climbing successfully upward, Love, Life is always there for us no matter how far we fall. Listen to what Christ is telling you about working out your problem.

The following experience illustrates how "letting go of the rope," pausing, rethinking, and praying in a new way can lead us into healing channels:

After eight years of struggling with chronic, debilitating back pain, I acted on the request of my husband (an agnostic) to see an osteologist. Long story short, after an examination that included an MRI, the doctor said I had a serious problem that would only get worse, but that surgery for it was so risky that I should hold off on that until the condition was truly unbearable. Driving home with my husband, who had gone with me to hear the results of the MRI, I expressed my disappointment. He responded, "Well, now you know what you're dealing with, and you can face it squarely through the healing tradition you've always relied upon." Then it hit me that I'd been thrown back into the arms of Divine Love. For the first time in years, I felt peaceful about the challenge. After that, I began and ended every day with a very simple thought: "Wholeness is your normal and natural state of being." Many layers of insight came through that essential conviction. And bit by bit, within a year, I found healing.

There is a way in the wilderness. "There remaineth...a rest for the people of God." Hebrews 4:9 KJ21

Summary

There are no easy answers in this chapter to a difficult subject. It is the author's belief that if important questions are raised, and the varied experiences of Christian Scientists are freely shared, then any one of us can be helped or guided to a healthy conviction about what to believe or what course might be taken.

Early Christians wrestled with the moral dilemma of how much of a sacrifice they were willing to make in the face of an opposing political system, the Roman Empire. Some became martyrs, while others fled from the Roman authorities out of a desire to survive. Today Christian Scientists face a more subtle challenge—the medically exacting expectations of their surrounding society, together with their own individual needs and those of their larger church body. Wouldn't Jesus ask us individually and collectively, as he asked Peter: **Are you feeding my sheep?** And while we are considering that question, we can remember Jesus' willingness to satisfy the needs of the unbeliever, such as his student Thomas.

Questions for the "billboard" Christian Scientist and his or her family and friends:
- A friend of the author once shared this counsel: "Take your stand of conscience where you feel at peace." Where should we take our stand?
- Do I feel in my heart that I am getting somewhere, or am I just floating? Is spiritual growth going on or only a protracted martyrdom?

- Am I more afraid of what I anticipate a doctor might tell me about my condition than what a doctor would actually say?
- Does my desire to have physical healing outweigh other facets in my life to the point where my problem has become an obsession more than a heartfelt cause? Books about medical overtreatment in Western society include *Overtreated* and *The Treatment Trap*. Is the "billboard" church member working so hard to be a "good" church member that they are overtreating themselves metaphysically in a parallel way to what Benjamin Franklin once said: "Nothing is more fatal to health than an over care of it."
- Are prayer treatments that go on for years really the Science of Christianity in action or just a facsimile of that? What is the ultimate loss and gain in an extended pursuit of spiritual healing? How do we measure something like that?
- Do people become believers in a faith because of the spectacular and heroic achievement of their predecessors? The author has been impressed by various spiritual healings over the years (including that of his grandfather of a disease that was medically diagnosed as terminal), but those healings by themselves have not been what ultimately have given this author belief, conviction, or spiritual understanding.
- Is what I am pursuing spiritually based on dogma, the opinions of others, or based on an inspired sense of the Infinite?

Our health and its relation to others

In words of advice about marriage, Mrs. Eddy wrote: **"Consider its obligations, its responsibilities, its relations to your growth, and to your influence on other lives"** (*S&H* 68). Elsewhere she wrote: "To reckon the universal cost and gain, as well as thine own, is right in every state and stage of being" (*Mis.* 288:21). When we are engaged in any prolonged situation or struggle, it is in some ways a relationship, and these considerations are worthy of our thought and subsequent action.

REBUILDING TOGETHER

CHAPTER 5

"First restore friendship…"
Matthew 5:24 (Jubilee Bible 2000)
—reconciling differences in building unity

I will seek that which was lost, and bring again that which was driven away, and will bind up that which was broken…
Ezekiel 34:16

With a little more patience and a little less temper, a gentler and wiser method might be found in almost every case…[1]
Robert Louis Stevenson–writing about quarrels, 1892

JESUS PUT GREAT EMPHASIS on the need for his followers to get along with each other. Over **one-fourth of the Sermon on the Mount** (Matthew 5–7) is **devoted to forgiveness, loving our enemies, and reconciliation.**

Near the beginning of the Sermon on the Mount[2] is the command for Jesus' followers to **drop their offerings to God and forget everything else until they have cleaned their slate with any brother or sister who has a grievance with them.** Note here that this command does not apply to times when Christians have a problem with a friend. This passage applies when the friend has a problem with *them*.

Other reasons to reconcile

The act of reconciling with those who have a grievance against us is an especially powerful form of **"preaching the gospel to every creature."**

---
1. Stevenson, *Across the Plains*, 314.
2. Matthew 5:23-24.

Reconciling stirs up the compacted soil of resistant thought. Reconciling surprises and renews those who hear about it, and not only those personally touched by the action. It detoxifies bitter, ingrained prejudice. It preaches in a way that cannot be refuted because it is a deed, not a creed or speech.

One "reconciled" river

Truth is like the Mississippi River. That mighty current will flow to the Gulf of Mexico and will not be waylaid or diminished but instead be enriched by its fellow watery contributors. The Rock River, the Illinois, the Wabash, the Ohio, the Missouri, the Arkansas and other tributaries all contribute to the "Father of Waters," but **none of these bodies of water are harmed by their mutual collaboration. We might say that all of these rivers become reconciled one to another. In fact, each body of water is reborn, transformed in some significant way** by peaceful mingling with its brother-sister waters.

Distrust of Truth's power

The Pharisee Gamaliel prevented the death of Jesus' disciples and intervened for them, saying to the High Priest's council:

My advice to you now therefore is to let these men alone…for if this teaching or movement is merely human it will collapse of its own accord. But if it should be from God you cannot defeat them [the disciples and their cause], *and you might actually find yourselves to be fighting against God!*

Acts 5:38, 39 J. B. Phillips

Gamaliel trusted universal Truth to maintain its own cause.

If we believe that infinite Truth is actually powerful and will endure no matter what, then we will not hover over our cherished religious views as Uzzah did (II Samuel 6) when he tried to steady the teetering Ark of the Covenant. If we believe that universal Truth, no matter what its particular form, will triumph in the end, should we fear joining hands with others whose views we fear might dilute or corrupt our own? In the spirit of Gamaliel we should all say that if our own creed or mother faith is of God, then nothing can stop or harm it. And if our life-faith is not fully based on enduring reality, we can be assured that it will either be corrected, evolve, or not survive, but ultimately yield to some higher, clearer, spiritual adherence.

Singular righteousness

Much of what makes reconciliation difficult is the conviction by at least one of the two alienated parties of **singular righteousness—a conviction that our own righteousness is superior to the sins or doctrinal misinterpretations of others.** This sense of righteousness is visible in the story of Elijah (I *Kings* 19:14 *The Message*). "I've been working my heart out for God," Elijah protested in answer to the divine inquiry of what he was doing, and the prophet noted that he was ***the only faithful one*** among his people.

In this narrative God corrected Elijah by pointing out that since seven thousand others were out there working for the Almighty's cause, Elijah shouldn't be patting himself so hard on the back. Not everyone is able to hear the divine correction as clearly as Elijah did in that instance. Can we all pray in the spirit of John the Baptist (John 3:30) to **decrease our own sense of righteousness** while we make corresponding room for an increase not just in Christ, but in the Christ-goodness that exists in others whom we may now look down upon?

Church people do the darnedest things

The best representatives of Jesus are Christians who care for nothing other than to bless and strengthen their fellow beings. But Christians often struggle to follow Jesus' forgiving love.

The problem is characterized by a story appearing in *Reader's Digest* of a man rescued from a remote island in the ocean. As the rescue boat pulled away from the shore, everyone in it looked back at the island where there were three grass huts. "What are those three huts about?"

the rescuers asked their new passenger. The man answered, "The one on the left is my house, and the one in the middle is my church." "So what is the third hut then?" the rescuers persisted. "Oh," the saved man offered. "That's the church I used to be a member of."

Bending, growing, or breaking off

While the story in *Reader's Digest* was fictional, pettiness in true life divides churchgoers. A branch church of our denomination in the Midwest elected a practitioner as First Reader, but a controversy arose over the audible clacking of this woman's false teeth. Another practitioner gathered together members of the same church who so intensely disliked the clacking of the First Reader's teeth that they started a break-off church in a nearby town. You might say they formed a rival clique, but at least there was no more clack. Unfortunately, that break-off church did not last very long, and can't we surmise that the founding impulse was improperly based?

The Chicago Tribune once anticipated doing a story on the founding of the various Christian Science branch churches in the Chicago area. The branches were all receptive to this idea, and they supported the story's concept until church members in their research discovered one disturbing fact—many of the churches started not because the pre-existent churches grew too large, but because members broke off in various states of dissatisfaction from other branches in neighboring towns.

Growth that results from division of thought, rather than genuine growth, proceeds from a "house divided" which ultimately cannot stand.

Partiality and getting past it

With favored teachings we sow the seeds of superior feelings and divisions. If pet teachings or personal doctrines just sat on our bookshelves like a collection of rocks, there would be no harm in them. But when those teachings become trophies, or when our "pet rocks" become weapons that exalt one teacher over another or establish one spiritual interpretation as orthodox and others as heretical, they become the antithesis of Christianity. Christ said that in his Father's house were "many rooms" (John 14:2 NIV), and he demonstrated this inclusivity in the conduct of his ministry. However, Christian history is littered with the carcasses of teachers who could not tolerate or be tolerated because of doctrinal differences.

What did Jesus say? **"The man who is not against us is on our side"** (Mark 9:40 J.B. Phillips). This was Jesus' response when the disciples found a man healing in the Master's name but not following Jesus as the disciples wished him to. **Another citation** in Matthew appears to contradict Jesus' earlier statement: **"He that is not with me is against me"** (12:30). However, this statement does not necessarily rebut the previous one, because this latter verse appears in a discussion about those casting out devils "by Beelzebub."

Does this apparent contradiction suggest that Christians should not partner with those who work at polar opposites from themselves, as distinct from those who differ in practice only in less significant ways? Though Jesus often expressed impatience with his disciples, **he tolerated a broad range of spiritual ignorance and mistakes within the company of his followers.**

Partiality is not erased or corrected by empty claims to impartiality. If a parent favors one child over another, the disfavored one can feel the difference. It doesn't matter what the parent says. If the favoritism is there, you can't hide it from a child. One way by which Mrs. Eddy put down partiality among her students was by first taking the role of "Normal Class teacher" out of the hands of one individual (Edward Kimball) and then later **rotating the job between different teachers**. She did this, according to Richard Nenneman, not to repudiate any particular teaching or interpretation but to subordinate any exclusivism attached to one teacher over another.[3] She established the standard of "rotation in office" (*My.* 254) as a basic rule for Christian Scientists to follow.

---

3. Nenneman, *Persistent Pilgrim*, 291.

Emulating fellow Christians vs. resenting them

Paul urged Christians to "eagerly desire" (I Cor. 12:31 NIV) the spiritual gifts of others, as opposed to being jealous of them. In this way Christians would broaden their appreciation of those different from themselves and also strengthen their own breadth of Christian "skill." But what has happened in the Christian world is a **broad division of churches and teachings, differing from each other, often in minor particulars**, but all claiming to be Christian. There is a church in England called the **Strict and Particular Baptist Church** whose very name, though it was bestowed by others as has happened to the Mormons and Quakers, indicates how Christians have attempted over the years to outdo one another in righteousness by name and proclamation more than by quiet actions.

The long, sad story of partiality in the Bible

It is remarkable that the earliest stories of the Old Testament describe first the Lord God favoring Adam over Eve, or at least creating the woman as an after-thought or a bi-product and helper for the man-creation. In the next generation the Lord God approves of Abel's work over that of his brother Cain, ending in bitter jealousy and murder, followed by generations of one parent after another, first favoring one sibling over another child, jealousy being created, and violence or threatened violence resulting. Noah disfavored his son Ham for a seemingly innocent mistake. Sarah, probably out of jealousy over her husband's concubine Hagar, demanded that Abraham exile Hagar[4] and Hagar's child Ishmael. Wasn't this the Bible's justification for schism among the Semitic peoples, between Jew and Arab? Isaac is seen as an ancestor of the Jews while Ishmael is seen by many to be the forefather of the Arabs.

In the following generation, Isaac favored his son Esau, while his wife Rebekah favored Esau's twin, Jacob. All of this resulted in conflict, threatened murder, and years of estrangement between Esau and Jacob.

---

4. Muslims consider Hagar to have been Abraham's wife.

Jacob favored his younger sons Joseph and Benjamin over the older siblings, though you would think he'd have learned not to do that, in remembering the bitter fruits of his own upbringing. This pattern of partiality haunts the practice of religion and serves as a negative model for worshippers down through the ages, for it justifies honoring one party or school of thought over another.

Jesus' parable of the prodigal son mitigates this tendency of unresolved tensions and favoritism by illustrating in his story **the relative merits and weaknesses of both** sons rather than highlighting and justifying continued enmity. Shouldn't Jesus' model of reconciliation be ours today, instead of the tragic earlier history of jealousy and mindless division?

Peter and Paul's reconciliation
*no greater burden than these necessary things...*Acts 15:28

Without a significant compromise of beliefs between Peter and Paul (see Acts 15), would Christianity have become a worldwide movement? While Peter's ministry focused on the Jewish Christians, and Paul's mission was directed to the Gentiles or non-Jewish peoples of the upper Mediterranean Basin, "Judaizing" Christians pressured Paul to demand that his converts to Christianity be circumcised. In Chapter 15 of Acts this question of the circumcision was resolved by the verbal and written approval of the apostles in Jerusalem. Peter and Paul concluded together that circumcision would no longer be required for gentile converts.

Instead, Peter and Paul reached a middle ground of agreement. A kind of **"basic kosher"** pact was decided between the disciples committed to the Jewish tradition and Paul and his co-workers.

The four common points of agreement were:
- prohibition from eating meats sacrificed to idols
- prohibition from drinking blood
- prohibition from eating things that had been strangled
- forbidding fornication.

Of course, this agreement hardly touched all the Ten Commandments, let alone other intricate demands of the Torah, but it **allowed both groups** of Christians, the traditional Jewish Christians and the Gentile-ministering ones, **to proceed together in mutual acceptance**. The King James Bible describes this agreement as "no greater burden than these necessary things" (Acts 15:28).

Today's Christians who reconcile potentially divergent practices within a Christian body would probably not pick Peter and Paul's four doctrinal points on which to converge. Sticking points for some Christians today might include whether to allow gays into the priesthood or not. But the spirit of what Peter and Paul accomplished in finding common ground in order to unify their Christian cause should remain a prominent model for all religious societies.

Compromise, condemnation, and hypocrisy

We will make no attempt here to trace the history of all Christian successes and failures in reconciling diverse teachings through the ages, but we can recommend that readers look into the life of St. Cyprian of Carthage (ca. 200-258 C.E.). Cyprian converted to Christianity around 245 C.E., and rapidly found himself in a leadership role in the church. Early in his career as a Christian bishop he fled from Roman persecution.

Later in life he verbally chastised compromisers who, under threat of death, had sacrificed meat to idols. But having himself fled Roman oppression, Cyprian wrote somewhat hypocritically. His letter "On the Lapsed" describes the conflicts of conscience that Christians were forced to wrestle with in that day, and their problems in reconciling Christian beliefs, especially during times of persecution.

We may find ourselves arguing with Cyprian's reasoning, given his decision to flee the Romans and lead his people at a safe distance while he remained in exile. Ultimately Cyprian bravely walked to his death at the hands of a Roman purge of Christians. His internal conflicts, eventual self-sacrifice, pangs of conscience, compromises, and even hypocrisy form part of the story of many Christians from before Cyprian's time up to the present.

Our very brief historical tour here helps explain somewhat why there are so many divisions among those who honor Christ. When Jesus was crucified, soldiers **"divided his garments, casting lots"** (Matthew 27:35). Is it the human ego or pride or an age-old form of idolatry that goads us to covet our own particular brand of religion, to choose the part of Christ's garments of teaching that we like the most, and to look down on the practices of others, instead of finding common ground as Peter and Paul did?

Fortunately, in the past century there have been movements toward Christian unity and definitely a trend towards Christians gathering together in communities for celebrations, or during times of tragedy and calamity, for the benefit of their respective communities, and for the mutual blessing of spiritual unity. May that trend continue, because Jesus would certainly want us to be one spiritual Body. Jesus himself had to reprimand his disciples for competing with each other over who was closest to the Master and over who would sit at his right hand in heaven (Matthew 20:21).

Paul's counsel

"Brothers, if anyone is caught in any sin, you who are spiritual [that is, you who are responsive to the guidance of the Spirit] *are to **restore such a person in a spirit of gentleness*** [not with a sense of superiority or self-righteousness], *keeping a watchful eye on yourself, so that you are not tempted as well."*

Galatians 6:1 (Amplified Bible)

Have Christians during the past two millenia worked sufficiently to maintain the "spirit of gentleness" that Paul commended to us? If not, another excellent admonition, often attributed to St. Augustine but actually written by an Italian theologian Marco Antonio de Dominis (d. 1624), may be helpful:

"In essentials unity, in non-essentials liberty; in all things, charity."

The large irony here is that Marco Antonio, born a Jesuit, ended up by alienating himself at different times in his life from both the Pope and the Catholic Church and later from the Anglican Church, and then at the end of his life leaving the Catholics again. So just because you can say nice things about unity does not always mean that your practice of religious unity comes easily.

> "Not excommunicating is the way we say that we are not the only church."
> New Order Amish minister[5]

Discipline and division among Christian Scientists

During the lifetime and spiritual leadership of Mary Baker Eddy, we have record of church members being excluded from fellowship only for extreme reasons. Here are two examples:

Augusta Stetson was quoted by one of her then-supporters as calling for the mental murder of those opposed to her.[6] While on the surface professing adulation toward Mrs. Eddy, Stetson attempted to build a spiritual monopoly, if that were possible, among the Christian Scientists in New York City. Mrs. Eddy wrote innumerable letters to this difficult student and visited with Stetson in attempting to win her back to normal fellowship, but to no avail.

Another Christian Scientist, Josephine Woodbury, had a child out of wedlock, then claimed it was an immaculate conception, and named the child "Prince of Peace." Both Stetson and Woodbury were asked to leave the Mother Church. After Mrs. Eddy's passing, we have any number of accounts of Christian Scientists who either resigned or were excommunicated for far lesser cause than was the case for either Augusta Stetson or Josephine Woodbury.

None of these cases that the author is aware of involved charges of mental murder or claiming immaculate conceptions. Rather, these incidents tended to involve shades of difference in spiritual teaching. In exasperation, Mrs. Eddy once wrote to her Board of Directors regarding the desire of some of her followers to remove from membership

---

5. Hurst, *An Amish Paradox*, 89.
6. Peel, *Years of Authority*, 339.

fellow worshippers for petty reasons: **"I see what you do not in these cases of discipline. If I were to have the students that break faith all excommunicated without sufficient effort on my part and yours to save them, how many members think you would be left…?"**[7]

The "Great Litigation"

Each one of you says something different. One says, 'I follow Paul'; another, 'I follow Apollos'; another, 'I follow Peter'; and another, 'I follow Christ.' Christ has been divided into groups!

I Cor. 1: 12-13, Good News Translation

What is called the "Great Litigation" (1916-1922)[8] never should have happened. First off, it wasn't "great" at all. It was a dispute or power struggle based on differing interpretations between two boards (Trustees and Directors) over deeds held in trust and church writings. Secondly, the litigation violated what Paul wrote about **intra-church legal disputes being taken before a judge outside the church** (1 Cor. 6). This ongoing dispute ran up against everything the founder of Christian Science taught about people getting along with one another:

> *"…**let your opponents alone**, and use no influence to prevent their legitimate action from their own standpoint of experience, knowing, as you should, that God will well regenerate and separate wisely and finally; whereas you may err in effort, and lose your fruition."*[9]

As the years-long legal wrangle within the Mother Church was winding down to a conclusion and final court opinion, an editorial appeared in the *Sentinel* (FEB. 11, 1922) entitled, "A Word to the Field." The writer stated, **"This is not a time for exultation or recrimination. It is the hour when every intelligent plea for closer unity and cooperation among brethren should be promptly heeded and wisely observed."**

---

7. L00317 11-08-1902 courtesy of Mary Baker Eddy Library.
8. While the actual legal battle extended from 1919–1922, the internal battle between the Board of Directors and the Board of Trustees had begun by 1916.
9. Eddy, *No and Yes*, 7–9. See especially 9:8–13.

Unfortunately, those words were not followed by deeds. It proved to be instead a time for recrimination. After the legal battle was concluded, letters were sent to practitioners with questions to determine whose side members were on.[10] Losers in the suit were excommunicated, and the aftermath of the suit has echoed down through the decades with a lawsuit within recent years echoing points similar to those in the "Great Litigation." The author is aware of two practitioners, excommunicated after the lawsuit's conclusion but later reinstated, who eventually "got over" the humiliation of their exclusion.

Again, would the litigation ever have occurred if both boards had heeded Paul's injunction that people of Christian faith should not haul their Christian brethren before a "pagan court" (I Corinthians 6)?[11] Instead of a public legal remedy, Paul had recommended that internal church disputes be settled by those "who are the least esteemed in the church."[12] Who exactly the "least esteemed" might be is open to different possible interpretations, but the message is clear from Paul that bringing church matters before courts is unseemly at best and should be avoided at all costs.

Even if both the warring boards had considered their battle to have been a war worth waging, and an appeal to civil courts to be proper, a broad spirit of reconciliation should have followed the concluding verdict. Jesus' parable of the vengeful servant speaks volumes to this kind of inside-the-church Christian contention.

In Jesus' parable (Matthew 18:23-25), a servant is forgiven his debt to his master, but then the forgiven servant goes out and treats mercilessly a fellow-servant whose debt is far smaller. Surely the argument between the Board of Trustees and the Board of Directors over the structure of authority within the Christian Science Church was **no battle over essential spiritual principles, but instead one that involved personal interpretations and no small amount of ego.**

---

10. Studdert-Kennedy, *Christian Science and Organized Religion*, 66–67.
11. I Corinthians 6:1, NLT, "When one of you has a dispute with another believer, how dare you file a lawsuit and ask a secular court to decide the matter instead of taking it to other believers!"
12. Ibid., verse 4, KJV.

Sadly, most religious disputes come down to relatively petty matters. Given this tendency, should not the final legal resolution of this church dispute have been an ideal time to bury the proverbial hatchet and to unify over spiritual essentials, rather than drive a lasting wedge of hostility into the body of our church's history? Mrs. Eddy had written quite plainly for Christian Scientists to "…hold no controversy or enmity over doctrines and traditions, or over misconceptions of Christian Science…." (*No and Yes 8:19*). Both boards in the quarrel violated these instructions—the Board of Trustees, by initiating the lawsuit, and the Board of Directors, by surreptitiously encouraging church members to stop subscribing to the Trustees' church publications.[13]

Should a portion of blame for the infamous litigation rest on the shoulders of the church membership? Was there not a responsibility to action on the part of the members when they saw their church being torn in half by the two warring boards? Were they not too much like sheep in the pejorative meaning of that word? There is no clear provision in our church by-laws for the congregation to register a vote, but surely there should have been concerted prayers, church meetings, and even spontaneous demonstrations from members telling both boards to drop their battle, find a compromise position, and carry on responsibly with church goals. Let's examine some of the negative consequences from that unfortunate era about which most Christian Scientists have only a vague awareness.

Squabbles over little matters with large consequences

More than creating a long-term basis for division among Christian Scientists, the "Great Litigation" did something far more tragic. It distracted the church from its primary spiritual field of duty. What happened in the world around Boston during the years of the prolonged litigation? "While men slept" what has been called the **Spanish Flu** (January 1918-December 1920) killed between fifty and one hundred million worldwide.

---

13. *Answer to Bill in Equity*, (April 4, 1920), 7. The Directors were found guilty of contempt of court and were fined for doing this.

Two hot spots of the flu outbreak were considered to be Fort Devens, Massachusetts, and Ayers, Massachusetts,[14] (respectively thirty-six miles and thirty-seven miles from the Mother Church). If you knew that something devastating was going on in your neighborhood that would kill 50 million of your fellows worldwide in a year, wouldn't you move heaven and earth to devote yourself to its eradication or remedy? By historical comparison, the Spanish Flu killed more people in one year than the Black Death did in one hundred years. It killed more in twenty weeks than AIDS did in twenty years. But instead of performing a prayerful watch, the Christian Scientists were caught up in strife over temporal power within their ranks.

The unjust settlement of World War I (1918-19) **and the failure of the League of Nations** laid the groundwork for the rise of Nazi Germany, World War II, and the Holocaust. In the United States, during this period Prohibition was passed as a national law, with its ensuing side effects of massive scofflaw attitudes and gangland ascendency. The **Ku Klux Klan** was re-founded in 1915, and peaked in popularity between that year and 1925, when the Klan openly marched on Washington, D.C. Not only did our church not defend itself against the racism of the Klan, it imposed institutional racism in 1926 by segregating its American churches—a stain on our history that lasted formally for the next thirty years and longer in at least our nursing homes and southern churches.

We will not argue that all the ills of the world at this time occurred as a result of one church denomination descending into internecine strife and abandoning its post of spiritual alertness. Let's just say that the negligence of Christian Scientists during that period was at least in some measure tantamount to indifference towards the evils and troubles that occurred in that era. Can we ask if the founder of the Christian Science Church had personally been at the helm during that dark period, might she not likely have sent the offending parties on both sides of the controversy packing their bags and leaving Boston for a one-way trip back to their respective homes?

Let's look now at a few creative ways to mediate church battles.

---

14. http://www.newenglandhistoricalsociety.com/the-1918-flu-epidemic-kills-thousands-in-new-england/

Tools for reconciliation

Most churches and religious groups could benefit from Paul's advice to the Christians at Rome. Paul recommends mutual toleration of Christian meat-eaters and their vegetarian counterparts. This advice could apply to reconciling any diversity of practice within a religious body. Rather than the meat-eater sitting in judgment over the vegetarian, Paul writes, **"Destroy not him** [the vegetarian] **with thy meat"** (Romans 14:15). Verse 14 would be controversial in many churches today—**"Nothing is intrinsically unholy"** (J.B. Phillips). That verse brings to mind some very unconventional young Christians I've read of who were willing for a short while to smoke cigarettes, which they detested, in order to better relate to teenagers they were trying to encourage and pray for. Verse 19 **"Build each other up"** (The Living Bible) is the Golden Rule in action.

Keeping focus and "plowing around" smaller issues

What prevents religion from being relevant to an increasingly large number of people especially in the West is that church controversies **tend to not be central to the core of a faith teaching, or even to life itself.** Paul labels these controversies as **"foolish arguments, which only upset people and make them angry."** [15] Putting focus and energy on issues of minor importance tends to drive away all but the most die-hard church attendees. Often these ongoing quarrels come down to a feud over who is right, more than over what is right. A little child can see that.

From Abraham Lincoln's life In 1862, Lincoln was focused on the prosecution of the battle to preserve the Union. Opponents of the Mormons and polygamy urged the President to send federal troops into Utah and go after the Mormons. An anti-bigamy act was passed by Congress. Lincoln fully realized that the attention of the federal government could not be distracted by the "Mormon problem" if there was any hope of a successful conclusion to the country's civil war. This is what Lincoln told a Mormon emissary:

---

15. II Timothy 2:23, TLB.

"*...when I was a boy on the farm in Illinois, there was a great deal of timber on the farms which we had to clear away. Occasionally we would come to a log which had fallen down. It was too hard to split, too wet to burn and too heavy to move, so* **we plowed around it**. *That's what I intend to do with the Mormons. You go back and tell Brigham Young that if he will let me alone, I will let him alone.*" [16]

In a different era and quoting a different cultural (Chinese) precedent, former presidential advisor Henry Kissinger offered a slightly similar proverb:

"When there is turmoil in the heavens, little problems are dealt with as if they were big problems. And big problems aren't dealt with at all. When there is order in the heavens, big problems are reduced to smaller problems, and little problems should not obsess us." [17]

"Teach men patiently and wisely to stem the tide of sectarian bitterness, whenever it flows inward."   S&H 139:12

Keeping the "Matthew code" in perspective

Too often the "Matthew code,"[18] a three-step process apparently intended to resolve church disputes, has been misconstrued by treating the three salient passages in isolation and separating those verses from the context of the rest of the chapter—whose over-arching theme is one of **reconciliation at all costs**, and not one of recrimination or punishment. Chapter 18 of Matthew's Gospel addresses the need for patient and nearly unlimited, persistent forgiveness as well as a demand to avoid hypocritical condemnation of our fellow Christians.

---

16. Widmer, "Lincoln and the Mormons," *New York Times*, 11-17-2011.
17. Kissinger, "The Nature of Diplomacy in the Contemporary Period," April 8, 1999.
18. The Living Bible, Matthew 18:15–17. If a brother sins against you, go to him privately and confront him with his fault. If he listens and confesses it, you have won back a brother. But if not, then take one or two others with you and go back to him again, proving everything you say by these witnesses. If he still refuses to listen, then take your case to the church, and if the church's verdict favors you, but he won't accept it, then the church should excommunicate him.

Undermining ego with humor

As mentioned earlier in this chapter, Mrs. Eddy spent endless hours trying to corral into positive channels the ego and promise of one of her students, Augusta Stetson. Unfortunately, Stetson's efforts to simultaneously flatter and yet undermine her teacher didn't yield to Mrs. Eddy's pleadings to be more humble and act accordingly. Mrs. Eddy commented to her student Emma Newman: "**If only Mrs. Stetson had had a sense of humor, I could have reached her.** I could have required no other virtue through which to work."[19]

The humor that undermines entrenched ego is the kind of gentle needling that Will Rogers applied generously to the whole class of politicians in the 1930s and which endeared Rogers to the American public.

"Love your enemy" taken to new heights

An article in the *Atlantic Magazine* describes an African-American jazz musician, Daryl Davis, who has managed to befriend a large number of members of the Ku Klux Klan. Not only has Davis found friends among the Klan members, but their friendship has produced a very surprising result—several of them have resigned from the Klan, and a few have even given Davis their old Klan outfits. What was Davis's approach that accomplished this amazing feat? **He listened to them**. Davis notes: **"The most important thing I learned is that when you are actively learning about someone else you are passively teaching them about yourself. So if you have an adversary with an opposing point of view, give that person a platform. Allow them to air that point of view, regardless of how extreme it may be."**[20]

We could add the Daryl Davis story to a pantheon of "how-to-achieve-reconciliation" stories that every church and nation can take to heart. Peace among peoples is not rocket science, but it does require conscious desire and effort. Look for good in another's reasoning. When

---

19. This was told by Mrs. Newman's student, Winifred Arbogast, to the author's Christian Science teacher, Daniel Jensen.
20. Friedersdorf, "Audacity," *Atlantic*, 3-27-2015.

you see the good in the thinking of your opponent, you begin inevitable change in yourself. Surely that approach is common to almost all religious traditions. It only requires participation.

Remembering what life is all about

A friend of the author became wound up in an emotional rant about church controversies in the presence of a long-time practitioner. At one point in the conversation the elderly listener appeared distracted from my friend's complaint, looked out the window into the distance, and in what we might call a Zen moment,[21] she remarked, "Aren't the evergreens beautiful this time of year!"

Recommendations for action

Throughout religious history, we find that the heretics of a particular age are often seen decades or centuries later as ahead of their time, as pioneers, or as prophets, even if they were gadflies to the establishment of their time. The following are ideas for consideration by both a local church as well as by all our churches.

Cast a wide net in bringing back into the fold excluded students A net of support, grace, and inclusion should be thrown out far and wide to embrace the unorthodox of all folds. In our church there are those de-listed practitioners excluded for holding minor points of belief among themselves, different from that of either a local church or officials in the Mother Church. Happily, **in recent years some of these individuals have had their official status restored**, but in our denomination's history there are far too many who have been neither healed nor comforted by the treatment they received from their fellow Christian Scientists. A **significant apology from the church is required**. There are many former members who simply feel excluded, hurt, or not good enough. A former First Reader who had surgery told me: "I had trouble going back to church."

---

21. "In Zen practice, deliberately irrational statements are sometimes used...to jar persons into realizing the limits of the common uses of the intellect." (Urban Dictionary)

Toleration of divergent or different teachings For example, British practitioner John Doorly was by many accounts a very good healer. However, he developed a fascination with the importance of the numerical order of the synonyms for God. (See *S&H* 465:10.)

Can our church be magnanimous enough to put up with that idiosyncratic teaching, honor Doorly's good works, but without feeling obliged to promote the numerological theory he espoused? Would Doorly's theory have been too outlandish for Jesus to accept him as a student, or not?

Similarly, Bliss Knapp's divergent theory about Mrs. Eddy as one of the great lights, together with Jesus, referred to in Genesis 1:16, seems to lie outside what most Christians could accept. Knapp's theory also has no basis in either Christian Science or Bible teaching, but Knapp married into huge wealth. He offered the Christian Science Church millions of dollars if the church would publish his book and maintain its regular availability for decades. The resulting controversy about the church's acceptance of the Knapp book divided many Christian Scientists and their churches in the 1990s.

Paul wrote to the Thessalonians: **"Do not stifle inspiration, and do not despise prophetic utterances, but bring them all to the test and then keep what is good in them and avoid the bad of whatever kind"** (I Thess.5:19–22 NEB).

> "Let both grow together unto the harvest."
> Matthew 13

Again, can't we work to tolerate divergent theories, embrace the theorist, even while we withhold judgment on the theory in question and not mainstream teachings that are dubious? Mrs. Eddy's aforementioned advice on pages 7–9 of *No and Yes* should be used as a template on this subject. Loving our brother and sister and "plowing around" points of contention or controversy is the way human families learn to get along with each other. Church families should be able to do the same.

"Listening sessions," not lectures, for the alienated Catholics have set up what they call "listening sessions" where former members are encouraged to come and vent their sorrows and complaints with the church. At these sessions there can be no judgment, no quoting at one another, no lecturing, no looking down on anyone. Only seeing the Christ in everyone.

Here is another nugget of wisdom from Abraham Lincoln: "The Civil War was in its last days, and the North was the apparent victor. An aide approached the President and inquired, 'What shall we do now that the South is conquered?' Lincoln replied, 'I will treat them as if they never left.'"[22]

Hearing both sides of any situation (*Mis.* 146:6–25) The following verse from the Gospel of John summarizes this precept of withholding judgment of any kind until all evidence is presented: "…surely our Law does not condemn the accused without hearing what he has to say, and finding out what he has done" (John 7:51 J.B. Phillips).

Here is a small example of how this can be accomplished: Rose Henniker-Heaton, a well-known practitioner and lecturer, successfully intervened with church officials who were going to exclude a practitioner from the *Journal* for having an occupation in addition to her practice. After inquiry it turned out that the prospective practitioner's other "occupation" consisted of her one-time sale of a litter of puppies.

Understand Jesus' teaching (Matthew 12:30) about parting company with those who insist on healing by "opposites" such as witchcraft, voodoo, etc. But cherish a willingness to **see the validity of others' views rather than to abruptly condemn slight theological differences in our fellow worshippers.** Presumably any exclusion in these circumstances must also include the steps mentioned earlier from the Matthew Code (Matthew 18:15–17); the Matthew Code passages cannot be separated from the spirit of reconciliation and forgiveness in the whole of Matthew 18.

> **You had correct teaching but not the *best* teaching.**
> a Christian Science teacher to his pupils

Carefully discuss in our church magazines issues of contention when the occasion arises, with regular reminders and examples of reconciliation and forgiveness. To date, our examples of reconciliation have tended to involve the peacemaking and prayerful efforts of Christian Scientists and others in their communities and the world, but not the specific reconciliation of differences of teaching and practice among our fellow church members.

---

22. Epperly, "Abraham Lincoln and the Quest," *New York Times, 2-17-2012.*

Practice* deep *rotation in office in making Mother Church (and branch church) appointments. Make a practice of selecting different students from a variety of Christian Science teachers all of whom would be expected to not stay on in Boston or at the church headquarters for longer than a few years at a time.

It would then be abnormal to move to Boston and remain there for any but unusual reasons. Rotation is meant to weed out obstacles to mutual understanding and respect among Christian Scientists. "Rotation in office promotes wisdom, quiets mad ambition, satisfies justice, and crowns honest endeavors" (*My.* 250:5–6).

Also helpful with this issue is the Baha'i first principle of consultation: "A broadly based consultation [when making church decisions] **is a healthy barrier against the opinions of the forceful."**

A Jubilee[23] ***year devoted to reconciliation*** In March, 1897 Mrs. Eddy asked that Christian Scientists stop teaching formal classes for a year and unite in reading her newly finished *Miscellaneous Writings*. It is a recommendation here that Christian Scientists do something similar today—delineate **a year devoted to self-knowledge and reconciliation** within the circle of our present fellowship and include those former Christian Scientists who have become estranged from fellowship for whatever reason. This constitutes a re-setting of the foundation for our church that is necessary in order for a new beginning to take place.

Must the "vineyard" have better tenants?
Matthew 21:33–44

Jesus' parable of the vineyard occupied by violent tenants is a parable rarely read in our Lesson-Sermons. It contains a very challenging message. The parable contains serious implications for Christians and Christian Scientists since it basically concludes that if Christians act in a hateful, spiteful way towards the representatives of the vineyard's

---

23. Peloubet, *Bible Dictionary*, 333–334. A special year of remission of sins and universal pardon is first mentioned in the Bible in Leviticus 25:9. According to Peloubet, its purpose was "to be a remedy for those evils which accompany human society and human government."

owner (God), they will be removed, and new "renters" will be brought in. One implication might be that if we in our church cannot behave in a way worthy of our teaching, then **what is best in Christian Science may well be given to more worthy people to love and practice.** This is not an easy message to digest, but an important one.

So we have a choice…establishing and rebuilding the spirit of real unity in a church is not an easy matter. There are practical ways to work on that building project, and fortunately significant steps have been taken in recent years to this end. Large-scale reconciliation should be a very high priority for us as a Christian body.

CHAPTER 6

Sitting at the end of the pew
—community and individualism and why spiritual life requires teamwork

We neither live nor die as self-contained units. At every turn life links us to the Lord.

Romans 14:7,8 J. B. Phillips

God setteth the solitary in families.

Psalms 68:6

WHY DO CHURCH MEMBERS sit at the end of a pew? To make an early exit from the service? To "claim" that pew and unintentionally make it hard for others to join them? Because of shyness? To be alone in prayer? To get to the bathroom easily? There are lots of reasons. Let's set aside for a moment the positive and very legitimate reasons for seeking solitude in church and ask, "What should be our connection, not just with the Holy Presence, but with our fellow churchgoers?"

Are we a church of the Lone Ranger? Even the Lone Ranger needed help from his reliable partner Tonto.

In an arresting critique of the practice of Christian Scientists, Prof. Bryan Wilson writes: "The sect provides a metaphysical philosophy to which a votary must become intellectually committed for his own advantage…rather than that of a group or of the wider society…Communal involvement is low. ***There is no real community*** [my emphasis added], only an association of those seeking and employing a particular regime of mental hygiene and therapy…The votaries may not even know each other except as passing acquaintances: there is no expectation that the adherents form a family-like community."[1] This is a scary picture if true. While the author has not experienced this lack of community in the various churches of which he has been a member, he is very aware of churches in our denomination that have behaved to visitors and members as cold as ice. If Prof. Wilson's depiction of Christian Scientists is the case in a local branch church, the worshippers are penalizing themselves in ways that they may not realize.

If any church or social group becomes a very loosely-knit gathering of rugged individuals, then it starts to attract mostly its own cultural self-stereotype of those who are shy, somewhat anti-social, and introverted. Before long, without anyone putting out an announcement, this gathering then self-selects and perpetuates an organizational image, and you find people there who are content to mostly be left alone, having minimal contact with one another. This organizational model does not bode well for any social entity, let alone a church, since dynamic growth, vitality, and progress rest on strong social cohesion. We'll look at counter-models of this "rugged individual" model shortly.

Do you know what it is like to walk into a church and not one person talks to you, not one person touches you, and no one even acknowledges your presence? I do. You can cut the rejection with a knife. You cannot imagine how alone you feel.[2]

Messy Spirituality, 64

Do those words describe any of our churches?

A visitor to a Christian Science church commented that in eleven years of attending his local congregation, no one from that church had ever engaged him in a real conversation. If that happened to me, I would not have waited eleven years to hit the door. Aren't we supposed to be spir-

---

1. Wilson, *Social Dimensions*, 198.
2. Yaconelli, *Messy Spirituality,* 64.

itual family? If we are isolated individuals, what is the Body of Christ? The following is why this translates into a big problem:

From a former member:
"I love Christian Science, but my wife and I need a church where people will be there for us if we really need them."

People go where they feel welcome, really welcome. Love in a church is more important than the church's apparent theology, because love is real theology. A friend of the author is a very warm, engaging man. When he served as First Reader in his branch church, he enthusiastically began the service with a Southern-accented, "You are all *most* welcome!" Trouble was that a few members heard this as, "You are *almost* welcome."

And therein is a potential problem. If everyone was as truly warm and sincerely inviting as my friend, there would be no problem. It's that feeling that the visitor or even a member senses that he or she is *almost* welcome…that threatens the family feeling which belongs at the heart of every church.

Christ's model of teamwork

Cast thy burden on the Lord, and he will sustain thee.
Psalms 55:22

Bear ye one another's burdens, and so fulfill the law of Christ.
Galatians 6:2

In the Gospel of Matthew, Chapter 11, Jesus puts forward a model of Christian action. Are Christians weary and "heavy-laden"? Then take the yoke of Christ in order to get your work accomplished. Work animals in Jesus' time were usually yoked in pairs. It's so much easier to accomplish many of life's tasks when working with partners. Are we not teamed up with Christ, and doesn't this heavenly teamwork make our task very doable? The author has felt the close Christian support of many good friends who have been an encouragement and blessing in every year of his ministry.

Jesus commissioned his disciples to **work together in teams of two**. Acts 3 describes Peter and John "going up together into the temple" where healing resulted. Look at Acts 12, where the prayers of the church were directly related to Peter's freedom from imprisonment. For starters, it can be a joy to share churchgoing, or performing any number of tasks or a journey with a friend, rather than doing so on our own. Jehovah's Witnesses go door-to-door in teams of two. Mormon missionaries work and live in pairs. This is especially necessary for moral support when working in a foreign country, and this partnership provides crucial encouragement when doors are slammed in the missionaries' faces.

> Two are better than one…for if they fall, one will lift up his fellow.
> Ecclesiastes 4:9, 10

Jesus told his followers to **wash one another's feet**, and to feed the Master's sheep—to nourish and protect the congregation of believers. James urged Christians to **confess their faults one to another** as a foundation for healing (James 5:16). These duties could hardly be performed if there existed a **wall of safe, private distance between worshippers**.

So we're not just talking about a social hour after church, though that could be helpful. We're talking about **unconditional love, felt by and for members, newcomers, and strangers**. This love is life-giving and Christian, and without it we can hardly call ourselves Christian. If this love is felt strongly, an "all are welcome" sign might be seen outside our edifice, but it wouldn't be absolutely necessary.

A Christian Science society in the South has made a practice of getting together on a regular basis for meals and occasional volleyball games after services. They believe in Paul's message to the Christians at Thessalonica: "We ask you, my brothers, to get to know those who work so hard among you" (I Thess. 5:12 J. B. Phillips).

A church that doesn't pray and live its way into the hearts of its adherents and its community has put up **an invisible electric fence** around the church perimeter. The fence literally keeps people out, and nobody is the wiser—even those who drive by.

"*I always mean to visit your church, but I don't know why I never go in.*"   a friend of the author

The action of this "electric fence" is sometimes recognized by Christian Scientists. But too often the problem is pigeonholed and dismissed in the following way. A church member will say: "We have to handle animal magnetism" (i.e. specifically pray about what influences others negatively), and maybe the discussion of this problem ends right there. This Christian Science terminology parallels what a Christian might say about the negative influence of Satan or the devil. In both instances, evil or negative action as an influence is typecast. To the Christian Scientist that negative action is a mental push or pull running counter to good or spiritual intention. In the Christian's case, this influence tends to take on a more personal nature in challenging the supremacy of a divine, good power.

Unquestionably we see the signs of evil or negative action in the world around us, but the real question is how do we deal with that? Evil is not really mysterious and elusive, but Christians and Christian Scientists need to do a better job at not only slapping stereotypes on a problem but proceeding to counteract negative influences with both concerted prayer and lively follow-through that fulfills prayer.

An inside job

Does the Christian or Christian Scientist recognize how **the devilish action works from the "inside" of the Christian gathering and not from a supposedly "outside" position?** C.S. Lewis shows in his classic *Screwtape Letters* how Christians subvert their own cause from "inside" their own hearts and congregation.

The all-powerful love of Christ melts the wall of worldly apathy or ignorant prejudice that would separate anyone from spiritual discovery. A sense of family can definitely happen in church experience, but divine Love requires our cooperation. It requires prayers accompanied by footsteps, and by big hugs, in order for love to be expansive and activated and felt.

Here is an example of how a church member made a very meaningful contribution for others by stepping out of his comfort zone:

Mario and Ray
—Christian supports and follow-through

Mario was incarcerated in the county jail near where we live. He had been in and out of trouble with the law for some years because of his drug addiction. Ray was a Christian Science volunteer chaplain who met Mario and gave him spiritual support and encouragement there in the county jail and followed up with him. When Mario got shipped downstate to serve out his prison sentence, Ray kept in touch and also did what he could to help Mario's family.

Mario returned from prison a new man. He had been healed through prayer and the Holy Spirit, and his friends and family noticed. They also noticed the help he had received from his

> The faith reposed in these things [drugs, etc.] should find stronger supports and a higher home. *S&H* 169

chaplain friend. Ray was there to meet Mario at the time of his discharge and took him to his church. Ray did not just give his friend a single cup of cold water from Christ; he showed Mario the "restaurant" where more cold water could be found. Over the next few years, over sixty kids and about two dozen adults attended Ray's church largely because of what they had seen touch their friend Mario.

How do we follow through?

Ray's *follow-through* with Mario is not that different from the follow-through practiced by the Good Samaritan in Jesus' well-known parable. The Good Samaritan not only gave the wounded stranger (1) **immediate aid and tangible help with his own resources, but also** (2) **provided for the stranger's future care and paid for it out of his own pocket**. Though Luke's Gospel mentions nothing in this parable about the Samaritan praying for the wounded stranger, didn't the helper's actions constitute the highest form of prayer in action, yet without words?

Christian Scientists are told not to leave those to whom they minister without follow-through: "**Let your loving care and counsel support all their feeble footsteps, until your students tread firmly in the straight and narrow way**" (*S&H* 454:26). These words from *Science and Health* are especially addressed to teachers of Christian Science in regard to those whom they have taught in what's called "primary class instruction," but this counsel could just as easily apply to any number of situations, such as that of Ray and Mario. Of course, whatever form this follow-through should take will differ with the circumstance and people involved.

Where did the dogma of "rugged individualism" come from?

It's hard to pinpoint any one source or teaching that has encouraged Christian Scientists to be less gregarious than other Christians or more apt to be loners in their spiritual journey. For whatever reason, prayer for Christian Scientists tends to be a one-on-one matter, with church members praying for themselves and communing with God when they are hurting, or calling a friend or practitioner for prayer help. Prayer in churches is intended for "the congregations,"[3] but, possibly for reasons of confidentiality, Christian Science churches do not customarily read a list of those seeking prayer from the congregation as do other churches. In the absence of that, there are often church care committees that are intended to let members know of those among the membership who may need special help or may be housebound, and then provide some of that help with visits by the members of the committee or by the church as a whole. If any of our churches fail to meet those needs, that is a serious omission.

Is there church teaching which favors individualism? Maybe. *Science and Health* twice cites Paul's instruction, "Work out your own salvation with fear and trembling" while leaving out the second part of that scripture—"for it is God which worketh in you both to will and to do of his good pleasure" (Phil. 2:12,13).[4] Are those partial quotations read too frequently by church members? It's obvious from reading all church texts how important the eternal support of

> **It is by** [Christ's] **grace you are saved through trusting him; it is not your own doing.**
> Ephesians 2:8 NEB

---

3. Eddy, *Church Manual*, 42:1.
4. Two other passages in *Science and Health* and one in Mrs. Eddy's other prose writings cite the full quotation from Paul.

God's love is in upholding our individual efforts for salvation. Salvation in the Greek means "safety, deliverance, rescue, health, and defense." Don't the most profound instances of our being saved proceed from sources outside of ourselves? So it's not a matter of us saving ourselves, but stunning help coming from others and from spiritual resources quite beyond anything we could have anticipated or even hoped for.

As we've pointed out in the chapter on "radical reliance" (Chapter 3), words taken out of context can cause trouble. There is also a phrase in *Science and Health* "self-reliant trustworthiness" (*S&H* 23:29) which could give a reader of that book the idea that we are a self-help faith, if the reader glossed over the next words—"which includes spiritual understanding and confides all to God."

A *Journal* article from the early 1960s cites the "individualism" in Christ. Specifically, the writer critiques his era's "social order tending progressively away from the **individualism of Christianity as Jesus taught and lived.**"[5]

Is that what Jesus taught and lived—"the individualism of Christianity"? Jesus' great dual commandment (to love God with one's all-in-all and love one's neighbor as one's self—Matthew 22:36–39) urges upon Christians both the **primal importance of the individual's relation to the divine and the necessary attention and care that we owe to others.** Mrs. Eddy wrote succinctly, "[Jesus'] mission was both individual and collective" (*S&H* 18:5). The individual, spiritual, and collective interests are not favored one over the other, but work together inextricably as co-partners for spiritual and human progress. Note that Jesus told his disciples to go into their closet and shut the door (in prayer and solitude), but also to "preach the gospel to every creature." Here is the natural balance between individual devotion and a Christian's obligation to the larger community. None of us can be blessed without our brother or sister being blessed. The follow-through by Ray for Mario (see above) shows how important are one-on-one connections in churches and society in general.

---

5. "A Recompense of Profit," *C. S. Journal*, Dec., 1960.

If present-day Christians and Christian Scientists were really fishermen, they would quickly go out of business. Here's why....

It has been the experience of the author that too often church evangelism, not just in our own denomination but in others, consists of throwing a fishing net overboard but neglecting to draw fish into the boat. Is the handing out of tracts or literature, or giving a yearly lecture in our community all we're supposed to do in order to "preach the gospel to every creature?" How many of us would honestly attend a church just because a church member dropped off a pamphlet at our door? One poll has shown that two-thirds of non-churchgoers would start attending a church at **the urging or example of a good friend**, and not because of a religious television show or from reading a tract left on their doorstep.[6]

The road of evangelism less taken

A white pastor friend of the author was once a severe alcoholic. This man ran a meat-catering service, and he employed two African-American men in his business. One day after a catering job, the boss asked his two employees why they were not enjoying some of the fine cuts of meat left over after the guests had left. The two gentlemen said they were not hungry, but when their boss pressed them again to eat up, they replied that they were praying and fasting for him. This jolting experience was a crucial first step in that man becoming not just a healed Christian and recovering alcoholic but the pastor of an interracial congregation in our racially divided city.

Now what if those two employees had just left a tract on the desk of their boss—"*How to overcome your drinking habit by the Holy Spirit?*" The boss might possibly have read that, but his heart, not just his mind, was truly and deeply touched by what the two men quietly did for him that day. The boss read and devoured the tract written in his two employees' lives.

---

6. Lifeway Research and the North American Mission Board, 2009.

Your very lives are a letter that anyone can read by just looking at you. Christ himself wrote it—not with ink, but with God's living Spirit; not chiseled into stone, but carved into human lives....

II Cor. 3:2,3 The Message

Religion is nothing but friendship; friendship with God and with man.

Washington Gladden

All life is related

*"The urge to form partnerships, to link up in collaborative arrangements, is perhaps the oldest, strongest, and most fundamental force in nature. **There are no solitary, free-living creatures: every form of life is dependent on other forms.** The great successes in evolution, the mutants who have, so to speak, made it, have done so by fitting in with, and sustaining the rest of life."*[7]

Dr. Lewis Thomas

The theologian Reinhold Niebuhr makes a similar point: "**Nothing we do, however virtuous, can be accomplished alone**; therefore, we are saved by love."[8] To claim sole achievement for anything good, or to take full blame for its opposite, is to be blind to the amazing context of life and its web of relatedness. Read an interesting book and very often the book's pages are filled with stories, ideas, research, and proofreading from so many quarters that the author is clearly just one teammate in a large team. And that is the way in life—no one deserves sole credit or blame.

Surprising benefits of community—the "Roseto effect"

How does community relate to health? If you want to know how important togetherness, community, and social cohesion are to our well-being, look no farther than the little town of Roseto, Pennsylvania. Malcolm Gladwell describes in detail how this small community,

---

7. Thomas, "On the Uncertainty of Science." Phi Beta Kappa *Key Reporter,* 1980 6:1. Phi Beta Kappa address at Harvard University.
8. Niebhur, "Happiness, Prosperity, and Virtue," *The Irony of American History*, 63.

seventy miles west of New York City, gradually transplanted itself from the bootheel of Italy to the United States beginning in the late 1800s. Roseto's new immigrant residents unknowingly created within their local confines an island of health.[9]

In 1961, an Oklahoma internist Dr. Stewart Wolf stumbled across the phenomenon of Roseto, having been inspired by a conversation he had with a Pennsylvania physician who told Wolf about the lack of heart problems he found in that small town. Follow-up study by Dr. Wolf and others over several decades found Roseto residents suffered half the incidence of heart-related deaths compared to similar towns in Pennsylvania and the United States.

What might have puzzled the researchers at first about Roseto residents were the townspeople's apparent negative prospects for long life. The men worked in the local slate mines, smoked cigars, and did not exercise more than others in their age groups. The fat content of the local diet included lots of cheese, sausage, meatballs fried in lard, and large quantities of wine.

So what factors did the researchers identify as maintaining the general health of Roseto residents? **"The community," Wolf says, "was very cohesive. There was no keeping up with the Joneses. Houses were very close together, and everyone lived more or less alike."**[10] Almost everyone attended the local Catholic church and spent leisure time in the Marconi Social Club.

There were other positive side effects of this tight-knit community spirit seen in the infrequency of suicide, alcoholism, drug addiction, and the relative absence of crime. With little economic stress in the community, the study couldn't find subjects with peptic ulcers. "These people were dying of old age, that's it," noted John Bruhn, a sociologist who helped Dr. Wolf in his study.

A downside to this story is that modern Americanization eventually caught up with Roseto. Year by year researchers found young people moving away from the town and a gradual "erosion of traditionally cohesive family and community relationships." With these changes came

---

9. Gladwell, *Outliers*, 3.
10. Cassill, "The Town Heart Disease Passed By," *People*, June 16, 1980.

a change in the health picture of Roseto, and the residents' longevity. By 1975 the town's heart-healthy statistics paralleled those of other neighboring communities.

Learning from Roseto

The **"Roseto Effect"** points conclusively to the health benefits of people living in cohesive communities that sustain and encourage their residents. Christian Scientists shouldn't require this kind of study to know that Jesus **preached and lived cohesiveness**—oneness with the Father-Mother God, oneness with his spiritual brothers and sisters, and day-to-day togetherness with his followers. In case we need more reasons to value community, here are more.

Other facts supporting the need for community

A recent study of social relations which analyzed 148 other studies of over 300,000 people indicated: "Not only are people who need people the 'luckiest people in the world,' they also live the longest." This study discovered that people with strong social networks "are 50% less likely to die early" and that "being reclusive is harder on physical health than smoking or being an alcoholic." And this is the conclusion of the research put in startling quantitative terms: **"Being socially isolated is the equivalent of smoking fifteen cigarettes a day."**[11]

Robert Putnam's book *Bowling Alone* addresses the increasing alienation and friendlessness prevalent in modern Western life. An American newspaper reported statistics that flesh out Putnam's observations: "In 1985, the average American had three people in whom to confide matters that were important to them." By 2004, "that number dropped to two, and one in four had no close confidants at all." This is a relatively recent phenomenon, since a 1982 study revealed that only 3% of Americans polled reported that they had no close friends.[12]

---

11. "Social Relations Linked to Longer Life," *Food Consumer,* 7–28–2010.
12. *USA Today,* 6-24-06.

Given the negative side effects of these increasingly privatizing and isolating social trends | **Hell is eternal apartness.** Harper Lee[13]

in our society, wouldn't it be appropriate for church participants to encourage an opposite trend among themselves—a trend towards increased and natural fellowship among their own congregations and surrounding community? This sense of regular communion and close bonds among worshippers lies at the very root of why Christian Scientists and other Christians have founded churches.

The neglected part of our purpose —the soil of early Christian spirit

"Friendship is the nearest thing we know to what religion is," wrote Henry Drummond. Christian Scientists may say that they have many friends and that their fellow church members are friends. Does the river of that friendship flow deeply enough?

The founding purpose of the Christian Science Church was two-fold: to **"reinstate primitive Christianity and its lost element of healing."**[14] When this phrase is repeated by Christian Scientists, the latter phrase tends to receive the emphasis. **Primitive or early Christianity was the culture or soil out of which early Christian healing began, but healing was just one expressive form of that spiritual soil which Christians link with their church's early history.** Sociologist Rodney Stark summarizes the contributions of the early Christians to their surrounding society:

> *To cities filled with the homeless and impoverished, Christianity offered charity as well as hope. To cities filled with newcomers and strangers, Christianity offered an immediate basis for attachment. To cities filled with orphans and widows, Christianity provided **a new and expanded sense of family**. To cities torn by violent ethnic strife, Christianity offered **a new basis for social solidarity**. And to cities faced with epidemics, fire, and earthquakes, Christianity offered effective nursing services…For what they brought was not simply an*

---

13. Lee, *Watchman*, 225.
14. Eddy, *Church Manual*, 17:12.

urban movement, but a new culture capable of making life in Greco-Roman cities more tolerable.[15]

Christianity started with the example of Jesus and his love. Jesus identified his followers not by their doctrine but by their love for one another. The healings performed by Jesus and his disciples were not a demonstration of a doctrine so much as a natural expression of divine Love meeting extreme human needs amid dire conditions.

By this everyone will know that you are my disciples, if you love one another.

John 13:35 New International Version

This is the soil of primitive Christianity from which healing spontaneously grows. This is the foundation of the Christian experience. Farmers will tell you that the quality of their soil is crucial to their success, so you cannot revive the "lost element of healing" without the proper, quality soil of Christly love to grow it from.

During a period of plague, Christians were seen ministering to the dying, and those who noted this said in awe, "Behold how they love."[16] Richard Rubenstein observed, **"Christian bishops and their congregations fed the hungry, housed the homeless, cared for plague victims, and offered sufferers membership in a tight-knit compassionate community."**[17]

Healing, if it is to be established from generation to generation, requires this soil of love, a groundwork or foundation. The soil of love requires constant rejuvenation. Otherwise healing becomes lost in urban legend and is stereotyped, then mythologized in tales about grand and less grand healing personalities. Until we live in space, grow all food hydroponically, and clone the entirety of generations, humans will require a context for progress.

The unity of spirit, love shared generously in deeds—these active in-

---

15. Stark, Rise *of Christianity*, 161.
16. From a report by Aristides to Emperor Hadrian.
17. Rubenstein, When *Jesus Became God*, 19.

gredients—form the natural atmosphere of Christian practice. A small illustration of the Christian spirit that existed early in the Christian Science movement was our church membership application. When it was sent out from Boston, it was not addressed to some Mr. or Mrs. The greeting line read, "Dear Brother....," or "Dear Sister....," and the church clerk signed it "Yours in bonds of Christ." Just a little item, but an indication of the warmth of fellowship that was expected early in the 1900s.

What new and reborn forms of Christian practice are needed today in the practice of Christian Science?

The great difference between solitude and isolation

Jesus advocated the virtue of prayer in private, but he lived in the company of twelve mortals for three years. The founder of Christian Science lived in a tight-knit household of several people for many of her later years. Isolation is one of the most severe penalties inflicted on prisoners, and it can drive a person crazy. Is there room for solitude? Absolutely. Here is a view from Albert Einstein on how solitude and community can interrelate:

"Although I am a typical loner in my daily life, my awareness of belonging to the invisible community of those who strive for truth, beauty, and justice has prevented me from feelings of isolation."[18]

There is a Christian necessity for solitude, and those of us who tend to be more introverted than extroverted personalities require relatively more time alone than do others. But the following contains a caution about solitude.

Dangers of Christian insularity vs. the need for solitude

The Interpreter's Bible urges Christians to, "(A)void...excessive preoccupation with the culture of our own souls. We forget ourselves into Christlikeness through caring for others...Jesus made friends with publicans

---

18. Einstein, "What I Believe," Speech to the German League of Human Rights.

and sinners. **The true safeguard of character is not isolation; it is in caring so much about the spiritual interests of others that we shall be proof against moral infection…**salt cannot purify anything with which it is not mixed."[19] Jesus prayed not for his followers to be taken out of the world, but for them to be kept from evil (John 17:15).

What all this means in practical terms will vary with our individual experience. Here is a fragment of a conversation that some Christian Scientists in our area had several years ago that relates to our private selves and connection with others:

> *We're not just praying for ourselves but for the world out there. Someone came up to me once at the train station and offered, 'I was praying for you.' My fellow Christian Scientists didn't do that. Our churches are losing members. We need to change our dialogue. We need to not just be into self-healing. We have a castle mentality like we have the secret. But there are less folks in the castle, and the moat* [the separation of ourselves from our surrounding community] *is getting wider all the time! We should be able to freely say to the guy next to us on the bus: 'I want to pray for you.'* (This last comment brought on a back-and-forth discussion about when and how we pray for others.)

There are times and seasons when the Christian needs a **monastic time of solitude** that may even last for years, and there are other times when intense involvement with others and the world around us constitutes the salt acting as saltness or purification. One thing is clear—going into one's closet and shutting the door is not a permanent state of being but is a time of solitude or preparation in order to prepare for a larger blessing for the world and ourselves. Otherwise, Jesus would have urged his disciples to hide their light under a basket.

Henry Drummond (with some help from Johann Goethe) helps summarize for us the important distinction between our need for both solitude and joining hands with our world:

---

19. Laymon, *Interpreter's Bible*. See commentary on Paul's question: "What accord has Christ with Belial?" Vol. 10, p. 353 (1953, rev. 1980).

Do not quarrel, therefore, with your lot in life. Do not complain of its never-ceasing cares, its petty environment, the vexations you have to stand, the small and sordid souls you have to live and work with. Above all, do not resent temptation; do not be perplexed because it seems to thicken round you more and more, and ceases neither for effort nor for agony nor prayer. That is your practice. That is the practice which God appoints you; and it is having its work in making you patient, and humble, and generous, and unselfish, and kind, and courteous. Do not begrudge the hand that is moulding the still too shapeless image within you. It is growing more beautiful, though you see it not; and every touch of temptation may add to its perfection. Therefore, **keep in the midst of life**. Do not isolate yourself. Be among men in the stream of life and among things, and among troubles, and difficulties, and obstacles. You remember Goethe's words: 'Talent develops itself in solitude; character in the stream of life.' Talent develops itself in solitude— the talent of prayer, of faith, of meditation, of seeing the unseen; **character grows in the stream of the world's life**. That chiefly is where men are to learn love."[20]

The Greatest Thing in the World

The following are some modest recommendations (and questions) for steps that aim in the direction of kindling the spirit of Christ-love in our church or refreshing that spirit where it is already alive and well.

Recommendations

Get to know those who work so hard among you.
I Thessalonians 5:12 J.B. Phillips

Do we create the space and approachableness where we dare open up to our fellow church members and our neighbors? Do we provide adequate venues for this free opening up one to another?

---

20. Drummond, *Greatest Thing*, 42-43.

Beyond "lobby love" to close friendship The people you are talking with amicably after church, do you know them? Do they really know you? Can you find occasions to get to know your fellow church members better? Would you happily turn to your church friends if you had a great need?

If you were in a deep, dark pit, would church friends be there for you?

Should you have to call a Christian Science practitioner to find someone who cares about you? Shouldn't church be a close circle of friends, and a circle that opens up and includes the world around it? How do we get there?

Theologian Henri Nouwen writes about a time when he was feeling spiritually dry and bereft of inspiration and vision. He wrote to twelve close friends in his community of faith and asked them to pray for him for a month. During that time he felt a wonderful influx of inspiration that re-nourished his soul.[21]

Friendship circles that sustain one another An answer to dependence on drugs is mentioned in *Science and Health* (and cited above): "The faith reposed in these things ["drugs and rules of health"] should find *stronger supports and a higher home*" (S&H 169).

What forms are there among our congregations for stronger supports? From the Ostlings' *Mormon America*: "Mormon people encircle each other in a loving community, seeking to make sure that everyone has a divinely appointed task and that no one's needs are overlooked. In modern, fractionated American society, those are accomplishments as impressive as building a city-state on the Mississippi, hauling handcarts across the prairies, or making the arid Salt Lake Basin bloom."[22] Are Mormons and other faith groups helpful social examples for Christian Scientists?

Developing close brother and sister partnerships in Christ The Rev. Billy Graham never went on an evangelical crusade alone, but had a prayer partner working with him. **"Two are better than one…for if**

---

21. Nouwen, *Discernment*, 28–29.
22. Ostling, *Mormon America*, 393.

they fall, the one will lift up his fellow" (Prov. 4:9,10). Is this kind of partnership practical for our church lecturers or any of our other workers? Our church services feature two readers working together.

Note to practitioners: How many of those who call you do that for friendship, more so than for prayer. Do not belittle the importance of supporting your spiritual brothers and sisters in friendship.

Is your Christian Science association a real "association"?[23] **Not exclusively a metaphysical lecture.** Many associations do include time for questions and answers and testimonies from the participants. An association meeting day can be a time not just for formal questions and answers, but an in-depth breaking of bread among fellow disciples.

Sharing association addresses with members Too many Christian Science associations let their members know that they will not have access to the yearly address or notes unless they attend in person. On the surface it may seem logical to follow this practice in order to encourage personal attendance, but does that type of policy send a very non-inclusive message to those members who are either incapacitated or embarrassed to ask for financial help in attending the meeting?

Compare this to a meal. Let's say that a couple is invited to a dinner, but the husband or wife is ill or too busy and stays home. The dinner's host will often send home goodies from the dinner, so that the one staying home feels included. The enriching of affections of all mankind should start with those who should know Jesus' way and therefore know better than to let any member of the Body of Christ feel mentally or physically left out from fellowship, especially in the case of any kind of disability. Jesus said for the disciples to go out into the field and far corners and **gather in anyone who could possibly attend his supper... or be sent a "plate" from the supper.**

And speaking of food...do your church members get together fairly regularly over a meal? It's an excellent way to develop closeness and mutual support. If food was "too material" for the spiritually minded, then we never would have read in the Bible about the Passover meal, the Last Supper, Christ's feeding of the multitudes, his evening meal af-

---

23. Associate— "to unite in action; to keep company, implying intimacy" Webster's.

ter the resurrection at Emmaus, and his feeding the disciples breakfast at the Sea of Galilee. Church gatherings over a meal are also a wonderful means of including single individuals, spouses of members, and those who have not yet joined the church.

Mentoring from generation to generation[24] Notice the importance, truly, the ***obligation*** of **"passing the torch from one generation to another"** cited in the following psalms:

One generation shall praise thy works to another, and shall declare thy mighty acts.[25]

Ps. 145:45. See also Ps. 71:18.

Important note

There are Christian Science churches that do not need the recommendations or narratives included in this chapter. These are very blessed congregations that are truly "aflame with divine Love" (*Science and Health* 367:8). These pages are for those churches where the ashes of Christly fire require stirring and nourishing to the ultimate goal that all churches share in that loving, inclusive spirit.

---

24. The author was helped considerably in the beginning stages of his ministry with freely offered advice and encouragement from two practitioners who were already established. This type of mentoring should be recommended to practitioners wherever there is a need, or someone is reaching out for help from a fellow worker.

25. More on this topic in Chapter 12, "Waking Eutychus."

CHAPTER 7

Peter's distraction
—evolving needs and church forms

An architect, in discussing the Spanish mission-churches in California, posed an interesting rhetorical question: **"When did a 'mission' become a building?"**

If the Christian apostles, St. Peter or St. Paul, could return to the Vatican, they might possibly inquire the name of the Deity who is worshipped with such mysterious rites in that magnificent temple.[1]

Edward Gibbon

A MINISTER FRIEND of the author pastored a modest-sized congregation of about forty people in our small Illinois town. His church rented space in a community building for Sunday worship. Despite their small size, this congregation held out-of-doors outreach services in the local housing projects and engaged in other community-minded activities. In boxing terminology, they "punched above their weight."

One day a member of my friend's congregation commented to him, "Pastor, you know we've got a lot of nerve to be doing what we're doing with these services in the projects when we only worship in a little rental space and don't even have a church building of our own?" My friend thought about that for a moment and answered, "Well, yes, but Jesus had a lot of nerve to feed five thousand people with a borrowed boy's lunch." My pastor friend had **not confused his church building with his church mission**. He knew his congregation could survive without a building of

---

1. Gibbon, *The Decline and Fall of the Roman Empire*, Vol. 6, Chapter 50, 250.

their own, but the congregation could not exist for long without possessing a mission that extended far beyond the walls of a building.

Shouldn't this lead us to central questions about church direction: Is my church mainly struggling to survive in a building and perpetuate itself? Or does my church focus primarily on its mission—to expand blessing for its community, the world, and also its church members?

The answer to those questions may determine the likelihood of our success and progress.

Size and numbers

Christians and Jews should be the last people in the world to be impressed by membership numbers and building size. Doesn't the Bible warn against numbering the people (II Samuel 24) and say that sometimes three hundred warriors are better than ten thousand? (Judges 7) And when Jesus is shown the beautiful temple buildings in Jerusalem, his only comment is that those buildings would all be thrown down (Matthew 24:1, 2).

For the first two hundred years of Christian history, Christians "met in enlarged private houses or rooms."[2] Only after that era do we find any evidence of a Christian church being built. Think of that—two hundred years with the Spirit active, but no settled church building.

And as for the Christian Scientists, when Mrs. Eddy was driven by the Extension of the Mother Church in Boston, an elaboration of the smaller church built ten years earlier, her only words were, "Too much matter."[3]

Commemorating and participating

On the mount of the transfiguration, Moses and Elijah appeared to the disciples with Jesus. The patriarch and prophet "were in deep conversation with" Jesus when "Peter broke in, 'Master, this is a great moment! What would you think if I built three memorials[4] here on the moun-

---

2. Fox, *Pagans and Christians*, 269.
3. Gottschalk, *Rolling Away the Stone*, 364.
4. Mark 9:5 NLT. "Shelters as memorials."

tain—one for you, one for Moses, and one for Elijah?' While he was going on like this,…a light-radiant cloud enveloped them, and sounding from deep in the cloud a voice: 'This is my beloved Son…Listen to him'" (Matthew 17 *The Message*).

Twenty centuries later, the divine voice is still interrupting distracted, busy mortals and reminding them that listening to, and participating in, the highest inspiration is far more important than building memorials to inspiring and divine occasions and persons. **The voice of God did not say, "Build me a tabernacle, Peter, and then return and worship here." The voice of God broke in upon Peter's construction project and said, "Hear my Son."**[5] During the greater part of the history of the Jewish people as recorded in the Bible, as was also true with the Christians, there were only brief periods when temple-centered worship was the focus of the Bible narrative. In the New Testament, we read of Christians congregating, but not often in church buildings. The author suggests that *during the greatest periods of spiritual growth for Christianity* in the past two thousand years, the open sky was the favored Christian spire, and caves, forest glens, catacombs, plain apartment walls, and too often prison cells have been common church surroundings.

Are temples graven images?

When the Apostle Stephen reproached his listeners over their disobedience to God (Acts 7:44-51), he struck a sensitive nerve by directly connecting prideful disobedience of the people to the building of physical temples in which to honor the Holy. The Holiest required none of that. Most translations of Stephen's last daring words do not quite catch this connection between church building and worshippers' "stiff-necked" resistance to God's guidance.

The little-known *Cotton Patch* free-spirited rendition of Acts makes Stephen's emphasis clear:

Now David got the idea of putting up a more plush sanctuary for the

---

5. The Message, Matthew 17.

God of Jacob, but Solomon actually built it. But—The Almighty does not live in man-made buildings.[6]

The prophet [Isaiah] bears this out when he says,
   'The sky is my office
   The earth is my den, says the Lord,
   What kind of a house could you build me,
   Or what kind of a resting place,
   Seeing as how I've made everything already?'

...you are forever turning a deaf ear to the Holy Spirit. You are just like your fathers before you.[7]

Acts 7: 46-51

Stephen pointed out this presumptuous sin of trying to build physical enclosures for an unenclosable, divine Entity. Then the beloved apostle uttered the ecstatic vision he was beholding of Jesus in the heavens with God. To the irate mob this final utterance was the ultimate blasphemy, and they stoned him to death. Far be it from us to risk receiving a similar response when we suggest that the building of temples can distract us from the Holy! However, Stephen's accusation certainly should make congregants of all denominations question whether their time spent on temple building, repair, and maintenance, and the priority placed on those activities, might defy the second commandment of Moses to not create or honor graven images.

Why have temples or church buildings not been important to long-run spiritual prosperity? The best answer to this is found in the words of Scripture:

Ye are the temple of God, and...the Spirit of God dwelleth in you.

I Cor. 3:16

God that made the world...dwelleth not in temples made with hands.

Acts 17:24

---

6. Dickey, *Memoirs*, 41. In a discussion between Mrs. Eddy and her secretary Adam Dickey regarding the Lincoln Memorial in Washington, D.C., Dickey offered, "Mother, I think people should be constructing a memorial to you and your work." In this offhand comment Dickey proved himself unknowingly to be following in Peter's steps.
7. Jordan, *Cotton Patch Version of Luke and Acts*, 107.

Could the Bible be any more specific? If God's children are the "temples" or vessels of God, why need those temples go into temples weekly or more frequently to be more "temple-like"? Garrison Keillor addresses the issue this way: "Anyone who thinks sitting in a church can make you a Christian must also think that sitting in a garage can make you a car."[8]

So how does church or temple worship enter into the Christian picture at all, given that early Christian preaching cited above indicates that temple worship is redundant?

The substitution of the lesser for the greater

As mortals are very easily misdirected in their lives, so we have church buildings—**material structures all built for the glory of a spiritual being**. What churchgoers often fail to recognize is that the time they devote to church buildings and their maintenance is generally time taken away from emulating the central purposes and original ideals of the founders of those churches.

This all shouldn't seem surprising. As we pointed out in discussions earlier in this book, the problem of dogma is related to the problem with church building. That is, **human nature is willingly distracted away from its primary calling and duties**. Human nature quite readily **buys high, and sells low, or sells out to the ways of the world, instead of helping elevate those ways.**

In the reverse of Jesus' parable of the precious pearl, the human mind is quite willing to sell its pearl of great price for pearls of lesser value. So a church's mission is exchanged for bricks and mortar buildings that are supposed to be the physical gathering spot for a mission. Similarly, dogmatic beliefs sell off the original inspired teaching for a less inspired crafting of that preaching, or a rule-bound mock-up of the original message.

---

8. Derived from similar words by Dr. Laurence J. Peter.

Is Christian gathering a true communion?

Christians *do need to gather together* for fellowship and spiritual unity most definitely. Paul kept in supportive contact with the widespread Christian churches that he patiently and lovingly nurtured. We are fed by loving contact with our fellow believers. The importance of our spiritual relations one with another was the focus of Chapter 6, "Sitting at the end of the pew." How do we best do that gathering?

In our services, spiritually hungry congregations **require immediate experience and spiritual intimacy**, more than a replica or re-run. Could that be one reason why churchgoers get easily distracted, even bored, in church? Our minds wander because what we are watching at the altar or in the front of the sanctuary, what we mistakenly call a "service," has too often wandered and has been misdirected. Like Peter's distraction, the "service" often strays from the immediacy of the spiritual and instead attempts to **replay the spiritual,** repeat prayers, read familiar passages that provide a temporary comfort to those listening.

Many of us have attended church services that have been so full of the presence of divine inspiration that the service has been at those times in no way a "re-run." Those services truly fed our souls. But for too many former or occasional church attendants this is not the case. We should ask, "Why?" and not dismiss those who are not getting what we may get from church as we know it.

The honored repetition of the holy or ancient cannot be an exact replica of the ancient. It must continually grow, thrive, evolve, and be transformed in order to "catch" the spirit of the original occasion or inspiration from which it is derived. It **must be bread, baked fresh and a little differently, every moment of eternity**.

The ancient Jewish temple separated the holy from the less than holy by a huge, thick veil. But the veil is not the only religious form that has attempted to make this separation. **Our churches may today have too many veils and walls of the invisible kind.** Veils and walls that isolate the spiritual life, that pull us away from our surrounding community, that attempt to confine the holy to a building or certain time frame. Are our church services more for the convenience of church members than the public?

A pre-historic motivation for church buildings

Long before the time of Jesus, there was the legendary tower of Babel. Why was it built? To honor God or to serve a holy purpose? No. The Bible relates that it was **the first statement building**. "Let us make a name for ourselves" (Gen. 11:4 Moffatt) "…Let's build a city and tower that reaches Heaven. Let's make ourselves famous…." (Ibid. *The Message*). The Bible text suggests that in part **the motive was fear**—"lest we be scattered." So the tower was an attempt at unifying people in one geographical spot, but it **served to commemorate both pride and fear**.

The mantra of what is crucial in real estate is often stated "location, location, and location." Shouldn't the key question regarding religious process be rather "motivation, motivation, motivation?" Religious endeavors should spring from inspiration. A veteran Christian Scientist once posed the important question about newly planned church structures, **"If something isn't worth doing, is it worth doing well?"**

Modern motivations for church-going

The motivation for a church activity or worship service directly affects the inspirational value of that activity or service. This is why, the author believes, that church services held in housing projects, jails, and mental health centers can feel full of the inspiration from the Holy Spirit possibly more so than regular weekly services held in formal, "regular" church buildings. The motivations can be quite different in the different locations.

In the "normal" church service held every week, those attending the service may carry along with them into their church building thoughts and feelings that hinder the action of inspiration such as: (1) the placid doldrums of the **habitual** and customary, (2) **personal expectations** of how church members behave and appear in church, (3) **monetary motivation** if attendees are paid to read or sing or play an instrument, (4) **obligation**, if they are going to church to please a family member, (5) even fear, fear of what not going to church might do to their personal reputation or spiritual progress.

To be sure church attendees may well be able to park all these unholy thoughts and desires at the door as they go in, and dive into a sense of sweet fellowship and the Holy Presence. That heavenly space is what we seek wherever we may be, and we hope for it to be right there in our church.

It is possible that church volunteers visiting state facilities or elsewhere have a built-in advantage in seeking the holy because they know that they go to give and not to just receive when they engage in their church services. They, like so many of our selfless readers in branch churches, put together services mostly because they love the activity and the sincere people who attend. They have nothing to gain financially. The clients or inmates who attend those services generally don't do so out of compulsion. Some may attend for lack of anything better to do, but many are sincere or just plain curious. Those attending these services as patients or inmates tend to care little about their appearance. They may have prejudicial expectations about the service or the type of church they're attending, but possibly not as much as those attending their own churches out in the community. The incarcerated attend because they want to worship. They are looking for new meaning in their very difficult and often impossible lives, so they frequently share outspoken gratitude for what they get from the church experience.

The services in prisons and mental health centers don't have to wash the feet of the participants because everyone's feet, the motivations of both those conducting the service and those attending, tend to be cleaner or washed of any self-absorption than those of your average church participant out in the world.

Are too many of our churches too full (not empty)…of the less than worthy motives? Yes, too full, not too empty. How do we "empty" our church lives of the less than worthy motives and aims, and fill them with substantial aims and motives?

Making changes to our church methods of operation?

Ask yourself: "What is my church all about?" The Christian Scientists' definition of "church" is full of action words—"rests upon and **proceeds from divine Principle**"…"**affords proof** of its utility"…"found **elevat-**

ing the race"…"**rousing the dormant** understanding"…"**casting out devils**, or error, and **healing** the sick" (*S&H* 583). If your local church is doing all or many of these things, you can safely skip the rest of this chapter. If, on the other hand, you worry more about utility bills than proving utility, engage in too much "resting upon" and too little "proceeding from" the divine, seek more soothing than elevating, desire more human comfort and less rousing, then there's work to be done.

Let's think about church as we think about our clothes

We wear clothes that fit, are functional, or make us feel comfortable. We wear clothes that work for us, either at our job or in relaxed settings. We should feel at home in our clothes, just as we should feel at home in our churches. Church and its accompanying structures and activities need to be like that.

In 1991, scientists discovered a fifty-three hundred year-old mummy in the Tyrolean Alps. The researchers were particularly interested in what this man's clothes could tell them about life thousands of years ago. They analyzed "Iceman's" clothing and why he was wearing what he did shortly before he became frozen for centuries on that fateful day in the mountains. The scientists concluded that "Iceman" wore clothing that had: (1) **necessity** (2) **function** (3) **availability** and (4) **symbolism**. So what has that got to do with church?

Other scientists, social scientists, have looked at why people, especially young people, go or don't go to church. What these scientists have discovered parallels why people wear the clothes that they wear: (1) necessity—Is my church experience a crucial or necessary element in my life? (2) function—Does my church experience give my life meaning, maybe a sense of home? Does my church bless my local community, and does it harmonize with where my life needs to go? Am I happy there? (3) availability—Does my church fit into the pattern of my life, and do my friends feel comfortable there? (4) symbolism—Is my church a "team" that I enjoy identifying with, even feel very close to, and to whom I feel indebted and want very much to support?

Necessity
Maybe in prior generations, the bonds of family and custom, even the fear of going to hell, kept people attending churches even when there was no individual desire to do so. There certainly used to be far fewer distractions and options in previous generations. The Sabbath meant that life on that day was devoted to the Lord and was devoid of buying and selling, sports activities, etc. Today, not so much. Churches must be not merely relevant. They must be as vitally important as **the company of our close friends or our kids' soccer games**. There have been years and seasons in my life when I felt that church embodied the comfort of close friends, and that feeling has kept me coming back over the years to offer friendship to others as well as receive that friendship.

Function
Does our church experience bring happiness to our lives? Does it encourage our forward movement? Does it have a mission and purpose? If so, then we are in a truly operative and active body of encouraging believers.

Availability
Is the church reachable, not just geographically, but emotionally? If we are in a low point in life, are there church members whom we can call on who are there to really help? That is availability. Do the forms of worship in our church connect with our heart and soul and connect with those friends close to us so that we feel the church message is really meant for us, meeting our spiritual needs and the needs of our friends? Does our church allow us to deeply engage with our fellow churchgoers?

Symbolism
People have a need to feel that they fit in somewhere, whether in a family or a bond of close friends. In ancient times, when the "Iceman" we mentioned lived, it was probably important to know friend from foe without modern forms of communication, community organization, and technology. In the same way that modern people identify with a local sports team or school, the "Iceman" probably had some kind of insignia that showed what tribe he belonged to. Do we have a core

of family or friends with whom we feel a deep kinship, and does our church experience intersect with that core and those bonds of belonging? Is our church dear to our hearts?

"Young adults are starved for community. What they aren't starved for is church as we know it, the community we are used to. They are looking for authentic community." [9]

Rev. Jan Barnes, United Church of Christ pastor

The groundwork for our mission

The founder of the Christian Science Church once wrote, "It is **not indispensable to organize materially Christ's church**…but if this be done, let it be **in concession to the period** and not as a perpetual or indispensable ceremonial of the church…**The real Christian compact is love for one another**" (*Mis.* 91:4).

No matter how often we may need to say it, this is the essence of the religious experience, the love we feel from the lives of Jesus and other earthly saints, the infinite care we feel that flows from the Almighty to all creation. Whatever we do in the name of our faith always redounds to this core principle of God's infinite love for all and our sharing of that love.

Therefore, everything we do in the name of God must fall in line with this founding principle. All the temporary forms of religious expression we are led to employ have to bow down to their original motivating power.

The perils of big buildings

Mrs. Eddy wrote in 1875, **"A magnificent edifice was not the sign of Christ's church"** (*Science and Health*, 1st Edition, 167). Though Mrs. Eddy loved the simple elegance of the original Christian Science Church in Boston, the imposing structure called the Extension, which followed it several years later, did not win her affections, as we have noted.

| A society that can pay $1 million for a building ought to drop the name Christian Science.
Mary Baker Eddy, 1903 (courtesy of Mary Baker Eddy Library) |

---

9. Barnes, "I Refuse to be a Member of a Dying Church," Sermon.

Somehow the founder's sentiment did not manage to reach the general population of Christian Scientists, who went about building modern urban Greek temples that often resembled banks more than they did the original Boston structure. Typical of the larger early Christian Science churches was the second Christian Science Church in Los Angeles. It was a magnificent building whose builders had "spared no expense"[10] and was reminiscent of the Mother Church Extension. The church was under construction when Mrs. Eddy penned this message to the Christian Scientists:

> **Are you striving, in Christian Science, to be the best Christian on earth, or are you striving to have the most costly edifice on the earth?... The more modest and less imposing material superstructures indicate a spiritual state of thought; and vice versa.... Mrs. Eddy has continued to declare against the display of material things and has said the less we have of them the better.**[11]

This statement suggests that the inspiration derived from a church service may be in inverse proportion to the grandeur and expense of that church's edifice. This strong caution against modern towers of Babel, cited above, was too late for many Christian Scientists. Large urban churches had already sprung up by 1908. Have these buildings, a century later, been held onto for far too long?

> **Pass ye the proud fane** [temple] **by,**
> **The vaulted aisles by flaunting folly trod,**
> **And 'neath the temple of uplifted sky**
> **—Go forth, and worship God.**[12]

So how do we proceed with our church structures? This book could not possibly fill in all those answers. But as long as we ask why we do what we do, and wait in prayer for solid answers, those answers will come.

---

10. Newman, "Meditation and Yoga," *Los Angeles Times*.
11. *C. S. Sentinel*, 12-5-1908, Vol. 11, No. 14. The editorial appeared under the by-line of an editor Archibald McClellan, but Mrs. Eddy wrote it.
12. Eddy, *Miscellany,* 151:17. Quoted from the controversial poet Rufus Wilmot Griswold.

How about the Reading Rooms?

Our churches have reading rooms that were early on in our church history intended to share Christian Science as available and stationary missionaries when church services were not going on. Are these rooms in keeping with the needs of our age? Do they rouse, prove, elevate, and heal? Each individual church may have a different answer to that question. A skeptical friend told me, "The reading rooms constitute too often (but not in all instances) testimonies to institutional failure, a failure to let forms evolve." Similarly our large, near-empty urban churches stand like the remaining teeth in a hockey player's smile. The reading room that does not spontaneously reach out in spirit to its surrounding community speaks more of the past and what is missing, whereas our church forms should speak to and aim for the future.

On the contrary, there are reading rooms that definitely rouse, elevate, and heal. They welcome underserved communities, they support their visitors who bring with them a variety of needs, and they fortify them with human encouragement and spiritual food. So does the form of what we are doing need to be transformed or do we merely uplift the spirit with which we express that form? **Mrs. Eddy altered structure when a practical need became evident.** She wrote with skepticism about holding onto organizational forms that have outlived their value.

Christian Scientists of today should be willing to change their approach when a current strategy proves to be inadequately fruitful or useful. What work, by whatever name, can substitute for many, but not all, of today's reading rooms and accomplish the same intended purpose, only doing it better? Or can our current reading room models adequately evolve so as to meet the need of humanity today?

The Rock and the church fence

One summer Sunday evening several years ago I was visiting with family on an island off the Massachusetts coast. After dinner we walked past the island's modest Methodist church, with its weather vane in the shape of a great bass. Through the church's screen door we could hear strains of a vesper service. The moment was mystical and sweet, and we would have joined the service, but it had been going on for some time. My mother and I sat on the church porch stairs listening to the holiness flowing out into the evening.

Absentmindedly I found myself admiring the church's white picket fence, its posts weathered by sun and hurricanes. The builders of that fence had encountered in the path of their construction a giant New England rock near the church entrance. This rock probably emerged from the island soil before pilgrims had thought of a new land. So with great respect and some common sense the Methodist fence-builders tapered the bottoms of the white posts and gracefully arched them over the giant rock, fashioning a straight top railing, but leaving the ancient boulder settled below in its place.

Since that summer evening Mom has left us, but the rock and its humble white fence remain, accompanied on some special times by the vesper choir. **"Oh, be careful how you build upon that sacred Rock."** If you must add on or improve, do so in deference to the Rock's leading and not in defiance of its simple, steadfast beauty.

Recommendations Few. The following may be helpful guidelines:
- Emphasize substance over form, and the importance of close and mutual support gained from gathering together with like-spirited fellow travelers.
- Ask what form is most appropriate for our individual needs and our community's need for spiritual communion.
- Be willing to let go of impractical traditions and impractically sized buildings.
- Keep focused on what the hearts of our church members are doing and can do where they are now planted, more than what physical impression our church building makes as a "statement" to our community.

Other than these thoughts, the author would be happy to turn over the task of making other recommendations to all those inspired to fill those shoes. Our local churches should be guided by their own inspiration always. However, the following questions may be useful for us:

Where to build, how, and why?

Ask yourself, "What was the scene of some of the holiest moments of my life?" How many of us would answer that the most sacred moments occurred in a church sanctuary? There are other sanctuaries in life. Sometimes a county jail meeting room, a mountain top, an emergency room, a remote seaside, and sometimes in a sick room where great internal soul-struggles are being waged.

Those sanctuaries and many others can be sites of the Most Holy of holies. Let us keep that in mind in whatever and wherever we are guided in our honoring of the Most High and Infinite.

What kind of physical setting is suitable for the band of worshippers in my community? For Christians in recent decades on different continents, the answers to this question will vary widely. A home-church experience, a scaled-down and environmentally friendly structure, a rented community building, or a far larger structure as with what we call megachurches? With any of these, form should closely follow substance and conjoin with the aspirations and character of the congregation. **Are we moving into an age where denominational lines become blurred, and churches of different stripes gather together in the same building?** A church that the author has been a member of shared space with three different denominations, all gathering at different times. If the divine is one, could a form like this be a possibility?

CHAPTER 8

"As wide as the love of God"[1]
—caring for others

If we want revival in our church, let there be a revival of invigorating Christian affection.[2] DeWitt John

MOST PEOPLE WANT to be caring neighbors, but Jesus' story of the Good Samaritan points to specific responsibilities that may be demanded of us if we desire to truly love our neighbor. This chapter is a short collection of questions that explore **dimensions of caring**.

Are we aware of our friends' lives?

From a church in the western U.S.– *I thought you might enjoy knowing about an experience we had several years ago at our church. We wanted to deepen our awareness of how to better pray for each other as we believed the early Christians did, so in one of our workshops we asked people (if they were willing) to list the problems that they were dealing with on a piece of unsigned paper and drop it into a box. Afterward the lists were read to the group.* ***I can't describe the raw emotion of learning about the severe challenges that our church brothers and sisters were facing.*** *Here was this sweet little group meeting every week for services with most of us thinking that we were sort of alone with our problems, and we came to find that so many of us were dealing with really heavy stuff—all the*

> Bear ye one another's burdens, and so fulfill the law of Christ.
> Galatians 6:2

---

1. Barclay, *Daily Study Bible*: Luke, 167. Barclay writes that our help for others, as the Good Samaritan offered to the injured stranger, must be "as wide as the love of God."
2. John, *C. S. Journal,* December 1981, 16.

major incurable diseases, gender identity issues, victims of abuse, etc., etc.

What did we do with the information? Those issues became topics for our Wednesday services, and we also had working sessions that delved into what we had heard from our people and how we could better pray for and support one another. Whether we knew the details of what each of us was wrestling with, we could still together prayerfully tackle as a Christian body the various problems our brothers and sisters were facing. It was indeed a profound experience.

So this was a creative way in which one congregation worked at becoming more supportive of its own people. But what if church members keep their private issues to themselves and don't want to burden others with their problems?

Are we too shy to ask for help…and then receive?

In Chapter 6 we discussed the need for Christian Scientists to establish stronger bonds of connection with their fellow congregants and not hunker down in a rugged individualism that prevents others from helping us. Mrs. Eddy wrote: "When we are willing to help and to be helped, divine aid is near" (*My.* 166).

When not to hide away from others— excessive admiration for secrecy

There are plenty of times in life when secrecy is precious—a sweet surprise kept in our heart, a precious confidence between friends, some bit of horribleness in life that would only serve to demoralize others. But if we go overboard on secrecy in certain situations, we stifle love. **Do we too often fear the thoughts of others more than we believe in the power of prayer and good thought?** Secrecy then becomes an entrenched superstition that lurks in the corner of our mind and shuts out the light.

Don't let **excess respect for secrecy** keep you from asking others for their prayers, or seeking help when help is needed. There are times, important times, when it's very right not to shelter others from our struggles because we believe erroneously that each of us is a fortified island of courage, independent of our brother and sister birds, and in need of little encouragement, cheering up, or breaking our dream of solitary confinement. To let others into our lives at those times is to let Christ in as well. Who wouldn't want to do that?

Do Mary and Martha have to battle it out over who is the best Christian?

What is the best kind of Christian work—prayerful, metaphysical, and spiritual, or human, charitable giving? I read an article a few years ago in one of our church magazines that advocated against allowing charitable giving to consume the commitment of a Christian Scientist to the detriment of individual dedication to spiritual healing. The writer suggested that it was a devilish suggestion to allow "good works" to compete with a church member's healing activity.

I can empathize with that writer's view in that I once became very involved in working on the board of a local chapter of Habitat for Humanity, an organization that builds houses with and for those who can't ordinarily afford to buy a home. As good an endeavor as Habitat is in its blessing for individuals and communities, I reached a point where I knew I had to turn over most of my board work and time to others, since ever-increasing duties involved with that charitable work were negatively displacing my progress as a Christian Science practitioner. As I backed away from the Habitat work, new members in that organization took my place and did a better job than I had done, while new fruitful opportunities turned up in my spiritual practice.

My Habitat experience notwithstanding, must we draw a sharp delineation between charitable giving and healing work? Love is healing, not ever separate from "good works." Mrs. Eddy once wrote:

> **Love cannot be a mere abstraction, or goodness without activity and power.** As a human quality, the glorious significance of affection is more than words: it is **the tender, unselfish deed done in secret**; the silent ceaseless prayer; the self-forgetful heart that

overflows; the veiled form stealing on an errand of mercy, out of a side door…lighting the dark places of earth.[3]

Notice here that Mrs. Eddy doesn't make any clear distinction between prayer and the loving expression of goodness that takes charitable forms. No doubt Mrs. Eddy herself was the beneficiary of such charity during her years of divorced impoverishment and widowhood.

Her statement (see above) contradicts the notion of love that is solely metaphysical but gives second-class status to tangible forms that touch people's lives. The visit that the author once received from church members bringing homemade cookies when I was laid up is never to be forgotten. It was a small but very meaningful gesture of the love that Christians should naturally express.

Not "either-or" but "both-and" Christianity

In the Gospel of Luke, directly after Jesus' parable of the Good Samaritan, is an interesting counterpoise to that parable. Jesus visits Mary and Martha, who are believed to be the sisters of Lazarus. While Mary seems focused on Jesus' spoken message, her sister Martha works hard at preparing food for the visit. But when Martha complains to Jesus that her sister should help out more with the food preparations, Jesus tells her, "Martha, you are fretting and fussing about so many things, but one thing is necessary."[4]

Was Martha's busy work in the kitchen not similar to the rescue that the Good Samaritan in the parable had offered to the wounded traveler? Possibly. However, Jesus seemed to sense an element of ego in Martha's attitude that needed reining in. The Master himself on different occasions shared food with his disciples, so he was not above helping others in mundane tasks, even feeding multitudes. Isn't it the spirit with which we do our tasks in life, more than the nature of the work itself, that should be in question?

"Either-or" Christianity says that we must choose between good

---

3. Eddy, *Miscellaneous Writings*, 250:20.
4. Luke 10:41, 42 NEB.

human works and spiritual healing. Jesus did "both-and." He healed and preached to the masses, but he also recognized human hunger and fed that condition as well as its spiritual counterpart. Jesus' parable of the sheep and goats (Matthew 25) makes crystal clear that feeding the hungry, housing the stranger, clothing the poor, and visiting the ill and imprisoned person are all Christly duties, not activities that in any way downplay the importance of healing work. So there is generous space for both Mary and Martha at the table of Jesus.

The importance of showing up

A friend of the author was in a motorcycle crash while on duty as a policeman. His fellow officers spent hours with him in his hospital room during his recovery. His fellow church members did not visit the hospital but said to my friend's parents, **"Tell your son we're thinking of him."** How hollow do those words sound in comparison with actually being there for friends when they need us. This in no way belittles the role of prayer as a primary means of blessing the world, but Christ demands that we pray and follow up that prayer with various appropriate actions such as personal visits wherever possible.

Another church member said out of exasperation: "If I'm in dire distress some day in my home or in a hospital, I don't want anyone to only 'silently support me,' thanks just the same." Mrs. Eddy wrote, "Human footsteps leading to perfection are indispensable" (*S&H* 254:1), and tangible love, showing that you're praying for someone, is indispensable as well.

A Christian Science teacher told his students: "If there is ever a time when Christian Scientists need the help of their brothers and sisters, it is when they are in the hospital. Do not abandon them." This teacher once excused his class that he was teaching a little early one day because one of his students from an earlier class, had been gang-raped, was in a local hospital getting an abortion, and there were complications. The teacher was going to the hospital to be with that woman. This kind of ready compassion should be the commend-

> "I named it Christian because it is compassionate, helpful, and spiritual."
> *Ret.* 25:10

able norm in the practice of all Christian Scientists.

The prophet Isaiah foreshadowed the words and works of Jesus when he wrote about the spiritual practices of his people:

> How anxious are they to worship correctly; oh, how they love the Temple services! 'We have fasted before you,' they say. 'Why aren't you impressed?… Why don't you hear our prayers? We have done much penance, and you don't even notice it!' I'll tell you why!… The kind of fast I want is that you stop oppressing those who work for you and treat them fairly and give them what they earn. I want you to share your food with the hungry and bring right into your homes those who are helpless, poor and destitute. Clothe those who are cold and don't hide from relatives who need your help. If you do these things, God will shed his own glorious light upon you. He will heal you; your godliness will lead you forward, and goodness will be a shield before you, and the glory of the Lord will protect you from behind. Then, when you call, the Lord will answer. 'Yes, I am here,' he will quickly reply…And the Lord will guide you continually, and satisfy you with all good things, and keep you healthy too; and you will be like a well-watered garden, like an everlasting spring.
>
> Isaiah 58:2-11 The Living Bible

CHAPTER 9

Guilt, blame, responsibility, blessed assurance

Did no man condemn thee?... No man, Lord.   John 8:10,11 ASV

Prayer is taking a chance that against all odds and past history, we are loved, chosen, and do not have to get it together before we show up.[1]

Anne Lamott

IF I AM SICK, IS IT MY FAULT? Jesus did not blame disaster or disease on the victim. When asked if victims of a well-known calamity were more sinful than others, he said they were not. And when he came across a blind man and was asked who was to blame for the man's blindness, he said it wasn't the fault of the blind man or his parents.[2] Now there was more that Jesus said, which we will get to shortly, but again: **Jesus did not blame disaster or disease on the victim. He did not blame the death of Lazarus on the young man or on his family.**

In Jesus' time illness was believed to be caused by sin,[3] and this tendency to judge the sick person continues today, especially among religious folks who should know better.

Why Christian Scientists should not blame a patient

When a student doesn't heal [his patient], *it's his own fault* [the healer's fault, not the patient's]. *I am out of patience at hearing a*

---
1. Anne Lamott, *Help, Thanks, Wow*, 5–6.
2. Matthew 5:45, Luke 13:3, John 9:3.
3. John 9:2.

student ask his patient to work [i.e., to study spiritual passages or otherwise use metaphysical treatment on his own behalf] **when the patient is up to the ears in the waves. Don't ask anything of your patient. Show him your Science, and when he is healed, he will work.**[4]

Mary Baker Eddy

This statement by Mrs. Eddy describes why practitioners should not put burdens where they don't belong—on the backs of their patients.

A friend of the author commented to his Sunday school teacher that he had crashed his car that week. The teacher asked him, "Did you read the Lesson the day of the accident?" "No," he answered. The teacher looked at him with a knowing glance that indicated where the blame rested.

The Christian Science practitioner works from the standpoint that God has created innocence in creation and not something called "original sin." When we're seeking to be right with the Infinite and our world, our past mistakes or omissions are no God-sanctioned basis for the action of evil in our experience. This fact provides a moral foundation for the Christian to overthrow the assumed legitimacy of evil in any form as either a cause or an effect.

A widow from Zarephath, when her child died, plaintively asked Elijah, "Did you come to remind me of my sin?" (I Kings 17:18 NIV) No, Elijah was not going to inflict guilt on an already desperately poor family. He wordlessly took the dead child to his room, and then, through prayer, revived him. No blame, just healing.

Lest human reason becloud spiritual understanding, say not in thy heart: Sickness is possible because one's thought and conduct do not afford a sufficient defense against it. Trust in God, and 'He shall direct thy paths'.[5]

Jesus often lifted burdens of guilt, self-condemnation, and societal condemnation from the backs of those whom he healed. Jesus spoke harshly towards those who foisted burdens on others (Matthew 23), but he did not blame the victims. A woman caught in adultery, a woman with

---

4. Von Fettweis, *Christian Healer*, 151.
5. Eddy, *Miscellany*, 161:23.

an issue of blood, and notably a woman who was bowed over. In the last case, Jesus pointed out that the woman was "held in bondage by Satan" (Luke 13:16 NLT), **and not enslaved by her own fault**.

What is our responsibility if we are ill?

Paul wrote to the Christians at Philippi, "Work out your own salvation with fear and trembling," and he pointedly added, "For it is God which worketh in you" (2:12, 13). This summarizes what Christian Scientists believe: that it is our spiritual responsibility to "work out" our life problems, including our sins and ills, but we can accomplish this only through the power of almighty divine Love. Christians believe in casting our burdens and sins before Christ and giving everything to Jesus. Christian Scientists might say this a little differently but would agree. There are times when life's problems are so overwhelming, often daily, that we feel we need the Almighty to do practically everything for us and with us, and at those painful junctures it would be wrong for a minister of any faith to tell us that we need to "pull ourselves up by our own bootstraps."

When *Science and Health* reads, "Take possession of your body, and govern its feeling and action…" (391), it can mean that we take stewardship of our being, but this can only be accomplished through "leverage" from a power above our own. Jesus told a hopeless cripple, "Rise, take up your bed, and walk" (John 5). Was that a cruel request, given the man's prolonged condition? Reading into the story we find out that this man had a chronic habit of blaming others for his situation, and he very much needed, with Jesus' aid, to take a stand, for himself. Jesus healed many others of whom he asked nothing but their outstretched arms.

Could a measure of guilt be instructive for our spiritual growth? People naturally blame themselves if they have brought upon their person or on others an illness or injury by some foolish action or inaction. But wallowing in guilt never moved anyone forward.

Guilt over sin

I knew a young man who had never heard the word *conscience*. He was rudderless and always in trouble with the law. Conscience is another name for the angels of Goodness which keep watch over our lives. When we get off track, those angels prick our soul and turn us back onto a constructive path. "The sensitive, sorrowing saint thinks too much of [sin]; the sordid sinner, or the so-called Christian asleep, thinks too little of sin" (*Mis.* 108:1). Sin is less a list of bad deeds or inclinations and **more a state of separation or alienation from our divine Source,**[6] and it will vary for each of us, given our path. Feeling guilty about being away from our divine home tends to forcefully nudge us homeward. There is a safe, narrow way between wallowing in our sorrow, or on the other hand, blithely forgetting how we have hurt ourselves and others when we have lost our way.

Unburdening the terrified

Florence Nightingale, the renowned British nurse, once comforted a dying prostitute who was terrified of going to hell. The frightened woman told her nurse, **"'Pray God, that you may never be in the despair I am in at this time.' Nightingale answered her, 'Oh, my girl, are you not now more merciful than the God you *think* you are going to? The real God is far more merciful than any human creature ever was or can ever imagine...'"**[7] What a burden those words must have lifted from off the poor woman's heart.

Unbelievable grace

This is about grace almighty. Without the consolation of an ever-loving higher power there is little hope for most of us. Without grace we might be forced to accept that "few are saved," but that teaching contradicts the inclusive competence and love of the Almighty.

---

6. Strong, *Exhaustive Concordance*. In Greek, the word *sin* means "to miss the mark."
7. Nightingale, ...*on Women*, 7, 48–49, 414.

Is a good or wise teacher one who flunks a large proportion of his class? The Bible tells us that God is "the greatest teacher of all" (Job 36:22 *Good News Translation*). Great teachers lead their students to successful learning and not to failure or frustration. Some driver's education cars allow the instructor to "overrule" the erring student driver and slam on the brakes when necessary. Likewise, the larger truth of the Almighty overrules our fluctuating lack of faith or what we feel is the inadequacy of our prayer.

No shame in illness

"If any man suffer as a Christian, let him not be ashamed..."[8] Ever. Paul marveled that the Christians at Galatia looked past his diseased condition to hear the essence of his message (Galatians 4). Remember the Christian Science practitioner who helped the critically wounded construction worker and whose prayers led to his speedy recovery in Chapter 1? That practitioner was a quadriplegic woman, paralyzed from the neck down. We hope she felt no shame about her physical condition at all, but, **hampered as she might have been, she was able to bring glory to God through another's healing**.

When the author injured his leg and was on crutches, a church friend told him, **"You better show up at church before you get that cast off."** My friend didn't want me laying low until I was back in good shape, having shown no sign of weakness or disability to my fellow members. Let's have the church spirit everywhere that would meet all brothers and sisters at their bedside, or at the hospital, while visiting them, helping them into the car, lifting their burdens and making them light.

Clearing out the closet of needless guilt

"Sickness must necessarily be largely the result of sin." This statement appeared in the *Christian Science Journal* in November of 1899. Somehow it slipped past the editors. By this questionable standard, if a

---

8. I Peter 4:16

Christian Scientist is ill, then they have sinned and need forgiveness or atonement in order to be healed. Then if they resort to medical treatment for their "sin-caused" illness, have they doubly sinned? We're blessed that this is not in the foundational writings of our church, but our church has a problem, as long as this automatic pairing of sin and sickness persists in any printed or spoken form.

Jesus never said that most disease was the result of the moral failure of a diseased person. Again, even the woman "caught in adultery" was not verbally abused by Jesus but forgiven by him.

> Neither blamed nor lectured, she is left to ponder the meaning of her rescue."
> Stephen Harris[9]

Consequences of guilt mongering

There's a real stigma attached if we have not healed with prayer. Tremendous guilt. — A mom and grandmom

For those unaware of how the church blame game takes shape, here are a couple of too-typical examples.

- A Christian Scientist resorted to medical treatment for cancer after seeing two friends pass on from that disease. She worked through that tough period and is doing well today. Another church member, who was told in an anonymous fashion about this, remarked about her fellow church member: **"Well, she probably wasn't a very good Christian Scientist."** I realize that condemnation happens in many different churches, but that fact does not excuse its presence anywhere.
- A church member who opted for some minor surgery returned to church only to find that she had been removed from her church position.

Could we please get away from all labels that try to identify whether we are "good" Christian Scientists or not? **Did Jesus ask suffering**

---

9. Harris, *The New Testament: A Student's Introduction,* 180. Commentary on the adulterous woman in John 8.

individuals if they were observant Jews before he healed them? No. But Christian Science practitioners have done that very thing. In far too many instances, the author has heard of practitioners telling their patients, **"I will pray for you if you stop taking any medication. That is how you will be healed."**

Is that a formula for healing, when we supposedly don't use formulas in healing? (*Church Manual* 43:5) But far more importantly, **a statement like that would attempt to attach dogmatic pre-conditions to the healing process in place of a practitioner's unconditional love for their patient.** If a patient of ours is wavering back and forth about taking some meds instead of praying for their condition, let's support their prayer for mental clarity, but not attempt to willfully push them into a conviction that they haven't yet reached on their own. We can keep in mind the point observed in the first chapter—that today's age, especially in Western society but truly around the globe, is many more times medically-minded, when appraised by the sheer amount of money per person spent on medicines today, than was the case in the early 1900s. Then there are the ubiquitous pharmaceutical commercials that only existed in print form a century ago. Wouldn't it make sense that influences and pressure move the average person to seek out medical solutions far more readily today than was the case for everyone in past decades? Our unconditional love and support should be proportionately greater to compensate for that highly increased social influence working on each of us.

What business do we ever have throwing our fellow brothers and sisters under the metaphysical bus or over a cliff because they don't "qualify" for God's mercy? Paul puts it this way: "There is no one who is righteous, not even one" (Romans 3:10 NRSV).

Let's look now at some subtle ways in which the seeds of inappropriate guilt are sown in the minds of our church members.

Subtly blaming the patient

Which of you, if your son asks for bread, will give him a stone?
Matthew 7:9 NIV

A long-time Christian Scientist wrote to the *Journal*[10] about a physical problem he had been stuck with, and he asked why he couldn't find a practitioner who could heal him. That's the kind of question that is difficult to answer. The editor answering this man tried her best, but part of her response missed the mark when she said: **"Jesus demanded a change of thought in his 'patient.'"**

What is off-base with that statement? Weren't there any number of people, multitudes we are told, whom Jesus healed, apparently without a word exchanged between the Master and the ones healed? Yes, Jesus told a blind man to go and wash in the pool of Siloam and told a lame man to pick up his bed, but throughout the Gospels the vast majority of those healed were just healed. Maybe gratitude or inspiration blossomed as the rescued individuals left the Master's presence. What Mrs. Eddy says along these lines is quite distinct: **"Jesus demanded a change of consciousness and evidence *and effected this change through the higher laws of God"*** (*Unity of Good* 11).

So again, it's not patients pulling themselves up by their mental bootstraps. It's Christ providing the spiritual power for what we call "change" or healing to happen. The full quotation suggests that a would-be healer brings the sense of Spirit to the occasion and doesn't try to wring a mental change out of the person who needs healing. Healing is seeing oneness of consciousness. A practitioner is neither seeing nor thinking about their patient: "My healing words are going to heal this poor soul and get him to reform his mental framework."

Another statement in the above-mentioned article: **"Each [healing] involved a transformation of thought."** Yes and no. Many healings surprise us. Healings may spring from no obvious prayerful work on our part, but from pure grace. Not all healings transform our thought. When our thinking or character is transformed, we tend to remem-

---

10. *C. S. Journal*, "Questions and Answers," August, 2012.

ber the transformation almost as much or more so than the physical change, but we are grateful when we are blessed by God, whether we remember a healing experience as a transformation or not.

Now back to the man who wrote to the *Journal*. He would not have written if he wasn't hurting and needing encouragement. **We, as Christian Scientists, collectively need to own our church's shortcomings**, and that questioning man pointed to the necessity for stronger healers among us. Here is what Mrs. Eddy wrote about the demand for practitioners to take responsibility when there is no healing:

Mrs. Eddy "teaches her students that they must possess the spirit of Truth and Love, must gain the power of sin over themselves, or they cannot be instantaneous healers themselves" (*Mis.* 40:22).

"[T]he practitioner may not always prove equal to bringing out the result of the Principle that he knows to be true" (*Mis.* 41:29-31). No blame foisted on the patient here, but the responsibility in both passages is placed on the would-be healer.

Dealing with a demanding faith

The challenge in a faith-practice that **demands much of its followers is that guilt and blame can set in without any special invitation or announcement of this development from anyone.**

From a southern church member: "Christian Scientists hold themselves to very high standards. What other religion expects its adherents to view each headache or broken toe as a call for prayer and increased spiritualization of thought? What other religion expects its adherents to ask the ambulance driver to take them home, instead of to the ER? What other religion expects its adherents to heal every conflict at work, every instance of financial instability, every limitation of mind, body, or spirit, the family, national and world economy, and the weather with an ever-expanding understanding of the laws of God?"

The "just-world phenomenon"

Melvin Lerner, a professor of social psychology, coined the theory *just-world phenomenon* in 1977, to describe the belief by which people expect that you get what you deserve in this life. Lerner's theory could lead us to blame people who have tragic events occur in their lives and attribute those tragedies to their personal failings rather than to consider circumstances that are beyond their control. As we have noted, Jesus questioned this belief.[11] His parable of the beggar and the selfish rich man (Luke 16) suggests that Jesus believed rewards for earthly goodness may await until after we have died.

Mrs. Eddy agrees with this idea that the reward for goodness is not necessarily realized during our human lives.[12] I confess that many times I have fallen into the above-named bad habit of expecting "bad things" to happen to "bad" people (as I might have classed those 'things' and those people), and I am sure I have been tempted to hope for those "bad" people to be punished in some way in this life. John Lennon sang about "instant karma." Christians, when facing tragedy or injustice in their own lives or the lives of others, could consider adopting Jesus' longer, kinder view of the when and how of divine justice and mercy, and how that plays out in the earthly experience.

The following is a critical observation from a university professor about Christians preaching what we could call a "health-wealth" message.

"Everything in your life becomes your fault or your reward."[13]

Great grace is an open door to all, an antidote to facile judgments, and we should feel that grace flowing from God and among our fellow church members.

---

11. Luke 13:1–5.
12. Eddy, *Science & Health*, 36:21-24.
13. Bowler, "On dying…" *Christianity Today,* 2-23-16.

What is blindness?

Our church has made some big steps since the following incident happened. Extreme forms of self-righteousness and condemnation are lessening, this author believes, but the shadows of old thought-habits and practices still haunt our premises. There is a need for a full-scale repentance from old sins and for reform towards a renewed Christ-like unconditional love and support for one another.

Do we really need to revisit the collective sins of our church's recent past? Yes, as long as by doing this, our church members gain a new humility and commitment to love for one another. If the tendency to casually put one another down, even subtly, is not pointed out, how will we move forward? We do this revisiting of bad examples in part to realize why we are where we are today as a body of faith…and where we need to travel in order to progress. Consider the following example from a friend of the author.

> In the early 1950s, my father-in-law Ted, who was blind from childhood, had discovered Christian Science and was attending a branch church. During a testimony meeting Ted spoke about his healing of a severe bodily condition. As he left the church with his seeing-eye dog, a man (later determined to be a *Journal*-listed practitioner) accosted him, grabbed Ted by the collar and shoved him up against a wall. You can imagine how alarming this would be, especially if you couldn't see someone coming after you. This practitioner told Ted to never give a testimony again until he had had a healing of blindness.
>
> During his lifetime, my father-in-law never did have a healing of blindness, but he remained a Christian Scientist, serving as a Sunday school teacher and board member. He went on to join the team that invented the very first computer (a mainframe). He co-invented the Braille computer. He was the first blind professor at MIT. He deciphered the scrambled Watergate tapes which led to Nixon's removal from office, and worked as a consultant for the NSA during the Cold War as one of the top five code-breakers

in the world, helping keep the US and Russia from pushing a red button and starting a nuclear war.

So who was blind?

"Love more for every hate…"[14]

A diseased culture supports or condones what happened in church to my friend's father-in-law. We can only imagine what our Savior would have said to the offending practitioner or what the founder of the Christian Science Church would have thought. The problem is more than this one person. Consoling and protecting and healing the "little ones" whom Jesus loved, begins with identifying and rejecting any skewed teaching or cruel views of humanity that would allow incidents like the one above to ever happen. A church department head once told his fellows: "The world will stop thinking of us as a cult when we stop acting like a cult."

It is not only important to re-tell and remember what happened to the blind man cited above; it is necessary, if Christian Scientists want the spiritual essence of what they believe to survive. Dogma and dogmatic behavior are why churches die. There are reasons why new churches take the place of ones that have grown self-content and dormant.

Christian Science defines a church as something that "affords proof of its utility." If the function of church not only isn't functional or blessing but abuses those who come to it for healing, that abuse must be thoroughly identified and removed, or the church will perish. That is why we tell uncomfortable truths in this book. No one wants to hear bad news, but if the bad news is so bad that it must be uncovered, so be it. In similar fashion, controlled prairie fires are started in order to burn off the old and prompt the rebirth of a new field.

---

14. *Christian Science Hymnal*, 209, verse 3.

No condemnation now hangs over the head of those who are 'in' Jesus Christ. For the new spiritual principle of life 'in' Christ lifts me out of the old vicious circle of sin and death.

Romans 8:1, 2, J.B. Phillips

…without the gospel—the union of justice and affection—there is something lacking.…

Science and Health, 592:13–14

There is a better way

The following is a brief memoir from Gilbert Carpenter, Jr., describing his father, a man who worked with Mrs. Eddy in her New Hampshire home during the later years of her life:

> When Gilbert Carpenter [Sr.] first came to live at Pleasant View he was much disturbed in his mind when he gained the knowledge that perhaps once or twice a year Mrs. Eddy had an experience of pain that was so severe that an M.D. was called in to give her morphine. Strange to say he never knew her to suffer in the daytime. It came to her at midnight when everything was dark, and she seemed in great fear.
>
> It was interesting that Mrs. Eddy made no effort to cover up this human experience as she might easily have done. She never made excuses afterwards to her students like saying that she endured all she could before calling the doctor. Furthermore, she never lost one bit of her spiritual authority, thereby showing that these experiences to her were merely part of the human side of things which she was daily putting out of sight. She indulged in no self-condemnation and when the experience was over, she appeared serene and untouched, with no mark left upon her, which is remarkable considering her years and her sicknesses.[15]

---

15. McNeil, *A Story Untold*, Vol. I, 486. "The younger Carpenter typed this note on the reverse side of a photostat copy of an inscription by Mrs. Eddy to Dr. Granville Conn."

Let's sum up what Carpenter was noticing about Mrs. Eddy's approach here:

- No attempt to cover up any compromises she might have made.
- No excuses given.
- No loss of spiritual authority.
- She considered these compromises in her use of morphine to be part of the human side of things that she was daily letting go of.
- She indulged in no self-condemnation over them.
- She appeared to have not been hurt in the long run by these incidents.

Condemnation and blessed assurance

It is central to Christian belief and Christian Science teaching that people can be, and must be, reborn through the Spirit. It is central to those teachings not to capriciously judge others for their mistakes, but only to point out mistakes for the purpose of healing. Who but ourselves can best know the history of any of us? Who can fully understand the multitude of considerations that motivate and underlie the actions of another person?

Martin Luther said that temptations are like **birds flying overhead which no one can entirely prevent, though we can deter those birds from nesting in our hair**. None of us has been spared from temptation circling over our lives. That is one reason we pray for forgiveness and rebirth and are so very grateful for the infinite grace that allows for rebirth, second chances, and the loosing our brothers and sisters from what would otherwise weigh down their souls.

Eugene Peterson's rendering of I John says all this so very well:

> My dear children, let's not just talk about love; let's practice real love. This is the only way we'll know we're living truly, living in God's reality. It's also **the way to shut down debilitating self-criticism, even when there is something to it. For God is greater than our worried hearts and knows more about us than we do ourselves**.

And friends, once that's taken care of and we're no longer accusing or condemning ourselves, we're bold and free before God! We're able to stretch our hands out and receive what we asked for because we're doing what he said, doing what pleases him...he told us to love each other, in line with the original command. As we keep his commands, we live deeply and surely in him, and he lives in us. And this is how we experience his deep and abiding presence in us: by the Spirit he gave us.

I John 3:18-24 *The Message*

The author has heard the following note of encouragement at the beginning of a Christian Science church service: **"Here in our church we want you to know that wherever you are in your spiritual journey, you are respected, accepted, and loved."** That statement sets the table properly. If anyone wanders into church worrying that they may have to run out at some point, words of unconditional support tell visitors that they can put their guard down. Would Jesus offer any less grace than that to the frightened, mistake-laden masses who came to him in their need?

Fanny Crosby, the blind hymn writer, wrote the following verse in her beloved song "Blessed Assurance":

Angels descending bring from above
Echoes of mercy, whispers of love.

A minister's observation
"By trying to interpret natural disasters and terrible circumstances, we easily convert them into a sort of **weaponized religious propaganda**... we end up assigning to God all our fears and prejudices and hangups..."[16]

What is a reason that some Christians 'weaponize' blame and guilt in the first place? We may find an answer in the following Bible rendition:

---

16. Pavlovitz, "No, Christians, God doesn't send storms and disease," johnpavlovitz.com, 9-8-2017.

She [the woman who bathed Jesus' feet with oil and her tears of repentance] **has been forgiven of all her many sins. This is why she has shown me such extravagant love. But those who assume they have very little to be forgiven will love me very little.**

Luke 7:47 The Passion Translation

Do Christians who assume that they are well on the way to spiritual perfection turn on those whom they see as not measuring up to a church standard, and do this in a way that conflicts with Jesus' teaching about self-righteousness, humility, and "extravagant love?"

A remaining question

Rabbi Harold Kushner, in his deeply thoughtful book *When Bad Things Happen to Good People*, raises the age-old problem of evil and its causation in the world. There is no facile answer to the ancient questions: "What is the cause of my problem or tragedy? And is life or God just?" Christian Scientists turn to Jesus' answer in response to his disciples' question about the man born blind: "Neither hath this man sinned nor his parents: but that the works of God should be made manifest in him" (John 9:3). Eugene Peterson in *The Message* captures the spirit of this verse: "**You're asking the wrong question** ['who did sin?']. You're looking for someone to blame. There is no such cause-effect here. Look instead for what God can do."

Parental guilt?

The author has heard of instances where parents caring for their child's sickness have been made to feel as if it is their personal fault that their child is ill. Didn't Jesus turn away this condemnation when he exonerated the parents of the man born blind? Yes, parents will be more instinctively concerned and therefore prayerful over their children than a typical child will be for his or her own well-being. But that's no occasion to blame anyone. Rather we "cast the burden" of concern for our kids before the great heart of divine Love and lean on the strengthening power of the love steadily flowing from our divine Father-Mother.

CHAPTER 10

Longevity, vision, life celebrations, and comforting those who mourn

Where there is no vision, the people perish.   Proverbs 29:18

IF THE PRECEDING WORDS from Proverbs are true, then so are these words: **"Where there is vision, the people thrive."**

This chapter is about stirring up the fire of spiritual vision and how Christian Scientists can better support their brothers and sisters dealing with death and the hereafter.

How do Christian Scientists relate to each other over the subject of death? The following four items may surprise church members, since they run counter to an inclination among many Christian Scientists to skirt over the subject of death:

- Mary Baker Eddy had an open-casket funeral.[1] Why? Were Christian Scientists more transparent about difficult issues one hundred years ago?
- The Christian Science *Church Manual* mandates an autopsy if a Christian Scientist passes on suddenly, and the cause of death is unknown (*Manual* 49-50). How come? Did we have more scientific curiosity and accountability when the church was first established?
- The Mother Church published the death-rates of Christian Scientists in 1902 and 1903, as compared with the death-rates of the general population of Boston.[2] Why were those statistics relevant? Did we

---
1. Peel, *Years of Authority,* 513.
2. *C. S. Sentinel*, Vol. 5, No. 45, 712.

value both accountability and longevity at that time?
- The Christian Science Church in Concord, New Hampshire, hosted a memorial service conducted by the local veterans group in 1907, when Mrs. Eddy lived in Concord (*My.* 284:12). And on September 19, 1901 a memorial service had been held in the Mother Church in Boston (*C. S. Sentinel* 9-19-1901), in honor of President McKinley who had just been assassinated. Were we less reluctant back then to celebrate and commemorate those who had died?

Four items and questions about them. Years ago did the Christian Science community deal with death differently than Christian Scientists often do now? It appears that the answer is a qualified "yes." Death, funerals, memorials, and vital statistics were maybe not subjects that Christian Scientists avoided a century ago, as they have tended to do in recent decades.

Let's start by looking at a factor that inspires morale in churches and society in general—longevity.

The function of longevity

"For I know the plans I have for you," says the Lord. "They are plans for good and not for disaster, to give you a future and a hope."

Jer. 29:11 NLT

Longevity is a building block of the faith community. It encourages and fortifies confidence in spiritual resources and faith in our Christian purpose. In Revelation we read, "Blessed are the dead who 'die in the Lord'" (Rev. 14:13 Moffatt). More encouraging to fellow Christians than "dying in the Lord" may be living, overcoming, and surviving, with spiritually inspired vitality. Historian Robin Lane Fox makes the points that Christian **martyrs did not immediately foster growth in the early church by the sacrifice of their lives,**[3] and that the greatest church numerical growth occurred during a time of legal approval, not persecution.

If Mrs. Eddy had died shortly after writing *Science and Health*, would the Christian Science movement have caught on as it did in the

---

3. Fox, *Pagans and Christians*, 441.

late 1800s? If she had passed on at a relatively young age, might that fact have belied some of the practical value of what she wrote, at least in the eyes of many of her would-be readers?

The Apostle Paul at times desired to depart from his mortal life of struggle, and he certainly had his share of deprivations as he worked to establish the fledgling Christian movement. But Paul realized that his persistent endeavors and self-sacrifice served as comfort and guidance to his fellow Christians. He wrote to the disciples at Philippi, **"For your sakes, it is better that I continue to live…so that I can continue to help all of you grow and experience the joy of your truth"** (Philippians 1:24,25 NLT). This summarizes the virtue of longevity in a nutshell. Longevity is **not a matter of prolonged years, but of fulfilled contribution and support to those around us.**

The prophet Isaiah envisioned a time when "no longer will adults die before they have lived a full life" (Isaiah 65:20 NLT). What promotes both length of days and fulfillment of life-purpose?

Life and purpose

A writer from BBC News interviewed British citizens over the age of one hundred years and collected nuggets of wisdom from these centenarians.[4] **Living for others** was named as a recipe for longevity. When Jesus told his followers that they were the light of the world, couldn't that light include being a living, loving encouragement for those around us and not living solely for our own benefit? Isn't that life-motivation the essence of Jesus' "Golden Rule"?

We learn from success and from the good example of others. For this reason we read the proverbs, the recommendations of wisdom in the Bible, and derive guidance from them. The following are extra-scriptural gems of advice on living a satisfying, unselfish, and long life, from the centenarians quoted in the above-cited BBC article:

- **Stay curious**
- **Be an optimist**

---

4. Wallis, "How to Live Beyond 100," BBC News, 7-2-2012.

- **Stay young at heart**
- **Cultivate friendships**
- **Learn what you can do without**
- **Do not take yourself too seriously; we are just a drop in the ocean**

Family and longevity

Epidemiologist Leonard Sagan put forward a thesis in his book *The Health of Nations* that strong family relationships, better education, and childcare are "measurably more critical than modern technology in promoting human lifespan."[5] Family and friendship form a context for our lives. We are not loners in the desert of mortal life, but we live in the context of the lives of others as well as in communion with the divine.

Mormons don't bowl alone
—friendship, family, and support

Mormons live, on the average, eight to eleven years longer than other Americans.[6] Researchers attribute this longevity at least in part to the church's prohibition of alcohol, tobacco, and caffeine. There may be other factors, including the church's social network, which helps insulate church members from some of the stresses of isolation and fractures within families experienced by so many Americans. Also, Mormons possess a comforting vision of the afterlife. In the hereafter, Mormons believe they will be surrounded by their families.

> The plan of the Father is that family love and companionship will continue into the eternities.[7]

This vision among Mormons is more complicated than the above quotation depicts, but the basic expectation of Mormons is that they will expe-

---

5. *San Francisco Gate* 12-12-1997.
6. Enstron, "Lifestyle and reduced mortality," 2007.
7. Hales, "The Eternal Family," Oct. 1996.

rience family togetherness after death. For many people that is a thought which encourages them in their earthly experience, alleviates fear, and may be a factor towards promoting longevity. Doesn't that vision of the afterlife help to remove the common dread of death—that it will be some kind of pointless void, involving separation from those we love?

Life after life—the biggest context and vision

Can we be confident of the continuity of life after our human lives are over? The American president John Adams, with touching faith and logic, penned an interesting perspective on his belief in the hereafter, after the passing of his beloved wife Abigail:

> **I know not how to prove physically that We shall meet and know each other in a future State…My reasons for believing it, as I do most undoubtingly, are all moral and divine. I believe in God and in His Wisdom and Benevolence: and I cannot conceive such a Being could make such a Species as the human merely to live and die on this Earth. If I did not believe in a future State, I should believe in no God. This Universe; this all; this** [totality] **would appear with all its swelling Pomp, a boyish Fire Work. And if there be a future State, why should the Almighty dissolve forever all the tender Ties which Unite Us so delightfully in this World and forbid Us to see each other in the next?**[8]

Mrs. Eddy appears to agree with President Adams: "Where God is we can meet, and where God is we can never part" (*My.* 131). She engaged this issue in the following way: "In [Christian] Science, individual good derived from God, the infinite All-in-all, may flow from the departed to mortals;…" (*S&H* 72:23-24). She wrote in her other prose writings: "When we shall have passed the ordeal called death… and shall have come upon the same plane of conscious existence with those gone before, then we shall be able to communicate with and to recognize them" (*Mis.* 42:12). What are distinctions in these strands of

---

8. Cappon, *The Adams-Jefferson Letters*, 530.

thought between Christian Science and the more intense exploration of the next world engaged by spiritualists?

In recent decades there have been many published accounts of near-death experiences (NDEs). While skeptics have attributed these phenomena to brain hyper-activity, NDEs give many people of faith a window into the possible dimensions of what we call the "hereafter." These phenomena also serve to allay the fear of death.

Those who have died, and then have been revived, possess a certainty of life beyond this one.[9] The revived ones also have learned from their tenuous experiences that there is more urgency and value to their earthly life than they had realized before their NDE. As a result, these survivors often find their life-purpose rekindled with a renewed vision.

Vision is everything. Without it, whole societies lose their footing, and individuals give up on living.

Premature death and calming the contagion of fear

Folks been dyin' around here that ain't never died before.[10]

When anyone reads the obituary page of a newspaper and notes the passing of an acquaintance who has reached ninety years or more, what is the reaction? It might be, "Oh, my friend is gone, but what a wonderful long life!" Take the same obituary page, and we spot someone who has passed on in their forties, or younger than an average lifespan, and immediately we wonder, "What did they die from? What happened?" We think to ourselves, "Could this happen to me? Am I next?" We check the birth year of the deceased to see if they are in our age group. This is an age-old tendency, to measure ourselves in relation to our fellow mortals. If the deceased is a friend or associate of ours, the news of the death casts a pall of concern over us and tends to create a contagion of fear and mystery, especially when that menacing shadow is accom-

---

9. Moorjani, *Dying to Be Me*. See other NDE experiences such as that of Reverend Howard Storm.
10. Johnson-Coleman, *Just Plain Folks*, radio KWMU, 12-14-98. *Just Plain Folks* shares homespun sayings, such as this one from the author's aunt. Ms. Johnson-Coleman commented that she wasn't exactly sure what her aunt's saying meant.

panied by unresolved questions regarding the departed. So if longevity can promote morale, and can encourage fellow travelers in a cause, and the premature death of our co-workers and the contemplation of the death-shadow erode our confidence, what's to be done to fortify the one and break the spell of the other?

A helpful prayer: *"Lord, make my life an encouragement to others."*

Thinking outside of ourselves

Here is a very brief review of big thinkers in the Bible whose senior years were momentous: The pioneering periods of the lives of Abraham and Moses appeared to only commence after they reached their senior years. The prophet Elijah thought expansively, but he had to first cross a bridge of deep depression related in I Kings 19. As he lay and slept under a juniper tree, ready to quit his life, he lamented, "I am not better than my fathers."

Are any of us better than those who've gone before us? Perhaps our indulging that comparison is needless. Isn't it more important that we absolutely do our best in the niche of time where we find ourselves? Comparisons of our lives with those of others can only be helpful if doing that prods us to exceed the limits imposed on us by the ghosts of unfulfilled promise of prior generations.

What did finally push Elijah into fulfilling his mission was the nurturing mercy of the Lord and a kind of spiritual to-do list that God issued to him after Elijah complained persistently about his woeful lot. There's nothing like being given a list of tasks to complete for the benefit of others. That call to duty serves to kick us out of any discouraged stupor. But what if that end-of-life stupor finds no uptick, and the prophet or individual succumbs to death?

If death can't be overcome, sorrow can be comforted

Decades ago during the author's childhood, we held our breath when passing graveyards, funerals were generally depressing, and the last job you ever aspired to was that of an undertaker. Social thought in the West has advanced since then in some arenas, at least in recognizing the importance of those who minister to the dying and the dead. Some of the shadow of death is yielding today to a different view of both the hereafter, how to treat those in the last years of their lives, and the needs of the mourners left behind by the deceased.

What we could learn from others and nature

In other cultures such as Japan, India, and Korea, reverence of the elderly and the deceased is a long-established tradition. Americans are more willing to relegate their senior citizens to nursing homes, to forget those who are gone, and even to construct housing over neglected or forgotten resting places of the dead. Humble geese remain loyal to their mates whom they partner with for life. A goose may refuse to leave the side of a sick or injured mate or chick even if winter is approaching and other geese in the flock are flying south. The goose will stay with the injured until there is recovery or until his or her comrade's final breath.

Jesus wept at the tomb of Lazarus. Exalted as the Savior was, he was not so high above others that he could not appreciate the pain of others and work to alleviate it. The author of Hebrews wrote: "We have not an high priest which cannot be touched with the feeling of our infirmities" (Heb. 4:15). Jesus was both sensitive to the suffering of others and understanding of their sins, even as he lived an exemplary life.

Consolation that truly consoles

Though Christian Scientists firmly believe that death has no enduring authority in our lives, our church's founder was willing to console mourners in their state of grief.

Mrs. Eddy wrote to the widow and daughters of church member Noyes Whitcomb:

> My beloved ones, my soul pleads for your consolation and peace, pleads that now, in this deep affliction, 'you acquaint thyself with

God and be at peace.' Dry your tears and be comforted because of his fitness for Heaven—the rich reward of his having been one of the best of all mankind on earth. Tenderly, lovingly thine…[11]

Mrs. Eddy wrote to President McKinley's widow:
"He [President McKinley] awaits to welcome you where no arrow wounds the eagle soaring…." (*My.* 290)

Mrs. Eddy did not consider it to be beneath herself in any way to utter words that she felt would be comforting to the bereaved, though these words might be labeled "old theology" by some of her students.

Coming to the bosom of Christ

A Christian Scientist had been sexually abused by a family member, and the wounds from that experience tormented this young woman's life. She cut and burned herself, though she survived. Some well-meaning church members encouraged this woman to see past the abuse that had happened, but those attempts at comfort did not reach her heart. One day she attended a Christian Science lecture given by a woman who herself had experienced abuse and had an understanding of what abuse does to people. Speaking to the lecturer after the talk, the young woman showed her the burn marks on her arms. The lecturer's response was, "Isn't it horrible?" The lecturer wasn't just talking about the burn marks. She sensed the suffering this woman had gone through and her need for deep consolation before the pain of her past could be dismissed as history. Recovery did happen for this young woman, but she found it necessary to first go through a period of grieving, supported by others' understanding.

Job's friends are often associated with the wrong kind of help for their grieving friend. In fact their first actions showed great wisdom and compassion for Job. When Eliphaz, Bildad, and Zophar saw their barely recognizable friend after his various personal tragedies, they too mourned and wept, and "then they sat upon the ground with him si-

---

11. L02617 courtesy of Mary Baker Eddy Library.

lently for seven days and nights, no one speaking a word; for they saw that his suffering was too great for words" (Job 2:13 TLB). Probably before it was too early for him to say something, Zophar is recorded as encouraging Job, "You will forget your misery; you will remember it as waters that have passed away" (Job 11:16 NRSV). Apparently Job was not ready to listen to this promise from Zophar that, at a later time might have been comforting. Job responded curtly to Zophar and the others, "You are all worthless physicians" (Job 13:4 NKJV). The right truth at the wrong time may be the wrong truth.

"Make no unnecessary inquiries relative to feelings or disease" (*S&H* 396:5). Notice that it says "unnecessary inquiries," not "make no inquiries." Even Jesus inquired as to how long a young man had been suffering what appears today to have been epilepsy (Mark 9:21). A frequent complaint about Christian Scientists is that they don't care how you feel, or they are insensitive to the feelings of their patients or family. A well-meaning church member in a stumbling effort to console the spouse of a friend said in reference to the friend's death, "Let's know this didn't really happen." The bereaved spouse responded, "Before knowing that, I'll know that this conversation never happened."

Ellen DeGeneres:
"I never knew how anybody was feeling."

Comedian and talk show host Ellen DeGeneres, was raised in a family of Christian Scientists, but her parents divorced when she was in high school. Ellen commented in a *Parade Magazine* interview: "I didn't see deep emotion from my parents. It was all very polite and very surface. I never knew how anybody was feeling."[12] Until her parents' separation, Ellen had assumed that all was well in her family.

A reader of the DeGeneres interview, who had grown up as a Christian Scientist, wrote to *Parade*: "When I was a kid and I'd watch something on PBS that said it was okay to be sad or angry, my mom would always say 'you know you don't really have to feel those things. That's

---

12. Rader, "Ellen DeGeneres Talks Feelings, Fun and Finding Dory."

just a false belief? She meant well, but of course psychologically that leads to repression and avoidance!"

Is there an important point stemming from the interview with Ellen DeGeneres and the comment made in response to it? Even if a minority of church members get the impression from their version of Christian Science that Christian Scientists are supposed to suppress feelings and emotions, and that is the way to happiness, shouldn't this cause concern for those who respect and appreciate the church's teaching? Where does the approach originate that we suppress human emotion, and shouldn't it be challenged? Jesus advocated forgiveness over revenge and hate, but he expressed human emotions such as joy, sorrow, and even anger against hypocrisy. Coldness, impassivity, disdain for the feelings of others have no part in the practice of Christian Science.

Is there a reason that Ellen's parents didn't allow into their home a normal exchange of emotion, feeling, sadness, and discussion over life's difficulties? What Ellen describes in her family has been reiterated by writers whose books have lambasted Christian Science for similar reasons. While most Christian Scientists might not believe that they should repress their feelings and inner thoughts, shouldn't we acknowledge that a logical extension of some passages from Christian Science writings could encourage the repression of emotion, hurt, or grief?

An incident described in *Science and Health* of a little girl falling on carpet could suggest to parents that they should brush off a child's accident as no big deal, regardless of how the child feels. The wording there on pages 154–5 could seem too curt or unsympathetic to any reader though it makes a good point that parents shouldn't over-react to their children's accidents. Mrs. Eddy wrote "sorrow is without cause" (*S&H* 386:27), and yet she endured deep grief over the passing of her husband Asa Eddy.

There's another passage that might feed a Christian Scientist's conviction that they not show feelings: "The pent-up elements of mortal mind need no terrible detonation to free them…they should be stifled from lack of air and freedom" (*Mis.* 356:5). Archie Bunker said to his poor, suffering Edith, "Stifle it!" Can we acknowledge that Christian Scientists may have been led to believe that they should stifle their human emotions? Shouldn't we make clear to our people that stifling grief and normal human feelings is not something we believe in doing?

After Asa Eddy died, Mrs. Eddy retired from her work for a time, and stayed with friends for two months in Vermont. She confessed her feelings about her husband in this way: "I never shall master this point of missing him all the time I do believe, but I can try…"[13] Does this comment suggest that Christian Scientists should make nothing of their feelings of grief? Not at all. Mrs. Eddy also addressed the need for healers to be sympathetic and approachable and to console those in need. The first few pages of the chapter on "Christian Science Practice" reinforce the need to be compassionate, to exercise "common sense and common humanity" (*S&H* 365:11).

When silence is not golden

I know of a branch church that set a policy which explicitly stopped the normal act of informing their members when a fellow-member had died. Muffling the news of a friend's passing in no way serves to comfort surviving family and friends. The author has heard church members say, when asked about the circumstances of the death of a friend or fellow member, "We don't need to know, do we?" A church friend writes about this: "People disappear, and we find out about it months later. This general silence does not recognize the church as the community that surrounds our faith lives."

Unfortunately, or not, the human mind tends to want to know, for good reasons and for less than noble reasons, when one of our fellows is ill or has not been in church for a while. The good reasons may be an expression of interested concern and sympathy and a desire to know what to say to the family of the deceased. The less blessed reasons may fall into the category of "I want to know either from a desire to gossip or from a fear that I might suffer from the same cause." In either case, it is right to be open and honest about what has happened.

Just imagine how awkward it can be when a church member asks

---

13. Peel, *Years of Trial*, 117.

a recently bereaved friend where their spouse is, after months of not seeing that man or woman in church. The Golden Rule should be able to guide us on these issues, but sometimes that rule is overridden by a dogma-ridden desire to avoid uncomfortable subjects at any cost.

The value of memorial services

Comfort ye, my people, saith your God. Isa. 40:1

Not having a memorial service or funeral does not make death any less difficult than it already is to those surviving the death of their family members or close friends. Instead it raises questions with those mourning: "Why is there no service? What was the cause of death?" So the lack of a memorial, and even of a church announcement for members

> Journalist David Halberstam wrote: **"A great journalist, a great editor, balances what people want to know with what they need to know."** [14]

in many ways reinforces the impact of death, instead of releasing family and friends to happier memories of the real meaning of the life of the deceased. Our church's founder had no objection to cherishing memories, as she writes:

> *...perpetuate no ceremonials except as types of these mental conditions,—remembrance and love...* Mis. 91:14

The grieving women who first saw the risen Christ had been on a mission of honoring the dead. They desired to anoint the body of Jesus. If this respectful deed and tradition was insignificant, why did Jesus condescend to appear to Mary Magdalene right there by his tomb?

There is a tradition that the author encountered among African-American Christians that may still prevail today. One friend told me, **"We weep when a baby comes into the world, and rejoice when a brother or sister passes through the veil."** Are not the birth and death of God's children both worthy of commemoration, whether we mourn or rejoice? More and more in American society, funerals take the form of celebrations of life rather than magnifying the sadness of the mourners' loss. We

---

14. Halberstam, *Monitor*, 11-8-2001, 18.

celebrate human and spiritual achievement just as an audience cheers for a strong performance by an actor or athlete, or applauds a beautiful song. Our lives are all expressions of divine wonder and are worthy of celebration, from the most meek among us to those honored by the whole world.

Author Allison Gilbert writes: "Grief experts agree that taking steps to appropriately remember loved ones is actually essential for healing. Individuals who keep the memory of loved ones alive almost always fare better emotionally than those who don't."[15]

When life was not memorable

What is the value of remembrance? In what we commonly refer to as the Dark Ages, individuals lived lives unknelled and therefore unremembered by future generations. European peasants did not have surnames. They lived and died in little villages and on feudal estates. William Manchester comments about this age: "Anonymity approached the absolute…so did [the peasantry's] mute acceptance of it."[16] Why resurrect, even in part, that spirit of ultimate disrespect for the identity of God's making? Do we see our individual lives as so devoid of importance that there is no need for anyone to celebrate our experience and what we have meant to those around us?

From a pastor who studies Christian Science: "I think many Christian Scientists brush death under the rug, and it is denial, denying the community a chance to celebrate the person's life, and a denial of the resurrection doctrine of the Gospel."

Honoring our "father and mother"

I can't imagine not having had a service for my mother…

—from a church member

---

15. Interview for CNN with Gilbert, author of *Passed and Present,* 4-12-17.
16. Manchester, *World Lit Only By Fire*, 22.

Memorial services, or celebrations of life, honor the memory of those who have gone before us, so they are a form of obedience to the fifth commandment of Moses. Commemoration of those who have passed on is a solemn duty in many cultures in the world. Certainly, both the treatment of elders and respect for them during life and after their passing should receive greater emphasis in the West.

Compassion for the bereaved…and celebration of life

Memorial services commemorating the value and meaning of those who have passed are often considered to be a fulfillment of the wishes of the deceased, but their Christian and compassionate function is not merely to honor the memory and life of the departed. Those services comfort and assure those who remain that both our lives and our enduring spirit have great value. In one sense the commemoration is all about the person who has moved on, but in a very real sense *the commemoration is not for the departed*. It is for the living, and it is for those who need to remember, or grieve, or rejoice over the life of their loved one and cherished friend.

What if a Christian Scientist requests that no memorial or service be held in their remembrance after they are gone? Perhaps this is solely a matter for the individual's family to consider. But before any Christian Scientists make this kind of end-of-life request, shouldn't they ask themselves: **"Is my human experience so empty of good that no one exists who cares to recognize any of my life's goodness or its value in the company of my lifelong friends?"** Again, if we celebrate the arrival of infants into this experience, why would it be of less value to honor that same grown infant's experience years later? Human experience is not a zero, a void of no significance to be forgotten or denied. No Christian teaching preaches that message of nihilism.

But what if the deceased is in their late nineties, has no friends or relatives nearby or living, has no one who cares deeply about them, and even has lived an unfortunate life full of misdeeds and tragedy? All the more reason for Christians of any stripe to stand in the gap for the deceased and dig for redeeming morsels or mustard seeds of good they can discover about the deceased, in order to honor the "least of these." The vision of eternal or ongoing life beyond the grave begins with a visionary appreciation of what we have already seen here in our existence.

And while we're on this subject, why should we wait until someone is gone in order to totally appreciate who they are, what they have stood for, and much of what they have brought to this life? Shouldn't the Christian experience include a regular celebration of the Body of Christ including the precious members of that Body who are alive and blessing in our midst? A friend of the author celebrated his ninetieth birthday with a large party organized by his family. This man's friends and family truly enjoyed getting together to celebrate their loved one, especially given that he was still with them and participating in the celebration.

The substance of a memorial service

The heavy shrouds and gargoyles are long gone. Life celebrations or memorial services reflect the joy of life in the Spirit and the joyful essence of the life of the deceased, but sometimes our church members need a little coaching along these lines about the new normal. The author has attended memorial services that were as devoid of spirit as any corpse could be. A memorial service should never be an excuse to merely read some traditional Scripture such as the 23rd Psalm, only because many others before us have read that passage. The funeral service for one Christian Scientist was so "impersonal" that the son of the deceased commented to me, "It was cold. I felt nothing. There was no mention of my mother's humanity, character, or lovely qualities, and other family members noticed this as well."

Lucia Greenhouse noted similar problems in her book called *fathermothergod* which tells the story of her rejection of Christian Science. In looking back at her growing up, Lucia was particularly disturbed by the dysfunctional way in which her family dealt with the death of her mother. While there was a memorial service, it failed to capture anything of personal remembrances of her mother. It included readings from the Bible and Christian Science writings but apparently lacked the spirit and vitality of the deceased. Greenhouse writes, "There was no reference to my mother's personality, or to anything she had ever done or said…no sharing of anecdotes."[17] If services like these are cold, then those presenting them are doing a serious disservice to their departed friend and to their Christian roots.

I used to believe that the way you did funerals was to read a few passages from the Bible, then *Science and Health*, pause for the Lord's Prayer, and maybe end the service with reading a hymn. Does it make any sense for us to read several passages about the insubstantiality of death to a gathering of those mourning their friend or relative, when the spirit with which we read conveys little in the way of consolation, spiritual promise, or joy over the life of the departed one? Are we afraid to show our humanity and tender care for those who have passed on and for their families?

A memorial service is also no occasion for trying to convert any unsuspecting attendant with a deluge of church writings. Friends or family of the deceased are not a captive audience, fish in a barrel, waiting to be hauled in with a large net of Christian Science theology.

A memorial service is a time to **comfort, encourage, celebrate** a friend and dear one, even laugh or share music that was precious to the departed, but it is not a time to lecture anyone. The following poem, written by an Anglican priest, is a thoroughly comforting statement. After the startling first line, this poem consoles grief in an intriguing way. It deals very much with our humanity and attempts to convey the ongoing presence of life, identity, and remembrance.

> Death is nothing at all.
> I have only slipped away to the next room.
> I am I and you are you.
> Whatever we were to each other,
> That, we still are.
> Call me by my old familiar name.
> Speak to me in the easy way
> which you always used.

---

17. Greenhouse, *fathermothergod*, 280.

Put no difference into your tone.
Wear no forced air of solemnity or sorrow.

Laugh as we always laughed
at the little jokes we enjoyed together.
Play, smile, think of me. Pray for me.

Let my name be ever the household word
that it always was.
Let it be spoken without effect.
Without the trace of a shadow on it.
Life means all that it ever meant.
It is the same that it ever was.
There is absolute unbroken continuity.
Why should I be out of mind
because I am out of sight?

I am but waiting for you.
For an interval.
Somewhere. Very near.
Just around the corner.

All is well.

Rev. Henry Scott Holland (1847-1918)

Picking up the yoke of our friends and making it our own

Memorial services are a time to rededicate ourselves to the cause and causes that the departed held dear and which we cherish as well. Elisha picked up the mantle of his mentor Elijah and sought the spirit of Elijah to pass along to him. When Jesus returned, what did he tell Peter who wanted so much to follow Jesus? "Feed my sheep, Peter." Carry on my work. Stay in my vineyard and labor there.

The following was shared by a Christian Science friend of the author who read these words at the memorial service for Charlotte, a young close friend of her daughter. Charlotte faced a fearsome diagnosis with an exuberant desire to love life and cherish others. It's certain that she not only touched many lives, but she also inspired those who knew her to carry on her joy. Beginning with these lines from Mary Oliver's poem "Felicity," the service also included the dedication of a bench in Charlotte's memory as well as other remarks:

> *Everything that was broken has*
> *forgotten its brokenness. I live*
> *now in a sky-house, through every*
> *window the sun. Also your presence.*
> *…Every day has somsething in it*
> *Whose name is Forever.*

This bench is made of American Heart Pine, as old as the land that Charlotte loved…It is rooted and grounded in the love this community has for Charlotte and her family.

The growth circles speak of eternal life and the ripple effect of just one of Charlotte's huge smiles, one of those unforgettable belly laughs, the inspiration gained from her immense courage and tenacious love of family, friends, and fun in the face of such trial.

In 1 John 4 in the Bible we read, very simply, that "God is love."

"Where love is we can meet, and where love is we can never part." [18]

I took the following words from a thank-you letter Charlotte wrote. This signature is what she's giving us this very moment. What is written in the letter to each of us will be different, but it is always signed off with this love. It's an undying legacy that is felt in small and large ways, helping us to be kinder where we might have been harsh, to hold a hand in quiet consolation, or to spread fun and joy where drudgery or submission seem the only options. This is her gift.

Love, Charlotte. Heart. Forever.

---

18. Eddy, *My*. 131. The exact quote: "Where God is we can meet, and where God is we can never part."

Recommendations

- The celebration of the lives of our fellow Christian Scientists at their passing can be an appropriate and constructive occasion when spontaneous expressions of appreciation, honor, and even humor transform what could be a mournful occasion into a very comforting and inspiring one. The avoidance of this recognition of one another after someone's passing *may*:
    - increase the mystery, and thus the fear, surrounding death
    - make our faith practice look like a cult, and
    - abandon a primary duty of the Christian Body to honor and respect the life and individuality of its family members

- **A too-studied avoidance of the subject of death does not erase the thought of death, but the full living of love naturally reduces the thought and fear of death.** Recognize the importance of longevity in encouraging the vitality of the Christian community. The author suggests here that there are some mental/spiritual factors involved with premature death among Christian Scientists that our brothers and sisters are capable of confronting in a better manner. Here are two of those factors:
    - excessive fear of the negative thoughts, or what we term the "mental malpractice," of others. This book does not contend that people aren't capable of thinking ill of their neighbor, but we affirm that thinking, praying Christians and others can certainly, with divine help, protect themselves from any believed-in effect of negative thinking, from whatever source it may originate.
    - demoralization resulting from dropping numbers of churches and membership. As we point out in other chapters, the decline of any entity, organization, or movement can be a time for thoughtful reassessment and renewal.

- There are pressing needs among our church brethren. If those needs are met, longevity can be stimulated. Consider the following goals that aim to truly comfort and lead forward our fellow church members:
  - increase unity in our church and the mutual prayerful support one for another
  - actively dismiss superstitious fears regarding believed-in causes for mortality
  - displace demoralization with vision
  - highlight awareness of, and rejoicing in, a present sense of eternal life in a saving Christ and forever life that is far more than a doctrinal tenet that we believe

Speaking of the big, enduring picture of life, Jesus once said to his disciples, "You have sorrow now, but I will see you again; then you will rejoice, and no one can rob you of that joy" (John 16:22 NLT). This vision fuels not just longevity, but more importantly, inspires a loving life. Love can truly meet human needs. "Stronger supports and a higher home" (S&H 169) include the natural demand that our church members are really there for each other in sickness, in our senior years, and when we need comforting the most.

CHAPTER 11

Shutting the door on progress
—Christian Scientists' views of class, race, gender, and identity

The rich and the poor meet together: the Lord is the maker of them all.   Proverbs 22:2

If the soft palm, upturned to a lordly salary, and architectural skill, making spire tremulous with beauty, turn the poor and the stranger from the gate, they at the same time shut the door on progress.
Science and Health, 142

Stranger 1. one unknown; 2. *one not admitted to any communication or fellowship*   Webster's Dictionary (1828)

CLASS

THE REVEREND TONY CAMPOLO has devoted years to urban Christian ministry. He tells this fascinating story of a city encounter.

> *One day I was walking down Chestnut Street in downtown Philadelphia. Coming at me was a schizophrenic man. He was one of those dirty street people who make me feel so uncomfortable that I often pretend not to notice as I pass by. This particular man was usually yelling at an invisible presence, and his tirades were filled with the "F" word, as though that were the only adjective in his vocabulary.*
>
> *On this summer day, however, there was something different about him. He had in his hand a Styrofoam cup filled with coffee*

from McDonald's. As he approached, he screamed at me, 'Hey, mister! Ya wanna' drink some of my coffee?'

Needless to say, I gave him a patronizing smile and said, 'No, thank you.' No sooner did we pass each other than I felt this strange impulse. I got about ten steps or so past him when I felt compelled to turn around and yell, 'Yo, mister! I've changed my mind! I really would like a sip of your coffee.'

I walked back to him as he held out the cup with his arm at full length. I took the cup and sipped a little of the coffee. Then with an inquiry meant to be cordial I asked, 'How come you're giving away coffee this morning? You're getting extra generous, aren't you?'

He answered, 'Well, the coffee is especially good this morning, and I figure that when God gives you something especially good, you ought to share it with people!'

I was blindsided by his answer and asked, 'Is there anything I can give you?' I thought he might hit me up for five dollars. Instead he answered, 'Yeah, you can hug me!' Actually, as I looked at him, I thought that I would have preferred the five dollars.

As I hugged him on that busy street, I realized he wasn't going to let me go. People passing us stared at that bum hugging this embarrassed, establishment-looking man. Then slowly, I became aware of something mystically wonderful. I gradually sensed that this was no bum I was holding in my arms. Instead, I grasped the reality that I was holding in my arms the one who once said, 'Whatever you do to the least of these—ye do to Me!' He was in my arms.[1]

This chapter is not about being politically correct or being open-minded and tolerant. It is about **recognizing Christ in our midst**. "The stone which the builders refused is become the head stone of the corner" (Psalms 118:22).

---

1. Campolo, *Revolution and Renewal*, 85–86.

A tale of two churches

There's a Christian Science church in the Midwest where fifteen years ago a homeless man wandered into the Wednesday night service and stayed. "They probably don't want me in here," he thought to himself as he walked down the church aisle and headed for a pew. Joe had been sleeping under a bridge. That evening he had a strange feeling that he wanted to go to church, but he had only his old clothes, no money, and a pocket full of meds.

"I walked into the building in the middle of the service. I was going to turn around and leave. I thought, 'What am I doing in a Christian Science service with my pockets bulging with pills?' The usher touched my arm and offered me a hymnal, 'Come on in!' After the service another member offered me a ride home. 'Oh, yes, thank you!' But I don't want to tell him that home is under the highway, so…'I'll get off here.'"

"'You're coming back on Sunday, right?' It was hard to say 'no' to that much love." Joe kept coming back to the church. He wore the same clothes for six weeks. Pretty soon, members realized what his situation was, and one of them offered Joe a job working for a water softening company. Others helped him find an efficiency apartment. Two years later he was the church's liveliest usher and the church's janitor. Four years later he was chairman of the board…and still the janitor. Five years after that first night he wandered into church, he became a *Journal*-listed practitioner…still helping take care of the church.

Joe goes back to the bridge that was his home. Only he takes with him copies of *Science and Health* and a lot of love. Not long after Joe's new birth, he took a bus down to New Orleans. It was the fall of 2005, shortly after Hurricane Katrina devastated that city. Joe got past the National Guard barriers and found his way to a Christian Science church. There he spent the next few days cleaning hymnals, pews, and staying in the empty church building until the Guard told him he had to leave. It was a mission of thanks and going home.

Would that every congregation in our country be blessed enough to have a treasure like this man as part of their church body. Notice

> Not many mighty, not many noble, are called.
> I Corinthians 1:26

from our story how Joe was welcomed by the church that he visited in many small but crucial ways that showed tender Christian empathy and alertness. When we look past people's appearances, and we see their spirit and heart, we are seeing Christ in our midst.

Another church, another story

About the same time that Joe was finding his way home, there was another Christian Science church with a less-blessed outcome. A homeless man was camping out behind the bushes that surrounded the church's auditorium. What was the members' solution? The church board voted to spend a considerable sum of money to tear up the bushes in front of their building and plant shorter shrubbery that would reveal if someone was sleeping there. The board then considered a motion to install an automatic sprinkler system that could activate in the middle of the night and baptize any unblessed intruder at occasional intervals. When this latter motion was being discussed, a friend of mine, a member of the board, felt that enough was enough, and she quit that church.

Which church action would Jesus love and why? And further: **Which church would *accept* Jesus?** Let's be very clear that homeless people can have issues that defy simple social solutions, just as some poor people may be more receptive to Christ's touch than others. Any of us should be justifiably alert to those who drop in on church services with the intent to hit up generous and unwary members, but suspicion of strangers should not be the order of the day for Christians.

One young member of the church that made life hard on its vagrant camper left a jacket out in sympathy for him, and who knows if the church which Joe discovered ever stumbled in their dealings with street people? But our question persists: **How in tune with Jesus are our churches?** Our answer to this question could determine whether we are **opening or closing the door on progress—and that is a huge choice**.

Christian Science churches have too often closed that door rather than opened it to the poor and the "stranger," and **we have paid a great price** for doing so. If we have failed to make our places of worship warmly welcoming to poor people, and people of color, and people of various sexual orientations, we have closed the door on Christ and his little ones, and have rejected not only "the stone which the builders refused…the head stone of the corner," but our very future.

Who is rich and who is poor? What is poverty and wealth?

There is a troubling passage in the book of Revelation. This verse contains a startling message directed to the Christians at Laodicea (located in modern-day western Turkey). The words could just as well be addressed to Christians in Western and developed nations today: "**You say, 'I am rich, with everything I want; I don't need a thing!'** And you don't realize that spiritually you are wretched and miserable and poor and blind and naked" (Revelation 3:17 The Living Bible).

This is the terrible paradox of Christianity in the West in our age—that while Western Christians are well-supplied with church texts and resources to carry forward the Gospel and exercise its power, their capacities are dulled by the relative material prosperity in which many of them dwell. The Revelator challenged the spiritual dullness that he felt existed in his time at Laodicea. How much more should today's "First World" Christians be alert to the greater problem of this "poverty of riches" with which Christians, including Christian Scientists, can be shackled today?

To preach the challenging gospel of the perils of material prosperity to today's Christians is no simple task. Christian pastor Heidi Baker and her husband have carried on healing work in Africa for two decades and have left behind worldly goods in their American homeland in order to do that.[2] Are we more apt to praise the works of such Christians than to emulate them? In following the path of self-renunciation we find the pearl of great price, but this pathway stands in conflict with many of the goals of the society in which we live. This problem existed in Bible times and is still with us.

---

2. Baker, *Compelled by Love*.

Faith without follow-through isn't faith

A pastor friend gave me the following: **"You cannot do more than pray until you have prayed; but you must do more than pray after you have prayed."** Another pastor says it this way: **"Put legs on your prayers."** These statements apply to many circumstances, though not all. Sometimes prayer alone does exactly what is needed, but notice how Jesus gave helpful counsel to some whom he healed. And notice in Paul's mission work how important human follow-through was to him.

The Epistle of James tells us that "faith without works is dead." Phillips translates here: "So you believe that there is one God? That's fine. So do all the devils in hell and shudder in terror!…Faith without the right actions is dead and useless" (James 2:18-20 J.B. Phillips). And earlier in verse 15: "If a fellow man or woman has no clothes to wear and nothing to eat, and one of you say, **'Good luck to you. I hope you'll keep warm and find enough to eat,' and yet give them nothing to meet their physical needs, what on earth is the good of that?**" Christian Scientists cannot skew these passages to suppose that "works," or "actions," mean only prayer and healing. Jesus did healing work as well as feeding the needy. So how can we pray without appropriate follow-through?

> From a young Christian Scientist in the western U.S.: **When a homeless guy came to one of our services, it was really awkward. People were angry that he was there.**

If Love is to meet every human need, what role do church members have in the meeting of those needs? Merciful, appropriate deeds are what typified early Christian practice just as much as spiritual healing was characteristic of that era. A friend of the author was unemployed for a while. He asked an elderly Christian Scientist who was a relatively new member of his church how he might be able to approach some church members to ask if they could help in his job search. His friend warned him, **"Don't be surprised if you get the cold shoulder. All they'll do is tell you to pray."** If those words seem blunt, recall the sermon of Martin Luther King: "Any religion that professes to be concerned about the souls of men and is not concerned about the slums that cripple the souls—the economic conditions that stagnate the soul…is a dry, dead, do-nothing religion in need of new blood."[3]

This is part of the attitude that James is reprimanding. **If we limit our sense of philanthropy, we have limited our prayer as Spirit in action. And if we have limited Spirit in action, we have mocked the grace of God.** Grace is so generously given to each of us that it cannot possibly be held onto and not be shared with others.

> *If we turn away from the poor, we are not ready to receive the blessing of Him who blesses the poor.*
> Science and Health 8:22

An ancient model of Christian evangelism

Thomas Cahill, in his tribute to sixth century Irish Christian courage, describes the contrast between what Columbanus and other early Irish spiritual "explorers" did for Christianity and what they encountered in the cooling ashes of continental European hierarchical religion.

> Still employing the old Roman episcopal pattern of living urbanely in capital cities and keeping close ties with those who wear crowns, the bishops tend their local flocks of literate and semiliterate officials, the ghostly remnants of the lost society. It has never occurred to these churchmen to venture beyond a few well-tended streets into the rough-hewn mountain settlements of the simpler Sueves. To Columbanus, however, a man **who will take no step to proclaim the Good News beyond the safety and comfort of his elite circle** is a poor excuse for a bishop.[4]

Christian Scientists who wish for their faith to maintain relevance in the twenty-first century should consider the example of Columbanus and be warned away from the fading forms of timid church life that he encountered.

---

3. King, "Why Jesus Called a Man a Fool."
4. Cahill, 188.

Unwanted visitors *from* the Kingdom

"A young man who came to a branch church to attend a lecture, approached the glass front doors to enter. The usher on duty barred the door. Another usher inside the auditorium watched in horror as a tug of war ensued, the visitor trying to get in, and the usher keeping him out. Finally, the head usher intervened and let the young man in. No doubt the front door usher considered the unkempt appearance and rumpled clothes unsuitable for their lovely church that was filling up with affluent members and those from other branch churches. Once again, the front door usher stepped in front of the unwanted visitor, insisting that he go to the men's room and 'wash up.' Exasperated, the young man refused and took a seat in the third row. After the talk, the lecturer put his arms around the young man."[5]

The author has witnessed in person a similar incident happening in an urban reading room with an attendant determined to exclude a shabbily dressed but unoffending street person. Where does the disdain for the poor come from among professedly Christian people?

Justification for mistreatment of the poor

After reading the Bible, it is practically impossible to justify treating poor people with open disdain (e.g. the poor widow's donation, Mark 12:41-44; "the poor of this world rich in faith," James 2:5; the calling of the poor to the "great supper," Luke 14: 12,13; and the reward of the beggar Lazarus, Luke 16:20-31). Christian Scientists have not tended to openly and explicitly scorn the poor as in the incident above. What has happened all too often has been **a subtle, though sometimes overt, honoring of human wealth** as a sign that a Christian Scientist has "demonstrated" or mastered spiritual truth—a kind of **presumed spiritual self-sufficiency or "dominion."**

Since **when does a very material bank account reveal a person's grasp of spiritual truth?** In the light of all that Jesus says about riches, and the spiritual difficulties that accompany riches (e.g. Matthew

---
5. *The Banner,* Spring 1988, a quarterly newsletter self-published by a Christian Scientist.

19:23), it is very problematic to equate our financial status with our spiritual well-being, but have Christian Scientists tried to make that equivalency? Have we too often been **indifferent towards those in poverty**, based on an unspoken assumption that the poor are somewhat to blame for their condition because they have not "claimed" their spiritual heritage and thus have lost out on the material wealth "proven" by their richer brethren?

An article entitled "A Recompense of Profit"[6] illustrates how Christian Scientists have found themselves justifying indifference to the human needs of their brethren. At face value this article merely builds a case for the admiration of profit.[7] The article's author does not blatantly say, "Profit constitutes socking away all we can of this world's goods." But the article gives readers the impression **that spiritual and human profit are virtually identical or synonymous**. And if not synonymous, then one, the spiritual, leads invariably to the other, the material. Does spiritual progress act as a law, producing material wealth?

> If material riches can be piled up successfully, how much more can a recompense of ideas be acquired by a truly studious man who seeks always to be taught of God, Mind, to profit. It is so right to profit![8]

Jesus explicitly points out in his parable of the "rich fool" (Luke 12:15-21) **that the piling up of riches is a futile, truly impossible task**, rather than an appropriate human model for spiritual work.

> We heap up wealth, not knowing who will spend it.
> Psalms 39:6, NLT

The incident of the gathering of manna by the Hebrews in the exodus wilderness stands as a warning against "piling up" material goods out of human distrust of future divine care, while Jesus' parable of the talents is a warning to anyone who would attempt to "pile up" their spiritual resources for some future time and not share what they have in the present, no matter how much or how little their "talents" may be (Matthew 25:14-29).

Again, looking at the "profit" motive in the above-cited article, the

---

6. *C.S. Journal*, December 1960.
7. "Profit" in the KJV means literally "to ascend" in Hebrew, or figuratively "to be valuable or useful" (*Strong's Exhaustive Concordance*) — not exactly the sense of financial advantage which that word has come to mean today.
8. Ibid.

article's author writes, **"Although Jesus asserted that the poor are always with us, he in no way endorsed poverty or set his approval on it…his whole life was affluent."** Jesus never "endorsed" any miserable human condition. Who would? But he said that the foxes had a resting place that he did not have. His challenge to Christians in all ages to take up the cross is hardly a promise of affluence.

Yes, to Jesus, spiritual living was a pearl of great price. But no, Christ experienced no easy life, and he warned his followers that they would have "many trials and sorrows" (John 16:33 TLB) in this world that we call human life. To say that Jesus' "whole life was affluent" is to deny the simplicity of his human lifestyle, his crucifixion, and to impossibly depict the Master's pathway as devoid of pain, scorn, suffering, and rejection. If the cross is the "central emblem [symbol] of history" (*S&H* 238:31) for the Christian Scientist, and the cross is larger than the crown on the very cover of *Science and Health*, we can hardly say to Jesus as Peter did, "God forbid it, Lord! This [miserable death] must never happen to you" (Matt. 16:22 NRSV).[9]

Most of the world's inscribed spiritual riches, including the written wisdom we find in the Bible, have been chiseled by "strangers in a strange land" and by people who would be classified as poor, or at best very low-income, by today's Western standards. The founder of the Christian Science Church lived as a widow in a semi-impoverished state for years, and while writing *Science and Health* was virtually homeless, having to move frequently from house to house, in large part because of her fragile financial condition.

One article in a church magazine does not a complete theology make. However, the thinking in the above-cited article has had a significant influence on Christian Scientists over the decades. The article's author taught dozens of classes including future teachers, and "A Recompense of Profit" itself has recently been recirculated by the Mother Church in an anthology of older articles. So, at the least, our church should feel obliged to make perfectly clear over time in its publications

---

9. Barclay. *Daily Study Bible*: Matthew 6, Vol. 1, 209: "It was certainly not material prosperity which Jesus promised his disciples. He in fact promised them trial and tribulation, suffering, persecution and death."

that any dogma portraying material profit or material wealth as an indicator of spiritual abundance is both untrue, spiritually misleading, and materialistic.

Not putting down the well-to-do or praising the poor

Our writing here **in no way disparages the wealthy, generous individual or church member.** Jesus befriended the wealthy Joseph of Arimathea as well as Zacchaeus, the tax collector. But there are plenty of Christians pushing the illusive ideal of "health-wealth" religion, and Christian Scientists have little business in that company.

> It is a serious mistake to suppose that the belief of poverty needs to be overcome, but that the belief of riches does not.[10]

Shouldn't our church's published words distance our denomination from that niche-stereotype of Christianity which is tantamount to materialism and essentially advocates worshipping *mammon*, the god of riches?

> **The love of money is the root of all evil.**   I Timothy 6:10

> **...level wealth with honesty, and let worth be judged according to wisdom...**   S&H 239:8

Opulence in the air

In 1899, a public official depicted the attendees at a large Christian Science Church in Chicago as "splendid representatives of the great and powerful class of successful business men."[11] Rolf Swensen notes that a similar predominance of the well-to-do among Christian Scientists also prevailed on the West Coast in the early 1900s.[12]

On the other hand, Ezra Buswell, a church teacher and student of

---

10. Buskirk, *C.S. Sentinel*, April 2, 1910, 599.
11. Mitchell, *C.S. Sentinel*, March 2, 1899.
12. Swensen, *Pilgrims*, 229-263.

Mrs. Eddy, observed that those of Buswell's Christian Science students who were not educated were "among my very best workers."[13]

St. Thomas Aquinas's comment on church wealth and spirituality

An incident attributed to the life of St. Thomas Aquinas (1225–1274 CE): Entering the presence of Pope Innocent IV… before whom a large sum of money was spread out, His Holiness observed, "You see, the Church is no longer in that age in which she said, 'Silver and gold have I none.'"—"True, holy father," replied Aquinas; "neither can she any longer say to the lame, 'Rise up and walk.'"[14]

What are the richest investments that Jesus recommends?

There is a striking theme in Chapter 16 of Luke's Gospel that rarely has been touched upon in our denominational magazines or our lesson-sermons. It is that the riches of this world are not only very temporal but that they should be shared by Christians with the understanding that **in the next experience or in life to come after death, the Christian may discover a very discomforting social role-reversal where the "first** [on earth] **will** [indeed] **be last, and the last first."** Jesus' parable of the selfish rich man and the beggar Lazarus illustrates this theme. Before Jesus tells that parable, he relates the story of the unjust steward (Luke 16:1–12) who hurriedly settles his master's debts in a way that would curry favor with people who could help that steward if he ever lost his job. The *Interpreter's Bible* comments on this section: **"The rich can help the poor in this age, and the poor man can help the rich in the age to come."**[15]

---

13. Buswell in a letter to Mrs. Eddy on June 18, 1898. Reprinted in "Journal of Religion and Spirituality" Vol. 1, No. 3.
14. Bent, S.A. (ed.), *Familiar Short Sayings from the Lives of Great Men.*
15. Laymon, *Interpreter's Bible*, Vol. 8, 284. The *Interpreter's Bible* specifically bases this commentary on a rather arcane verse: "Make to yourselves friends of the mammon of unrighteousness; that, when ye fail [die?], they may receive you into everlasting habitations" (Luke 16:9).

Have you ever felt the suspicion that those who seem especially deprived of material goods in this world and yet have a noble, warm nature, are really just preparing for a far more just and merciful future experience than the existence they have had here on earth? Christians who build their missions with and for these "future pillars" of Christ may possess the sharpest "investment" foresight of anyone.

> *Has not God chosen those who are poor in the eyes of the world to be rich in faith and to inherit the kingdom he has promised to those who love him?*
>
> James 2:5 NEB

> *Israel soon became fat and unruly;*
> *the people grew heavy, plump, and stuffed!*
> *Then they abandoned the God who had made them;*
> *they made light of the Rock of their salvation.*
>
> Deut. 32:15, New Living Translation

An inspiring living example from the Congo

From the February, 2011 *Christian Science Journal*:
> [One] aspect of Mrs. Eddy's life that has shaped my life-experience is her unselfish giving. I once read she donated shoes to children. That example helped me when my country, the Democratic Republic of Congo, came out of a war in 1994. My family and I lost everything except a Bible and a copy of *Science and Health*. Many women had lost their husbands during the war—either they died or disappeared —so, they struggled alone with their children. While I prayed and helped them find healing, I thought I could do something more. I was led to start a micro-credit project for women (with the little funding that I raised through my healing work) to help them.
>
> Later on, I felt that the children of these women needed to attend school. My wife helped start a school while I continued my work as a practitioner. The project culminated in the founding of a nursery school, primary school, middle school, and a vocational training school. Children are given uniforms free of charge and they are given food—at least a meal a day—something that is not

common in other schools in my country.

Following Mrs. Eddy's example, I saw that I could easily share with others whatever little I had. For instance, I was able to donate a substantial amount yearly to the school over the past five years. [Author's Note: The preceding testimony gives a slight taste of a major omission in this book—coverage of the promising frontiers of spiritual exploration being expanded by Christian Scientists in the Democratic Republic of Congo and the Philippines. It is the author's hope that others can fill that serious gap in our larger awareness of this pioneering work and all that it can teach our spiritual brothers and sisters in other countries.]

The problem of indifference

A wistful article in *Miscellaneous Writings* (*Mis.* 230-2) laments the sadness with which human happiness looks on its own contented holiday scene in contrast with the heaviness of others' life-circumstances. Christian Science has much to bring to the table of thought about society, but have Christian Scientists too often turned down or deferred the invitation both to think and, more importantly, to follow up their bold words with deeds that provide evidence of all they say they believe about God and creation? This Grand Canyon between aspiration and performance is especially obvious when we look at the issues of class, race, and gender.

A breadth of charity

"Our cause demands a wider circle of means for the ends of philanthropy and charity, and better qualifications for practical purposes. The latter lack in students of Christian Science is a great hindrance to our cause and it must be met and mastered."[16]

Included in the above letter was a suggestion from Mrs. Eddy to her church's board that they open a facility for Christian Scientists who

---

16. L05380 courtesy Mary Baker Eddy Library, 1-15-1906 Mrs. Eddy to Mary Longyear. This appeared in part in the *C. S. Sentinel* Oct. 7, 1916.

needed affordable nursing care. The church of her time put off this idea, but ten years later they saw fit to open the first "benevolent" facility. Care for those who are ill or poor is not just about being nice to those people. It's a crucial investment in the Christians' spiritual future (see Luke 16-17). It's directly connected to the progress of the cause of healing. Again, as Christ's parable of the talents points out—**the human problem is far less what can be called "supply" and much more a problem of withheld distribution.** So how do we best "freely give," having freely received? (Matthew 10:8)

> **"Christianity has withstood less the temptation of popularity than of persecution."**
> Retrospection and Introspection 45:24

Lingering quandaries and questions

Do cultural and social influences outweigh our religious and spiritual teachings? That question pertains both to the class views of Christian Scientists as well as to their views about race and gender.

Isaiah 58 points out that truly religious acts of self-denial are not physical fasting but actions that *"loosen all that fetters men unfairly."*
Isaiah 58:4 Moffatt

How much is too much? How little is too poor? These questions are encompassed in the following proverb: *"If I have too much, I might deny that I need you, Lord. But if I am too poor, I might steal and bring shame to the name of my God."*
Proverbs 30:9 English Revised Edition

When or how should Christians or Christian Scientists think about saving for the future, for their families, or for some emergency needs? If the piling up of wealth is not a Christian concept, how do we think about material savings or investment? After all, Jesus on the cross was concerned about the future welfare of his mother.

RACE

Influences on ethnic and racial prejudice among Christian Scientists

Christian Science does not subscribe to the teaching that Adam's son Cain or Noah's son Ham were "cursed" and in some way connected to the African race. Some Christians have justified their centuries-old racial bias as based on the biblical cursing of Cain and Ham. Christian Scientists teach and believe in the oneness of God, one Mind, and creation made in the image of that one Mind, without distinction of race or ethnicity. But ethnic and racial prejudice wormed its way into the history of the Christian Science Church incidentally, more than by explicit teaching.

Mrs. Eddy might well have been influenced by anti-Irish prejudice that was prevalent in eastern American cities of her era. An early edition of *Science and Health* (1887) made reference to the "filthy Irish emigrant" (p. 354). Its index was even more insulting. Under "Irish" in reference to this page is the elaborative wording "happy in dirt." Christian Scientists of today are happier for the succeeding editions of their church text that washed away both references in favor of the generic word "emigrant."

As to the matter of race, a highly influential church teacher Bicknell Young taught that African Americans were too emotional to be stable prospects as students of Christian Science.[17] Perhaps Young was influenced by his Mormon uncle Brigham Young who authored some of that church's early (and now renounced) anti-black teachings.[18]

Racial segregation of the Christian Science churches

From 1926 through 1955 the Christian Science Church quietly segregated its American churches and required African-American practitioners to be listed in the *Journal* as "colored."[19] There were two social factors that may

---

17. Young, Bicknell, 1936 Primary class personal notes, 132–3.
18. Turner, "'Any man having one drop of the seed of Cane [sic] in him cannot hold the priesthood,' Young declared in 1852." "Why Race Is Still a Problem for Mormons."
19. There was no official announcement of this policy, but the word "colored" appeared first in 1926 next to African-American practitioners, and in the following year next to predominantly African-American churches in the U.S. Race-labeling in the *Journal* continued until 1956.

have formed an underpinning for this move towards segregating the races in our church. The first was the great migration of African Americans from the South into cities of the North, Midwest, and West starting in the early 1900s. Prior to this era, southern American churches segregated their black worshippers, but white Christian Scientists in northern states were rarely exposed to other races attending their services.

The rise of the Ku Klux Klan in the 1920s and widespread discriminatory practices ("Jim Crow" laws) against African Americans in the United States helped establish a culture that was unsympathetic to black church members entering predominantly white churches.

Explaining segregation

Some of the reasoning or justification behind the segregation of Christian Science churches is contained in two letters (see below) sent in 1938 from the Mother Church in response to a "colored" branch church (Twelfth Church of Christ, Scientist, New York City) which had evidently questioned the segregation policy.[20] Reading the following paragraphs is difficult. It brings back some of the many tragic memories of our nation's history, but, more so, reading the following makes us shake our heads in disbelief at how Christian Scientists could have been so heedless of the mass prejudice they had swallowed about their spiritual brothers and sisters of another race. While the prejudice visible in the church letters is muted by euphemism and careful language, its clear disdain stands in stark contrast with what Christianity and Christian Science are founded upon.

> June 21, 1938
>
> Your letter of May 21 and its enclosure have had our earnest consideration.
>
> It seems necessary first for us to correct the impression you apparently have that this Board [the Christian Science Board of Directors] establishes branch churches. This Board recognizes

---

20. "Christian Science Church Adopts Jim Crow," *The Crisis Magazine*, December 1938, 386.

as branches of The Mother Church organizations which are formed by Christian Scientists which are formed in accordance with rules laid down in the Manual of The Mother Church and which can comply with the usual requirements for recognition. Twelfth Church of Christ, Scientist, New York City, to which you specifically refer, was formed by Christian Scientists in that city who are of the negro race. To have such a group designated "colored" when they are gathered together in a church organization and holding services is a means of informing those of their own race where to find them. It is simply a statement of information which is helpful, not only to the colored people but to those who are of the white race.

It has not been our purpose to segregate Christian Scientists who are colored from those of the white race. Experience has shown, however, that in sections of this country where the majority of the residents are white some designation is needed to indicate which churches have been formed and are maintained by Christian Scientists who are of the negro race. In a number of cities where the number of Christian Scientists of this race is insufficient to warrant the forming of a separate church, we believe these individuals are admitted into membership in the already established churches. Were the situation reversed, and churches composed of people of the white race the exception, it would doubtless be necessary to designate in some manner the churches composed of white people.

We feel that instead of looking upon the designation "colored" as a stigma or as prejudicial, the members of churches so noted should rejoice in the privilege extended to them to have a church of their own where they may perform all the functions of a branch of The Mother Church. Then they would realize the opportunity given for all those of their race in the city interested in Christian Science to know of their existence and to be able to seek association with them.

Experience has shown us that the ultimate ideal relationship between the white and colored people, even though they may be Christian Scientists, has not yet been demonstrated. It is a protection to Christian Scientists of the negro race for them to be associated in a branch church properly designated to which others of their race will be drawn. Our action is not a discrimination or reflection [meaning unclear]; it is more in the nature of a distinction which the public, whether white or colored people, is entitled to know. This distinction should not be interpreted or regarded as based on discrimination because of racial identity; for in relation to this Board, members of The Mother Church who are colored and members of The Mother Church who are white have equal standing and recognition.

In case the lightly suppressed racism contained in this letter does not make us feel uncomfortable today, there's another letter. It appears that the original letter writers from the "colored" church were not satisfied at all with the response from the church headquarters in Boston, so they wrote further, asking that, given what they had been told in the first letter, why was there segregation in the Mother Church Sunday school which was in Boston?

October 18, 1938

Your letter of October 10 has been received. In answer to your specific question we are glad to give you the following information.

    A few years ago, it seemed well to place nearly all the colored pupils in the Mother Church Sunday School in classes by themselves. The arrangement appeared to be a necessary expedient. It had a tendency to relieve the Sunday School of the attendance of some pupils who had not come really to get Christian Science instruction. It did not deprive the colored pupils who were in earnest of any of the privileges or blessings of the Sunday School, and it was satisfactory to the parents of some of the white pupils in certain cases where the parents did not wish their children in classes where there were colored children. The rule has never been enforced strictly and there have always been a few earnest pupils who were colored and who remained in classes made up of white children with the single exception of themselves.

As you perhaps know, in Christian Science each church is democratic in its government. Some Christian Science churches have found it advisable to place children of the colored race in classes by themselves, and children of the white race in classes by themselves. This is no reflection on either. And if the child and its parents are truly interested to learn something of Christian Science, the fact that the colored child is in a class with other children of its own race need not hamper its progress. Parents of the white children must be considered, as well as the parents of the colored children. Neither should feel that there has been discrimination because of some local arrangement in the Sunday School.

The Christian Science Board of Directors

These letters insinuate that segregation can be a local decision, but why then did the national church, the Mother Church, sanction something that was offensive to the teachings of Christian Science as well as to many other Christian Scientists of different races? The church writers used words such as "designation," "distinction," "protection," "consideration," "arrangement," and the unsupported statement "experience has shown," but resisted admitting that they were systematically segregating or discriminating against their own people, although that was exactly what they were doing. Finally, referring to the African-American child as "it" rends the veil from the race prejudice which our forefathers succumbed to.

The second letter above, if taken to its logical extension, would imply that some "colored" practitioners, like their "colored" school-age counterparts, therefore might not be sufficiently "earnest" and should be given separate designations in the *Journal*. However, if individual practitioners who were African-American were really and truly "earnest," they might be able to be listed as not "colored," but instead allowed to pass as white practitioners because they had become sufficiently "earnest" or spiritual enough to be washed of their racial disadvantage. This was an absurd possibility and naturally did not occur.

A friend of the author questioned the segregation policy while it was ongoing. A church official's response to that question was, "Well, you wouldn't want them [African Americans] using your rest rooms, would you?" For all the careful language that tried to explain away segregation, this kind of blatant distaste for black Americans may have been at the heart of the church policy.

The Mother Church made a conscious three-decades-long commitment to violate its spiritual ideals and grossly offend people of color rather than ruffle the cultural sensibilities of its prejudiced members and white society in general. This was not a problem confined to the southern United States. New York City, Chicago, Los Angeles, and Boston churches were all affected by the policy. So it hurts today to look back at articles in the church magazines of that era and read, "There are no barriers of race or creed to the activity of the Mind 'which was also in Christ Jesus'..."[21] And a decade later: "The separation of the ideal and the practical finds no endorsement in the teachings of Christ Jesus."[22]

"Following a multitude to do evil"

The Bible reads: **"Thou shalt not follow a multitude to do evil"** (Ex. 23:2). *The New English Bible* translates this: "You shall not be led into wrongdoing by the majority." But that is what happened. A former Mother Church official told the author, **"This [segregation policy] was a major sin and a gross violation of a holy trust. The church reflected its surrounding culture more than its own ideals."**

The following observation came from another church member:
> We lived in [a southern U.S. city] from 1979 to 1987 and were active in the Christian Science church there. There was a lovely black woman who couldn't be elected reader because the community 'wasn't ready for it.' I then realized that the local southern culture went deeper into the soul of most church members than did their understanding of Christian Science.

---

21. "Fellowship," *C.S. Sentinel*, 9-16-1933, 47.
22. "Universal Fellowship," *C.S. Journal*, May 1943, 291.

Learning from the courage of other churches

At the same time when the Christian Scientists were making life hard for their African-American brethren, the Jehovah's Witnesses in Germany were committing themselves to defend the Jews whom Hitler was busy attacking and planning to destroy. The Witnesses by and large shared no Jewish heritage, but thousands of Witnesses went to concentration camps and over two thousand Witnesses died there for their solidarity with their Jewish brethren.[23] In 1934, there were 20,000 German Jehovah's Witnesses and fewer than 100,000 worldwide, whereas today there are over 5.5 million in the world. Could Christian Scientists in the 1930s have benefited from the example of other churches' stand on behalf of justice for other peoples and faiths?

More collateral damage from segregation

From a practitioner:
> *Overcoming discrimination was a long, hard struggle for me. One little word 'colored,' beside my name in the* Journal *tried to tell others that my race was inferior—that members of my race couldn't practice Christian Science healing with the same degree of success as others whose mortal bodies were another color.*

From an African-American woman who attended church in East St. Louis, Illinois, when it was a mostly white community:
> "How could I continue as a Christian Scientist? I knew they [those segregating the church] weren't practicing. **I looked past those people to the soul of the religion.**"

Another "colored" practitioner:
> "**As I became clear who I was, regardless of the 'colored' listing, the resentment faded.** It's not what others think about ourselves, but it's what we think about ourselves that matters."

---

23. Engardio. "Jehovah's Witnesses' Untold Story of Resistance to Nazis." *Monitor*, 11-6-1996.

An odd offshoot of traditional prejudice

During the 1950s a Christian Science teacher in the southern United States taught his classes that if black Christian Scientists became spiritual enough, their skin color would lighten. In other words, this theory embodied the concept not just of Caucasian racial superiority, but that non-Caucasian skin color was tantamount to a sin or disease. A woman in that decade gave a testimony in a Texas branch church of her skin turning lighter as she progressed spiritually.[24]

The demand for full-scale apology and atonement

Were there white Christian Scientists who opposed the segregation policy? The author has no doubt that there were. One board member William McKenzie is rumored to have worked to reverse the policy, but church records are unavailable to confirm his stand. A *Sentinel* article, published in 1943 entitled "Love hath one race," says clearly that racial distinctions are inappropriate for any mortals since those mortal distinctions are unknown to the Almighty. However, the article in no way pushes for the quick removal of racial barriers in society but states, "What the human steps may be in the appearing of equity and justice for all races only the all-loving Mind can determine."

Many American churches of other denominations openly discriminated against African Americans during the Jim Crow era, but is that an excuse for the bad behavior of Christian Scientists? The Catholic Church has apologized and asked publicly for forgiveness for the Crusades and Lutheran churches have issued public apologies for the damage that Martin Luther's anti-Semitic writings caused and the influence of those writings on the Holocaust. It is highly appropriate and requisite for a church that recognizes the importance of "practical repentance" (*S&H* 19:23) over one's sins and straightening out one's "snarls" (*S&H* 240:30) before progress can happen, to **fully and in a heartfelt manner**

---

24. The Mormons' original teachings included the concept that skin pigment would lighten as a person repented of their sins (3 Nephi 2:15 *The Book of Mormon*). So this bizarre view of "racial progression" was not unique to our church.

apologize for our institutional treatment of African Americans. It is remarkable and without excuse that this apology has not already been given. Atoning for collective or individual sins helps establish the heart's foundation for new life in Christ. So the possibility of our church's atonement over this collective sin could be a potentially reviving blessing for individual Christian Scientists and our entire church.

We will see similar problems and personal convictions in the following discussion about church views regarding homosexuality.

GENDER AND IDENTITY

Several articles and editorials have been written explaining why homosexuals cannot be admitted to membership. One of these I wrote myself, the title: 'Homosexuality Can Be Healed.' All I can say in defense of myself for writing it is that it was based on information I thought was authentic, but which later was disproved by further studies. If I were to write another article on the subject now, I would probably entitle it, 'We're ALL God's Children.'

by Carl J. Welz, C.S.B.

What Jesus has to say…

…there are eunuchs who were born that way, and there are eunuchs who have been made eunuchs by others—and there are those who choose to live like eunuchs for the sake of the kingdom of heaven. The one who can accept this should accept it.

Matthew 19:12 New International Version

Opponents of homosexuality often cite the Bible's opposition to it. That is comparable to saying that the United States Constitution is against black people. Yes, in Article 1, Section 2, of the original Constitution, black people ("other persons" not free) were given the political worth of 3/5ths of a free person. However, later amendments to the Constitution (amendments 13, 14, and 15) made clear that former slaves were then given the rights that their white counterparts had enjoyed under the original law.

So while churchgoers have been told by their clergy that "the Bible condemns homosexuality," (and that there are eight passages in the Torah and Paul's letters that address this subject), **no words of Jesus condemn homosexuals**. Possibly as close to the theme of gender in any of Jesus' recorded sayings is found in remarks he makes regarding marriage and divorce. Branching off from the subject of marriage, Jesus addresses the nature of eunuchs (see above Matthew 19:12). Clearly, being a eunuch and being gay are not the same experience. **The Mosaic Law discriminated against eunuchs and excluded them from congregational fellowship** (Deut. 23:1), and no eunuch would have desired to be classed in that disdained social category. The reader should decide whether Jesus' observations about eunuchs relate to the social acceptance or rejection of homosexuality. Jesus notes **three kinds of eunuchs: some born that way, some made that way by others, and some who made themselves so "for the kingdom of heaven's sake."**

Did he then say that one class of eunuchs was favored by God over others, or that one kind of eunuch was more spiritual than another? No. **He simply stated what was the observable social fact of his time.**[25] Jesus concluded this discussion about controversial, hard-to-define social do's and don'ts with this interesting comment: **"He that is able to receive it, let him receive it."** Moffatt renders this: **"Let anyone practice it for whom it is practicable."** The *Interpreter's Bible* describes Jesus' comment as **"a warning against forced interpretations of the teaching. It is an appeal to spiritual intelligence."**[26]

Notice here that Jesus does not say, "You all must treat eunuchs in this specific fashion." Rather than dictate a social or religious preference or create a new commandment regarding this question about sexual formation and practice, he refuses to either commend or chastise, but merely states what he observes.

---

25. Minor, "Who Are Those Eunuchs…" *Whosoever* Magazine, 5-16-2020. Dr. Robert Minor points out that Matthew 19:12 depicts "…a Jesus who just didn't judge these people no matter where else in Biblical literature or in the history of the Christian Church someone else did." Minor adds the observation that in Acts 8:27, we see that the first gentile convert to Christianity was a eunuch from another nation and ethnicity. (*Whosoever* is an online magazine dedicated to the spiritual growth of LGBT Christians.)
26. Laymon, *Interpreter's Bible,* Vol. 7, p. 482.

It is a discredit to Christians when they have forced interpretations on issues such as gender and homosexuality in a manner most unlike the first Christian. **Jesus was continually tempted by his opponents to micro-define and explain his interpretations of the law and rules of human conduct** (Matthew 22:15-46). Jesus' enemies were eager to catch him in a gross divergence from either the Torah or the common Pharisaical interpretation of the Jewish law. His answer to the question regarding marriage and the topic of eunuchs is typical of his manner of eluding these verbal traps: **"Not all men can accept this statement, but only those to whom it has been given"** (Matthew 19:12 New American Standard).

Before Jesus' comment about eunuchs, he put forward his thought about the way in which divorce had been corrupted during his age, and how that standard or practice could be elevated. He then used the varieties of experience and human history of eunuchs as a parallel to the subject of marriage, *possibly* to point out that different mortals approach these sensitive social questions from very different standpoints, and that **everyone would not necessarily arrive at the same social or even religious conclusions.**

Jesus' observations do not establish any artificial, man-made classifications. When his disciples sought preferred status for themselves in the life to come, Jesus rebuked them (Mark 10:40). But aspiring followers of Christ have both attempted to set up theological rankings that Jesus declined to do, and they have ranked Christians by benchmarks that Jesus did not employ.

Not damaging wheat while uprooting tares

Too much Christian energy is spent on endless controversies that have damaged wheat and overlooked weeds. The Gospel parable of the wheat and tares is a beautiful admonition to **trust the "harvest" and to exercise patience in order to properly distinguish between right and wrong in Christian practice.** "Give a thing time; if it can succeed, it is a right thing," wrote the Scottish philosopher Thomas Carlyle.[27] The

---

27. Carlyle, *Works*, Vol. 5, 143.

author interviewed a veteran practitioner who had healed a man with an advanced case of AIDS. As we were sitting by her computer which that healed man had given her fourteen years after his healing, we talked about gender and sexual orientation.[28] She was very emphatic: **"The problem is not heterosexuality or homosexuality. The problem is sensuality!"** For emphasis, she pounded her fist on the desk.

Christian Scientists habitually depersonalize moral and physical problems and break down issues into their mental components for the purpose of healing, so it is ironic that they have tended to categorize, personalize, and generalize about homosexuality in a way that they do not tend to do in relation to other issues.

Too often Christian Scientists have done two things which Mrs. Eddy did not do: (1) citing certain portions of the Bible as spiritual authority that we generally do not consider to be "inspired" but reflecting dogmas of the times in which they were written, and (2) lumping the spiritual identity of individuals in with an assumed "lifestyle"—whatever the word "lifestyle" suggests. Let's examine these two problem areas.

What is the "inspired Word of the Bible"?

This question opens up a huge discussion, but we will try to summarize a few ideas here. The "inspired" Word may be what inspires me, but maybe not you. Christian Scientists see the Ten Commandments as inspired teachings. However, we question different aspects of the six hundred plus commandments included in the Torah, or Law of Moses—for example, the prohibitions from eating shellfish, wearing mixed fabrics, or trimming one's beard.[29] We would also question both the applicability of all the provisions of the Torah to modern life and the severity of punishment involved in many of the six hundred commandments. That doesn't mean that Christian Scientists would disagree with all of the Torah's ethical prohibitions, but when critics of homosexuality, especially Christians, rest their case on passages from the Torah and not on the preaching of

---

28. The healing was witnessed by four physicians.
29. Leviticus 11:9-12; 19:19; 19:27.

Jesus, shouldn't Christian Scientists at least question that basis for reasoning?

Do gays or lesbians "find their sense of identity in their sexual practice"?[30]

The author doesn't know any Christian Scientist who wakes up in the morning and says to himself, **"Boy, do I feel like God's perfect heterosexual idea today!"** It should come as no surprise that gay Christian Scientists don't glory in a mythical "gay identity" either. What has happened to gay people is similar to what happened to people of color in the past centuries. When African Americans were typecast by predominantly white American society as "colored," "darkies," and worse, those people of color felt it to be only right to define and defend themselves and their race, using terms of their own choosing. Out of that feeling arose social movements such as "black power" and "black pride." But people of color likely would not have felt a need for their own **racial self-identification** if they had not needed to defend themselves against a hostile society that looked down on them as inferior.

Have homosexuals and lesbians used terms such as "gay" and "queer" in order to defend themselves from hostile criticism and prejudice? Doesn't sexual or racial self-identification spring from a **conscious intent to counter negative images with positive ones, even humorous terms?** The current African-American usage of the "N-word," and the gay community's use of "queer," may be forms of taking word-weapons used against one's race or personal identification and turning them into weapons of sometimes **jesting self-defense.** Jesus possibly used a similar form of sardonic self-deprecation or self-defense when he compared himself to the brazen serpent that Moses lifted up as a healing talisman in the wilderness (John 3:14).

There would likely be little need for a Christian or Christian Scientist to prominently self-identify as a racial, ethnic, or gender type, unless that individual was feeling attacked by reason of their race,

---

30. Spirituality.com, Live Chat, May 9, 2006.

ethnicity, or sexual identity. Jesus stressed the far-reaching spirituality of his followers in saying they were "the light of the world." No doubt he saw great possibilities for these children of light and did not limit his followers to one social class. We don't hear Jesus say, "Go forth and be outstanding Jews!"

A Christian Scientist once asked the author if he "endorsed" homosexuality.[31] My response to that question was that I did not see it as my business to endorse either homosexuality or heterosexuality, but that I did endorse God's ideas wherever or whoever they may be.

Do heterosexuals have one lifestyle?

Just as Jesus recognizes in Matthew 19 that there were different kinds of eunuchs, some born that way, some made that way by people, and some who made themselves celibate, so there are different lifestyles of heterosexuals and homosexuals. **There is no one homosexual or heterosexual lifestyle**. Any gay or straight person can tell you that. So on what grounds does any Christian Scientist attach to gay people the judgment that they have made a "lifestyle choice"?[32]

Is it a choice?

Abraham Lincoln once remarked after he had been attacked for being two-faced, **"If I had another face, do you think I would choose this one?"** Lincoln's self-belittling remark doesn't apply to gays and lesbians who are at peace with their "face," or how they believe God has created them. Lincoln's words might apply, however, to those who don't feel at home in their gender of birth. Many gay and lesbian people have tried very hard to conform to the straight world around them but have found nothing but frustration and heartbreak in doing so. Marrying someone to conform to society or staying "closeted" out of fear of the opinions of

> Gender is mental, not material.
> Eddy, *Science and Health*, 508:13

---

31. The author had recently addressed Emergence, an organization of gay, lesbian, and transgender Christian Scientists.
32. Ibid.

one's family, friends, or employer is fortunately becoming less frequent as American society becomes more tolerant of individual expressions of sexual orientation. Why should Christians or Christian Scientists stand against the innate emotional happiness of individuals? The arguments against gender transformation run something like this: "If God had wanted to make you a man, then why were you born in a woman's body?"

Must the Christian Science Church or any Christians have one human viewpoint on these fluctuating issues of gender and sexual identification, when Jesus did not establish any exact standard on this subject?

"In my Father's house are many rooms." John 14:2 RSV

The preceding words from Jesus may constitute one reason why Christians do not have to have fixed opinions about every controversy, especially not if having that fixed opinion causes damage to the wholeness and oneness of the Body of Christ.

Acts Chapter 5 tells us how a wise Pharisee named Gamaliel, who taught Saul before the latter's conversion to Christ, expressed a very sensible view when he urged great restraint from his fellow Jews as they threatened to punish the Christians. Gamaliel harked back to the recent fate of rebellious factions in Israel and concluded from this history that truth would prevail. Gamaliel trusted in God's power to exalt truth, demote false teaching, and resolve controversies and heresies. Here are his words.

> *Keep away from these men* [the Christians] *and let them alone; because if this plan or this undertaking is of human origin, it will fail; but if it is of God, you will not be able to overthrow them—in that case you may even be found fighting against God!*
> Acts 5:38, 39 NRSV

What we can unabashedly preach

"Look long enough, and you see male and female one—sex or gender eliminated; you see the designation *man* meaning woman as well, you see the whole universe included in one infinite Mind...."

(*My.* 268:29) These words of Mrs. Eddy are promising and visionary. Could Christian Scientists take them to heart when considering the subject of gender and gender classification?

Why do mortals attempt to super-define both the genders and the mortal sense of marriage? Don't these limited, distorted definitions spring from the same ground of thought that in our era conflates the sensual with the romantic and the romantic with what constitutes enduring love? No wonder that people today are confused about sexual identity and are afraid of the marriage vow.

Teaching about the "healing" of homosexuality

Hardly any topic brings up more emotion in the discussion of gender than the prospect that homosexuality is a disease or sin which should be healed. An explicit editorial in the *Christian Science Sentinel* entitled "Homosexuality can be healed" (April 22, 1967), was hailed at the time of its publication as a bold approach to the subject, though the title and conclusion of the article were later renounced by its author Carl Welz, as cited at the start of this chapter.

The concept of healing homosexuality has an interesting cousin in the history of the Christian Science Church. Bizarre as this concept may seem to us today, it might not have been considered outlandish to some Christian Scientists during the era of racial segregation when a black complexion was a problem and an obstacle to social progress.

Does *Science and Health* condemn homosexuality?

Some Christian Scientists have claimed that Mrs. Eddy condemns homosexuality in a phrase from the church textbook: "Man in Science is neither inverted nor subverted, but upright and Godlike" (*S&H* 200:19).[33] The reasoning here is that "inverted" can mean "homosexual." But there is a problem with this argument. In the dictionary that

---

33. The author has heard this argument put forward in formal and informal branch church discussions. Those doing so have attributed the claim to their Christian Science teaching.

Mrs. Eddy turned to, *inverted* is not equated with *homosexual*.[34] Furthermore, in the fifteen-some references to "inverted" in Mrs. Eddy's writings, the context suggests nothing related to gender or sexuality. Finally, the passage so often cited as proof-positive of Mrs. Eddy's condemnation of homosexuality is surrounded by nothing suggesting the topic of social mores.

The experience of gay and lesbian Christian Scientists

In June 2004, a Christian Science branch church set up a booth at the St. Louis Gay Pride Festival. The following are some notes from the report on their booth:

- "A man asked, 'Are Christian Science churches and reading rooms open to gays?' He told us of his early teen experience of entering a reading room and being told they would pray for him, but he couldn't join unless he was healed."
- "A young transgendered male asked if ours is a 'safe' church. This gave us [those staffing the booth] a chance to think about what a 'safe' Christian Science church is!"
- "A man, an ex-First Reader, had left Christian Science because his teacher told him it was not okay to be gay. He said, 'That was the end for me.' We had a nice, long chat. He and his partner attend a Methodist church now. His daughter studies Christian Science. He was very surprised to see our church represented and happy to see us. He said, 'I didn't know Christian Scientists reach out.'"
- "A man stopped by to say it seemed incongruous to have our booth there. We talked about church and his experiences where he had seen Christian Scientists act in a cruel fashion to gays and lesbians. He said he was glad we were there, but he wasn't sure he trusted us."

Given what my friend found in participating at the St. Louis Gay Pride booth, it's no wonder why some Christian Scientists have formed

---

34. The term "invert" to mean a homosexual, did not come into use until the late 19th century, and lasted until roughly the middle of the 20th century. The term seems to have come into play in 1886 by a psychologist.

an informal organization called Emergence International, with satellite sub-groups meeting around the US, as a means of spiritual fellowship and protection from those of their faith who would shun or discriminate against them. One friend of the author faced a blatant form of this kind of judgment at a Wednesday night testimony meeting where the First Reader read a series of passages from the Bible about homosexuality, all the while occasionally looking right at my friend. That evening sent my friend away from that church for three years. He wasn't aware at the time of any support group for gay Christian Scientists.

A gay Christian Science nurse: "I don't want the focus to be on my sexuality. I want the discussion to be on my spirituality."

Summary

From a friend: *I was at a church committee meeting one Saturday morning several years ago. One of our members had passed by a large church with a full parking lot on her way to our meeting, and she piped up, 'What we have here is so good. I don't understand why those people go to that church and are not coming here.' I had to bite my tongue, but the answer to her question was a simple one. That other church lets those people in.*

The answer may be more than merely letting people into your church building, of course. It is **letting Christ into our hearts**, and that means letting in those whom Jesus considered friends. The cross, and all that it stands for, are a blatant contradiction of the material standards of our world, but too frequently Christian Scientists have hesitated to embrace the cross and its implicit denial of the fundamental affections of this world. The two are woven together.

"A higher and more practical Christianity, demonstrating justice and meeting the needs of mortals in sickness and in health, stands at the door of this age, knocking for admission" (S&H 224:22-25). **Will we let that Christianity in?**

Recommendation

Christian Scientists twice a year read a lesson-sermon entitled "Doctrine of Atonement." As this chapter has pointed out, there is a substantial amount of **atoning for collective discriminatory practices** that is in order for our church. This chapter in no way assumes that all Christian Scientists have been party to the negative practices outlined in these pages, but even current church members, no matter how loving or inclusive their attitudes and lives have been, are obliged to deal constructively with the issues addressed here.

Church members' attitudes are changing over the years, but unless we as a Christian body recognize the grievously damaging attitudes that we and our forebears have been party to in the past, and to some extent the present, the damage to individual lives and to the church will continue. Whatever collective acts of atonement will be seen as appropriate by our church should include open recognition of the mistakes or sins of the past and present, and a statement of our resolve to turn over a new leaf for the future.

Remaining questions and problems

Is your branch church or society welcoming to all people?

If churches in your area provide services at jails or prisons, does your church's institutional committee make efforts to connect interested inmates who are leaving incarceration and rejoining the community with a church nearby where they will be living upon their release? How is this important transitional need best met by our church members?

CHAPTER 12

Waking Eutychus
—youth leadership and mission work

Your young men shall see visions, and your old men shall dream dreams.   Acts 2:17

EUTYCHUS WAS A YOUNG MAN who, together with a large crowd of others, came to hear the Apostle Paul preach in the area of Troas that today is in northwestern Turkey. Paul was long-winded, especially when the Holy Spirit got him going. Unfortunately for Eutychus, he was sitting precariously on a window ledge listening to Paul. The young man dozed off during Paul's sermon, and fell some distance to the ground. The account in Acts 20:10 (NRSV) describes Paul "bending over him [and taking] him in his arms." No doubt he prayed for Eutychus, who eventually revived before Paul left the area.

If the church causes our young people to fall asleep, whose duty is it to wake them up, nourish their souls, or spiritually resuscitate them?

This duty can be accomplished. When I was Eutychus' age, I was very blessed to have many "Pauls" waking me up and keeping me awake.

Learning from Sara Talbert

Having left college and while living in a religious commune, I befriended a ninety-year old woman, a "shut-in," or so I was told. This woman was a member of our local church but couldn't easily attend services. She had moved from her native New York City to northern California to be near her only daughter.

Sara Talbert was a wonderful character. "Crusty New Yorker" might have described her. She had been a young woman when Mrs. Eddy was leading a vibrant religious movement, with New York City being one of its epicenters. New York was central to both the faith's prominence and controversy. Mrs. Talbert, as I called her, rarely left her two-room apartment. When she would greet me at the door, her eyes would squint into the sunlight as if she was peering out of a cave.

Actually Mrs. Talbert's cave was a sanctuary for me. Her most conspicuous furnishing items were stacks of old church magazines that lined the walls of her catacomb. She must have had these magazines, her crown jewels, shipped out from the East Coast with little regard for other belongings. There were two simple chairs and a small table, a bed and a dresser in the other room. I would bicycle to the grocery store, get a few small food items, and when I returned, Mrs. Talbert would have fixed something for both of us to share for lunch.

However, food was not the main course. Mrs. Talbert would be clutching in her hand a favored article, maybe written in the 1940s or 50s. She would have underlined many of its sentences. **"Look at this!"** she would say as she pushed it in my direction. "Now read that!" She wouldn't say this sternly. A beaming, proud, not quite toothless smile would be telling me that I must, really for my well-being, absorb the message of the crown jewel of the day. "Look where Mr. Seeley says, 'There is no hurt mortal and no mortal doing hurt in the kingdom of our Father.' What do you think of that?"

Nobody had a better Sunday school teacher than I had in Mrs. Talbert, and I have been blessed with a number of amazing mentors. **If you want to grow a good crop, make sure you have rich soil, and that soil consists of those who deeply care about the spiritual prosperity of the next generation and the future.**

Mentors before our time

Passing the torch of the Spirit from one generation to another is a holy, precious, supremely vital task. A labor of love. Most of the major achievers in the Bible had support forces who mentored their successors. Elijah mentored Elisha, but there's more to that story. Remember that, according to I Kings 19, Elijah had nearly given up on the usefulness of his life and was ready to throw in the towel. At that juncture, the Lord reminded him that he was not an island of strong belief, but that seven thousand others were open to God's message, and that Elijah had more work to do and more people to bless before his time was done. Armed with this vision, Elijah passed the torch to Elisha who was no clone of his mentor, but who shared the same Spirit.

We all have a similar duty to perform today, to be attentive to and supportive of the "Elisha-apprentices" in our path. These "apprentices" are needed to continue the race that we have run, for the benefit of generations to come.

Eli mentored the young boy Samuel, or was it the other way around? Naomi fostered Ruth's progress. Priscilla and Aquila helped Apollos achieve his potential. Of course, Jesus taught his disciples, and Jesus' spirit mentored Paul who had earlier been mentored by Gamaliel. Paul in turn nurtured any number of other budding Christians, notably Timothy.

Why are those interpersonal connections so important for the development of any cause? **Because most significant causes cannot be fully established during the span of one lifetime**. So if you want to plant an orchard that's going to grow and thrive, you had better find young friends or budding future farmers in the next generation who want to take care of your fruit trees as much as you do.

Was Harriet Tubman the lone abolitionist and slave liberator? Hardly. Was Martin Luther King the sole civil rights champion? Not at all. The nature of life requires successive generations of hard effort in order for a substantial cause to succeed. Nazism did not die in a Berlin bunker. Racism did not succumb in Montgomery, Alabama, though both those evils have been diminished over time by the committed lives and ongoing work of countless servants of the good.

A lion of divine law—Daniel Jensen and others

I had been a war protester and in trouble with the law because of it, so it was ironic that my Christian Science teacher was a former lawyer. Even more ironic was the fact that Mr. Jensen's nephew, David Harris, had inspired me in the anti-war movement of that era.

Daniel Jensen possessed both a joyful and warm character and a vehement, judicial intolerance of anything that would mock God or God's creation. He conveyed firm but happy, supralegal enthusiasm with his large association of students and with his patients. His spirit of strong God-faith and understanding empowered those who knew him. Mr. Jensen was clear about what he was here on earth to do—to heal and to teach. He had opportunities to take on other church positions, but he turned those down in order to focus on the care of his people.

In our formative years we all should spend a goodly amount of time in the presence of elders who believe in us more than we believe in ourselves.

Character as much as healing touches our hearts

It isn't necessarily spiritual healings that validate and reveal to us the authenticity of the spiritual guides in our life. For this author it has been character, honesty, sincerity, warmth of love, even insightful humor that have persuaded me of the authenticity of my mentors. Healings have been the side effects of that spiritual rainbow of mental qualities.

There have been other "Pauls" in my life: Winifred Seymour, a Sunday school teacher who impressed me very much because she told our class that she first read *Science and Health* with one hand holding a cigarette and in the other hand a glass of whiskey. I'm not sure where she put the book.

Bob Lydiard, another Sunday school teacher, made me feel pre-approved by the Lord while just sitting in his presence. Jack Hubbell and his wife Carol invited Christian Science college students from around the San Francisco Bay area to their home for a lasagna dinner with no agenda other than happy fellowship.

Byron Shideler was the first practitioner I met who was happy to work with people who were hospitalized. That fact might not seem very unusual today, but he was a pioneer in honesty and mercy, and I knew he was a busy guy because he was the only person I'd ever seen who had a telephone extension in his bathroom. Each of these blessed individuals imparted to me a clear sense of friendship, unselfish dedication, and spiritual community.

Jan Barnes writes: "**Young adults are starved for community**, authentic community." If we let our young people feel that they are a crucial part of our church family and needed for our future, we have passed a basic test in church-worthiness.

A very impressionable time—"the reminiscence bump"

In case churches need another reason to take good care of their teens and twenty-somethings, there's something called the "reminiscence bump."[1] Various studies have found that the teen years and twenties are some of the most memorable times of a person's life. In interviewing older adults, what times do they remember and look back on as significant? Their teen years and twenties.

New parents are told how significant the earliest years of a child's development are. Shouldn't we let our churches know the same thing about the "bump" years, and ask ourselves, **"What are we doing that shows our total commitment to the upcoming generation? What opportunities are we giving to the next generation to show our increasing trust in their ability to take on the mantle of spiritual progress and church leadership?"**

Empowerment versus entertainment —how churches succeed

What do the Mormons, Jehovah's Witnesses, and a number of Evangelical, Protestant, and Catholic churches do that Christian Scientists have yet to do on a regular basis? **They care enough about their young people to challenge them with missions and give them an honorable role, and expect them to fulfill that role.**

Rick Warren, the pastor of an American megachurch was inspired and mentored by Reverend Billy Graham over a period of forty years.

---

1. Henig, "The Reminiscence Bump," *Psychology Today*.

Veteran preachers have seen the potential in young protégés and have helped their ministries develop from little storefront start-up churches to large congregations. Whether or not Christian Scientists aspire to have megachurches is beside the point. Too rarely do we show young people that we care about them by giving substantial attention to their activities, outside of one hour on Sunday. **We provide little in the way of transition for teens between Sunday school and church attendance.** Is it any wonder that young people feel adrift about attending church when their parents are not there to take them to Sunday school anymore?

> *Tell me, and I will forget. Show me, and I may remember. Involve me, and I will understand.*   Confucius (ca. 450 BCE)

A challenge for all churches today

"The problem arises from the **inadequacy of preparing young Christians for life beyond youth group,**" and most teens lack **"mentors or meaningful friendships with older Christians,"** writes David Kinnaman, author of *You Lost Me* and researcher for the Barna Group that has done extensive surveys of young people in relation to religion and religious affiliation.

> **While other Americans yield to the demands of youth, adult Mormons impose high demands on their next generation, requiring them to ingest church teaching an hour a day through high school and expecting the boys to save up their own money and spend two years in hard-core mission work. The system produces young adults with pride and commitment.**[2]

By asking their young people to train and prepare to be the engine of their church, Mormons are telling their youth that they really matter. The demand and challenge of Mormon missions says to young Mormons: "You are our future and hugely important to us." In the absence of this kind of spiritual investment in the next generation, what message are young people hearing from our church?

---

2. Ostling, *Mormon America*, 392–393.

"If we're not needed, look for us elsewhere"

Thom and Sam Rainer[3] have studied what motivates young people in regard to church activity, and they conclude the following reasons for non-attendance and involvement by those under age thirty:

- Church members seemed judgmental or hypocritical
- Moved to college and stopped attending church
- Did not feel connected to the people in my church
- Chose to spend more time with friends outside the church
- Was only going to church to please others
- Simply wanted a break from church

The Rainers further observed that young adults are likely to stay if they see church as **truly essential**. To the majority who drop out, going to church is less important than work, leisure activities, or simply doing nothing. **Most churches are doing little to become essential to the lives of their members.**[4]

How does the Christian Science Church fit into this analysis of being essential or not essential to our young people?

What the Christian Science Church has done that is future-looking

In the past fifteen years, the Mother Church in Boston has taken some forward-thinking moves to focus more on youth. The Church established an Internet site called Spirituality.com, and more recently TMC Youth. They have sponsored conferences around the world called Summits that have used local talent and local organizers to address and reach out to, not just young church members, but people of various ages with big ideas about church. All of this is to be applauded.

---

3. Thom Rainer is President and CEO of Lifeway Christian Resources, and his son Sam is a Baptist pastor.
4. Rainer, *Essential Church*, 160.

The contribution of summer camps

Since the 1960s and earlier, summer camps for young Christian Scientists have actively encouraged youth leadership in the church. The camps that my family and friends have observed have done a tremendous amount of good for the Christian Science Church. They have nurtured kids from troubled families, inspired whole families, and jump-started any number of kids towards a lifetime of spiritual dedication.

Camp counselors in Christian Science camps are given a fair amount of autonomy to prove that they can be both innovative and gifted youth leaders. Camps are way more than just "doing cool things for kids." More local churches, after summer camp is over, have to let their young people grow into leadership roles in church that parallel what those young people have learned in their camp experience. Shouldn't this mean **more than ushering** or heading up a youth committee? This is where the gap seems to be—between the leadership role that the camps have encouraged among young people and the void of responsible activity which those same young people sometimes, but not all the time, face when they return home.

In recent years Adventure Unlimited has set their creative sights on this "gap" problem, initiating a National Leadership Council (and a more recent similar program called Compass). The NLC aims to develop future leaders in the church, organize service projects, and keep a select group of high school age Christian Scientists engaged in their activities and discussions during the whole year. Can we as a church aim to broaden this kind of work to include as many as possible of our young people? The following is a concept that our church might be able to ponder for its viability with the purpose of not just filling a gap between Sunday school and church, but giving vision and renewal to all our church members:

What if…? The challenge to us from Tony Campolo

The Rev. Tony Campolo challenges Christian youth: "If the Mormon kids can take off two years of their lives to do missionary work, I want to know why you won't take off one year and give it in service to God and to those God calls you to serve."[5]

A mission-year proposal

Rev. Campolo initiated what is called Mission Year in New Jersey, and it has been active for over forty years. It's a non-denominational endeavor with the purpose of "Christian leadership development and church renewal," and it aims to join together needy city churches with volunteer youth workers. To envision this program, consider what the Mormon Church does in preparing their early teens for mission work until they go out at age eighteen and older. Or think of Peace Corps trainees preparing to work in foreign countries.

How could this be constructed for our young volunteers?

When young people leave home on a mission, they require some support. Early in the twentieth century eager Christian Science lone missionaries took the message of their church's teaching to Germany[6] and elsewhere. In the early 1900s new practitioners were mentored by veteran ones. I know of one Chicago practitioner who housed at minimal cost a new worker until that novice practitioner was ready to go out on his own.

What if Christian Scientists were to put together a Mission Year program? It should probably **start small** and operate as a pilot program with the intent of weeding out potential problems early on. It could begin with a board of forward-thinking Christian Scientists including certainly twenty-somethings, and probably a practitioner. Call it a youth ministry or mission, or non-military chaplaincy. It would require a clear vision, purpose, and a defined scope of what work would be done, including even the eventuality that such an activity might ultimately not need its "fathering-mothering" framework.

Whether the program remained autonomous or became part of a

---

5. Campolo, *Revolution and Renewal*, 76.
6. Seal, *Christian Science in Germany*.

more formal church network could be left up to the oversight of those most involved with it. Our churches' prison ministry currently is organized by various states, and that system seems to work well where it has been established.

Possible initial steps in establishing this idea: (1) recruit young adult "mission year" workers who have graduated from high school, and demonstrated leadership potential at camp or in other comparable venues; (2) seek out branch churches in various locations, starting in the United States but eventually going international. These branches would sponsor a "mission year" worker who would work as an "apprentice" practitioner (see more on this point below), living in a home or room near the sponsoring church.

The workers could be sponsored partially by their home churches. They could be paid for by their own savings as the Mormons do it, or other funding possibilities could be explored. Should they bring their own car, but get paid for mileage?

Activities

The volunteers' work would consist of (a) time for prayer and taking on practitioner work for their community possibly in the mornings; (b) working in consultation with an established practitioner of their own choosing hopefully in the target area, but not necessarily from that area. This would be a kind of intern-mentor relationship conducted for free by this practitioner; (c) besides this, the worker would have a "calling" of anything from music ministry (helping local Sunday schools with diversifying music and encouraging kids' involvement in the music), to nurses' training, to prison or mental health ministry, to Bible education, to another ministry of the worker's own calling, or a combination of the above. The worker would also be expected and encouraged to be involved in local community service or inter-faith activities such as Habitat for Humanity.

The host branch or society would not be allowed to relegate the youth worker to be full-time Reading Room librarian or to fill a position which would naturally fall to the local members. This doesn't mean that the worker would be "above" helping out in the branch when needed.

Other potential activities
A worker could organize a Bible workshop for kids and adults, or help the regional chaplaining effort in the jails, and very possibly work with local ecumenical groups as our church representative, all with an eye toward developing future participation from fellow Christian Scientists in the region rather than the mission year worker becoming individually indispensable; (d) over time, if this "mission year" effort was successful, it could grow naturally nationwide, work in concert with or be coordinated by the Mother Church and have volunteer regional supervisors who could troubleshoot and intervene if, for example, a housing situation needed adjustment or there were other needs.

Note
The purpose of a "mission year" would not be just to train young workers to become practitioners. We all have different gifts, and one size does not fit all. But our young people require both a challenge and to feel that their church looks to them for leadership. One young practitioner told me recently that one of the first steps in her career that led her to the healing work was leaving her "comfort zone," and a "mission year" type of experience could definitely serve to take volunteers out of their comfort zone. **Consider what a program such as this could do for the spirit of our church vision—to know that we had a dedicated group, even a small group, of workers blessing our church's work in this way?**

Broader possible applications

The shepherding activity described here applies specifically to the progress of our young people, but of course ideas such as Mission Year could apply to the development of all our church activities and age groups. Paul nurtured and helped develop and encourage the infant Christian churches, which he patiently supported in those churches' early stages of development. He did this in mentoring Timothy and, through his letters and many visits to the various "start-up" churches that he inspired in some way.

Paul was continually making recommendations to the infant Christian gatherings in regard to the conduct of their members and the quality of their spiritual instruction. As an example of this kind of Pauline work that Christian Scientists have recently been engaged in, one of our church-associated camps has done an excellent job of encouraging and supporting spiritually and financially Christian Science outreach in a state nearby, with good results from that effort.

Questions about a Mission Year:
- **Should young workers be sent out in pairs?** The need to maintain morale is significant. The author was a former VISTA volunteer and found quickly that life can be very lonely in an unfamiliar community.
- The preceding brief outline is a bare-bones proposal. I believe that we need to be bridge builders. The connections between our youth education and the building of future workers in a church or any organized activity should be natural, but ideas such as the above will always need proper thought, planning, evaluation, and revitalizing. **What other possible actions could be taken to further the ends of fostering youth leadership and supporting important efforts that are already ongoing?**

The foregoing suggested program is to encourage thinking beyond the boundaries of what is present. It is not an exact model for action, but more a basis for discussion.

Question:
Should Sunday school end at age twenty, at a time when people still have huge questions about their lives and their faith-life?[7]

Limiting the growth of Eutychus

"We have sinned by not allowing Sunday school to go on after age twenty."   Comment of a long-time church member

---

7. There is a by-law in the Christian Science *Church Manual* (62) that specifically restricts Sunday school attendance after the age of twenty.

Does the limitation on Sunday school age constitute a quenching of the Spirit? From *Science and Health*: "I would not transform the infant at once into a man, nor would I keep the suckling a lifelong babe" (*S&H* 371:20). One branch church the author has visited offers an informal discussion group at the same time as the church service for those over the age of twenty. Another church has allowed some church attendees over Sunday school age to act as "student teachers" together with a regular teacher in Sunday school classes.

Related questions:
Paul wrote: "Quench not the Spirit. Despise not prophesyings" (I Thess. 5:19). Are the rules and customs in our church geared to putting "Eutychus" to sleep, marginalizing him, or is our church gathering the energy, questions, and ideas from its young people into fresh channels for the purpose of developing and improving the spiritual Body that those young people need to be a vital part of?

CHAPTER 13

Earth helping the woman[1]

I've always subconsciously looked out for the total Christian and when I found him, he turned out to be a non-practicing Jew.[2]

William F. Buckley, Jr.

OUT OF THE GOODNESS of his heart, my neighbor often plows the snow from our driveway on winter mornings, and he risked his safety to keep our house from flooding when we were out of town. I don't think he goes to church. Does it matter if he does or doesn't, if the spirit of his life expresses what most of the world's religions espouse?

Some of our best help can flow from unpredictable sources, frequently from outside our circle of fellowship. Jesus pointed out, to the severe displeasure of his hometown congregation, that outsiders were receptive of healing from the prophets Elijah and Elisha more readily than Jesus' people. In Jesus' well-known parable of the wounded traveler, the official religious men in the story failed to rescue the crime victim. Help instead came from a Samaritan, whose people were considered to be heretics at that time.

---

1. This chapter title refers to Revelation 12:1–16, in particular verse 16 of that chapter, wherein aid for the figure of a woman is provided by the earth which "swallowed up the flood which the dragon cast out of his mouth." The author suggests that help for spiritual causes can come from surprising places, people, and backgrounds.
2. Buckley, Congressional Record Online through the Government Publishing Office [www.gpo.gov], S5455, May 21, 1996. Buckley's comment was part of his eulogy at the memorial service for Richard Clurman (1924-1996), a journalist, editor, and administrator best known for his long association with *TIME* magazine.

Throughout the Scriptures are stories of non-Jewish and non-Christian "saints." In Numbers, the semi-heathen soothsayer Balaam blessed the children of Israel (23:18).[3] In Genesis 20, Abimelech, the polytheistic king of Gerar, heeded the voice of God warning him not to take Sarah as a concubine, and Abimelech appeared more noble than Abraham in this brief narrative. We are told in II Kings (5:1) that the Syrian military captain Naaman was not only healed by the Hebrew prophet Elisha, but the Lord empowered Naaman, a non-Hebrew, for the deliverance of Syria.

After the ascension of Jesus we find Gamaliel, a Pharisee, advocating for impartial treatment of the Christian apostles, and on another occasion a pagan city official holds off a mob that fancies retaliation on Paul and other Christians.[4]

Here is a pattern of help and encouragement coming from outside the favored congregation or culture. Why should it not be a continuing phenomenon?

During a New Hampshire legal battle in early 1903, a bill that would have punished Christian Scientists was withdrawn after opposition to the measure arose. Friends of the Christian Scientists, and not our church members themselves, led this opposition to the punitive law. Irving Tomlinson described the New Hampshire action in a letter to Mrs. Eddy, as follows:

> The Judiciary Committee…by a vote of 12 to 1… reported to the House 'Inexpedient to legislate.' This favorable report was adopted by the House… This…victory was won by your friends who are not yet [Christian] Scientists. No legal counsel was engaged to manage the case. Not one of your representatives visited the Legislature Hall or called upon the Judiciary Committee or one of the legislators. **Your many friends outside the church gladly enlisted in your behalf and attended to every needful detail.**[5]

---

3. Dummelow, *The One-Volume Bible Commentary*, 114.
4. Acts 19:35.
5. Tomlinson, "A Brief Account." *C. S. Sentinel*, 2-5-1903.

Interesting observations from a physician

Christian Scientists may find confirmation and support in intriguing places. Lewis Thomas, a veteran physician and author, wrote a fascinating overview of medical practice in the twentieth century. In reflecting on his decades of experience, Dr. Thomas described an illness that hospitalized him, and how that illness led him to consider the meaning of his inner life. Performing his own physical and spiritual self-examination during this time, Dr. Thomas wrote the following:

> I have seen a lot of my inner self, more than most people, and you'd think I would have gained some new insight, even some sense of illumination, but I am as much in the dark as ever. I do not feel connected to myself in any new way. Indeed, if anything, the distance seems to have increased, and I am personally more a dualism than ever, made up of structure after structure, over which I have no say at all. I have the feeling now that if I were to keep at it, looking everywhere with lenses and bright lights…I would be brought no closer to myself. I exist, I'm sure of that, but not in the midst of all that soft machinery…I now doubt that there is any center, any passenger compartment, any private green room where I am found to be in residence…I am glad that I don't have to worry about the details. If I were really at the controls, in full charge, keeping track of everything, there would be a major train wreck within seconds…I'm glad I'm here outside, wherever that is.[6]

Dr. Thomas's humility and frankness are quite astounding. Though he does not profess to be religious in any special way, his conclusions, clothed in a clinical vocabulary, wind down paths shared by metaphysicians.

Three points stand out here:
- The deeper and longer Dr. Thomas looks at his physicality, the greater he feels removed from his actual identity as a person, and he senses a dualism between his body and his selfhood.

---

6. Thomas, *Youngest Science*, 232.

- Dr. Thomas very modestly assesses a physician's ability to competently control all the necessary functions of the body—even if this control was mechanically possible.
- Most surprisingly of all, the doctor concludes that, not only does he not feel that his essential selfhood is headquartered in his physical body, but that he, Dr. Thomas, is "outside, wherever that is." Again, this is a man who wears no religious convictions on his sleeve.

Three fairly remarkable conclusions from a supposedly non-religious source. Dr. Thomas is no longer living, but he left behind a small hieroglyph of how physicians and metaphysicians can arrive at similar crossroads. Mrs. Eddy wrote that man lives in Soul, and that Soul is "outside the body" and "outside of finite form, which forms only reflect" (S&H 510:16–17 and 71:7). While Dr. Thomas might not have uttered the word *Soul*, did not his words approximate Mrs. Eddy's observation?

Look again at the second point above—the doctor's judgment that the functioning of the human body far exceeds human capacity to regulate it. If creation possesses an intricate, complex ability of apparent self-sustenance, then could mortals consider that there may be an over-arching, governing intelligence in the universe? As a believer who tends to use some traditional, religious forms of reference, I find Dr. Thomas's insights helpful because they are **secular on the surface but possess deeply spiritual implications**. Therefore, they speak to a secular world in parable form.

A wide variety of helpers

The following is a brief, informal list of some books, organizations, and individuals whose purposes and thought corroborate or run concurrently with elements of Christian Science. They represent pioneering and innovative thinking in the fields of medicine, religion, philosophy, psychology, history, and humanitarian endeavor that not only complement the best aims in those fields but look towards the future. Readers can no doubt come up with their own list and may feel free to question some of the author's choices:

Dr. Patch Adams—The reader shouldn't be put off by any simplistic characterization of Dr. Adams from the eponymous film about him. Dr. Adams sees, as does Dr. Leonard Sagan (see below), the relationship of wellness to one's environment.

Reverend Rob Bell—an evangelical preacher with unorthodox views on subjects such as the nature of hell.

Brother Yun (Liu Zhenying)—His autobiography, *The Heavenly Man*, tells his remarkable story. Brother Yun is a Chinese evangelist and his life experiences in his homeland parallel New Testament accounts.

Sir Winston Churchill—"Never yield to force; **never yield to the *apparently overwhelming* might of the enemy.**"[7] Note how Churchill's phrase parallels the biblical language: "When the enemy shall come in *like* a flood, the spirit of the Lord shall lift up a standard against him." "Yea, though I walk *through* the valley of the shadow of death, I will fear no evil." Christian Scientists are sometimes mocked for their claim that evil is a *claim*, a *belief*, in a way, a phantasm. There are other great thinkers whose words are similar to the view of Christian Scientists that evil is not now and never has been what it has been reputed to be.

Norman Cousins—*Anatomy of an Illness*. In his book Cousins writes: "It is doubtful whether the placebo—or any drug, for that matter would get very far without a patient's robust will to live…The placebo is only a tangible object made essential in an age that feels uncomfortable with intangibles…The placebo, then, is an emissary between the will to live and the body. But the emissary is expendable."[8]

Dr. Vince DeVita—*The Death of Cancer* explores the bureaucratic and personal issues that have inhibited progress in medicine and have kept promising therapies from reaching patients. Books like DeVita's are a tough read for a Christian Scientist and many other lay people, but they can give an insight into factors that are important for us to come to grips with, no matter how we are approaching disease.

---

7. Churchill, Speech at Harrow School, 1941.
8. Cousins, *Anatomy of an Illness*, 66–67.

Doctors Without Borders—This organization's work is a selfless example of Christian love, whether or not the individual doctors have any religious background. Similarly, in Syria and in other countries, unaffiliated physicians are serving people under horrendous conditions for caregiving.

Dr. Larry Dossey—Before his book *Healing Words* was published in 1993, only three U.S. medical schools had courses devoted to exploring the role of religious practice and prayer in health. Currently, nearly eighty medical schools have instituted such courses, many of which utilize Dr. Dossey's works as textbooks.

Henry Drummond—*The Greatest Thing in the World*. Another book by Drummond, *The Changed Life*, is a short remarkable work as excellent as Drummond's better-known writing.

Fambul Tok—an organization that aims at reconciliation and forgiveness in communities affected by the long-running civil war in Sierra Leone.

Robin Lane Fox—*Pagans and Christians* focuses on early Christian history, and is intriguing for Christians in part because of the author's avowed atheism.

Edward Gibbon—The 18th century historian and author of *The Decline and Fall of the Roman Empire* described acts of faith and even the raising of the dead in the early Christian church. However, according to biographer David M. Low, Gibbon "had no belief in a divine revelation and little sympathy with those who had such a belief. While he treated the supernatural with irony, his main purpose was to establish the principle that religions must be treated as phenomena of human experience."[9] Perhaps readers of Gibbon's work may find more authenticity in his "pro-Christian" message in part because Gibbon was not a church partisan.

Health Wagon—Virginia-based Appalachian nurses in a van who minister to disadvantaged rural communities.

---

9. Low, "Edward Gibbon," *Encyclopedia Britannica*.

Hope Ships—similar to Doctors without Borders in their desire to serve the underserved, only with a more ostensibly Christian mission. These ships travel to countries especially in coastal Africa, bringing the work of primary care physicians to countries in great need of them.

Immaculee Ilibaghiza—*Left to Tell* is a stirring, remarkable memoir of one woman's survival of the Rwandan genocide. Her faith and ability to forgive are inspiring beyond words.

Tracy Kidder—*Mountains beyond Mountains* tells the story of Dr. Paul Farmer who established medical clinics in some of the most challenging parts of the globe, including Haiti.

Anne Lamott—author of *Traveling Mercies* and other writings relating her faith journey.

Dr. Robert Lanza—*Biocentrism*

Dr. Bruce Lipton—"The Biology of Belief"

Kelly McGonigal—Her TED talk about stress indicates that stress doesn't have to be the enemy most people believe it to be. Dr. McGonigal: "182,000 Americans died prematurely, not from stress, but from the belief that stress is bad for you."

Anita Moorjani—*Dying To Be Me* is a fascinating narrative by a woman raised in the Hindu tradition. It describes the author's journey in healing her case of cancer. Moorjani's book, together with the message of other near-death experiences (NDEs), illustrate the following statement from *Science and Health*: "The relinquishment of all faith in death and also the fear of its sting would raise the standard of health and morals far beyond its present elevation...." (S&H 426:23). The vision that Moorjani experienced in her NDE evidently healed her of a very late-stage of cancer to the astonishment of her doctors and family. While Christian Scientists view death as an opponent of sorts, and Moorjani's healing "foiled" death, yet her experience and that of many others indicate that we have no reason to see death as a state to be feared.

Pierre Pradervand—*The Gentle Art of Blessing*

Dr. Lissa Rankin—*Mind over Medicine* and her research on the placebo effect

Dr. Leonard Sagan—*The Health of Nations*. Dr. Sagan was an epidemiologist with unorthodox views of the causation of sickness and health. He attributed recoveries and wellness to psycho-social factors such as education, family strength, and environmental surroundings.

Eckhart Tolle—*The Power of Now* and *The New Earth*

Barbara Von der Heydt—*Candles Behind the Wall* points to spiritual and religious elements involved in the transformation of communist governments in 1989 and 1990.

Margaret Wheatley—*Leadership and the New Science* challenges for the better much of what we have tended to believe about organization.

Philip Yancey—*What's So Amazing About Grace?* Yancey's writing frees Christians from the thought that they can earn heaven or even healing just by behaving well. While grace is implicit in the life of Jesus, would we know that by assessing the attitudes of many of Jesus' professed followers?

Notice the number of interesting doctors cited here. Nurses are amazing though under-represented in our list. I'm talking not just of Christian Science nurses, but RNs. In all my visits to patients and others in hospitals over the years, I hear again and again immense thanks for nurses voiced by Christian Scientists and others of different backgrounds. In any profession, you will find the "brusque," over-businesslike, and uncompassionate person, but it's been my experience that the large majority of nurses express deep dedication, amazing patience, and enduring cheerfulness in the face of very difficult conditions. This goes for doctors as well, whose days are stretched very thin among all their duties.

More support from medical sources

Here are statements by Dr. William Osler[10] to his students. Dr. Osler was the Regius Professor of Medicine at Oxford University and the first Physician-in-Chief of the Johns Hopkins Hospital.

> I would urge you to care more for the individual patient than for the special features of the disease…To keep your own heart soft and tender…Keep a looking-glass in your own heart, and the more carefully you scan your own frailties the more tender you are for those of your fellow-creatures…In charity we of the medical profession must live and move and have our being…While doctors continue to practice medicine with their hearts as well as their heads, so long will there be a heavy balance in their favor in the bank of Heaven…not a balance against which we can draw for bread and butter, or taxes or house-rent, but without which we should be poor indeed.
>
> In all ages the prayer of Faith has healed the sick…The modern miracles at Lourdes and at Ste. Anne de Beaupre in Quebec, and the wonder workings of the so-called Christian Scientists are often genuine and must be considered in discussing the foundations of therapeutics. We physicians use the same power every day…Faith is a most precious commodity without which we should be very badly off.[11]

A sentiment similar to that expressed by Dr. Osler once came from William Mayo who, with his brother Charles, founded the Mayo Clinic in Rochester, Minnesota. William Mayo is quoted as saying the following:

> I have sent people to Christian Scientists [typically meaning 'practitioners' involved in the healing practice] and they have got relief.[12]

---

10. Dr. Osler (1849-1919) has been described as the "Father of Modern Medicine."
11. Thom, *Johns Hopkins*, 83–84.
12. Powell, *A Life Size Portrait*, 38.

Encouragement and novel approaches from medical studies

While Christian Scientists are often reluctant to read about medical studies or research, sometimes interesting tidbits emerge in the news that provide encouragement for those who practice healing from a spiritual basis. Consider this excerpt from *The New York Times*:

> Many cancers, researchers now recognize, grow slowly, or not at all, and do not require treatment. Some cancers even shrink or disappear on their own. But once cancer is detected, it is impossible to know if it is dangerous, so doctors treat them all.[13]

This observation is a part of the *Times*' story that garnered little attention in the headlines, but should be interesting to many people, especially Christian Scientists who don't see diseases acting similarly in all cases and can fully appreciate the phenomena that the writer points out here.

Similarly, a *60 Minutes* story provides helpful information for the metaphysician:

> Dr. Matthias Gromeier: **So cancers, all human cancers, they develop a shield or shroud of protective measures that make them invisible to the immune system. And this is precisely what we try to reverse with our virus.** So by infecting the tumor, we are actually removing this protective shield. And…enabling the immune system to come in and attack.[14]

Most people don't think of cancer as coming with its own "defense mechanism" that protects it from the body's immune system. In *Miscellaneous Writings* (352:15) Mrs. Eddy points out that it can be helpful for a practitioner to be aware of what "claims to produce" the problem. I share these small items with that motive in mind.

---

13. Kolata, "Vast Study Casts Doubt," *New York Times*, 2-20-2014…
14. "Killing Cancer, Part 1," *60 Minutes* segment on recent cancer treatments being tested at Duke University.

Thoughts about the brain

Mortimer Adler was a philosopher, and not a neurologist, but his following observation is thought-provoking:

> The most that can be said of the brain in relation to the human mind is that it is an intellect-support organ upon which the intellect depends, without which it cannot think, but with which it does not think.[15]

Scientific understanding of the action of the human mind is still in its infancy, which means that it is a frontier for both physical scientists and Christian Scientists.

Logic and reason: human devices for divine purposes

Religiously inclined peoples tend to cite ancient sacred texts and sayings to validate their beliefs and practices. Jesus did that as well, but often he cited logic or **reason alone as sufficient grounds for doing or not doing something**. Logic is not necessarily considered a mark of the holy or divine; on the other hand, *logic* is derived from the Greek word *logos* that is synonymous with Christ in the New Testament (John 1:1).

The following are instances where Jesus employs *logic* as a way of making his case to his listeners:

Luke 17:10 J. B. Phillips "We are not much good as servants; we have only done what we ought to do." When a person obeys a divine command, should he or she expect any special reward or status as a result? Rather we should feel humbly obliged to serve more than be served as we labor in the spiritual vineyard.

Paraphrase of Luke 7:41–43 If two men are forgiven their debts, who will show the most appreciative love in return, the man with the larger debt or the one with the smaller debt?

---

15. Adler, "Is Intellect Immaterial?" *Self-Educated American*, Part One, 9-6-2011.

Matthew 16:2-3 New International Version "When evening comes, you say, 'It will be fair weather, for the sky is red'...You know how to interpret the appearance of the sky, but you cannot interpret the signs of the times." If you can forecast physical events, why can't you forecast events of larger significance?

Matthew 7: 9,10 New International Version "Which of you, if your son asks for bread, will give him a stone? Of if he asks for a fish, will give him a snake?"

Logic and guidance

A friend of the author uses logic this way: "If I'm not sure which direction to take in life, I think to myself, 'When did I last feel the leading of the Almighty?' And then, 'Did anything come up recently that would change that leading?' Because if nothing has, then I'm going to go with the spiritual leading that I last felt and feel secure that I'm heading along the right path."

This reasoning works in hiking. If you get lost along the trail, you can sometimes return to the last marker you saw on a tree or rock, and proceed from there, if you're not sure you're following the correct way.

A litmus test using logic from *Science and Health*

Mrs. Eddy similarly turned to logic to bring out a point in her overall spiritual arguments. In her chapter entitled "Marriage" she counsels those considering marriage to not rush the decision, to consider their responsibilities and prospective obligations and how a marriage might affect their own growth and their connection with others (*S&H* 68). All of that is human advice that makes eminent sense. Practical counsel does not need to be explicitly based on metaphysics or a divine truth or biblical command as it implicitly expresses an inspired sense of wisdom.

Similarly, Mrs. Eddy quotes Thomas Carlyle in her other prose writings: "Give a thing time. If it succeeds, it is a right thing."[16] There's nothing here in Carlyle's words that's grounded on a metaphysical basis, but his observation does spring from what we might call reliable human experience.

We have heard Christian Scientists use the idea of reason or logic in the following way: "I felt ill, but I reasoned that as God's idea I could not experience anything that God did not make or know." While that reasoning can be drawn from a spiritual interpretation of the first chapter of Genesis, there are more expansive possibilities in reasoning than that statement of deductive logic.

Christian Scientists tend to feel comfortable starting their metaphysical reasoning from a high, what we term *absolute*, standpoint and then conclude something from that. That is deductive reasoning. But Mrs. Eddy says that, "Christian Science must be accepted at this period by induction" (S&H 461:4). **The world may call our deductive reasoning *circular logic* and may criticize us on that basis**. Our critics say: "You are going to arrive at your predetermined conclusions no matter what is going on or what happens. Therefore, you are living in your own cloud." Isn't this criticism the reason we need to work and speak more frequently with inductive reasoning if we wish to be understood? Truth is still true, but most people, including Christian Scientists, need to be led gently, step-by-step to what spiritual truth can accomplish.

Learning from nature

Jesus pointed to birds and lilies and mustard seeds as models for human behavior and reliance upon God. Most Christians don't realize that Buddha turned to earth as a "testifier" as well. When Buddha's tempter demanded who could attest that the Buddha was worthy of reaching ultimate wisdom, the noble monk touched the earth, and the earth answered, "I am your witness."[17] That response sent the tempter in retreat.

---

16. Stephen, *Hours*, 255.
17. MacPherson, 131.

Birds are beautiful examples of the divine. Migrating birds literally save energy (and decrease their heart rate) when they fly in a "V" formation. Is that flying formation an inspirational basis for our church's precept of "rotation in office?" (*My.* 250:4) **What are sometimes condescendingly called lesser species can warn the human species of impending natural disasters by their sensitive awareness of natural forces that are insensible to most humans.** Volumes could be written about all that we have to learn from nature. Doesn't nature speak to mortals with bilingual, earthly and divine tones?

| **What fools to cry for signs when creation harbors nothing else!** [18]

Not afraid to borrow good ideas

Ideas do not have to originate from our own tribe, faith, or from predecessors of our faith in order to be valid and useful. President Dwight Eisenhower, having seen the German Autobahn in the conclusive months of World War II, borrowed from the German concept a plan for an American interstate highway system that was then realized in the United States (1953). American drivers didn't object that they would be forced to drive on roads inspired by a Nazi regime or drive a "people's car" (the Volkswagen) which Hitler helped popularize.[19]

Borrowing from other religious traditions

Bible readers do not usually realize that the first words in the Holy Book are deeply influenced by the creation writings of the Babylonians. Scholars generally believe that the first verses in Genesis 1 and 2, called the Elohistic writing, were due in part to the captivity of the Jews in Babylon, circa 600 BCE. The writers of the Bible's first creation story, however, notably differed from both the Babylonians' vision of many gods, and from the anthropomorphic, tribal narrative in Genesis called the Jehovistic version.

---

18. Smith, H., 222.
19. Reid, *Healing of America*, 14.

When St. Paul addressed the Athenians on Mars Hill, the apostle did not consider it beneath him to quote a Greek poet in order to confirm his message that we live in the God-presence. What many Christians don't realize is that the Greek poet Aratus, whom Paul quoted, had written: "Everyone is indebted to Zeus, for we are indeed his offspring." It was sufficient to Paul that Aratus' words paralleled the Christian message even though those words honored a "pagan" supreme deity. The comparison was close enough to be able to reach Paul's Greek audience, and perhaps there weren't enough touchy Christians in that crowd to object.

What are the most helpful "gifts" from other faith traditions and practices? The author has been deeply grateful for his friendship with those from a diversity of backgrounds. We all have so much to learn from one another. Paul says to "covet" the spiritual gifts of others, almost in the spirit of collecting treasures. From the *New Living Translation:* "You should earnestly desire helpful gifts" (I Cor. 12:31).

What Krista Tippett saw…

American journalist Krista Tippett wrote in her book *Becoming Wise* about the collective **"coveting" of spiritual gifts** that she was privileged to witness in the 1990s at the Collegeville Institute for Ecumenical and Cultural Research, near the Twin Cities in Minnesota. There aren't too many venues where Americans of spiritual mindset from a great variety of backgrounds can gather for thoughtful discussion, but Tippett found one of these venues at Collegeville:

"At St. John's we had hours to tell our own stories and listen to others, days to unfold the 'why' and 'what next' and 'so what' questions that followed—and take them up together…The friendship between these former religious strangers was in itself remarkable. **They all remained as distinct and impassioned on their spectrum of belief as ever. And yet the delight, curiosity, and esteem they had acquired for each other's minds and journeys changed everyone profoundly**. It humanized doctrine. It invigorated their sense of their own tradition, and simultaneously imparted them with a grateful sense of mystery about what other traditions bring into the world. They took these new ways of seeing and being back into their lives in their own communities."[20]

A hint of future possibilities

A psalm reads: "Open thou mine eyes, that I may behold wondrous things out of thy law" (Psalms 119:18). Life can be full of surprises. It's important for all of us to be open to the divine surprises.

A few years ago, a friend of the author was visited by an emergency medical technician regarding an insurance claim from an accident. The EMT asked my friend, who is a Christian Scientist, who their regular physician was. My friend replied that she didn't have a regular physician, and she was a Christian Scientist. The EMT looked a little surprised, and asked her, "Do you read *Science and Health*?" It turns out that the EMT had stumbled across a copy of the Christian Science textbook and shared it with members of her crew and friends without realizing that there was a church associated with the book. The EMTs found *Science and Health* to be very helpful for them in dealing with cases of infection.

Are there Christian Scientists today who could imagine something like this happening? Do we instead tend to think that those in the medical field find very little in common with the teachings in our church textbook?

Summary—notes in a bottle

This chapter is an accumulation of notes in a bottle. Don't these notes form an unexpected message whispering to us that the "divine" is a very large tent? A physical tent could hardly contain what is infinite. It is a tent fashioned by those who think of themselves as religious as well as by many who do not. Firm believers of spiritual teachings tend to belittle or merely overlook what other believers and non-believing atheists and agnostics have found in other teachings. There is a usefulness and blessing that flows from curiosity and openness to the virtues

---

20. Tippett, 20, 22.

of others and not maintaining a condescending "we've found it" view towards those who have much to teach us.

St. Paul wrote about those non-Jews who became a "law to themselves" (Rom. 2:14) by the manner in which they lived. **"God's laws are written within them,"** as the Living Bible renders this verse. Paul was speaking of people who did not require a set of religious precepts in order to know the spirit of how to live in a way that religious people call "righteous." It is right to honor those lives that stand in quiet, eloquent compliance with some of the most valuable religious teachings in the world without requiring a brand of any set of religious teachings to define them.

Recommendations:
When referencing other faiths and their ideas and practices, do our church members and publications cite others mainly for the purpose of validating our own beliefs and practice? The *Christian Science Monitor* is continually pointing out good deeds and ideas sprouting around the globe no matter what the religious orientation of the doers and thinkers.

Can our other church publications and our members in their church gatherings be looking to regularly point out what is admirable in other faith practices whether or not Christian Scientists are modeling the same practice? In our church discussions we can do this **cross-referencing** of the vocabulary and ideas of other religious thinkers, and do this not to point out any believed-in superiority of our terms of reference or religious beliefs but to allow others to understand our faith tradition more clearly through the lens of others' language and thoughts.

Suggestion from a friend who studies Christian Science:
Would it be feasible to put together an evolving registry of Christian Science-friendly MDs around the U.S. and other countries who are supportive and not judgmental of their patients who are Christian Scientists? Is such a thing practical or even ethical? The Principia, a school for Christian Scientists, has in the past kept an informal list of local physicians who have been supportive and helpful enough to set a student's leg and put it in a cast, for example.

CHAPTER 14

The Great Inclusion
—modesty in religion

Other sheep I have which are not of this fold: them also I must bring, and they shall hear my voice; and there shall be one fold and one shepherd.
John 10:16

Enlarge the place of thy tent, and let them stretch forth the curtains of thy habitations: spare not, lengthen thy cords, and strengthen thy stakes...
Isaiah 54:2

The expanded flock and unbroken net

TO THE CHRISTIAN, Jesus was not merely a pacifier of partisan hostilities. His actions embodied large-scale inclusion. He chose disciples from opposite ends of the political spectrum—Mathias, a tax collector for the Romans, and Simon (not Peter) the Zealot whose sect hated the Romans. He patiently rebuked his disciples' rivalries.

He dealt with the partisanship issue directly in his parable of the Prodigal Son, where neither brother was sinless, yet the Father loved both of his sons. In one of his parables Jesus used a Samaritan as a foil. The parable targeted the prejudices of the Master's listeners who looked down on Samaritans. Jesus spoke with a Samaritan woman (Luke 4) to the consternation of his disciples.

Jesus was not defensive of his own personal righteousness. We find him making the amazing statement, "Why do you call me good? There is none good but one, and that is God" (Matthew 19:17 New Matthew Bible). There was **no personal pride** in his words. No lording over others.

Paul welcoming Gentiles into the tent of Christ

Paul followed Jesus' example of inclusion and expanded the net of inclusion beyond the borders of Israel to the non-Jewish world. His model of impartial evangelism should have become the model for all Christians. Peter eventually came to a revelation that paralleled Paul's vision: "I see very clearly that **God shows no favoritism**. In every nation he accepts those who fear him and do what is right" (Acts 10:34, 35 NLT).

Christians have been busy dividing the teachings of Christ for a long time…since his crucifixion, really. The Gospel writers themselves reveal some of the various "schools" of Christianity in their infant stages: Luke, scribe of a "social" Gospel; Matthew, addressing his writing to Jewish Christians; John, the metaphysical deep-sea diver. Gregory Riley, the author of *One Jesus…Many Christs*, argues that the multiplicity of Christian teachings and denominations are natural by-products of what Jesus taught. But did these different schools and interpretations have to be so unsupportive of and hostile towards one another? The spirit of Christianity requires new and unpredictable forms. Throughout the centuries the ever-new wine of the Spirit has entered new bottles or forms in many places.

> …when they had crucified him, they divided his garments among them by casting lots.
> Matt. 27:35 ESV

There are over seventy denominations in the United States that believe they are the one and only true faith. Why has the Second Coming not arrived at any of these churches? Is it possible that the stone and stones that these builders have rejected have become the cornerstone at more humble locations? Jesus could have warned us that this might happen when he reminded his home synagogue that Elijah and Elisha had found a receptive audience among the Gentiles and not among those to whom the Covenant was given (Luke 4:24). Paul continued along this vein in Romans 10: "By a foolish nation [maybe without perfect spiritual teaching] I will anger you…and I was found of them that sought me not" (vv. 19, 20).

Dummelow's vision of the unbroken net

J. R. Dummelow presents a remarkable and beautiful vision of the possibilities of spiritual fulfillment in his commentary on John 21:11. At Jesus' reappearing by the Sea of Galilee, the Savior came across his disciples struggling to return to their old occupation. Fishing in their customary ways had left his followers with an empty net. But at Jesus' direction, not only was their net filled, it was unbroken by the great weight of one hundred and fifty-three fish.

Here Dummelow's words startle us:

"The earlier draught of fishes (Luke 5:6) with the breaking net symbolised the Church on earth, imperfect in its organization and methods, and allowing many souls to escape from its meshes. This draught, in which the net is unbroken (John 21:6)…symbolises the Church triumphant in heaven, freed at last from all earthly imperfections, and **embracing** in its membership **all genuine servants of God…**"[1]

Has the spirit of our church's spiritual fishing often lacked the loving care that filled the nets that Christ fills? Have we sought "fish" who looked like us, and disdained many whom we might have welcomed and who could have been leaders in our ministry and fellowship? Have we marked out distinctions that were not substantial differences between one church or teacher and another?

Why should all Christians wait for the "Church triumphant in heaven" in order to realize something of this unbroken net? The prophet Micah foretold a time of international accord when every man would sit peacefully "under his fig tree" and, even more remarkably, Micah adds, **"For all people will walk every one in the name of his god, and we will walk in the name of our Lord our God for ever and ever."** (Micah 4:5)

Micah's prophecy here doesn't include the more typical religious conclusion of a favored group of believers defeating the less-favored unbelievers. The Interpreter's Bible comments that **Micah, "…could not see a real peace for his time which did not bring some sort of truce**

---

1. Dummelow, *Bible Commentary*, 811.

amid the warring religions of the day... The spirit of freedom and tolerance must find some kind of creative approach to the fact of religious differences."[2]

What could the "unbroken net" look like?

I remember one Sunday morning church service when I was sitting towards the rear of the church, noticing different people walking in. It didn't seem like an ordinary Sunday at all. There was a former teaching colleague of mine from our local middle school. I didn't know that he ever went to church. Then a friend we rarely saw from out of town, followed by another friend who hadn't been there in quite a while. This last man had been rescued from destructive addiction in the previous two years. I wondered to myself if this was some small foretaste of the life to come where we would be pleasantly **surprised at the generous inclusion of heavenly company**, because the divine net stretched so much farther than the imagination of our human minds and hearts.

"No prophecy of the scripture is of any private interpretation"

II Peter 1:20

When Christian Scientists discuss healing work, and the circumstances of a particular healing experience, I have sometimes heard a church member ask in slightly condescending and skeptical tone, "Was it a real '*Christian Science*' healing?"

A church institutional volunteer shared the following:
> At the end of our service at the jail on Saturday, in response to our asking if any had questions, one lady asked us what had brought us into Christian Science. I shared that when I was in high school, in the process of joining the Presbyterian Church, my mother was healed of cancer through Christian Science. That was all I needed to want to learn more about it...

---

2. Laymon, *Interpreter's Bible,* Vol. 6, 925.

This prompted one of the ladies to share that her mother had also had cancer in its last stages and, with the help of prayers from her Catholic church, had dumbfounded the doctors by making a complete recovery. She had only received chemo for a week. The doctors and nurses were so joyous, and said that there were some things that could not be attributed to medicine. Everyone at that service acknowledged that it had been God that had healed her.

After our last hymn, we gathered in a circle, held hands, and each briefly shared gratitude. It was simple and sincere.

"God is universal; confined to no spot, defined by no dogma, appropriated by no sect. Not more to one than to all, is God demonstrable as divine Life, Truth, and Love; and His people are they that reflect Him—that reflect Love."   Mis. 150:25

The truth is to one as to all. It knows no copyright.[3] If a listening, inspired individual hears the word of God and knows that to be a truth, imagine how broadly does the Infinite Wisdom dispense inspiration to multitudes unseen by us. "And I, when I am lifted up from the earth, will draw all people to myself" (John 12:32 NRSV).

Wherever and however that Christ-spirit is lived, uplifted, we are "drawn to" the Spirit, and the earth is newly blessed because of that lifting up. The large impact of this divine thought-influence and its possibilities are hinted at by the well-known "butterfly effect" coined by Edward Lorenz.

Lorenz's idea postulates that small causes can lead to large effects. We don't have to be afraid that precious truth has only been entrusted to a private club of especially spiritual listeners. **The more universal and blessed the "prophecy of scripture," the more universal its dispensation and potential effect**. This is the nature of a universal Science. This is why Nobel prizes have been awarded to different individuals on different continents who somewhat simultaneously have stumbled across important, world-blessing discoveries, while unaware of the universality of Wisdom which their discoveries pointed to in the lives of others.

---

3. Eddy, *Retrospection*, 76:2; "Christian Science is not copyrighted."

"All religions are equally false and equally true, depending on how you use them." [4]
Eckhart Tolle

Is Tolle right, or wrong, or over-generalizing? If any of us are more "fully persuaded" (Romans 14) by one faith over others or none, there's no fault there. The author happily identifies as a Christian Scientist because the essentials of that faith practice make eminent sense to me and have been proved "sea-worthy" in my life experience. My Christian Science faith is a lens through which I can clearly see the Infinite. Nonetheless, I empathize with the spirit of Eckhart Tolle's words that call all religions to critical self-appraisal.

"I, even I only, remain a prophet of the Lord..."
(words of Elijah) I Kings 18:22

Does any one religion have it all?

Does any one torch along the mountain trail shine brighter than all the others combined? Can any one religious body lay claim to a spiritual exceptionalism over all others? The Pew Foundation commissioned a huge study in 2008 based on interviews with 35,000 Americans. Here are some highlights of the Pew study:

Religion is deeply entrenched in the American culture; 56% say religion is very important in their lives; 82% say it's somewhat important. And only 7% say it's not important at all.

While **one in four (24%) believes their religion is the one, true faith** leading to eternal life, **most (70%) believe that many religions can lead to eternal life. A similar percentage (68%) believes there is more than one true way to interpret the teachings of their own religion**.

Americans believe in prayer; 93% pray outside of religious services and nearly 60% pray at least once a day.

Of those who pray, 90% believe they have received a definite answer to a specific prayer request; 62% believe they receive direct answers to their prayers at least once a month.[5]

---

4. Tolle, *The New Earth*, 70.
5. Pew Forum, "Religious Landscape Survey."

We can learn from and exchange with our fellow believers from other religious "brands" just as cooks may exchange recipes, even while those cooks add their own style to borrowed recipes. Gandhi, by his *satyagraha* or 'truth force' and practice of non-resistance, borrowed elements of Jesus' teaching, and in so doing he taught Christians something they had hardly practiced over the ages, though it was integral to the teachings of their Master.

Brands already possess decreasing meaning

By "enlarging the place of our tent," we discover commonality, and we find out that what is dear to others is also important to ourselves. *Mara*, the tempter in the Buddhist tradition, distracts humans from practicing the spiritual life by making ordinary things attractive, and making the negative seem positive. In different words Christians call this tempter Satan or the Devil, while Christian Scientists call it *animal magnetism*. Here's to the day when no translations from one practice to another will be needed because of our increasing familiarity with and support for our brothers and sisters of other faiths.

Possessing pieces of the one, grand puzzle

Might not each of us, each church, denomination, mosque, synagogue, and temple have received one piece or more of the grand puzzle of being? In Jesus' parable of the workers in the vineyard (Matthew 20), some workers complained because all those who labored, regardless of when they joined the workforce, received the same wage. By this parable Jesus was not setting a new standard of non-hourly pay scales. Was Jesus suggesting rather that all those who join in spiritual endeavors are entitled to parallel standing, regardless of their spiritual "seniority?" John the Baptist similarly chided notions of spiritual pride when he said that God could fashion sons of Abraham out of stones (Matthew 3:9).

Need for one another's spiritual contributions

The usefulness and blessed function of the one or more "puzzle pieces" that we have been given may depend on our joining together with others whose different pieces are absolutely needed to complete the puzzle of life. Yes, maybe some faiths appear on the surface to have received a few more pieces of spiritual substance or inspiration than others, especially the most humble of faiths and congregations, but I suggest that none have received all of the pieces.

Moral of this part of the story: **We must honor and "covet" and seek to express the wide expanse of universal spiritual gifts. What if all the energy poured into burnishing the image of our various denominations and sects was poured into positive efforts to honor and emulate the admirable gifts of** *other* **churches and denominations?**

No surprise that the pieces of the puzzle change over time

Religious practices evolve and devolve, reform and decay. A practice that might have shined brightly with unselfish inspiration and soaring exaltation yesterday may have cooled into a cold mass of inert cinders today, and another faith-practice that struggled severely with moral inconsistencies at its founding may have reformed some of its practices and today could have blossomed into a beautiful flower of God. Of course, these fluctuations happen within denominations and sects since no spiritual movement changes as a monolith but experiences over time both spiritual heights and depths within its own body.

Though Jesus communed with Samaritans and used a Samaritan as a prime example of unselfish love, that doesn't necessarily mean that he favored the Samaritans' theology (see John 4:22). Jesus suggested in his conversation with the Samaritan woman that, theological differences aside, the future we all would eventually see, could be glimpsed in Jesus' time. "The hour cometh, and *now is...*" He envisioned that **"the true worshippers... [would] worship the Father in spirit and in truth,"** (John 4:24) if not necessarily in the same fashion or building.

What would heaven on earth look like if all the pieces of the puzzle fit together? Many "people like ourselves"? Not at all.

Would there be a thousand-piece puzzle of the Holy Spirit, with five hundred blue ocean corners, and three hundred identical green palm leaves, and one hundred versions of the same toucan resting in the palm tree's branches? That is the vision that some of us have cherished over the years—a vision of **people like ourselves** drawn by supernatural guidance to join our church fellowship. We imagine that the world will eventually worship as we do. But might that not be a dreary landscape, tedious with pride, sameness, and inflexible customs?

How about an alternative to that vision being a vast congregation of small pockets of supportive fellowship composed of all the best qualities of the faith practices of which we are aware…and then some?

Look for a moment at the jewels of admirable qualities, practices, and thought that we can see around us in various spiritual traditions: Look at the **Amish** and their value put on simplicity, modesty, humility, and hard work. The **Mormons** embody a willingness to engage their youth, cherish their families, and possess a generous ability to help their fellow beings in distress. The **Quakers** and **Mennonites** have contributed immensely to efforts towards peace and reconciliation in the world far beyond their denominational confines. **Baptists** and **Pentecostals** both knew that something was missing from the staid ritual in church, and it was called the Holy Spirit. They believe that an intensity of joy belongs in our intimate experience with God. **Catholics, Methodists, Lutherans**, and **Episcopalians** revere the sanctity of holy rites and they all believe in and do much good for their respective communities, establishing hospitals and educational institutions. **Jews** explain roots of the Muslim and Christian traditions, especially monotheism, so Muslims and Christians should honor their spiritual ancestors. Jews have survived mass persecution, more intense than that experienced by practically any other faith tradition, and they have shown us the meaning of courage. **Buddhists** demonstrate what inner stillness can be. The **Baha'i** love unity and cherish what is good in all faiths. While my far too superficial characterization of these faith practices is so very limited, think of the power of the qualities mentioned, if and when they could be combined, or at least allied together in mutual support.

So let us look for the all-redeeming Spirit acting in all faiths and overpowering both the letter of religious teaching and its relative significance when compared with the importance of a person's actual life.

Borrowing from surprising quarters

In our **borrowing of outstanding spiritual elements from the faith and actions of others,** does a precise theology play a crucial part in the lives of those people we most admire? Florence Nightingale, the inspiring British nurse, was devoted to Christ, but she believed also that what we call Eastern and other religious teachings, as distinct from the Christian churches, contained substantial revelations. She maintained a strong stance against any prejudice that Christians might have felt in her time against those different religions and practices.

Since the first can also "be made last," denominations who fancy themselves to be the best in heaven and on earth, may have to take a back seat to those children of God who possibly don't know the letter of any "holy writing" but are wonderful living examples of God-likeness, whether they're aware of it or not.[6]

The magic singing beach

Have you ever walked near a beach where all the stones were singing as the tide rolled back over that jostling, glistening orchestra? **All the rough edges had been knocked off** by the timeless rubbing together of one stone against another under the steady crashing of the waves. What if all the world's people were a beautiful singing beach, one that John Lennon could barely dare to imagine? This ongoing smoothing action has been going on through the centuries, working over sharp edges of distinction between mortal egos, foiling human pride between the hardened beliefs of one person, distinct from those of his neighbor.

---

6. Eddy, *Retrospection*, 65:25; "…practical manifestations of Christianity constitute the only evangelism, and they need no creed."

Jesus' saying that **it rains on the just and the unjust** refutes the persistent superstition among religious peoples that the spiritually minded ones are instantly blessed and shown preference in this world. We may reap what we sow, but the timing of that reaping rests in the infinite wisdom of the Almighty and not in the possession of mortals.

"Detribalize religion...dogma is the war-paint and battle insignia of the tribes of religion."   T.A.

The following is a poem by an unknown author which is ostensibly about marriage but can apply to our mutual support for, and understanding of, all those in our world.

Understanding

They say a husband and a wife bit by bit
Can rear between their lives a mighty wall
So thick they cannot see with ease through it
Nor can they look across, it stands so tall.
Its nearness troubles them,
And each in his own way
Had longed to find for such a wall
A magic word to say.

So let us build with master art, my dear,
***A bridge of faith** between your life and mine,*
A bridge of tenderness, and underneath
The ties of understanding deep and fine
Till we have reared so many lovely ties
There never will be room for walls to rise.

Author Anne Lamott expresses beautifully how faith practices may inter-mingle in the progress of our lives:

> My coming to faith did not start with a leap but rather a series of staggers from what seemed like one safe place to another. Like lily pads, round and green, these places summoned and then held

me up while I grew. Each prepared me for the next leaf on which I would land, and in this way I moved across the swamp of doubt and fear. When I look back at some of these early resting places—the boisterous home of the Catholics, the soft armchair of the Christian Science mom, adoption by ardent Jews—I can see how flimsy and indirect a path they made. Yet each step brought me closer to the verdant pad of faith on which I somehow stay afloat today.[7]

---

7. Lamott, *Traveling Mercies*, 3.

AN EXPLANATION

CHAPTER 15

An Explanation: Isaac on the altar... and the ram in a thicket

Abraham called the name of that place Jehovah-jireh
[the Lord will provide]...
Gen. 22:14

Why Abraham, Isaac, and the ram?

THE LAST THING in the world that Christian Scientists might imagine is that either their children or themselves would be sacrificial offerings to God. Christian Scientists see in their faith-practice safety from the threat of danger or death, healing for life's ills, and a vision of God who is both Wisdom and Love.

So how do Abraham and Isaac enter the picture? For well over a century the stereotype of Christian Science practice as a modern-day form of sacrifice to God has been thrown at members of my church and its founder. This book attempts to deconstruct the basis of that destructive stereotype by challenging church dogma and its resultant malpractice, which has formed a rational basis for the pernicious meme. In this chapter we will take a fresh look at the historical and textual origins of the Abraham-Isaac narrative itself.

Abraham's near-sacrifice of his son Isaac (Gen. 22) stands as the most heart-rending story in the Old Testament. For all the scholarly and religious debate over what might have happened on Mount Moriah where the sacrifice was to take place, the part of the story most neglected by authors, artists, and theologians is the ram in a thicket. While our attention falls on the tormented patriarch, the helpless Isaac, and the upraised blade, a solution to this terrible moral quandary lies nearby—a ram caught among the thorns. The **entry of surprising grace**, too often absent in the early Biblical narratives, reveals to Abraham an unexpected path of sacrifice that rescues the patriarch and his son from disaster.

Thomas Cahill writes: **"It is our lives, not our death that…God wants."**[1] The ram in the Abraham-Isaac narrative introduces divine mercy, the hope of a creative turning point in life—life delivered from a cruel doom. In the incident on Mount Moriah, Bible readers open the pages of a new beginning in humanity's history, an **unexpected, merciful step away from mindless, cultic practice**, an advance in the evolution of worship, an elevation of both thought and practice which rises above the threat of stoic self-destruction.

| I have found a ransom.
| Job 33:24

The ram is the solution in the Genesis story, but the ram represents no spiritual ideal. It is still a blood-sacrifice for the patriarch to make. Abraham feels compelled to perform a very physical alternate sacrifice, although no divine voice or sign demands that to happen (Genesis 22:13). At least Abraham will not kill his own son.

J.R. Dummelow comments, "The substitution of the ram…preserves the spirit which prompted Abraham's act, while at the same time it indicates the objectionableness of human sacrifice."[2] The appearance of the ram to Abraham foreshadows the words of Israel's exilic prophets that were echoed later by Jesus. From Hosea we hear it first: **"I desired mercy, and not sacrifice"** (Hosea 6:6; Matthew 9:13).

The ram embodies a **moral bridge** leading out from savage customs and forming a progressive stage in human and religious development.[3]

---

1. Cahill, *How the Irish*, 141–142. Cahill refers here to the cessation of human sacrifice in Ireland centuries after Abraham.
2. Dummelow, *Bible Commentary*, 30.
3. The notion of child sacrifice to please a deity did not disappear after the age of Abraham. Jephthah's sacrifice of his beloved daughter, told in Judges, Chapter 11, is a tragic recurrence of the compulsion to offer living innocence to in some way honor God. There are also a few other biblical references to children being made to "pass through the fire" (e.g. Jeremiah 32:35) alluding to sacrifices to Molech, the pagan deity associated with child sacrifice. According to Otto Eissfeldt, the 7th-century B.C.E. reforms under Josiah abolished child sacrifice.

If there is a God that is Love itself, then there is a stern mandate from heaven: **this moral bridge out of self-destruction must forge a final and one-way exodus**. Fathers and mothers may sacrifice themselves or their interests for that of their children, but not the other way around.[4] Religious practice must ascend and leave behind barbarity.

As firmly as Lot was wrested by angelic hands out of a chaotic, violent community (Genesis 19), as securely as the infant Moses was shielded from a pharaoh's destructive power, as the wheat is stored and the weeds burned, so **the God that is Love demands the protection of the innocent and in no way makes a child's fate a test of whether a father loves his deity or not**. The test question for Isaac's father ends up being not how much Abraham is willing to destroy in order to serve his God but **how closely is Abraham willing to listen to the saving message from a God that is a God of the living**.

The prophet Micah poses a fearsome query: "Shall I give my firstborn for my transgression, the fruit of my body for the sin of my soul?" Then he answers this agonizing question with an encompassing definition of moral and religious conduct: "He [God] hath shewed thee, O man, what is good; and what doth the Lord require of thee but to do justly, and to love mercy, and to walk humbly with thy God" (Micah 6: 7, 8). This answer implies that the era of child-sacrifice is nearing its end, since it never had a purposeful or merciful place in worship.

A century or more after the prophet Micah, Jeremiah specifically denounces the burning of the sons and daughters of the Baalites to honor their deity Molech. In the words of the Lord: **"…a thing I never ordered, a thing that never entered my mind, this abominable practice that led Judah into crime!"** (Jeremiah 32:35 Moffatt). So how could a practice abominable to the God of Jeremiah and the God of Micah have been a reliable litmus test of faith to the God of the dutiful Abraham—the spiritual forefather of those later prophets, and spiritual "first-father" of the Hebrew people?

---

4. Eddy, *S&H*, 518:14. "…the higher always protects the lower."

Was God behind Abraham's temptation?

The divine command, as related in Genesis 22:2, is explicit in directing Abraham to take the son whom he loves and to offer him as a burnt offering.

If we assert that every word of Scripture is divinely inspired, there is no evading the stamp of divine authority on the command to kill Isaac. In the Christian Gospels, Jesus was tempted by the devil in the wilderness with unreasonable requests that ran absolutely contrary to the well-being of the Messiah's mission and that mission's integrity, but Jesus answered those temptations by refuting them. In Genesis, we see Abraham acceding to the terrible command without an obvious word of protest, though surely his heart must have been overwhelmed in anguish and turmoil.

If we, as strangers, are immersed in a foreign community or in a sensual era that is engaged in a cultic practice, **it may be hard to distinguish our own impulses from our neighboring influences**. Wouldn't any of us, given certain surroundings, be capable of doing what we would never do in another environment?

Alternative explanation 1

It wasn't God that was demanding the killing of Isaac, but more likely **it was Abraham's surrounding culture** that subtly implanted that deadly notion in the patriarch's mind. From commentary in the *Interpreter's Bible*: "Here was a great soul living in a crude age. He saw people around him offering up their children to show their faith and their obedience to false gods."[5] Was Abraham too close to the noise of his neighbors' battle? Was he moved by that noise to do the unthinkable?[6]

---

5. From Quartz Hill School of Theology (California): "Philo (Hellenistic Jewish philosopher c. 25 BCE–c. 50 CE) portrays El (the Canaanite Father God of the ancient Near East period) as a bloody tyrant, whose acts terrified all the other gods, and who dethroned his own father, murdered his favorite son, and decapitated his own daughter…(T)he astounding characteristic of Canaanite deities, that they had no moral character whatsoever, must have brought out the worst traits in their devotees and entailed many of the most demoralizing practices of the time, such as sacred prostitution, child sacrifice and snake worship."
6. Laan, *Prophets and Kings,* 28. "At times of crisis, Baal's followers sacrificed their children, apparently the firstborn of the community, to gain personal prosperity. The Bible calls this practice 'detestable' (or abominable) (Deut. 12:31, 18:9–10). God specifically appointed the tribe of Levi as his special servants, or place of the firstborn of the Israelites, so they had no excuse for offering their children (Numbers 3:11–13). The Bible's repeated condemnation of child sacrifice shows God's hatred of it, especially among his people."

The *Interpreter's* commentary continues: "In spite of the torment to his [Abraham's] human love he could not help hearing an inward voice asking him why he should not do as much; and because that thought seemed to press upon his conscience *he thought it was the voice of God.*"[7] Today we might call this phenomenon herd mentality, or herd thinking.

A moral crevasse opens wide between hearing what one believes is the voice of the deity, and the actual signature of the divine leading. Sages through the centuries have listened patiently to discern the difference between a surrounding influence, as opposed to a higher, what we may call divine, guidance. In the wilderness, the prophet Elijah apparently could distinguish the "still, small voice" of the authentically divine message from the anger and destruction embodied in the wind, earthquake, and fire (I Kings 19).

Alternative explanation 2
It was a **tempting thought apart from God that suggested to Abraham that he should sacrifice his son**. So the notion of Abraham's sacrifice of Isaac originated neither from God nor from Abraham's surrounding society. There is a fascinating version of the Abraham-Isaac narrative contained in the Dead Sea Scrolls that contradicts the more orthodox and familiar Old Testament translations. In the Dead Sea Scrolls' version of Genesis, the **"Prince of Malevolence (Mastemah) came [to G]od, and brought his animosity to bear against Abraham because of Isaac."**[8]

The text goes on to imply that Mastemah is the source of the suggestion to kill Isaac, the motive being some form of devilish jealousy. Is there a parallel between this Bible account and the narrative in the Book of Job (Job 1:6–12) where Satan goads the Lord into afflicting Job in order to try Job's faithfulness? The Gospel temptation of Jesus in the wilderness (Matthew 4) also involves the devil's temptations, but there is no direct assent from God.[9] Similar to the orthodox interpretation of

---

7. Laymon, *Interpreter's Bible*, Vol. 1, p. 643. Emphasis added.
8. Wise, *Dead Sea Scrolls*, 262.
9. Matthew 4:1. The Spirit "leads" Jesus into the wilderness of temptation but does not communicate with nor collude with the tempter.

Abraham's trial, this second alternative explanation of Abraham's motivation suggests that the divine can co-conspire with a demonic force. This leaves us with a disturbing question: **Can God fall "under the influence"** and work with a countervailing power to potentially undermine the very creation?

Alternative explanation 3

Abraham deep down remained confident that God would somehow protect Isaac and his father in this terrible dilemma. Was Abraham willing to begin to go through with what he was told to do because of his **certainty of divine rescue?**

> He trusted on the Lord that he would deliver him.
> Ps. 22:8

When Abraham instructed his servants not to follow him to Mount Moriah, he added, "I and the lad will go yonder and worship, and come again to you" (Genesis 22:5).[10] Abraham may not have had any idea how his rescue would take place, but could these words imply that he trusted that deliverance would happen? Is Genesis 22:5 adequate proof of Abraham's confidence? The author of Hebrews writes that Abraham "believed that God could raise his son up, even if he were dead" (Hebrews 11:19 J.B. Phillips).

Whatever may be our interpretation of Abraham's trial on Mount Moriah, fresh moral and religious ground is broken there in the ultimate outcome. **Mercy and grace are found outpacing the brutal and pointless.**

Ritual sacrifice is a blood-giving, but the mercy and sacrifice embodied by Jesus in a later age is a self-giving that sacrifices not other mortals or a favored animal, but one's own cherished ways, human will, and, in Jesus' case, his own life. The submission of Jesus to the crucifixion was not blind compliance with a mindless command but a deed, forged out of a great mental struggle and pure purpose, and done for the progress of the world.

What cannot be justified

So is there a moral or theological basis for seeing God as the cause in the near-sacrifice of Isaac at the hands of his human father? Theologians

---

10. Berlin, *Jewish Study Bible* commentary, 46. "He (Abraham) may be expressing his profound trust in God's promise, casting his faith and hope as a prediction."

have struggled for centuries to arrive at this conclusion or to challenge it.

We can understand Abraham's attempted sacrifice of Isaac in the context of a child-sacrificing world, but we cannot justify it. We cannot justify God proposing such a thing for the following reasons:

- That threatening suggestion or command acts in conflict with a God of life, mercy, blessing, and protection ever-acting on behalf of those needing protection.
- It violates the near-universal moral teaching— "Thou shalt not kill."
- And it grossly offends the universal trust of an innocent child in parent-wisdom. This point is true, whether a person's trust is invested in a human parent or a divine Being.

Therefore, in the absence of any moral or religious reason for God suggesting the perverse and unthinkable, religious thinkers need to look at a more plausible cause behind the temptation of the patriarch.

The Christ connection

"Surely he has borne our griefs and carried our sorrows."
Isaiah 53:4, ESV

Students of the Abraham-Isaac narrative will differ on how they interpret the divine role, actions, and motive. It is the view of this author that, as the events on Mount Moriah marked the beginning of the end of religiously sanctioned victimhood, so Jesus Christ, and the power of his life, transformed and uplifted the meaning of sacrifice. To Jesus his self-sacrifice was not a mindless ritual to appease an angry Father-God, nor was his deed solely a vicarious sacrifice for all humanity. His sacrifice embodied a history-shattering action of immense unselfishness. And his sacrifice became a proving ground for the immortality of life and the saving power of the divine.

We can never really know the personal torment which Jesus endured in his self-giving, especially considering that he could quite possibly have escaped his great trial.[11] To imagine that Jesus walked through his

---
11. Matthew 26:53 cites "legions of angels."

torture at Calvary while maintaining an unshaken assurance that his heavenly Father would both rescue him and allow him to escape the world's wrath runs up against the Gospel verse depicting Jesus' final words: "My God, why have you forsaken me?" (Matthew 27:46 TLB) But just as Jesus confronted the religious meaning of the divine law in many ways that set him in conflict with the religious authorities of his day, so he also recast the meaning and purpose behind sacrifice.

The ram symbolizes more than a moral and religious bridge of progress. **Christian scholars have seen in the ram on Mount Moriah, a symbol of Jesus Christ** in his supreme mercy and self-offering at the cross.[12]

Jesus reaffirmed the protection of the innocent in his love for children. He said that it would be better to be pulled down to the bottom of the sea by a millstone than to offend a little child (Matthew 18:6). Many Christians see Jesus' self-sacrifice and death on the cross as imposed by the Master's heavenly Father—a kind of cruel echo of both the Abraham-Isaac narrative and the sacrifice of the paschal lamb in Exodus 12. Isaiah as well as some New Testament texts affirm this theme (see Isa. 53: 4,5,10; Acts 2:23; and Acts 4:28). The author questions that assumption for the following reason:

The Gospel of John presents Jesus' understanding of his sacrifice as self-sacrifice with a moral and vision to it, not the mystifying death of a loyal son at the command of or by the foreknowledge of his Father-God.

> *Therefore doth my Father love me, because I lay down my life, that I might take it again.* **No man taketh it from me, but I lay it down of myself.** *I have power to lay it down,* **and I have power to take it again.** *This commandment have I received from my Father.*
> John 10:17,18

In the midst of Jesus' agony on Calvary, might his courage have been powered by an inner faith that spiritual power could overcome the world's evil even there on that desolate hill, the scene of a most brutal form of hatred? For the author, who is a Christian and Christian Scientist, the ram

---

12. See Clarke, *Commentary on the Bible*, Genesis 22. See also Linden Wolfe's blog, *Captivated by Christ*, which compares the ram's entrapping thorns with Jesus' crown of thorns.

embodies not only the redemption and rescue of Isaac and Abraham, but it points prophetically to **a higher way of faith practice with more divine means and ends**, all of which Christians see in the life of Jesus.

Surprising grace

The most divine solution to a moral quandary is often **an unexpected one**. Our attention is so riveted on our problem or on the goal we are seeking, or the fear we are fleeing, that at first we overlook the saving grace at hand. When Jesus' ministry began, those anticipating a very different messianic figure were disappointed by the arrival of a mere carpenter's son (Matthew 13:55).

Herein is another dimension to the ram figure. When stubborn will becomes entrapped, no amount of effort can rescue mortal, willful misdirection from itself. This is because mortal misdirection must always look outside of itself and its own terror or moral failings to find a solution to its dilemma. Something above our mortal abilities is required to rescue us from life's most cruel occasions. Abraham was shown a way out of a self-destructive, extreme course of action, and that way was natural and simple, but divinely above what Abraham had anticipated or feared.

Was it not grace that enabled him to be receptive of a different direction? When Abraham uttered those amazing words, "Jehovah jireh,"[13] (in Hebrew: "God will provide"), we know that he was willing to be redirected and thus his life-direction and his son were preserved.

To Abraham's eternal credit, he sensed that the ram was his way out of a terrible quandary. God had indeed provided for him, for Isaac, and their spiritual and human progeny. Grace and humility had conquered self-destruction and opened an expansive chapter of reborn life. So the ram is not so much a compromise of Abraham's conviction and principles, but more so **a path of grace**, a grace tinged with the divine mystery of **an unexpected but doable outcome**.

> On the mountain of the Lord, he will give us what we need.
> Gen. 22:14 ERV

---

13. Genesis 22:14, CEB. "Jehovah jireh" has also been translated also as "the Lord is seen."

Out from the thicket

The person of Abraham may no longer be with us, but religious people today still require saving grace to guide them safely away from their surrounding cultures and any dogma that might impel them to act in a self-destructive fashion. The ram of Abraham's surprising discovery shadows us in this book as we explore what that symbol means not just for Christian Scientists but for all of those eager to welcome evolving religious practice.

PROSPERING IN A SCIENTIFIC AGE

CHAPTER 16

❧

Time, place, and receptivity
—how our times and location relate to spiritual healing

TIME:
...the boy Samuel served the Lord by assisting Eli...in those days messages from the Lord were very rare, and visions were quite uncommon.
I Samuel 3:1 NLT

PLACE:
It is recorded that in certain localities [Jesus] *did not many mighty works 'because of their unbelief'* [Matthew 13:58] *in Truth.*
Science and Health, 400:32

CHRISTIAN SCIENTISTS SOMETIMES ASK, "*Why are the healings in our church not as prevalent or as earth-shaking as they were a century ago?*" Thus far we've offered indirect approaches to that question. Here we take a quick dive into a more direct search for an answer.

Time and place are not absolutes. There is an ebb and flow to history. Deeds that seem relatively easy to accomplish and are common occurrences in one age, or in one region, may be very uncommon elsewhere or at another time, though the universal laws of God remain a constant. What can we learn from anomalies of both time and region in relation to the constancy of universal laws?

There are spiritual constants in life, but the *context* in which those constants are lived influences the relative success or failure of human achievement. In his last book about Christian Science, church historian Robert Peel wrote of the need to take into account factors relating to healing such as "the social matrix in which decisions must be made, the family situations, the age, experience, and spiritual readiness of the individual who must make the decision."[1]

To put this in more common terms, **"You gotta know the territory."**[2]

Why did Jesus once say: **"The night cometh when no man can work"**? And why did Mrs. Eddy warn: "…the same 'Mind…which was also in Christ Jesus' must always accompany the letter of Science in order to confirm and repeat the ancient demonstrations of prophets and apostles?" (*S&H* 243:10) Isaiah reads: "Seek ye the Lord while he may be found, call ye upon him while he is near" (Isaiah 55:6).

Is this an elaborate way of making excuses for failure?

No. Recognizing factors of resistance and the relative ignorance in any age helps in mitigating those factors. Taking into account the relative difficulty of a task is not making excuses for not accomplishing that task. It's being realistic about life's circumstances. **But an explanation of a task's degree of difficulty is no excuse for not attempting to perform that task.**

Climbing a mountain in the Himalayas will require a degree of preparation and protection that wouldn't be required in walking over low-lying hills in a local forest preserve. A Christian Scientist takes mental and not just physical factors into account when praying for someone. Factors such as public hostility or community concern about an outbreak of a communicable disease are part of the "territory" that might be included in the prayers of Christian Scientists. These factors could be blithely dismissed by people unfamiliar with prayer work, but they are "safety factors" no different than the need to de-ice an airplane in bad weather.

Was the apostle Stephen not adequately aware of "the territory" when he so outraged a crowd that was already unreceptive to his message that they stoned him to death? (Acts 7) Jesus "knew the territory" when he

---

1. Peel, *Health and Medicine*, 132.
2. Willson, *The Music Man*.

told his brothers that he would be judicious about traveling to Jerusalem, given the hatred of those watching for him in that city (John 7:1–10).

Let's look at a modern example of the significance of where we live and its relation to public health.

The Lithuanian study: location or education?

In One Country, Chronic Whiplash Is Uncompensated (and Unknown)
New York Times[3]

It does matter to your health where you live, but not always for the reasons we expect. The following is a vivid example and tangible evidence of the importance of cultural and societal influences on health. In 1996, the *New York Times* reported a study by a Norwegian neurologist Dr. Harald Schrader and a team of researchers who uncovered the **virtual non-existence of chronic whiplash in** the population of Norway's Baltic neighbor **Lithuania**. The Norwegian study was prompted by an unusually large number of victims of chronic whiplash in Norway (seventy thousand victims in a country of roughly four million).

Dr. Schrader and his colleagues chose Lithuania for their research "because there [was] **no awareness there about whiplash or potential disabling consequences, and no, or very seldom, insurance for personal injury.**" Dr. Schrader's team compared a group of over two hundred Lithuanians whose vehicles had been rear-ended in the previous years with a control group whose numbers had had no auto accidents, and determined that there was no difference between the two groups in relation to chronic pain, though the groups were controlled for age and locality. "**No one in the study group** [those who had been rear-ended] **had disabling or persistent symptoms as a result of the**[ir] **car accident.**"

In Lithuania, unlike Norway at that time, the government paid most medical costs of individuals, there was no habit of personal litigation, drivers did not carry personal-injury insurance, and there was no incentive of financial gain by claiming chronic injury. "**Most Lithuanians, in fact, had never heard of whiplash.**"

3, Grady, "In One Country," *New York Times*, May 7, 1996.

Predictably, when Dr. Schrader's report was released, there was an explosion of criticism from the Norwegian whiplash victims' group that threatened to sue the doctor. This study prompts a number of questions:

- Has the Norwegian-Lithuanian comparison been adapted to the study of the prevalence or rarity of health conditions in other countries?
- Why aren't there more frequent and well-publicized country-to-country comparisons by epidemiologists researching other anomalies and phenomena related to health and disease?
- Is it possible that disease can be seen more often as "regional?" If disease is "regional," then we should be more alert to area-wide influences on health, including education.

Anita Moorjani has written an account of her healing from cancer. In her book, *Dying To Be Me*, Moorjani discusses the potential difference in recoveries from various diseases depending upon a patient's local environment including regional support for any particular approach to healing. She writes, **"Any modality that's wholeheartedly supported by the surrounding culture will be more effective than one without such underlying strength…."** (179). This could be a conclusion to be drawn from the Lithuanian study. Apparently in that Baltic nation not a modality but disbelief or ignorance of a common affliction and its cause and symptoms insulated a national population from the prevalence of that affliction and its symptoms.

The night seasons: uprooted from Jerusalem to Babylon

When the Jews were collectively taken hostage during what has been known as the Babylonian Captivity (ca. 600 BCE), many elements of their national practice changed. With the Temple in Jerusalem destroyed by the victorious Babylonians (586 BCE), animal sacrifice ceased, and synagogues rose into central importance. Teaching and study of the Torah, the singing of psalms, and prayer all altered temple worship.

Are changing societal conditions in the twenty-first century impacting the practice of Christian Science? Christian Scientists have not exactly been taken captive by a foreign power, but it can be argued that the multifold increase in the prominence of conventional medicine has made Christian Scientists feel that over the past hundred years they are living more "in Babylon, than in Jerusalem." The trajectory of human progress throughout history is not a straight, upward-trending line with no bumps or dips in that trajectory. The same holds true for the progress of social and religious movements throughout history.

When Christian Scientists talk about the spirit of healing leaving the early Christian church (S&H 328:14-17), do they imagine that the phenomenon of losing the spirit of healing could ever be repeated in history and possibly happen to their own church? Doesn't history repeat itself or at least rhyme?[4] Mrs. Eddy suggests this possibility of the decline of spiritual healing in our time (e.g. *No and Yes* 19:1-3).

Is the inspiration contained in the Christian Science textbook so clear and powerful that it could forestall any future intrusion of erroneous doctrines, unchristian practices, or demoralization in the church? **"Those who cannot remember the past are condemned to repeat it."**[5] Have Christian Scientists become indifferent to the importance of collective self-knowledge and knowledge of history, including their own, so that they risk repeating the mistakes of Christians in prior generations?

History is a harbor map of rocks and navigable channels and tides. A sea captain can guide his ship by the stars and believe that he needs no map and yet still wreck his craft on a long-forgotten reef. As a religious body, have Christian Scientists recognized that the social environment in which their denomination originated has changed significantly since 1910? Mrs. Eddy recognized that **different times require different approaches judging by her numerous adjustments to church practices**. In our church hymnal are the words of James Russell Lowell's poem: "New occasions teach new duties. Time makes ancient creeds uncouth."[6]

Here are some examples of **Mrs. Eddy's grasp of the impact that different eras have on the relative health of people**. She wrote the following in reference to common opinions about digestion in earlier times:

---

4. Inaccurately attributed to Mark Twain; source uncertain.
5. Santayana, *Life of Reason*, 284.
6. *Christian Science Hymnal*, 258.

"A man's belief was not so severe upon the gastric juices" (*S&H* 75:23–24). Does this not suggest that education may cause fluctuations in public views of and treatment for any number of diseases?

"Different dreams and different awakenings betoken [signify] differing consciousness" (*S&H* 82:27–28).

Mrs. Eddy seems to be acknowledging in these passages that human attitudes and beliefs change through the centuries, and today we should not be surprised to see that evolution in thinking continue. Consider this more explicit statement: "Entire immunity from the belief in sin, suffering, and death **may not be reached at this period**, but we may look for an abatement of these evils; and this scientific beginning is in the right direction" (*S&H* 219:29–32). In naming her discovery and practice a "scientific beginning," she seems to clearly imply that ages will continue in a learning trajectory.

"Until the advancing age admits the efficacy and supremacy of Mind, it is better for Christian Scientists to leave surgery and the adjustment of broken bones…to the fingers of a surgeon…." (*S&H* 401:27). Mrs. Eddy does not anticipate exactly when that progressive age might be, and she acknowledges the difficulties in swimming against the mental current of an era in her statement about Jesus' time: "[I]t was difficult in a material age to apprehend spiritual Truth" (*S&H* 350:17).

There is a reference in *Science and Health* (152:14) to the curing of a case of paralysis by Sir Humphry Davy (1778-1829). Davy's patient had assumed that the famous chemist's insertion of a thermometer into his mouth was a means of cure, and the patient immediately began feeling better. After two weeks of this simple treatment, the man fully recovered from paralysis. This would probably not be possible today in a Western nation where the average patient **because of education and enculturation would deny the possibility of such a placebo-like healing**.

> There are truths which are not for all men, nor for all times. Voltaire (1694–1778) [Attr.]

Along similar lines there are many references in the Christian Science textbook using words such as "increasingly," "to the degree of," and "in proportion to," which all suggest to the reader that what is learned of Christian Science will be applicable dependent on such factors as individual commitment, faith, spiritual understanding, and surrounding conditions. These words and phrases convey the natural ebb and flow of surrounding conditions potentially affecting the treatment of patients, and we ignore that potential fluctuation to our detriment. Do Christian Scientists desire to dwell in a world of absolute human stability wherein what has happened before or elsewhere is easily repeatable in any time and locale? Is that a reasonable expectation?

Healing today in other *places*

Why did Jesus heal more readily in some towns than others, and tell one blind man whom he had healed not to return to his hometown (Mark 8:26)? Should not the significance of **"thought-weather" be taken into account?**

St. Joseph of Cupertino—a spiritual phenomenon How would he be treated today?

Outside of the Catholic Church not many are familiar with St. Joseph of Cupertino. He was a fascinating figure whose lifespan included the first six decades of the seventeenth century. As a young man from the southeastern "bootheel" of Italy, Joseph felt deep spiritual yearnings, but his lack of education and apparent slowness of mind at first prevented him from becoming a priest. However, sincerity and persistence eventually won him the favor of church officials, and he was welcomed into the priesthood, circa 1625. What was especially unique about Joseph was his inclination to ecstatic inspirations wherein he **levitated even to the treetops**, often in the presence of his fellow priests and, at times, witnessed by visitors even including a cardinal from Rome. Joseph was so deeply involved in his ecstatic experiences that he was oblivious to onlookers.

His tendency to levitate, not always at the most appropriate times, caused Joseph to be **transferred from one monastery to another**. His levitating, though inspiring to many, was seen as a distraction from priestly duties in the eyes of Joseph's superiors.

How would Joseph be treated if he were living in our age? There were times in his adult life when the levitating didn't happen. Would trance-like flying be impossible in the West in our cynical era? During Joseph's time, he was looked upon with suspicion, and was even reported to the Inquisition[7] whose henchmen were apt to condemn as a witch anyone associated with flying. Joseph is considered to be the patron saint of aviators, astronauts, air travelers, people with a mental handicap, test takers, and poor students.

> **Every chapter of history has the capacity to illustrate, forewarn, and encourage other chapters of the human story.**

When to adapt to one's culture? When to take a stand?

No church, no religious teaching, nothing but our own conscience can answer the questions of when to "come out and be separate" and when to yield to the demands of our environment. A friend of mine was praying about the proper alignment of his broken leg and found healing of his injury without having a cast put on or having the leg set by a doctor. Another person might well have been more cautious and asked for medical assistance. It's the author's belief that **self-knowledge gained through prayer helps determine what anyone can or should attempt to heal through prayer.**

What is the right time and place?

Only God and our conscience know the answer to that question about time and place. "The methods of our Master were *in advance of the period in which he personally appeared;* but his example was right, and is available at the right time…remember that [Christian] Science is demonstrated by degrees, and our demonstration rises only as we rise in the scale of being" (*Mis.* 359:20–26, emphasis added).

Mrs. Eddy further cautions: "Peter's impetuosity was rebuked [re-

---

7. The Inquisition failed to find Joseph guilty of anything, and he was then assigned to the Sacro Convento in Assisi. While being close to the tomb of St. Francis delighted Joseph, he apparently fell into a spiritual drought of sorts, and experienced no levitating flights during this time.

garding Peter's attempt to walk on water]. He had to learn from experience; so have we" (*Mis.* 359:19–20).

This book does **not in any way endorse a new dispensationalism which would dictate that spiritual healing can only happen at a set period when the collective consciousness of an era or locality is spiritually mature and receptive enough for the touch of heaven to occur**. On the contrary, we believe that, while certain times in history appear more enlightened than others, still spiritual or divine healing can happen and has happened throughout the centuries, including in very materialistic eras. Individuals such as Joseph of Cupertino in some way were "being a law to themselves"—**a law of immunity, or exceptionalism to the trend of thought and practices of their age**.[9]

Those who advocate for spiritual healing should be aware that in different times and locations **receptivity to divine action will vary, and that receptivity or lack of it may affect their practice**.

All that said, the words of Martin Luther King resound in all ages: "The time is always right to do what is right."[10] King seconded that thought in a talk at the National Cathedral three years later when he said, "Time is neutral. It can be used either constructively or destructively."[11]

While it is important to understand the varying mental states and climate of an age or region, that is **no excuse for a Christian or a Christian Scientist to not exercise the discipline and expression of prayer regardless of the environment, the particular time, or location in which they live.** Again, maintaining awareness of our surroundings should never be an excuse for spiritual

> When the time is ripe for certain things, they appear at different places in the manner of violets coming to light in early spring.[12]

---

8. Dispensationalism is a religious approach to or analysis of the Bible that sees God as allotting certain events and actions to defined periods of history and doing this according to a larger all-encompassing divine plan.
9. Romans 2:14. We employ a slightly different meaning with this phrase than the way in which Paul used it in his letter to the Christians at Rome. See also Chapter 19 "The Law and Saul's Armor."
10. In a speech delivered at Oberlin College, Oct. 22, 1964.
11. King, "Awake Through a Great Revolution," March 31, 1968.
12. Li, *An Introduction to Kolmogorov Complexity*, 1st ed., p. 8. Farkas Bolyai (Hungarian mathematician 1775-1856) wrote this to his son Janos, urging him to claim the invention of non-Euclidean geometry.

inability or weakness anymore than bad weather justifies remaining indoors when work must be done outside, rain or shine. We gauge the tone of our environment so we can intelligently deal with it, work around its obstacles, and encourage others to work wisely as well.

Some remaining questions:
- What is the "night...when no man can work"? (John 9:4) Is it a particular time that is hard for Christians or Christian Scientists? Or is it a time when spiritual work of any kind is impossible? How do you pray or work around what seem to be insurmountable conditions?
- As we cited earlier, Mrs. Eddy identified a time when thought acted less "severe[ly] upon the gastric juices."[13] Does the collective consciousness of today "act severely" upon the brain?
- Is there more or less fear of contagion in our era than years ago? Does the prevalence of vaccination lessen the fear of contagious maladies or does it produce an unreliable trust only when there is a well-vaccinated public?

"...the age in which he [Jesus] lived..."

Mrs. Eddy was not reluctant to critique her church's magazine editors. In 1905 she corrected an editorial by Annie Knott in this way:

...you speak of our great Master [Jesus] eschewing [shunning] the use of material remedies'...(R)ecall his use of clay to anoint the eyes of the blind...(t)**he age in which he lived required what he did, and his wisdom caused his concession to its requirements in some instances.**[14]

The following chapter and ones after it provide examples both of how Christian Scientists have adapted to and can adapt to and bless the age in which they live.

---

13. Eddy, *Science and Health*, 175:23.
14. L04756 11/8/1905 courtesy of Mary Baker Eddy Library

CHAPTER 17

The 1902 "Change of Front"
—an unknown compromise

The prudent see danger and take refuge.
                                        Proverbs 27:12 NIV

The righteous are bold as a lion.
                                        Proverbs 28:1

HAVE CHRISTIAN SCIENTISTS as a whole ever compromised on medical issues? Yes. But few people know that. There was a time early in the church's history when Mrs. Eddy urged upon all of her somewhat reluctant followers a large-scale compromise regarding the medical versus non-medical treatment of patients.

In the fall of 1902 Mrs. Eddy changed the practice of Christian Science. There had been two large outbreaks of diphtheria in which hundreds of people died in the states of New York and California. Two victims in the outbreaks were the young patients of Christian Science practitioners. Both practitioners in quite separate cases were subsequently charged with manslaughter, but they were ultimately not convicted. No doctors were brought to trial over the other hundreds of deaths. What took place were two trials, one in White Plains, New York, and another in Los Angeles.

The Los Angeles case was described in the February 1903 *Christian Science Journal* several months after the case was settled. What we read there are thirty-five pages of supportive testimony consisting of various healings submitted for the court record by local Christian Scientists. Though the charges against the Los Angeles parents were serious and the situation a tragedy, the wave of healing testimonies supporting the Christian Science position did appear to briefly boost the church's cause. The White Plains case was another matter.

The White Plains case

If the Los Angeles case had been the first shoe falling, it was only a light slipper. The White Plains case fell like a large, heavy boot. Newspaper coverage portrayed a squirm-in-your-seats examination of the accused practitioner blazoned on the front pages of the *New York Times* only days after the death of seven-year-old Esther Quinby,[1] the daughter of two Christian Scientists.

The prosecutor grilled, baited, and toyed with John Lathrop, the practitioner. The back and forth questioning is as hard for Christian Scientists to read today as it must have been for Mrs. Eddy to see in the *Times* over a century ago. It's important to note that the practitioner had spiritually treated the mother, her daughter Bessie (who recovered from diphtheria), and the second daughter Esther who died.

Q: What condition did you find Bessie in?
A: *I found her under the claim of tonsillitis.* [Later determined to be diphtheria]

Q: What is tonsillitis according to your belief?
A: *Merely a mortal belief.*

Q: What is cancer?
A: *I would say that cancer was a belief of the human mind made manifest on a human body.*

Q: How about a broken leg?
A: *The same.*

---

1. The family name appears in the *New York Times* and other newspapers misspelled as "Quimby." *The Boston Herald* spells it accurately "Quinby," as do official branch church records.

Q: **What is consumption? Is the treatment the same in that case as in the case of a broken leg or cancer?**
A: *Yes.*

Q: **Do you believe that food is necessary to sustain life?**
A: *We believe as did Jesus in that respect, that is, that man does not live by bread alone, but by every word that proceeds out of the mouth of God.*

Q: **Do you think that a man can live without food, if he was high enough in Christian Science?**
A: *He probably could if he was spiritually high enough, although food would be needed in some material form.*

Q: **To what do you ascribe the death of little Esther Quimby [sic]?**
A: *Nothing from a Christian Science point of view, although I suppose from your view it was real.*

Q: [After this last retort, the prosecutor showed his growing frustration]: **Talk plainly; this scientist lingo is like a foreign language to us who are not in the fold.**[2]

Perhaps some of what the practitioner said in court would have made sense to Christian Scientists. Many church members today would question Lathrop's answers, including what he said about the nature of his treatments for various ailments being all the same. More significantly church members today might be astounded at the cavalier condescension in Lathrop's last remark to the attorney, cited above.

Paul urges those who speak in tongues to make sure that an interpreter is present, and in the absence of a clear interpretation, to keep silent in church (I Cor. 14:28). Unfortunately, John Lathrop lacked both an interpreter of his testimony as well as the ability to avoid shaky verbal and spiritual ground "where angels fear to tread." Elsewhere in his court examination Lathrop claimed to know one risen from the dead. This elicited an excited, if mocking and sarcastic, sub-headline halfway through the *Times* article: "Once Dead Person Now Alive!"

---

2. *New York Times*, October 24, 1902, p. 1.

What added to the hurtful weight of John Lathrop's ill-considered words were his mother's additional remarks, blurted out loud after the charges against her son were read in court. The *Times* reported that Laura Lathrop smiled and then dropped the following bombshell on the audience:

> While we do not welcome prosecution, yet we know it will do us great good. It gives us a chance to tell our belief, and that sets people to thinking. Once the people get thinking, they buy our books, and the result is that they are converted to Christian Science. We have nothing against medicine; it has served its day, and Christian Science is the only true treatment. This case…like all others… will…redound to our own good and the glory of God.[3]

So on the front pages of the *Times* of October 24, 1902, was a template for how not to present a serious religion. Christian Science or anything else that you want others to sympathize with or understand. Exaggerated claims? They are there. Red meat for your opponents to seize upon? There. Arrogant boastfulness in the presence of failure? There. The Christian Scientists at the White Plains hearing appeared totally disconnected from their surrounding world, unaware of how inappropriate their words and tone sounded to others. No contrition, no humility, no obvious concern over the deceased and her family, and no self-awareness. Only self-justification, and that, sounding quite absurd to the average newspaper reader.

From our standpoint over one hundred years later, we can only conjecture what Mrs. Eddy's household was thinking when the trial coverage from the *New York Times* arrived in Concord, New Hampshire. But rumblings of unhappiness were quick to surface. A letter from Mrs. Eddy's secretary Calvin Frye, November 4th, noted the "great harm JC Lathrop is doing with his tongue."[4] This letter was sent out after a week when Mrs. Eddy was both attacked in the pulpit by Rev. Charles Parkhurst, and was also threatened to be charged by the New York cor-

---

3. Ibid.
4. L15922 courtesy of Mary Baker Eddy Library.

oner as a principal in the White Plains case. Facing the unchastened mistakes of the Christian Scientists in White Plains and with threats from an irate public lingering in the air, it was clear that action of some kind needed to come from Mrs. Eddy's corner.

On November 5th, Alfred Farlow, writing in the *Boston Times*,[5] began the church's answer to the legal charges with an aggressive, defensive posture. Farlow repeatedly compared the one death of Esther Quinby at the hands of the Christian Scientists to the one thousand deaths under conventional care during the New York diphtheria outbreak, and he challenged the public to note the disparity in numbers, and perhaps to ask if orthodox MDs should not be brought to trial instead. His tone then softened in the direction of deference to the great majority of doctors and their accomplishments on behalf of public health. The stance that Mrs. Eddy was soon to take was not visible in Farlow's letter.

On the following day, November 6th, Mrs. Eddy's surprising view appeared in a three-line comment attached to Archibald McClellan's lead editorial in the *Sentinel*. If the *Sentinel* readers were not looking carefully, they might have missed the statement, since it appeared almost as an after-thought at the article's ending: **"Mrs. Eddy advises, until the public thought becomes better acquainted with Christian Science, that Christian Scientists decline to doctor infectious or contagious diseases"** (*My.* 226).

The wording was careful, a little vague. Did *doctor* mean "treat medically?" No. The note advised church members that they were not to spiritually treat infectious or contagious illness for a time, as was soon made clear. The seriousness of this adjustment in the Christian Science approach was indicated in local papers. The *New York Times* of November 14th trumpeted:

> **'Christian Scientists' Change of Front…'Healers' will not hereafter treat contagious disease**…Mrs. Eddy's 'advice,' it is admitted was doubtless prompted by the action taken in the Quimby [White Plains] case.

---

5. The *Boston Times* allowed liberal space for the views of Christian Scientists.

All the Christian Scientists whom the *Times* interviewed said they would cooperate with Mrs. Eddy's request, but there was an open question as to how they would distinguish what was contagious from what was not.

Was there a rebellion from Christian Scientists to the "edict," as some papers called it? Newspapers portrayed it that way. "**Revolt against 'Mother' Eddy**—Christian Scientists Resent Order Regarding Infection" headlined the *Boston Post* on November 15th, and the writer explained:

> Signs of revolt among the advanced Christian Scientists…Her writings, up to the present time, they cite, have been that their belief could cure all maladies, and that **to eliminate contagious diseases while under fire is a retrogression**. They will not come out in the open and defy the leader, but among themselves it is taken as a disagreeable command to relinquish the treatment of the infectious.

Former judge and church lecturer William Ewing rode on a special train with about sixty fellow Christian Scientists to White Plains, where Ewing pleaded on behalf of the unconditional rights of freedom of worship and practice for his fellow adherents.

Judge Ewing argued in his lecture: "The law furnishes absolute protection to us who are right…There is no law which can prohibit a Christian Scientist from practicing his profession anywhere beneath the sun."[6] Mrs. Eddy termed Judge Ewing's lecture "excellent," but she soon took issue publicly with his contention that the law allowed Christian Scientists free rein to do as they pleased. Three weeks after Mrs. Eddy's initial "advice," an article by her in the *Sentinel* entitled "Wherefore?" elaborated on the compound meaning of her advice. When reading this article, it becomes apparent that Mrs. Eddy's counsel was not limited to a mere retraction of a field of healing. Though there was no backing off in her words about the power of God to heal, **she drove home a**

---

6. *Boston Post*, Ibid. (November 15th) Judge Ewing's contention ignored the Supreme Court's well-known rebuke of the practice of polygamy in 1879—a ruling concerning which Judge Ewing should have been aware. In that case, *Reynolds v. United States*, the high court, citing Thomas Jefferson, noted the ability of courts to restrict religious action or practice which violated civil law, while allowing for religious belief by itself to go unrestricted. Supreme Court rulings such as *Prince v. Massachusetts* (1944) have since that time further restricted religious practice when it threatened the welfare of a child.

message for her congregants to become better acquainted with their own Christian principles and healing capacities just as much as the public needed to understand Christian Science more clearly. She pointed out that practitioners should know what they could or could not successfully treat and to assess their own readiness to heal before diving into a situation.

The article "Wherefore?" indirectly rebutted some of the statements by the Lathrops and Judge Ewing. Mrs. Eddy cautioned church members about what they say, and that, even if they healed a case, they were *"not specially protected by law."* This last statement was highlighted by her in italics. It was a forthright rejection of Ewing's contention that Christian Scientists could practice as they pleased "anywhere beneath the sun."

Conclusion and aftermath

Mrs. Eddy's "advice" was a small, but significant change in the history of the practice of Christian Science. It **did not change the theology of the church** she founded **or the theory behind Christian Science. But it was a timely rebuff to pride, ego, mispractice, and bluster**. It was a clear assertion of rights, with a give-a-little, take-a-little argument.

Sailors call it reefing the sails. When the wind is blowing wildly, there's an urgent need to expose less of the sails' canvas to the storm. According to the *New York Times*,[7] this was the first "change in front" or "retrogression" in the history of the Christian Science Church, and a serious, if temporary, curtailing of the healing activity.[8]

There is no public, historical record of Mrs. Eddy rescinding her advice at a later date, as in, "Now you can take infectious cases again." But

---

7. November 14, 1902.
8. Technically the *Times*' assertion may have been correct. But in the spring of 1888, there had been an incident parallel to the White Plains case. A Christian Science healer Abby Corner was spiritually treating her daughter during childbirth when both the daughter and grandchild died. Mrs. Eddy wrote to the *Boston Herald* rebuking the lack of training or "quackery" of the Christian Scientist (Abby Corner). After the Corner case, Christian Scientists ceased to include the field of obstetrics in what students were taught by their fellow church members. The 1888 "change of front" was not mentioned by the *Times*, though historians have cited it far more frequently than the White Plains case.

once the point had been made to both her students and the world, after a few months the issue was not discussed in the church magazines. We may assume that at least by the spring of 1903, when there was a final reference to the White Plains action in the *Sentinel*, practitioners went back to a more business-as-usual approach.

What is notable, as an aftermath of the White Plains case and Mrs. Eddy's ensuing decision to temporarily restrict the practice of Christian Science, is a series of legal decisions in various American states that endorsed the rights of Christian Scientists. In New Hampshire, North Carolina, and Texas attempts at discriminating against Christian Scientists and their ability to practice were defeated by legislators. Were these cases a coincidence or did they, in part, result from Mrs. Eddy's compromise? That is a question open for further historical exploration.

What is most striking about the 1902 advice of Mrs. Eddy is that **so few Christian Scientists and religious scholars know anything about it**. The incident is indirectly referred to in an article in Mrs. Eddy's prose writings, which most church members have on their bookshelves (*My.* 226-228). With some brief cross-referencing to the *Sentinels* of that era, it is not difficult to grasp what happened and how the church's founder responded.

Historian Stuart Knee briefly mentions the White Plains case in his little-known work *Christian Science in the Age of Mary Baker Eddy*. Stephen Gottschalk refers to the "Wherefore?" article, but does not cite its surrounding circumstances, the legal cases, or the implications of Mrs. Eddy's advice.[9] Other than these isolated references, the question is begged, **"Why would a startling anomaly of religious practice be of so little interest both to the proponents of Christian Science and to the church's critics?"**

Perhaps to those sympathetic to Christian Science, such as biographers Robert Peel, Sibyl Wilbur, and Lyman Powell, Mrs. Eddy's action defied the pre-conceived norm. Was her action too conciliatory to fit into the model of a young, brash church asserting its rights to practice? To ardent followers the Christian Science founder's advice also potentially opened the door to further compromises that, especial-

---

9. Gottschalk, *Rolling Away the Stone*, 350.

ly after her passing, the church was increasingly hesitant to entertain. For this reason, officially church-endorsed books about Christian Science could have shied away from discussing the White Plains "change of front" which the writers believed might have put the church's founder in a conflictual light.

What about unsympathetic biographers, such as Edwin Dakin and Georgine Milmine, and more recent authors such as Caroline Fraser? What stopped them from pouncing on this sensational episode and perhaps seeing it as an instance of waffling inconsistency or hypocrisy by Mrs. Eddy? All that can be offered to explain this historical omission are hypothetical answers.

In the view of impartial sources from that era the White Plains case and Mrs. Eddy's response conveyed the impression of a reasonable religious leader, willing to take public criticism upon herself and steer her followers away from a precipice of self-destruction. The *Chicago Public Reader* carried the following editorial:

> Why is it that so many educated men are so feeble at distinguishing differences? An example occurs to us in connection with the recent proclamation of Mrs. Eddy...in which **she advises her followers to bow before hostile public sentiment** to the extent of allowing the employment of physicians in the treatment of infectious and contagious diseases. It ought to be perfectly plain...that this is no recantation. There is nothing in the proclamation to indicate that Mrs. Eddy has not as much faith as ever in the efficacy of her teachings. On the other hand, **it is a manifest mark of respect for the rights of others**...Her conduct in this matter should command respect... (This editorial was reprinted in the *Sentinel* Dec. 18, 1902)

Mrs. Eddy's motives, as this impartial Chicago editorial suggested, appeared to be transparently constructive and Christian. But was that the image that critical biographers wanted to project about Mrs. Eddy? Most likely not.

It was as if this interlude in church history fell into a pool of cognitive dissonance where **it didn't exist because it was in no one's interest for it to exist**. There is no excuse for this story to not be widely known.

It is not so critical that the foregoing should have been known by Christian Scientists and students of religion in 1902 as it should be known today. It might have greatly benefited Christian Scientists to have been aware of and to have pondered the lessons of this narrative over the past several decades. In the 1980s and early 1990s a series of highly publicized legal cases involving children who died under Christian Science treatment presented a terrifying quandary to church members. If Christian Scientists during that recent troubling period had known of Mrs. Eddy's decision in 1902, it is quite possible that a similar "change of front" could have been fashioned that would have given church parents a different sense of alternatives than what they faced at the time. After all, the White Plains case, together with the one in Los Angeles, were cases involving children and were direct legal precedents and predecessors of what Christian Scientists would struggle with eighty years later.

What if the Board of Directors of the Mother Church had issued something similar to the following in a message to all Christian Scientists in the 1980s?

Dear Church Members and Friends,

In 1902, during a particularly difficult time, our church's founder Mary Baker Eddy sent out a directive (see Miscellany 226-228*) which 'advised' that Christian Scientists, 'until the public thought becomes better acquainted with Christian Science,' turn contagious and infectious cases over to orthodox physicians.*

We look back at that precedent today, and ask you all, that if there is a Christian Science child under your care with a physical illness that does not yield quickly to the prayers of the parents, family, guardians, and/or a practitioner, and the situation appears potentially serious or life-endangering, we encourage the persons involved to promptly confer with a physician and follow that physician's recommendations if necessary, in order to protect the welfare and health of the child.

> *In doing what she did in 1902, Mrs. Eddy made it clear that she was not denying the power and efficacy of prayer or of Truth, God. But she was recognizing that for the long-run prosperity of spiritual healing, for the protection of children, and for the world's understanding of the ethics of Christian Science, and its Christian priorities, occasionally steps may be taken which might not be the norm in all eras, but which are needed to care for our nearest and dearest, to buttress the reputation of Christian Science, and to secure its benefit of healing for present and future generations.*

In 1902, the founder of the Christian Science Church saw her followers severely damaging themselves in court and out of it. She took a leap of faith, or perhaps a calculated risk, and while requesting a step back in the public position of church practice, she took the heat of condemnation upon herself and off the backs of those whose steps were buckling under that weight.

She did not directly, publicly rebuke her students for their missteps, but those mistakes were dealt with in writing indirectly over a period of a few months. Long-range progress was more important to her than any short-term loss or gain. Mrs. Eddy's actions and example at that pivotal time over a century ago confront us today.[10] They raise a number of ethical dilemmas examined in other chapters of this book.

Questions for further discussion:
- Does the White Plains case and its aftermath hint of changes to the practice of Christian Science that might be needed in our time?
- Should any such changes be initiated from the "top-down," i.e. from church headquarters, or can change in religious practice emanate from the "field," or from Christian Scientists not commissioned by the Mother Church?
- What are the limits of concessions that religious organizations of all types can make while still maintaining the spiritual essence of their teachings?

---

10. See Appendix (p. 507) for a timeline of events described in this chapter.

On the way to seeking to do the best thing in life, we may be required by our conscience and by divine leading to do what seems far less than the best, but is the right thing to do.

CHAPTER 18

Getting Isaac off the altar

He shall gently lead those that are with young.
                                                        Isaiah 40:11

WHAT STEPS CAN the Christian Science Church take as an institution to counter the accusation that reliance upon prayer constitutes a potential form of abuse, especially when children are involved? The following are some possible positions that could be circulated among the Christian Science membership and churches: (1) No abuse of children is tolerated by the church, condoned by its teachings, or is acceptable to its members and adherents. "Abuse" includes **any actions or inaction that could put the life or safety of a child in jeopardy**. Christian Scientists should be willing to conform to any state requirements that might require physical examinations of children to ensure that no abuse is taking place. (2) No teaching associated with Christian Science should imply that children or their parents are expected to be "test subjects" of the possibilities of prayer. To the contrary, safety precautions similar to those put forward for the Maine legislature in 2005 (see Chapter 24, pp. 412–414) could be standard expectations for all parents, Christian Science nurses, and practitioners.

Further necessary precautions could encourage Christian Science parents to consult with a physician if they had any question as to whether their child's health was in jeopardy. (3) Christian Scientists in the United States could begin to re-examine the function and desirability of legal exemptions (see Chapter 19) as they relate to compulsory examinations, vaccinations, and other requirements that are common in American civil statutes but which our church has considered objectionable.

Is this capitulation or compassion for all?

Would greater conformity to civil law negatively impact the progress of Christian Science and spiritual healing and lessen the reliance on God for healing in the lives of Christian Scientists? The case study we examined in the previous chapter suggests that **conformity to the minimal expectations of national laws regarding children** (and also seniors under the care of an adult child or guardian) might reduce animosity aimed at our church without unnecessarily compromising the beliefs of Christian Scientists. At present in countries and American states where children are required to see a doctor if they are ill, Christian Science parents need to make sure they are keeping alert, and that their healing work is effective. Parents in all the United States could be asked to follow this lead or do something comparable.

Answering the tough questions

Just as Abraham was guided out of his frightening moral dilemma to an answer that he named *Jehovah jireh* ("God will provide"), so Christian Scientists can be led to actions that allow them to adhere to their core principles while meeting society's basic legal requirements of its citizens.

There are Christly answers to the world's toughest "what-if" questions and accusations that underlie criticism by others of Christian Science practices. Several years ago, on his national television show[1] Larry King asked a Christian Science church official the "what-if" question seven times in the same interview in different ways: *"What if your prayers are not working?"* King pointedly brought up this question in relation to prayers for children. Granted, it's very difficult to give a calm, complete answer to a question like that in front of a fast-talking media professional. That question is related to our chapter's heading: "Getting Isaac 'off the altar.'" The altar is a position of danger that some portion of the American public sees in our faith practice. Although a share of public opinion in the United States believes that Christian Scientists are willing to sacrifice their children for their belief system,

---

1. "Larry King Live," May 4, 2001.

Christian Science parents totally reject that notion and see their faith practice as inherently the best care they can offer for their family.

In defending and explaining Christian Science to others, it is wholly appropriate to tell of healing experiences we have had through prayer, but it's also proper to point out the various safeguard provisions outlined in our church writings which we have cited in this book—provisions dealing with surgery, pain relief, obeying the demand for compulsory vaccinations, conferring with physicians, and temporary or material means when prayer has not healed an individual.

Airplane passengers relax when they know that there are oxygen masks within reach and flotation cushions under their seat, and those passengers are shown on every flight how to use them—despite the chances of a plane crash being very slight. By our church members properly and fully answering, both in theory and example, the safety provisions that we have in our church teachings, the albatross that has hung about the neck of Christian Scientists can begin to be lifted off. This is being honest and merciful not just to our own people, but to a sometimes bewildered public. The author does not believe that the general public will be persuaded to accept all the basic premises of Christian Science just because of this shift in approach by the Christian Scientists. The author hopes that possibly by what is presented in these pages a religious teaching can become more understandable.

Is every child's illness a faith-test like Elijah's challenge to the prophets of Baal?

Of course not. Scriptural narratives such as the account in I Kings 18, where Elijah confronts the prophets of Baal to prove or disprove the power of Baal as opposed to the power of Elijah's God, do not have to serve as faith-models for Christian Science parents whenever their child has an illness. The following words from the daughter of a practitioner give a counterbalance to any fearful belief that parents or any Christian Scientist may entertain that makes them feel driven to "prove" themselves or their religious conviction through their child's experience:

> *As a Christian Science practitioner, my mother would tell parents of children who phoned her for prayer, 'If the child does not respond within 'x' amount of time, then find another practitioner or take the child to the hospital/doctor.' She did not believe in compromising the lives of children especially when they would not understand and were not in a position to dictate what kind of care they should be given.*

Sometimes there are relatively simple solutions and occasional concessions, to handle health problems with kids. Christian Scientists are not the only ones who can be unknowing of their children's health needs, but there is no spiritual excuse for letting a child's extended or serious illness go unimproved by that child's parents or guardians. We can get Isaac "off the altar." A child and the parents of a child should absolutely not be on the ramparts of our faith battles. If a child's illness is not quickly dealt with by the parents while working with a practitioner, or praying by themselves for their child, it would be wise to visit a doctor with the child.

From a Christian Science parent: "**In the 1980s** [during the time when there were several legal cases against Christian Science parents] **our burden fell on the young, tender parents. What England has in the way of laws that require a doctor's visit can protect parents like these from endangering their children and themselves.**"[2]

The responsibility of the village

An opinion column ran in the *New York Times* six years ago promoting the idea that Christian Scientists should be able to claim legal exemption from national health care practices for themselves and their children. The writer, a Christian Science practitioner, added that this accommodation should apply "in all cases no matter how serious."[3] The column brought out a host of angry emails in response, nearly all of which mocked the idea of spiritual healing, especially when it involved children.

---

2. The author is not convinced that the United Kingdom has current laws that require a doctor's visit.
3. "Let Us Follow Our Beliefs in Caring for Children," *New York Times*, 3-11-2015.

Jesus warned Peter (Matthew 17:24–27) from offending those public officials who don't understand your belief system. So today, if our public words cause large-scale offense, should we not adjust our approach? In 1902, Mrs. Eddy pointed out to Christian Scientists that they could not expect always to be protected by the civil law (*My.* 227:20, cited in our previous chapter). Have we considered Mrs. Eddy's counsel and Jesus' words to Peter, as we explain our faith practice to a questioning public?

One response to the practitioner's opinion column in the *Times*, cited above, was critical but positive in its tone:

> While I respect your perspective, I must disagree. My mother was introduced to Christian Science when I was very young and I was in Sunday school until age 18. I then went to church. While I learned that God loved and cared for me, my mother never used the exemption from medical practices. Her faith in God was unwavering, but she felt it was wrong to put others in jeopardy. She had me vaccinated against measles, chicken pox, and everything else. She knew God would heal her and this often happened. One thing we talked about before she died was that **too many people in the Christian Science Church try to do at the beginning of their understanding what Jesus did at the end of his** [see *Mis.* 215:23–29]. Relying on prayer completely is a step-by-step process/journey, not a leap from the bottom to the top.

Shepherds and guides

In our church are we adequately shepherding those who are entrusted to our spiritual care? It's one thing for Christian Scientists to say that our parents are not coerced by the church to turn to prayer and reject medical help. That is formally true. It is also true that our members have choice in these matters. But those assurances fail to deal with the fact that for decades we have suggested, implied, and recommended in our publications and in talks and members' conversations with practitioners that a Christian Scientist who goes to doctors is somewhat less than a full-fledged Christian Scientist.[4] The composite body of church articles, whether recent or written decades ago, that oppose anything but a total rejection of medical treatment under any circumstances constitutes a cache of peer pressure and education that is not easily overturned by words from our church's spokespeople that have suggested in recent years a more compliant or nuanced view about resorting to medicine.

It is commendable that we now say clearly and publicly that our church members have a choice about how to handle their own personal health situations, with no dictation or pressure from the church, but we must say and do more. We must deeply and sincerely apologize and ask for forgiveness from those whom we have wronged when our church used words like "forbidden," referring to the possibility of church members using any medicine.[5] We must apologize and ask for forgiveness from those whom we told needed to "restore their status" as Christian Scientists if they sought out medical care in an urgent situation.[6] What form could be best employed to voice apologies of this kind that cover a large period of time?

As for branch churches that have by-laws to this day that exclude from membership gay people and those using medicine, what's to be said? Maybe we could remind these churches that if Mrs. Eddy was alive today, any church excluding potential members over the issue of medicine essentially would have turned their back on the woman who wrote *Science and Health*, since during the last decade of her life she employed morphine on several occasions. Branch churches are autonomous, so they don't all have to dance to the same tune, but discrimination, for reasons of sexual orientation, race, and so on, is wrong. Our church headquarters has a duty to make that very plain to all within its membership.

---

4. See chapters 4 and 9. See also Rosten, *Religions in America*, 45.
5. Ibid. See also *C. S. Sentinel*, July 12, 1952, p. 1225.
6. Ibid. See also Rosten, *Religions in America*, 45.

Feeling safe

Simon Sinek is a motivational speaker whose TED talks have received much attention. In his presentation "Why good leaders make you feel safe" Sinek highlights two basic features of sound leadership that are very similar to the kind of shepherding recommended by Jesus in the New Testament. He says that (1) good leaders create an environment in their organizations where their employees feel supported and safe, and (2) they assure employees that their bosses would do anything for their workers. Jesus spells out a similar message in Chapter 10 of the Gospel according to John: "I am the good shepherd and know my sheep, and am known of mine" (v. 14). "The good shepherd giveth his life for the sheep" (v. 11). That chapter relates how the good shepherd goes "before the sheep," leading by example and precedent.

What spiritual leadership and protectorship means

For the Christian Science flock to feel truly safe, there are two special areas of need that have become apparent in recent decades. There are potentially vulnerable "sheep" who need to feel safer as Christian Scientists—our seniors and our parents with their young children. The shepherding hand of our church must be there for those in their senior years who should know that their church will give all for them, with only secondary concern over financial issues involved. Too many older Christian Scientists feel adrift in the sea of the American health-care system. The shepherding hand of their church is not sufficiently visible and tangible, leaving them in an uncertain limbo when it comes to decisions about private insurance plans, Medicare, and family help. For many seniors this is not working out well because of the expense of medical care, and uncertainty about what and how much support seniors can expect from their fellow church members.

Mrs. Eddy in her last years tried to get her Board of Directors to provide facilities for older folks and especially for those who were ill with little ability to pay. Six years after her passing the first "benevolent" home opened near Boston. Since that time sanatoriums for older

Christian Scientists have sprung up around the United States and in other countries, but the demand has tended to exceed the church's ability to provide support that was affordable for members in need. To this author, the problem appears to be one of misplaced priorities. There are efforts prior to the publishing of this book that have developed and are utilizing a large funding pool for the nursing and practitioner needs of senior Christian Scientists. These steps are very encouraging and inspiring to this author.

Shouldn't the care for our elders be as paramount as the fourth commandment to honor our fathers and mothers? Too much time and money has been spent on our church buildings and not enough on this crucial area of human need.

Another area of need for positive shepherding involves our parents with young children. Have there been changes in church approaches, attitudes, and possibly policies that have developed since the 1980s that could help prevent a recurrence of what the church, and especially its young members with children, went through three decades ago? Surely we have learned since that time how to better support those who are anxious about any problem they may face with their children's health. It would reassure church members for all of us to point out exactly what we have learned and hopefully have improved in our practice to prevent a repeat of that difficult period.

Examples of the "gold standard" of shepherding

In the following two instances, one of which involves a persistently caring individual and another that illustrates supportive love from our church headquarters, we see the spirit of shepherding that really works. While neither situation directly touches upon the interface of Christian Science, children, and the law, these examples of tender, persistent love and merciful "shepherding" depict the spirit that has succeeded and healed over the generations:

> My brother's kids grew up with some serious problems, but
> they grew through them thanks to my mother's loving support

regardless of their situations. My oldest nephew was deeply involved in hard drugs, and got into dealing them in his early high school years. He was busted in a police raid at his school as a "kingpin," but, thanks to a lenient judge and family lawyer, was sentenced to mandated residential treatment. My niece was hanging around with a dangerous gang and got arrested and sent to a special school for her involvement in a gang fight. My other niece was doing great in school and soccer (and headed for a college athletic scholarship) but ran away with a man several years her senior who emotionally abused her and had little money to support them.

As you can imagine the parents went through a seesaw of overreacting with punishments and at times looking the other way. They also were plagued with guilt and confusion over what to do. The one steadfast support through it all was **my mother's non-judgmental listening and caring**. Many people turned to her joyful and buoyant spirit when distressed. Her grandchildren also came to her regularly to confide their problems and feel some love. They would acknowledge, "I always feel good around mom-mom," and "I could tell her anything." My mother would tell me that her Christian Science faith enabled her **to discern and trust an embracing love at work, God's love**. It was more than just a personal "big heart." She was living the love her faith taught, not just talking or thinking it. She would say, Christian Science is "aflame with divine Love." It's the "tender word and Christian encouragement" that make the difference.

There was a long road between then and now, but all my brother's adult children are currently living loving and caring lives, with their significant troubles long in the past— married with kids of their own and helping others to avoid their problems. Their aim in the past was to live as far away from their parents as they could. Indicative of their change is that they all live near their parents and support them, and vice versa, in a tight family bond. And most of all, they each pay tribute to my mother as a guiding light throughout their past problems and confused selves.

Here's the second narrative:
The sister of a friend of mine had joined the Mother Church [the central Christian Science Church in Boston] as a young teenager but had done so without a great amount of thought or spiritual dedication. Later, when still in her teens, she fell into drinking and drugs and sensed an alienation from her earlier faith commitment. When she wrote to Boston to request withdrawal from the church because of what she saw as her moral failings, she received back a kind letter that said that while the church would be willing to honor her request to withdraw her membership, they would be happier to "wait for her." Years later, when this young woman felt a resurgence of the Spirit in her, that spiritual inkling was kindled by the memory that her church was still with faithful love "waiting for her."

Gently leading those that are with young

The following chapters include other examples of how our church can continue to clarify its approach and practice today as a spiritual family that is as conscious about the safety and well-being of its church members as it is about our desire to freely practice our faith.

A question for further discussion:

Who *should* be on the "front lines" of a church's legal battles? In the next chapter we'll look at legal issues, including exemptions for Christian Scientists as well as the Mormon controversy over polygamy in the late nineteenth century when a Mormon church official volunteered to be the test case for his church's cause.

CHAPTER 19

The law and Saul's armor

Just because something is technically legal doesn't mean that it's spiritually appropriate.

I Corinthians 6:12, The Message

What happens when Christian beliefs collide with the demands of the civil authorities?

IN A CONVERSATION WITH his disciple Peter concerning the relations of Christians with the state, Jesus asks Peter whether kings tax their own children or strangers. Peter naturally answers that sovereigns tax strangers. **"Why then,"** said Jesus, *"their own people are exempt"* (Matthew 17:26 NEB). Here Jesus appears to have established a basis for Christian exemption from state demands, **by comparing Jesus' own spiritual realm to a worldly government**. But on the heels of that justification, the Master cautions Peter to pay the state tax[1] **"so that we may not cause offense"**[2] (Matthew 17:27 NEB).

What did Jesus say about complying with unjust Roman laws? **"If a [Roman] soldier forces you to carry his pack one mile, carry it two miles"** (Matt. 5:41 CEV). Dummelow comments on this latter passage: **"Christians ought to pay their taxes and undertake other public burdens cheerfully and willingly."**[3]

---

1. Matthew 17:17. Gathered in by a surprising way of fishing.
2. The Greek word for *offense* is s*kandalizo*, which literally means a trap-stick or snare.
3. Dummelow, *One Volume Bible Commentary*, 643.

Can we conclude from Jesus' statements that when Christians claim exemptions for religious reasons, they may cause unnecessary consternation among non-Christians, even cause an offense or scandal? To claim exemptions might also hinder the public acceptance of any larger spiritual message that Christians may wish to convey to the public.

Scandals draw public attention to themselves and their associated personalities. When we remember a scandal, we generally recall names, the people involved, and a few sordid details. Rarely does the public gain any new spiritual or intellectual illumination from a scandal of any kind.

Jesus picked his battles wisely, and he was careful not to make a priority of fighting Rome or the common civil laws of his time. Had he done so, he would have forfeited his spiritual accomplishments for the sake of winning arguments of lesser value. **That approach could only have thwarted his spiritual mission** and brought him to an earlier crucifixion. A nineteenth century pastor wrote: "There are matters in which Christ's people ought to forego their own opinions, and **submit to requirements which they may not thoroughly approve, rather than give offence and 'hinder the Gospel of Christ'.**... There are occasions, when it shows more grace in a Christian to submit than to resist."[4]

This question of how religious persons relate to civil law is as relevant as recent controversial U.S. Supreme Court decisions.[5] Jesus urged compliance with the demands for taxation, giving to "Caesar what is Caesar's and to God what is God's" (Matt. 22:21). Jesus did not resist his own arrest, and Paul urged Christians to obey civil authorities and to pay taxes (Rom. 13:6, 7).

Paul, Christians, and the civil law

Paul's view about the appropriate interaction of Christians with the state takes Jesus' point of rendering to "Caesar" a step further than did the Master. The apostle wrote that it was a shame for Christians **"even**

---

4. Commentary on Matthew 17 agreeing with Dummelow by Rev. J.C. Ryle (1816-1900), the Anglican Bishop of Liverpool, England. From Ryle's notes on Matthew (1856), 217.
5. *Burwell v. Hobby Lobby Stores, Inc.* (2014) and *Christian Legal Society v. Martinez* (2010).

to have lawsuits with one another at all,…is in itself evidence of defeat. **Why not let yourselves be wronged? Why not rather let yourselves be defrauded?**" (I Cor. 6: 7 Moffatt)[6]

Paul's advice here is for Christians to settle their intra-church legal problems among their own people, and, similar to Jesus, he advises against going to the civil law for justice when Christians should be willing to humble themselves in temporary defeat rather than agitate their cause before local authorities. Granted, Paul sought the protection of Roman law for himself at a time of his own potential danger (Acts 22:25). Was that an ethical inconsistency by Paul, while under threat of punishment?

Jesus and fighting for our rights

Jesus said to Pontius Pilate: "My kingdom is not from this world. **If my kingdom were from this world, my followers would be fighting to keep me from being handed over…**" (John 18:36 NRSV). For centuries since these words were spoken, Christians have fought in the ways of the world to establish governments often in the name of Jesus, to take lands which they considered holy from Muslims, even to war against and kill their fellow Christians, and to do this in ways that Jesus told his disciples not to. "Put away your sword" (Matthew 26:52 NLT), Jesus told his disciples who tried to physically defend him in the garden at Gethsemane. He warned his followers then, (and, by extension, Christians of today) that **if you fight that way, you will also die that way** (Matthew 26:52).

Have Christian Scientists been willing to listen to Jesus and Paul?

Have Christian Scientists pursued legal exemptions and "protection" from various state-imposed requirements, especially in the United States, without sufficient regard for the counsel of Jesus and Paul? In

---

6. This approach by Paul was previously cited in Chapter 5.

explaining the position of the Christian Science Church in 1993, a church official stated, "Scientific prayer is diametrically [completely] opposed to medical treatment. That's the reason we seek exemptions from state law, so we can freely practice our religion."[7] There are at least two problems with this statement: (1) **Christian Scientists' prayers in no way collide with the ultimate intention of doctors or their work.** Prayers are metaphysical and, naturally, not physical actions though they possess the power to transform the human experience. Prayers are paths of seeking wholeness for those receiving prayer and are distinct from the methods of a doctor, but Christian Scientists have no basis to judge the methods of others, anymore than a graphic artist is opposed to a sculptor, or a mountain climber is opposed to an astronaut. Christian Scientists' prayers for themselves do not start or conclude with any denunciation of or opposition to the treatment of a medical practitioner. Their prayers are built on the allness of God, the universal Mind. The infinite Mind acts universally to the advantage of all and in harmony with the positive motives of all, regardless of religious affiliation, belief, or unbelief.

Therefore, even if a law required Christian Scientists to undergo medical treatment which they did not desire, that law's enforcement would in no way separate the Christian Scientists from either their closeness to God or from an adequate practice of what they believed.

> A genuine Christian Scientist loves Protestant and Catholic, D.D. [doctor of divinity] and M.D...It will be found that instead of opposing, such an individual [the Christian Scientist] **subserves** [helps to further or promote] **the interests of both medical faculty and Christianity, and they thrive together,** learning that Mind-power is good will towards men (*My* 4:14).

(2) **Can a civil law prevent Christian Scientists from "freely practicing [their] religion?" No.** Prayer cannot be stopped or quenched by any law, whether that law required a physical examination, a vaccination, or other form of medical treatment. Mrs. Eddy said as much in

---

7. *Battle Creek Enquirer,* MI, 11-28-1993.

giving her assent to mandatory vaccination in 1901 (see the following pages). Mrs. Eddy even used herself as a test subject of what she taught when she once allowed herself to be injected with morphine, and it had no influence upon her (*Mis.* 249:2–5).[8] Of course, Christian Scientists don't typically want any law requiring them to do something they don't have faith in, but as in instances in the Bible, as well as in more modern times, they believe persons can be protected by Truth and prayer from events or conditions thrust on them against their will and belief.

On what foundation should Christian Scientists base their rights?

The *New York Sunday Journal* of April, 1901, published Mrs. Eddy's interesting comment about Christian Scientists and vaccination: "Whatever changes come to this century [for example, changes in laws regarding vaccination] or to any epoch, we may safely submit to the **providence of God, to common justice, to the maintenance of individual rights, and to governmental usages** [customs or practices]" (*My.* 220:1–5). Notice that in her view, individual rights are only one of four considerations that properly influence progress in the laws of the land.

What is the cornerstone of our legal stance?

We have petitioned legislators to encourage our national and state governments to allow, on the basis of the Bill of Rights in the American constitution, that Christian Scientists be free from obeying laws which we consider to be in conflict with our religious beliefs[9] and trouble-

---

8. Eddy, *Mis*. 249. "...I experimented by taking some large doses of morphine, to see if Christian Science could not obviate [remove or oppose] its effect; and I say with tearful thanks, 'The drug had no effect upon me whatever'." This occurred sometime before 1897.
9. Because the basic teachings of Christian Science do not advocate the use of drugs and challenge medical premises, Christian Scientists have often opposed laws which insist on medical attention, such as compulsory vaccination and physical exams as "in conflict with our church tenets," but there are no church tenets which forbid Christian Scientists from going to a doctor, submitting to compulsory vaccinations, physical exams, and so on.

some to ourselves and our children. But instead of basing our arguments mainly on the American constitutional law, shouldn't we first and foremost look to the record and words of Jesus?

Vaccinations and the common good

A prime example of where Christian Scientists, particularly after Mrs. Eddy's passing, have sought legal exemption from state laws has been with the contentious issue of vaccination. At a time when mass public vaccinations were in their infancy, Mrs. Eddy made a statement that should surprise many who assume she would have rejected medical treatment of all kinds:

> **Rather than quarrel over vaccination, I recommend, if the law demand, that an individual submit to this process, that he obey the law, and then appeal to the gospel to save him from bad physical results.**
>
> My. 220-221

In a separate statement about the same time in 1901, she conceded to the requirement for children to be vaccinated where the law required it. The path that she carved out for her church lay between the extremes of total capitulation to a practice which Christian Scientists considered unnecessary for themselves, and rebellion against vaccination requirements, which the majority of American citizens believed, then and now, are necessary for the public welfare.

Since Mrs. Eddy's time, our church position has tended to reflect the following official statement: "They (Christian Scientists) oppose compulsory vaccination for Christian Scientists—as a trespass upon their religious convictions."[11] Does this official statement contradict in some measure Mrs. Eddy's willingness to accede to civil demands regarding the need for vaccinations? The author's local school district publishes

---

10. Eddy, *Miscellany*, 344:30–3. "Where vaccination is compulsory, let your children be vaccinated, and see that your mind is in such a state that by your prayers vaccination will do the children no harm."
11. Rosten, *Religions in America*, 47. Q & A from the Church's Committee on Publication.

the following summary description of what staff and faculty should be aware of and honor in relation to Christian Science students:

> Reliance on prayer for effective health care. Legal accommodation for strongly held religious beliefs including exemption from inoculations, vaccinations, and immunizations. No medications; no physical exams; no vision, hearing, intelligence or psychological testing; and no instruction in disease.[12]

While some Christian Science parents may seek exemption for their children from this list of standard school requirements for students, it's questionable whether the founder of Christian Science expected that the children of her fellow church members would need a list of exemptions insulating those students from requirements demanded of all school children in American towns and cities.

Are vaccinations safe for children?

While scientific organizations in the United States and elsewhere today almost entirely endorse the general safety and effectiveness of vaccines, they don't hesitate to mention that individuals can have bad reactions from shots, and as of this writing medical exemptions from vaccinations are available in all fifty American states. A minority of parents in the United States are "anti-vaxxers" (approximately nine percent), for reasons of health concerns as well as for religious and ethical reservations. The measles vaccine, according to a since-discredited scientific study, has been linked to autism in children, and as of 2015, it's estimated that only 13% of American parents of minor children do not believe in the safety of the measles vaccine.[13]

It is understandable to the author that safety concerns can be an important factor in Christian Scientists' objections to having their children immunized, whether or not those concerns are shared by a small

---

12. Illinois School District U-46, Elgin, Illinois.
13. Blake, "Here's how many Americans are actually anti-vaxxers," *Washington Post*, 2-9-2015.

minority of citizens in their respective countries. Most parents don't require a wave of peer support when they're considering what is safe or dangerous for their children. One reason that may keep more Christian Scientists from taking an anti-vaccination legal stance at this time is that evidence of harm caused by vaccines has not reached the level of what is called *critical mass*. It's conceivable that a *critical mass* level of objections to vaccination could be reached in the future if there was a disastrously defective vaccine made mandatory with widespread results made public, as took place with the thalidomide-caused deaths and the resultant banning of that drug in the early 1960s. Thus far a vaccine disaster on a par with the well-known tragedy of the thalidomide drug and its accompanying public condemnation has yet to happen in the United States.

How can a law that exempts from common civic requirements be a problem?

Answer: In the same way that parents excessively helping their kids with schoolwork can stifle the initiative and sense of responsibility of those students who won't mature until after the parents are no longer available to help out. When parents are not around to help in their children's future, hopefully they will have instilled in their sons or daughters the desire for self-sufficiency and have not imparted a need in those children to unnecessarily seek protection from others.

Do exemptions protect or weaken those that are exempted?

Professor Stephen Carter of Yale Law School charitably spoke out in a news column for the rights of Christian Scientists. He wrote that without special protections for their freedom to practice, "religious communities whose values differ sharply from the mainstream might be unable to survive."[14] The troubling assumption in Professor Carter's

---

14. Carter, "The Power of Prayer, Denied," *C. S. Monitor* 2-7-1996.

defense of protections for Christian Scientists is that our faith practice is fragile, like an **exotic, delicate species**, close to extinction, and therefore requiring special, watchful protection from the state. While Christian Scientists undoubtedly appreciate Professor Carter's sympathetic concern, should we agree with a view of Christian Science as an endangered species? I would hope not. Jesus contended for a Christian's faith and practice to be like mustard seed, that may be small at first but grows abundantly under unfavorable soil conditions.

Here's a comment from a young man who was not exempted from various school classes and vaccinations as a child, since his parents were Christian Scientists who didn't believe that exemptions were particularly useful: **"Those exemptions or accommodations make it easier to be scared** [of medical interventions] **later on in your life."** In other words, if we as church members have been sheltered since childhood from various impositions by the state and by the world around us, do those legal protections make us **sturdier trees in the future or hothouse plants that are apt to wilt under adverse social conditions?**

If our church members are more schooled in self-sufficiency, and expected to be able to heal successfully regardless of legal restraints, would there be little need for special protections from the civil law in whatever society we inhabit?

David and Saul's armor—using unconventional, but natural defense

David, before he went into battle with Goliath, refused to employ the conventional means of defense that others were pressing on him to use. He protested, "I cannot walk with these [the heavy armor and sword], **for I have not tested them**" (I Samuel 17:39 NKJV). David had leaned on divine empowerment and simple means (a sling and stones) to protect his sheep from marauding animals, so why would he want to use weaponry and means of defense that were foreign to him? Have Christian Scientists in the past century acceded to the conventional legal means of self-defense that they have deemed necessary for their survival more than relying upon precedents of defense employed by their spiritual ancestors? Have legal accommodations, also known as exemptions, really helped Christian Scientists and their cause over the years?

In summary, this book contends that Christian Scientists must recognize their own internal accommodations and protections from danger that Mrs. Eddy offered to her church members. These protections consist of both the overall help that divine Truth provides, together **with safeguards of temporary support in the event of our failures to practice successfully**. We have too often neglected to talk about these little-discussed accommodations in our collective forums (our church magazines, associations, etc.) nor have we as a whole and as individuals tended to follow these concessions for over a century (see Chapter 22). It is regrettable that we have not given attention to our "laws of limitation" (*My.* 229:26). Unheeded provisions from our church writings literally could have saved members' lives or kept them from unnecessary pain, injury, and ultimately the church's disrepute.

The following is a small timeline of some "laws of limitation" which Mrs. Eddy recommended that Christian Scientists accede to:

- November, 1902   Mrs. Eddy asked church practitioners to decline to treat infectious and contagious cases for an undetermined length of time after testimony by a practitioner in the *New York Times* indicated how arrogant the Christian Scientists had become over their presumed rights (*My.* 226).
- November, 1902   Mrs. Eddy pointed out that whether Christian Scientists were successful or not in their prayerful efforts *"they [were] not specially protected by law,"* and she emphasized that statement in italics (*My.* 227).
- 1901   Mrs. Eddy urged that Christian Scientists not "quarrel over vaccination," but submit to it when it is the law and know that their submission could in no way harm them (*My.* 219).
- 1901   Mrs. Eddy complimented the Ohio Christian Science practitioners who carried on while not being able to receive any remuneration for their work because of the restrictions of the then-current Ohio state law (*My.* 204).

"For their own good"—the Babylonian Captivity

How can a retrograde step for a people or nation actually be an avenue "for their own good?" The Book of Jeremiah describes the dilemma of Israel when the King of Babylon took the Jews captive and removed many of them to Babylon. Jeremiah surprisingly told his fellow Jews that this captivity would be **"for their own good"** (Jeremiah 24:5 NKJV), and he used the analogy of a basket of figs. To Jeremiah the rotten figs were the Jews who decided to stay in Israel, while the good figs were taken away. Was the prophet advocating the demise of Israel? Not at all. The Lord had told Jeremiah that **the captivity was a necessary consequence of the people's disobedience, and it would be only for a time**. As a symbol of the temporary nature of the Babylonian captivity, Jeremiah even purchased some land in Jerusalem—a dubious real estate investment, but nonetheless a symbol of the prophet's intent and commitment for himself and his people to return to their native land.

Let's examine how an American religious sect survived a period of ostracism, legal "captivity," and compromise due to the demands of state law.

The Mormon experience —where a setback led to progress

How could the Mormons' controversy over polygamy be instructive to Christian Scientists today? The first U.S. Supreme Court case to restrict the free exercise of religion was *Reynolds v. United States* (1879) that challenged Mormon polygamy. The Supreme Court charged George Reynolds, the Mormon First Secretary, a prominent church official, with flouting the Anti-Bigamy Act of 1862 passed by the U.S. Congress. Reynolds had openly married a second wife, while still married to his first wife. This case is often referred to in discussions regarding the rights of the religious to practice their faith. While the Mormons' religious and legal quandary differs in many ways from the question of legal exemptions for Christian Scientists, the gradual demise of church-sanctioned polygamy illustrates how a church can rebuild its public image when it is willing to humble itself, give up a publicly condemned church practice, but still maintain its essential belief system.

A brief history of the war against polygamy

Beginning with the Morrill Anti-Bigamy Act in 1862, and culminating in the legally enforced disincorporation of the Mormon Church, the seizure of church property, and the arrest of nearly one thousand Mormons in the late 1880s, the United States government waged a decades-long form of "holy war" against the Latter-Day Saints. The Mormons fought back. Church president John Taylor wrote: "We will contend, inch by inch, legally and constitutionally, for our rights as citizens and plant ourselves firmly on the guarantees of the constitution."[15]

In 1889, ten years after losing the *Reynolds* case in the Supreme Court, the Mormon leadership quietly stopped sanctioning plural marriages (polygamy), the main cause of popular antagonism against their religion, but they did not publicly announce this action. The government persecution continued until 1890, when Church President Wilford Woodruff announced in what was called a manifesto that polygamy would no longer be allowed by the church. Woodruff noted in his journal that the change in church teaching or policy was **"for the temporal salvation of the church."**[16]

In spite of ongoing dissension among Mormons over the end of polygamy, a softening of public sentiment towards the Mormon faith in Utah and in the rest of the country resulted from the church leadership's change of official policy. Utah was subsequently admitted as a state into the Union in 1896. Polygamy was secretly countenanced by church leaders after the 1890 manifesto and is still practiced by some "fundamentalist" Mormons today, but because of its official condemnation by the Mormon Church, it is no longer the burden to the church that it once was.

---

15. Arrington, *Mormon Experience*, 181.
16. Arrington, 183.

Polygamy "brought reproach upon the people,"[17] wrote President Joseph F. Smith in 1911, and the manifesto banning polygamy was recognized over time by Mormons as a revelation rather than an expedient political maneuver.[18] The Mormon Church today does not apologize for its past practice of polygamy, but asserts that it was done out of sincere religious conviction.

Bending before public sentiment

The Mormon example illustrates how the lightning bolts of animosity directed at a church have been deflected by the willingness of church leaders, for reasons either of pragmatism or divine revelation, to finally bend to government insistence and the norms of society. President Woodruff stated in his manifesto, "**The question is, whether it** [polygamy] **should be stopped in this manner** [as the state ordered]**, or in the way the Lord has manifested to us** [by the Mormon Church withdrawing its former doctrine]."

Many would argue that polygamy was indeed stopped primarily by pressure from the government and, only in desperation, by the Mormon leadership's action. What upheld the United States' continued pressure on the Mormon Church throughout the latter half of the nineteenth century was the distaste of the American public for "plural marriage." Public consensus on this issue gave the government sufficient cause to pursue the course of action it took.

Public sentiment carrying more weight than our rights

Abraham Lincoln spoke in regard to slavery: "**Public sentiment is everything. With public sentiment, nothing can fail; without it, nothing can succeed.** Consequently, he who molds public sentiment goes

---

17. Conference Report, April 1911, p. 8.
18. Snow, "Discourse," delivered at St. George, Utah (1899). Later published in *Millennial Star*, Vol. 61, No. 34, pp. 529-533.

deeper than he who enacts statutes or pronounces decisions. He makes statutes and decisions possible or impossible to be executed."[19]

Lincoln appeared to suggest in this statement that law requires a consensus of public opinion for its enduring support, and without that support any individual law must ultimately be remade or annulled. Though American public sentiment had condemned the Mormons over polygamy, once polygamy became no longer an official teaching of the Mormon Church, that adverse sentiment changed.

Mrs. Eddy used the Latin term ***vox populi*** (*Mis.* 245:11) which meant literally "the voice of the people" or public sentiment. She appeared to see public sentiment as generally a **moderating voice of wisdom** in our country that would ultimately prevail over temporary prejudicial policy and injustice. When Mrs. Eddy recommended that Christian Scientists let their children submit to compulsory vaccination, she was essentially recognizing where the consensus of public sentiment stood in her day, as it still predominantly does today. She wrote: "So long as Christian Scientists obey the laws, I do not suppose that their mental reservations will be thought to matter much. But every thought tells…" (*My.* 345:3–5). The American public thought is comparable to that of Pontius Pilate in Jesus' time in this way, that as long as religious persons follow what the public considers to be appropriate behavior for a citizen, the public will not care about the religious reasoning involved.

Reflecting on the Mormons' experience, we can draw one moral from their history: When churches bend, particularly when they alter conduct which the state or the *vox populi* finds objectionable, the state is more willing to accommodate the general practices of those churches.[20]

---

19. First Debate with Stephen A. Douglas, August 21, 1858, Ottawa, Illinois (Nicolay and Hay version). Robert Peel notes on p. 500 in *Years of Authority*: **"Favorable statutes [are] only as good and as lasting as the general climate of thought that sustain[s] them."**
20. Reid, *Healing of America*, 41. In India, astrologers are accommodated in the national health policies to the degree that they are paid for their services by health-care rupees. How does that work? A majority of citizens in India, or the *vox populi,* consents to that accommodation. In the United States a majority of citizens would likely oppose Christian Science practitioners being compensated by means of any national health-care system and not as the Indian astrologers have been compensated.

When the law frees you, but the court of public opinion does not

In what are referred to as the "children's cases" in the 1980s and 1990s, Christian Science parents and others, connected in some way with the deaths of seven children, were charged by the law with neglect and manslaughter, but most of them were not convicted, in part because American law contained exemptions for parents treating children with only spiritual means. A formal exoneration in court does not mean victory as far as the public and governmental authorities are concerned.

For example, after one of these cases, the Massachusetts legislature eliminated its state's "faith healing" exemption and "enacted a rule requiring all parents to seek appropriate medical care for ill and injured children."[21] The court in Massachusetts had ruled that the state law's provision for "exemption was ambiguous enough that it could have led the parents to believe that they were immune from all prosecution for child neglect, even in cases resulting in death."[22] In the preceding chapter in this book and other chapters, we make a case that there are various actions which Christian Scientists may take that can both guide church members to better protect their children as well as guide them in relation to American law. It is the belief of the author that if Christian Scientists can shepherd their own members and correct any elements of their church members' dogmatic behavior and writings which have directly or indirectly led to the deaths or injury of children, there is less likelihood that American law will need to be involved in prosecuting members of their church.

Self-policing by the religious encourages state tolerance

As we have noted, two thousand years ago, as is true today, civil authorities have tended to get involved with religious questions **only when**

---

21. Tuttle, "Faith Healing and the Law," Pew, Aug. 31, 2009. Q & A with Robert W. Tuttle, Prof. of Law and Religion at George Washington University Law School.
22. Ibid.

there are disruptions of the social order.[23] Pilate said to Jesus' accusers: "Take ye him, and judge him according to your law" (John 18:31). Long before the concept of separation of church and state emerged in the United States, the Roman magistrate Pilate, literally and symbolically, sought to wash his hands of a religious-state matter—the questions of Jesus' guilt or innocence and his fate (Matthew 27:24).

In Jesus' time as long as Jews and Christians kept order among their own people, the Romans were happy. Perhaps Pilate agreed to the crucifixion of Jesus because of the obvious tumult and controversy surrounding Jesus that was arousing both the church authorities and their people (Matthew 27:24). In our modern era, only when American courts have felt that public order is threatened have they tended to bring charges against the religious. American courts in the Mormon case in 1879, and throughout the twentieth century, have drawn a line in the sand if religious practice harmed persons or threatened social order. Justice Felix Frankfurter articulated the Supreme Court justices' concern in 1946: **"If one man can be allowed to determine for himself what is law, every man can. That means first chaos, then tyranny."**[24]

Other Supreme Court justices besides Frankfurter have used the term "law unto themselves." If a religious person has claimed to be a "law unto himself" or herself, that claimant has indicated to the U.S. Supreme Court that he or she was acting in defiance of the law and thus was following a personal code or law that challenged the legitimacy of the American democratic system. The Mormons had challenged the American law banning bigamy, and their defiance in part determined the anti-polygamy outcome of the *Reynolds* case.

---

23. Kostenberger, *Encountering John*, 179. "Throughout the proceedings, Pilate displays the customary reluctance of Roman officials to get involved in internal Jewish religious affairs" (Cf. John 19). Acts 19:35–41 describes a town clerk pacifying an anti-Christian mob on the basis that Christians had not violated local customs and religion.
24. U. S. vs. *United Mine Workers*, 330 U.S. 312, 1946.

Christians being "a law to themselves"

Apostle Paul used the phrase "law unto themselves" (Romans 2:14) nineteen centuries before the U.S. Supreme Court had done so, but he had clearly meant something quite different from how the Supreme Court employed that phrase. Eugene Peterson captures something of the spirit of Paul's words in his rendition of Romans 2:14: "When outsiders…who have never heard of God's law follow it more or less by instinct, they confirm its truth by their obedience. They show that God's law is not something alien, imposed on us from without, but woven into the very fabric of our creation" (The Message).

Paul advocated that Christians not attempt to determine their own definition of law that could lead to chaos. He urged Christians to be in super-adherence to the religious law (the Torah) and demonstrate such by comportment that would leave no room for criticism by the authorities or the public. In our own day, the U.S. Supreme Court has feared **the arrogant and potentially disruptive exceptionalism of religious persons**. Paul may have been addressing religious law, rather than civil law, but he envisioned Christians acting in super-compliance with religious law. The U.S. Supreme Court's sense of what constitutes "being a law to one's self" has steadily diverged from the sense of that significant phrase that St. Paul wrote about.

> "*They* [early Christians] **obey the prescribed laws, and at the same time surpass the laws by their lives."**
> Epistle to Diognetes c. 130 CE

Jesus and being "a law unto one's self"

In Jesus' words: "If I do not the works of my Father, believe me not [i.e. believe not my theological contention that 'I am the Son of God']. But if I do [the works of God], though ye believe not me, believe the works [for their own value or significance to you]: that ye may know, and believe, that the Father is in me, and I in him" (John 10:37, 38).

Now if Jesus was a modern-day Christian Science church member, would he have gone to a judge and said: "Believe me and let me live freely by my own code, because the First Amendment of the United States Constitution gives me the inherent freedom to live as I believe my religion dictates"? Did not Jesus instead rest his credibility on the moral and spiritual consistency of his life rather than on his human or state-bestowed rights?

Paul, when referring to the Gentiles, and Jesus, when referring to his own work, established criteria of acceptable **religious practice to be justified by substantial living proof or practice**. Neither Paul nor Jesus said that anyone may say or do anything as they please, regardless of whether their particular religious teaching is useful or practical. Performance counts. To be a "law to one's self" for Jesus and Paul meant that Christians were to **live in internal consistency with their conscience and religious profession, in order to fulfill the intent of the law where they lived.**

Therefore: Should not Christian Scientists, in relation to the laws of the various countries in which they live, always make clear to their local authorities that they should be assessed by their performance and strive to be "a law to themselves" in that their performance should attest the validity of their faith practice? They should never belittle the concerns of public health and civil authorities but communicate to these officials both how they practice and *that the Christian Scientists welcome an examination of the results of their own practice.* The author believes that our church has steadily for years stated the above intent of its practice. However, Christian Scientists have very infrequently submitted to before-and-after examination of their actual healing work but have relied almost exclusively upon their own collected records to speak for their church.

> *"To be a law unto yourself does not mean you write your own law; on the contrary, it's something altogether more humbling. You discover that the law, the universal law, is already written in your heart."* — E.R.

Recommendations and questions for further discussion:

- How our church can best follow Jesus and our church's founder regarding matters of the laws of the land is a large question. There is no obvious path for how changes should or could happen to our church's view towards civil law and exemptions, but in this chapter we have presented some ideas for the encouragement of that discussion.
- Before our church could possibly change its approach to the law, it would be wise for Christian Scientists to research and inform their members how the legal status for Christian Scientists in various countries around the world affects or has affected the church members' healing work going on in those countries.
- How "central" to our church's teaching and practice are exemptions and accommodations from the civil law? The "centrality" of a religious practice to its own theology has been significant to American courts in determining whether any element of religious practice should be curtailed. Possibly Christian Scientists themselves are the ones best equipped to determine, based on their collective experiences, how crucial, or not, exemptions/accommodations have been to the religious lives of their own people.
- Could the gradual reduction of our legal exemptions encourage or discourage better healing work by Christian Scientists in the United States?
- The *Church Manual* (70:10) allows for conferences within states to confer on legal changes. Forums, such as conferences like these envisioned in the *Manual*, might be suitable venues to discuss any changes in the law affecting Christian Scientists that church members might want to consider.

CHAPTER 20

Listening to our ardent opponents

During many years the author has been most grateful for merited rebuke.   Science and Health, 9

IN THIS HUMAN EXPERIENCE, there's nothing that compares to the heart-wrenching pain of burying a son or daughter. So, it is very understandable that someone who has lost a child under Christian Science care might turn their pain-filled grief into a crusade against those teachings.

Before Christian Scientists rush to defend their faith against those who attack it, they need to first put themselves in the attackers' shoes.

Brief historical overview

Rita and Doug Swan are ex-Christian Scientists whose son Matthew died of spinal meningitis in 1977. Matthew had been taken to a hospital shortly before his death, but his parents assert that the Christian Science practitioners who prayed with them before Matthew's hospitalization, together with the Swans' own religious training, created such guilt that they rejected medical intervention for Matthew until it was too late to save him.

There are conflicting views of the substance of interactions between the Swans and their Christian Science practitioners. The bottom line is that the baby's suffering was not relieved by prayer, and a desperate effort in taking Matthew to the hospital proved to be tardy help.

This book addresses issues that the Swans and their tragedy have raised. Some of the Swans' contentions have validity, which various chapters in this book address. Other contentions by the Swans do not.[1] Because some of what the Swans have said is untrue about Christian Science,[2] Christian Scientists have not attended closely enough to the Swans' grief and the deep harm that the traumatic loss of a child does to one's heart, relationships, and views about life.

The author contends that when we Christian Scientists have shown **coldness** or **indifference, or inhumane treatment to our own people, more than any lack of healing itself**, we have often turned wounded families and individuals into enemies of the teachings of our faith. Why should this be so hard for us to grasp?

As a practitioner, I have received a large number of calls from Christian Scientists who have been "dumped" by other practitioners. These church members might have had some surgery or gone to a doctor for diagnosis or treatment, at which point the practitioner who was praying with them bluntly told them they could not pray for them anymore. There is no Christian justification at all for this happening, and it illustrates a serious misunderstanding of how Christians should treat one another.

How the Swans are blessing the practice of Christian Science

The angriest critics of Christian Science are blessings in disguise. They are disturbing blessings, but blessings indeed, if we can learn from them. We have admitted the fact that attacks on our faith can serve the

---

1. *People Magazine,* March 31, 1980, Vol. 13, No. 13; Mrs. Swan stated that her own operation for an ovarian cyst after Matthew's birth was criticized by church members. She cited that experience as cause for discouraging her and her husband from seeking a doctor's help for their son Matthew. Other parents could potentially believe that a parent might forgo medical attention for themselves, but not be so willing to withhold medical care from their child in a crisis, regardless of others' opinions.

2. "Faith Healing Court Cases," *Religion and Ethics News Weekly,* May 15th 2009. Mrs. Swan, for example, said in an interview that it was a "law of the church" that keeps Christian Scientists from going to a doctor. There is no church tenet, or by-law, but only dogmatic belief, and Mrs. Swan is probably aware of that, though she is quoted as saying: "I know in many cases parents are relieved. It [a legal requirement of the state] takes the moral burden of decision-making off of the parents' shoulders. **They no longer have broken a law of the church.**"

cause of good, but have we been able to identify what kind of good those attacks may accomplish? In other words, **what are Christian Scientists actually learning from what happened to the Swans?** Evidently not enough so far. Our severest critics have pointed out our failures, and they may have exaggerated them, but on the other hand our friends and fellow church members may have been too timid to say to us anything that was constructively critical when we really needed the correction of our thinking and actions. Isn't it a fair-weather friend who hesitates to stop you while you drive over a cliff?

The numbers of Christian Scientists were already on a steep decline in 1979, when Rita Swan launched her efforts against American laws that both shield Christian Scientists from prosecution and protect other religionists who rely centrally on prayer, especially in cases involving children.

Rodney Stark, an American sociologist of religion, has charted the numbers of Christian Science Church members and practitioners. He points to the mid-1930s as the tipping point where membership began to decrease, and by the late 1970s the church had lost three-quarters of its practitioner workforce.[3] Stark attributes the decline primarily to the rise in modern medicine, but **the era of medicine's most remarkable developments, including the common use of antibiotics, lay decades in the future, long after the decline in church numbers began**. For example, although Alexander Fleming discovered penicillin in 1928, mass production and distribution was not a reality until 1945. The so-called "golden era" of antibiotic discovery is considered to be the 1950s, 1960s, and 1970s—with no new discoveries after the mid-1970s.[4] Therefore, the assumption that the decline in church numbers has been directly caused by advances in medicine requires closer analysis.

If you were a harsh critic of Christian Science in the late twentieth century, and you wanted to see its organizational demise, all you really had to do was…nothing. Just sit tight and watch it fade away. For reasons this book points out, Christian Scientists were doing damage to themselves unconsciously and unintentionally without the "help" of others.

---

3. Stark, "Rise and Fall," 189-214.
4. Aminov, "Brief History of the Antibiotic Era," paragraphs 8 and 10: https://www.ncbi.nlm.nih.gov/pmc/articles/PMC3109405/

Reforming bad practice

When the widow whose son had died asked the prophet Elisha, **"Are you calling my sins to remembrance?"** Elisha answered her agonized question with healing, not with a theory or judgment. That's the only satisfactory way to answer the most intense criticism of Christian Science. But in order for that healing to happen, there needs to be a systematic reform of harmful dogma and its resultant bad practice. (See Chapter 24 on accountability.)

It is understandable that writers like Caroline Fraser (*God's Perfect Child*) dismiss the idea of healing by prayer. They haven't seen it practiced consistently. But *these critics are not bitter simply because they weren't healed. Once again, before and after* **they weren't healed, they may not have been loved or listened to.**

We don't rebut grief. We console it. We work to repair the great damage, and alleviate the underlying causes of tragedy. We realize that grief can be like that of the widow in Elisha's time who was probably angry with God, while Elisha proved to be a substitute target for her anger.

Those who have railed against Christian Science are often our best friends **because they are showing us the way, both how to go and how not to go**. We must always bless those who grieve and bless all our opponents if we are going to be Christians. For us to dismiss the harshest criticisms levied against us is as pointless, in a very real sense, as it is to thumb our nose at God. "If a friend informs us of a fault, do we listen patiently to the rebuke and credit what is said?" (*S&H* 8)

This book contends that, had Christian Scientists listened honestly and patiently to the rebukes of their friends, they would not have to face today the onslaught of those who, in the guise of enmity, are still their **friends**, only **at a higher decibel level**. Our most vehement opponents are all singing a similar tune: **be kind, be merciful, be humane, listen to the quiet voices of your children**, as well as to the louder voices of your critics. Our critics' apparent indictment is: Christian Scientists are stoic, fanatical, and dangerous, and their legal protections should be removed. Had we, as a religious body, listened to the inside message of that attack, and corrected ourselves, our actions, and, above all, our spirit when it became misdirected, would we be facing the same barrage of attacks and open disdain today that we too often do?

"You can disagree with another person's opinions; you can disagree with his doctrines; you can't disagree with his experience."[5]

The next chapter describes one Christian Scientist whose life embodies various possible active answers to the challenge presented by the Swans' family tragedy and the similar experiences of others. The life of Cathryn Keith also illustrates the miles Christian Scientists may need to travel in order to better bless our current era.

---

5. Tippett, *Becoming Wise*, 22.

CHAPTER 21

Angel of mercy
—the work of Cathryn Keith

Quite possibly a crucial element of what was missing in the tragic loss of the Swan family's child can be found in the work of a Christian Science nurse named Cathryn Keith.

MRS. KEITH, AS SHE WAS known to generations of Christian Scientists,[1] was a Christian Science nurse whose life spanned nine decades of the twentieth century and beyond. Interested in training as a Christian Science nurse when she was just a teenager, Mrs. Keith found out that she would not be accepted for nursing work by her church until she turned twenty-one, so she took medical nurses' training instead, and then joined the Christian Scientists when she "came of age."

Mrs. Keith's contributions to the work of Christian Scientists covered more than one post of duty. She **nursed and taught other nurses**. Beginning by the late 1950s she **counseled new Christian Science mothers in proper care for infants**, and she did this with lengthy individualized letters without the help of a copy machine. In this role she resembled a religious-based combination of Dr. Benjamin Spock, the baby doctor (as Dr. Bill Sears does these days), and the advice columnist Dear Abby (Abigail Van Buren).[2]

---

1. The material in this chapter was drawn from a number of interviews with Mrs. Keith, from families and individuals whom she helped, and from friends of Mrs. Keith.
2. In a small example of her practical care tips, Mrs. Keith suggested that parents use corn starch when changing a baby's diapers, before it became known that baby powder caused physical problems.

"Mrs. Keith knew the right things to tell me in helping me bring up a very healthy baby."

From a mother who worked with Mrs. Keith

Another of her missions **was finding adoptive families for the babies of young pregnant, unwed women**. In all her extra-nursing roles Mrs. Keith helped those who might have fallen through the cracks of standard church or social welfare programs.

In part due to her unusual background of having nursed in an orthodox medical setting as well as for Christian Scientists, Mrs. Keith was particularly qualified for a highly sensitive and meaningful role which she undertook in the 1960s and 1970s as a **liaison between the Christian Science Church and parents whose children's health was in jeopardy.** When church officials were ever alerted during that period to a family in trouble, they had created a special role for Mrs. Keith who would then act as semi-official help from the Mother Church to the family at risk. It's been estimated by her friends that Mrs. Keith went out on between fifty and a hundred of these sensitive help-missions for children in harm's way.

Examples of Cathryn Keith's missionary work for families

Around the mid-1980s, after the time-period when Mrs. Keith was being sent out on urgent cases involving children, the following happened. A Christian Science nurse was called on for an emergency situation involving a seven-month-old child. The infant had been showing flu symptoms for a few days. The nurse called Mrs. Keith for advice on what to do for the family, and Mrs. Keith answered, **"We can't lose another one. Do what you need to do."** Keep in mind that this was the decade when there had been seven deaths of young or infant Christian Scientists. The nurse on duty with this family told the author, "I took off my badge and told the parents, 'I'm talking to you as a fellow Christian Scientist and as a mother. Your child needs more than I can do for her.

You need to take your child to a hospital.' The parents proceeded to do that, and the baby recovered."

From a mother who subscribed to Mrs. Keith's letters: "I never felt rebuked by her letters. I remember having comforting conversations with her that gave me **both practical wisdom but also metaphysical understanding**."

Was Mrs. Keith's baby advice appropriate?

There are Christian Science parents who contend that Mrs. Keith's advice to our church's parents of infants was not on target for kids, nutritionally or developmentally. Those parents believe that Mrs. Keith's information and counsel consisted of outmoded medical advice that dated back a few decades. The author cannot personally vouch for or against the usefulness or accuracy of Mrs. Keith's advice, but has heard more from appreciative voices than from critical ones. I will be interested to hear more on this subject from those who actually received the Keith letters and either found them helpful or not.

Standing in the gap with families in crisis

What does seem clear with Mrs. Keith's record is the vital need she met in visiting families whose children's health was in danger. In one particularly dire situation involving a child, a family was referred to a local hospital by Mrs. Keith, and although the child later passed on there, the parents remained very grateful for all that was done for them. Mrs. Keith was able to arrange for a large monetary donation to the family from a Christian Science association, since the father was out of work. From the parents of the child: "You can't imagine how much that meant. It was just such a symbol of love and unconditional support."

"Cathryn **did not stop at the door of a hospital. She went right to where the need was**. She was formidable."

From a mother who adopted a child with Mrs. Keith's assistance and who benefited from her counsel in rearing the child

Mrs. Keith was called in on at least ten cases where there was a bowel obstruction with children. In nine of these cases, the parents requested surgery, and the child came through well, but with one of the ten, the parents declined to have an operation, and the baby passed on.

From a co-worker aiding Mrs. Keith with unwed mothers-to-be:
"I think of the days in the 1940s when Mrs. Keith and I would take to the back roads when a girl was in labor, and we arrived to help. How can we 'clone' what she did?"

Mrs. Keith's own standard for herself and others

In the 1970s Mrs. Keith broke her arm, but she did not have it set by a physician. However, it healed very well. She was not against having bones set, but this particular healing was her "individual demonstration" as Christian Scientists call it. Others might call it pushing the envelope or even tempting the Lord, but Mrs. Keith was, like Paul, her own "body's sternest master" (I Cor. 9: 27). In another instance in her late eighties, she was hit by a truck and broke her hip. She had the hip pinned by a bone doctor, and was up and walking in three days. She was on pain medication, and couldn't get a Christian Science nurse to help her because of that.[3]

A friend of Mrs. Keith notes, "While she was kind and flexible to those she helped, Mrs. Keith was very demanding spiritually and humanly to herself." Again as Paul wrote, "I am my own hardest taskmaster."[4]

Though she fully recognized the power of Love to heal, she was magnanimous enough to assist in situations where healing was not taking place. She personally paid for an operation for the niece of a prominent Christian Science teacher, when the young woman involved was not improving as a result of prayer. If this could be called "mixing" by some, it was the kind of "mixing" or assistance that the Good Samaritan would have heartily endorsed.

---

3. See Chapters 22 and 23.
4. I Cor. 9:27, J.B. Phillips.

Interesting teamwork with Boston physician

Among her wide acquaintances, Mrs. Keith befriended a Boston OB/GYN Maybelle Hiscock. Dr. Hiscock was able to help Mrs. Keith in a number of the above-mentioned circumstances by referring patients to an appropriate and supportive physician. Dr. Hiscock told Mrs. Keith that she had arranged for a number of surgeries for practitioners after their husbands had passed on, including two spouses of church officials. The doctor herself eventually became a student of Christian Science, but perhaps her greatest help to Christian Scientists was her contribution as a regular physician.

Mrs. Eddy wrote in *Science and Health* of "the importance that doctors be Christian Scientists" (*S&H* 198:27). She also wrote that if one hires an M.D., it should be one who is "learned" and "skillful" and not a charlatan (*Christian Healing* 14:9). Dr. Hiscock was definitely "learned" and "skillful" in Cathryn Keith's estimate. However, the former quotation from Mrs. Eddy begs the question of how a regular physician might remain in that occupation and not leave their medical practice, but still embody the metaphysical and Christian approach to illness that any Christian Scientist would be expected to have. That is a question and discussion that could be very useful to delve into for Christian Scientists.

Help for unwed mothers in placing children

From an adopting mother: "We adopted our first child with the help of Mrs. Keith. We had contacted the New England Home for Little Wanderers. Mrs. Keith had a good relationship with the home. The young women who were expecting babies and wanted to give them up for adoption could request what faith they were willing to have their child follow in the adopting home. Outside our church there was great respect for Mrs. Keith." This facet of Mrs. Keith's work is an example of a Christian Scientist who saw a need that others might have ignored, and then did something about it. Her work with unwed mothers was also the fruit of her involvement in the Boston community beyond the walls of her church.

Disagreements with other Christian Scientists

Mrs. Keith spoke with a Christian Science teacher who told her that it was better to have a crooked arm than to have it set by a physician. She strongly disagreed with that view. Chapter 4 cited the example of Harold Hobson, the prominent drama critic and church member who worked for the *Monitor,* and all his adult life hobbled on a poorly set bone. Mrs. Keith considered these things very wrong and a misapplication of Christian Science, especially given what Mrs. Eddy wrote about surgery (see *S&H* 401:27).

We draw the line in funny places,"[5] Mrs. Keith told a friend in regard to medical compromises that Christian Scientists considered to be permissible. She continued, "All my life Christian Scientists are condemning doctors." She saw ignorance and hypocrisy in that unjustifiable condemnation, as well as an absence of common sense, humanity, and wisdom, all of which were recommended by the founder of Christian Science.

Her thoughts about nurses and practitioners: "If practitioners could see the things that nurses do, they would sing a different song. Practitioners don't comprehend what nurses go through. They too often give terrible personal advice to patients."

While this chapter details some of Mrs. Keith's agreement with the need for church members to sometimes make compromises in their spiritual convictions, she was very aware of what spiritual healing could accomplish. She was the nurse on duty when a child was stillborn but was revived and thrived through the prayerful work of a practitioner. She was also on nursing duty in a case where a child was healed of a heart condition. So her willingness to entertain the notion of medical intervention was not without her realization that wonderful things could be accomplished through whole-hearted reliance upon spiritual means for healing.

---

5. More on this subject in Chapter 22.

On a cancer ward for children

During the 1980s Mrs. Keith was told that her services were no longer needed as a liaison between the Christian Science Church and families with threatening health challenges for their children. After her departure would the presence of someone acting in the capacity of what Mrs. Keith did, intervening in critical health situations involving children, have saved the lives of any of the children in the publicized seven cases where children of Christian Scientists passed on? That is impossible to say for sure, but did the absence of anyone of Mrs. Keith's stature, performing the interventions that she did, eliminate a crucial watchdog role in our church that this book contends is critically needed today as well as decades ago?

The last mission of Cathryn Keith's life was her most unsung, but one that was exceedingly valuable. When her church had no more use for her skills, she found her way to a Boston hospital that specialized in treating children with cancer. Mrs. Keith was a ministering angel to many kids in this hospital, whether they were considered terminal or not. The doctors and kids there and the children's parents loved her. Her many experiences in nursing prepared her for this ministry to those facing life's toughest tests.

One of Mrs. Keith's friends sees her late-in-life ministry in the hospital as a kind of penitential journey, done for the good of all the world's children. Her hospital work was an intriguing capstone to a life-mission of alleviating pain and suffering. Cathryn Keith passed on September 20, 2007, at the age of 97. Many Christian Scientists and others were blessed by her lifetime of human contributions, but few church members have been aware of the extent of what she stood for and accomplished.

Recommendations for further discussion:
The author has examined the various "children's cases" involving the deaths of the children of Christian Scientists (1977 through the 1990s) and is persuaded that, had there been individuals acting in the same capacity as Cathryn Keith, acting in a role as liaison between the church and families, that most of those cases could have been resolved either

with the survival of the child or, at worst, with the families involved feeling unconditional love and support from their church, even in the face of their terrible loss.

In some of these cases, there were domestic situations in which a wise third party could have helped resolve what the Christian Science practitioner on duty was not able to accomplish. **This book recommends that the church quietly reinstate the role of individuals acting, as Mrs. Keith did, in an informed and loving manner, to whom families could turn as supportive consultants in severe emergencies when a child's health is at risk.** Of course, a practitioner can fulfill this role as well, but it seems that families can benefit by having an impartial third party, or sounding board, available and physically present, to help them decide on a proper and safe course of action for a child's well-being.

Cathryn Keith's gift to the world embodies the following words of Mrs. Eddy:

> Love cannot be a mere abstraction, or goodness without activity and power…it is the tender, unselfish deed done in secret; the silent, ceaseless prayer; the self-forgetful heart that overflows; the veiled form stealing on an errand of mercy, out of a side door; the little feet tripping along the sidewalk; the gentle hand opening the door that turns toward want and woe, sickness and sorrow, and thus lighting the dark places of earth.
>
> *Mis.* 250:20

CHAPTER 22

The lesson of the grass
—the how and why of concessions

Jesus' concessions (in certain cases) to material methods were for the advancement of spiritual good. — Science and Health, 56

God can be trusted not to allow you to suffer any temptation beyond your powers of endurance. He will see to it that every temptation has a way out, so that it will never be impossible for you to bear it. — I Cor. 10:13 J. B. Phillips

A concession: something allowed or given up; a gesture, especially a token one, made in recognition of a demand or prevailing standard. — Cambridge Dictionary

WHAT SHOULD CHRISTIAN SCIENTISTS do about unrelieved pain? About vaccinations? About surgery? Where should they draw the line on what they concede to? Where do they take a stand for what they believe can be healed through prayer alone? Are certain concessions a yielding up of our high ideals, or are they ever a wise choice? These questions connect us to the tortured difficulty of Abraham's trial on Mt. Moriah. The apostle Paul wrestled with these kinds of questions that led him to his message cited above—that there can be a God-guided "way out"—and a way forward through hard trials.

Concessions from strength…or from fear?

The Irish statesman Edmund Burke wrote: "The concessions of the weak are the concessions of fear,"[1] as contrasted with the concessions of the strong, done out of benevolence, not weakness. The concessions indulged by Jesus showed his willingness to meet those desperate for help right where they were. Those concessions arose from Jesus' vantage point of spiritual strength, and they were apparently **motivated by humility and consideration for others**.

Large sections of the Bible deal with compromise and concession

Throughout the early history of the Jewish and Christian faiths, the Bible chronicles major concessions to religious law and established customs. These concessions or compromises in two instances resulted in long-run forward movement for Judaism and Christianity.

The two largest books of prophetic writings in the Bible, Isaiah and Jeremiah, focus on the failure of Israel to honor God and the subsequent humiliating captivity of the Jewish people in Babylon, a country that was seen by the Jews as a pagan nation. This captivity betrayed much of what Jews believed that Jehovah had given them as their right, but Jeremiah assured his listeners that the compromise which their captivity entailed would ultimately be **followed by a return to the Holy Land**.

The Jews in Jerusalem did have an option to resist the Babylonian captivity, to flee elsewhere, or to remain in their land, but Jeremiah recommended that yielding to their captors would be the best path to take (Jeremiah 24:5).

New Testament writings, especially Paul's letter to the Galatians, describe the Apostle's efforts to reconcile Christian teaching with Jewish tradition and gentile practices. Paul worked hard to find a pathway around the customs of kosher demands and circumcision, whereby Gentiles could feel welcome in the Christian community. **Finding a**

---

1. Burke, "Conciliation with America," Paragraph 11.

compromise position between the traditions of the Jewish Christians and the non-Jewish Christians was crucial to the future growth of the Christian cause.

Good can sometimes survive not only compromises, but serious moral failings. Abraham and Peter managed to fulfill significant promise in their lives despite notable instances of moral lapses motivated by their fear: (a) Abraham twice offered up his wife to be a concubine (Gen. 12 and 20) in order to save his own life and (b) Peter, of course, denied that he knew Christ, which compromised Peter's moral sense completely. So why did Peter in Acts 5 curse to death a couple (Ananias and Sapphira) who had withheld money from the church, when Peter had not been condemned nor cursed to death by Christ after committing a far greater infraction?

Compromise, especially when the reason for that compromise is clear and well-motivated, need not entail spiritual failure. Nature teaches us that species succeed which successfully adapt to or yield to the demands of their environment. Let me repeat: **"Compromise need not entail spiritual failure."**

St. Cyprian: Early Christianity and compromise

In an earlier chapter we have touched upon the compromises of St. Cyprian (200–258 CE) who justified his flight from the Roman authorities in this way: "**...the Lord [Jesus] commanded us in the persecution to depart and to flee [see Matthew 10:23, 24:16, John 8:59]; and...taught that this should be done, and Himself did it...whoever abiding in Christ departs for a while does not deny his faith, but waits for the [right] time [to return]...**"[2] Cyprian's internal conflicts, ultimate self-sacrifice, pangs of conscience, compromises, and even hypocrisy form part of the story of many Christians from before Cyprian's time up to our present era. While Cyprian's early compromising flight from the Romans seemed motivated by fear, Cyprian eventually did not deny his Christian beliefs.

---

2. Cyprian, *The Treatises of S. Caecilius* Cyprian, 159-160.

The Savior's willingness to bend

Christian Scientists have described Jesus as being radical and uncompromising (see Chapter 3). In fact, his whole life embodied a compromise—**a willingness to stoop to the mental level of his associates in order to save them and to help them grow spiritually**. Note how patient Jesus was with the slowness of his disciples. He lifted up Peter when the brash disciple was sinking beneath the waves. Jesus put up with his followers' reluctance to believe and with their personal ambitions that exceeded their spiritual readiness. He was willing to show Thomas his scars after his own resurrection so that Thomas could grasp something of the reality of that event. Jesus applied mud and saliva (a common ointment in those days) to the eyes of a blind man who seemed to need that treatment, even when he healed others who didn't require that kind of aid. If Jesus truly believed the saliva and mud to be his customary treatment for blindness, why did he only use it in a couple of recorded instances and not in the case of others?

In the case of the Gadarene demoniac, Jesus "allowed" the devils to go out of the insane man and into swine, though there is no mention of this type of exorcism in any other instance of his healing work with the insane. Did the demons absolutely need to "go into" the swine? Maybe not. Did they actually go there? We will never know. Were the people around Jesus, including the insane man, helped or convinced by the authenticity of the cure when they saw the swine stampede into the water? Evidently. It appears that **Jesus was willing to adapt his healing work to the needs of patients and, in the Gadarene's case, to a local animistic environment (Mark 5: 1–20). Jesus' variety of means of treatment is illustrated in an array of approaches to healing the blind (John 9:6–7; Mark 8:24; Matthew 9:29–30)**.

Jesus spoke in language that his listeners could understand—parables for the crowds of followers who might have struggled to comprehend theology. He rested, slept, ate normally, and wept over the death of a friend (John 11). And though he preached non-violence (Matthew 5:39 and 26:52), in one instance he allowed his disciples to carry weapons to protect themselves (Luke 22:36).

The role of concessions

What are the concessions or compromises in the foundational writings of Christian Science? The description of these concessions is fairly plain and straightforward in *Science and Health* and elsewhere, and not hidden from our church flock like some dangerous contaminant. Our church members have been dancing around these passages for over a century, so that too few church members are even aware of many of the safeguard provisions visible in our written tradition.

I have referred to various concessions of a concrete nature already, but let's review some of them briefly here:

Some are broad in nature, such as the time (1) when Mrs. Eddy asked healers to stop treating infectious and contagious diseases (see Chapter 17). Other concessions are specific to a realm of medical treatment or counsel such as (2) pain relief (*S&H* 464), (3) conferring with a physician (*Manual*, "Duty to Patients," 47) and recommending the choice of a "learned…skillful" physician if that was a Christian Scientist's choice (*Hea.* 14:10) (4) use of an anesthetic (ether) during surgery[3] (5) vaccinations (*My.* 344:30) and (6) surgery (*S&H* 401) which has potentially broad application. Because statements such as (7) God guiding Christian Scientists into "the right use of temporary and eternal means" (*S&H* 444) are unspecific, they are subject to speculation among church members and require students of Christian Science to think for themselves, pray, and not base their actions on preset assumptions.

The fact that most Christian Scientists go to dentists and optometrists for help with their teeth and vision is rarely discussed in church writings. That practice is justified by church members because those fields of medicine are "mechanical," but is a root canal surgery any more or less intrusive than many types of laser surgery for problems outside the realms of optometry and dentistry? The exact function of physical exercise, and how much of a concession it is for a Christian Scientist, is another subject that needs more discussion in our magazines.

---

3. A10407 courtesy of Mary Baker Eddy Library.

The "why" more important than the "what"

When you notice the breadth of the above-listed concessions, you can tell that Mrs. Eddy over a period of years determined that there were humane allowances that would be needed not by all Christian Scientists maybe, and not on all occasions. As life jackets on a ship and guardrails along a highway are provided as safety features to protect ocean passengers and car drivers, so Christian Scientists might require some **fail-safe measures** to protect their lives as well as give them the assurance that their church really cared about their well-being in the event that their prayers and the prayers of others ever proved inadequate for them. Highway guardrails and life jackets are not intended to encourage bad driving or reckless sailing. Those safety measures are **thoughtful considerations** for everyone invested in safe travel.

Does a ship's passenger feel less confident or more confident in the abilities of a ship's captain and crew when lifeboats and life jackets are readily available? That's an easy answer. When Christian Scientists realize that those guiding their spiritual path have their overall safety in mind, their fear is lessened, and therefore they can pray and carry on with their lives, knowing that all of the above considerate provisions are part of "divine Love" meeting their "every human need" (S&H 494).

Let's say that we tell our son or daughter who is learning to ride a bicycle, "You need to learn to ride with no training wheels because that will show that you have both faith and skill. Training wheels are material props and are only for the faithless." Well, we're not being either merciful or honest about our own gradual learning experiences. Many children have become so skilled with training wheels still on their bicycle that they've found themselves not needing those supports before an adult removes the extra wheels from the bicycle.

When Christian Scientists disagree about concessions…

People who read the "concessionary" statements in this chapter tend towards three views on the statements. Those readers may conclude either that:
- The **concessionary statements are hypocritical evasions** and run

counter to everything else in the Christian Science textbook. Therefore, these evasions are only a weak attempt by Mrs. Eddy to avoid the legal prosecution of her church.

- **These statements do *not* mean what they appear to mean at all, and in any case are superseded by many other statements in Christian Science writings.** "Temporary" does not mean "material." "Surgery" only applies to setting bones, and is to be discouraged, and is an indication that those going to a surgeon are of lesser spiritual mettle and should repent after they have had a bone set, in order to repair their standing in the church.
- **These statements mean what each and every one of them says** in relation to temporary (i.e. material) means, pain relief, surgery, etc., and they should be considered seriously and in the context of everything else in the Christian Science textbook.

Those siding with the view of the first point tend to be harsh critics of the church. View of the second point is close to what some official church statements and other Christian Scientists have suggested, or said outright, especially beginning in the 1950s. This author agrees with the interpretation in the third point.

In this chapter we are merely raising the outlines of a large subject. It is the view of the author that helpful religious concessions: (1) do not concede to any imagined weakness in the divine power; (2) nor are they based on any assumed incapacity of a divine Christian method. Instead, concessions motivated by (a) **compassion for others** and by (b) **self-knowledge and honesty about any situation** tend to steer a sincere Christian or Christian Scientist in a forward-moving direction. If a religious teaching fails to take into account the potential fears and frailties of worshippers, as well as the mental climate of an age or region, that teaching is asking for trouble to occur.

Are there "no concessions?"

Various articles in the Christian Science church magazines over the past century have argued for a doctrinal position that downplays any substantial role for religious concessions in Christian Science practice. George Channing, a practitioner and teacher of Christian Science and father of the actress Carol Channing, in 1949 wrote an editorial in the *Sentinel* entitled "No Concessions to Matter."[4] Without exact reference to the particular passages where Mrs. Eddy alludes to the use of a painkiller to relieve suffering, or surgery, or "temporary means," Mr. Channing described these passages as "allowances" but not "concessions." The following is an excerpt from that article:

Why does Mrs. Eddy twice assert and at other times imply her lack of jurisdiction over any would-be follower of hers who lets circumstances convince him that he should turn to those very methods which are no part of his religion?

What is he saying here about Christian Scientists letting "circumstances convince [them] that [they] should turn to those very methods that are no part of [their] religion?" Why would Mrs. Eddy have planted a proverbial forbidden tree in the midst of her book, her spiritual garden, when that "tree" preaches the polar opposite of her book's message? This author believes that she did not do that. The reader of Mrs. Eddy's text has to read the full context of that book's contents, or the meaning is missed. Everything in *Science and Health* relates constructively to the reader's spiritual and human purpose in life. Mrs. Eddy says it clearly: "**…[I]n this volume of mine there are no contradictory statements…**" (*S&H* 345)

In *Science and Health* are statements of what we call "absolute" truth, declarations of the all-power and all-presence of the one Mind. There are also statements about such relatively mundane matters as to how marriages can be made more collaborative between the marriage partners. There are cautionary statements about everything from talking unnecessarily about disease, to knowing one's capacity to brave a storm, to making too much of one's age, and also taking a pain-reliever under circumstances of intense pain when the would-be Christian Scientist is unrelieved by prayer. Again, from the article by George Channing: "The implication is plain that recourse to other means than [Christian] Science will not do final or substantial good."

---

4. Channing, "No Concessions to Matter," *C. S. Sentinel* 7-9-1949.

If this statement is true, then why would "God guide" Christian Scientists into a course of action that possessed no 'substantial good' at all? (S&H 444:7–12)

Must we do semantic double flips to avoid any potential conflict in our church teachings? Our church can hardly tell its members to never take medicine if Mrs. Eddy wrote about the use of pain relief under certain circumstances, wrote positively about surgery,[5] engaged physicians for herself, and those physicians administered morphine to her on several occasions.

In trying to avoid that conflict Mr. Channing attempts to say that Mrs. Eddy didn't really concede to anything at all, least of all the "laws of matter." We cannot in the long-run get away with our denials since *Science and Health* says plainly: **"Jesus' concessions (in certain cases) to material methods were for the advancement of spiritual good"** (S&H 56). Note that this sentence does not read: "Jesus allowed the spiritually disabled and weak to use material methods, but only bad things happened as a result." Why have we tried so hard to justify the unjustifiable position that real Christian Scientists never concede to anything at any time, ever?

When dogmatism finds itself in its own trap

The irony about George Channing's article is that **his professional life was built on a concession** and a significant compromise with the culture of his times. Channing's mother was African-American.[6] Had this fact been widely known among his Christian Science colleagues and friends, Channing could have worked as a practitioner of Christian Science, but, since the church was segregated for most of his career, his star never would have risen beyond his work as a local healer.

In fact, Channing became not only a Christian Science teacher but also a lecturer, editor, and the Committee on Publication (public relations officer) for the whole church. None of those other positions would

---

5. Eddy, *Science and Health*, 401; and *Miscellany* 345:21.
6. Channing, *Just Lucky*, 8.

have been reachable for him had he openly gone public and openly admitted that he was part African-American and was "passing" as a white man. In appearance he did not look dark-skinned. An elderly friend of the author told me, "Mr. Channing wasn't black when he lectured in our church." Pictures of him indicate very little in the way of African-American ancestry, but in 1937 he told his daughter Carol the family secret, and the secret was kept within the family during his lifetime.

Why has it been so hard for Christian Scientists to say "compromise"?

In his excellent and thought-provoking biography about Mrs. Eddy, *Rolling Away the Stone*, Stephen Gottschalk goes to lengths not untypical of Christian Scientists to make the case that the author of *Science and Health* never underwent "medical treatment" after her discovery of Christian Science. **"While she herself never sought medical treatment for healing after her work in Christian Science began, she found it necessary on a limited number of occasions to use morphine for the relief of extreme pain."**[7]

When someone unfamiliar with Christian Science reads this, what are they thinking? To what extremes do we need to go to try to make the point that Mrs. Eddy never conceded to medical treatment at all? This kind of assertion, similar to the aforementioned article by George Channing, makes us look hypocritical in the eyes of the public. No, an injection of morphine is not surgery or a curative for kidney stones, but to argue that morphine is no form of medical treatment undermines all reasonable points we may have put forward, and it calls into question our **rational consistency** because of that one evasion. A medical treatment is virtually anything that a trained M.D. administers, whether it is a drug, pain reliever, or an over-the-counter medicine that we may take without a doctor present. Why bother arguing that morphine injections are not medicine of some kind?

Gottschalk, to his credit, points out that Mrs. Eddy left in *Science*

---

7. Gottschalk, 349.

and Health and elsewhere written guidance that was an anticipation of **"a dilemma that others might face in future years and** [would] **help...them to resolve it without evasion or guilt."**[8]

Compromise can be a hard pill to swallow

Bliss Knapp was an early practitioner, teacher, and lecturer for the church, and an ardent devotee of Mrs. Eddy. Nineteen years after her passing, when Knapp learned from an editorial in the *Journal* (March, 1929) that Mrs. Eddy had indeed taken morphine, his wife wrote that he was "*greatly* troubled."[9]

Knapp's diary showed his shock that Mrs. Eddy "took drugs!!!"[10] The *Journal* editorial had specifically, and incorrectly, cited Mrs. Eddy taking an anesthetic. Morphine, which Mrs. Eddy had employed on several occasions, is not an anesthetic but an analgesic (pain reliever) that reduces pain but does not block all feeling as an anesthetic does, which is why the latter is used for surgery.

Hadn't page 464 in *Science and Health* already made plain to Christian Scientists that material pain relief in critical circumstances was **no departure from the faith**? For indecipherable reasons, since the 1920s our church's official writings have gone to great lengths to skirt around the problem of concessions or compromise, when simply facing facts might have made Christian Science more understandable and self-consistent than trying to stake out an untenable "official stance" that only the most dedicated church members would accept. Has it been pride in our denomination, and not our actual closeness to spiritual truth, that has motivated our evasion of the subject of concessions and compromise?

No "stupefying cup of appeasement or concession"

To some of Mrs. Eddy's followers any concession to material means constitutes a spiritual loss, and they have believed that one's conduct

---
8. Ibid., 350.
9. Houpt, *Bliss Knapp*, 251.
10. Ibid.

of Christian Science practice must meet a standard that rejected any hint of medical intrusion. A highly influential Christian Science teacher wrote, "Jesus drank the cup necessary to demonstration, but not the stupefying cup of appeasement or concession."[11]

In another article this teacher wrote: "*Science and Health* concedes nothing to error. It makes no compromise with matter or material medicine."[12] Statements such as these contrast with some words in *Science and Health* where the tone is different. Again, "Jesus' concessions (in certain cases) to material methods were for the advancement of spiritual good" (S&H 56:4). So did Jesus allow concessions for the purpose of spiritual advancement, or did he make no concessions at all?

Reconciling apparent doctrinal contradictions

Instead of awkward attempts to justify any particular interpretation of a doctrine which may leave us on a shaky basis, representatives of our church and other faiths should pour more energy into examining and adjusting apparent conflicts in explanations of their faith practices and concessions. It's important to seek to resolve those conflicts in as honest and sincere a manner as possible. It's time to listen to our church's opponents, who have been rightly pointing out for decades the inconsistencies in our **convoluted self-justifications**.

According to the New Testament, Jesus says to "resist not evil," but in James we read an exhortation to "resist the devil."[13] When researching different Bible translations, we find that the first verse refers to people, so the apparently conflicting verses don't really clash with each other. In *Science and Health* we read, "You weaken or destroy your power [to heal] when you resort to any except spiritual means" (181:12–13). That verse appears to conflict with passages cited in this chapter regarding alleviation of extreme pain, surgery, vaccination, etc. Perhaps an attempt at reconciling here could be reached by seeing that the concessions we have pointed to are primarily palliative measures of care. That

---

11. "Consistency," *C. S. Journal*, January, 1952.
12. "Advancing," *C. S. Journal*, June, 1958.
13. Matthew 5:39 and James 4:7 KJV.

is they "lessen severity without curing" as Webster's describes *palliative*. This is one short note in a discussion that could and should be far more comprehensive than space allows here.

What are concessions that "slip-slide away" from faith?

A concession may be unhelpful to our spiritual progress **when fear is the prime and continuing motivation**, and when the illumination of our life's aspirations dims as a result of that concession. **When temporary or appropriate-at-the-time measures become permanent ruts** in our road of life, we are slip-sliding away from being honest with ourselves and what we deeply believe. There is no hard and fast benchmark for when we are selling out our soul to the world or losing track of our spiritual sense, but we can feel in our heart when that is taking place.

Mrs. Eddy writes, "Attempts to conciliate [win over] society and so gain dominion over mankind, arise from worldly weakness" (*S&H* 238:22). **Are we making concessions in order to make our cause more popular?** Isn't there a difference between seeking popularity for our cause and seeking what is merciful to our own people or others? Recall the distinction that Burke spoke of—concessions from a point of weakness being a result of fear, whereas concessions from a point of strength are motivated by the desire to be merciful. When Paul circumcised Timothy, was he trying to win approval from the Jewish-Christians, or was it an appropriate concession? Did Paul desire approval to support his own sense of insecurity? Or was he extending kindness, by way of reaching out toward Timothy and the Jewish community? These are the type of questions we must always be asking ourselves.

Here is a fork in the road expressed in biblical language, where Paul wrote: "As a Christian I *may* do anything, but that does not mean that everything is good for me [to do]" (I Cor. 6:12 J.B. Phillips). Also, from Paul: **"Don't let the world around you squeeze you into its own mould…"** (Romans 12:2 J.B. Phillips)

What was the "lesson of the grass"?

Daisette McKenzie remembered some life-saving guidance which Mrs. Eddy once shared with her and her husband-to-be William McKenzie: **"I had to learn the lesson of the grass. When the wind blew I bowed before it, and when mortal mind put its heel upon me, I went down and down in humility and waited,—waited until it took its heel off, and then I rose up."**[14]

Mrs. McKenzie noted that this caution from Mrs. Eddy **"practically saved our lives."** To what did Mrs. McKenzie refer when she said that this instruction "practically saved our lives?" We don't know. But we may intuit that this "lesson of the grass" is **the lesson of the cross**. It is the lesson of humility springing from self-knowledge and hard experience.

The lesson of the grass may include submission to powers, customs, conditions, or laws that a state law might insist on, even when a believer might find those conditions objectionable. This "lesson of the grass" and the demand for individual and church humility embodies much that Christian Scientists, especially in the present era, **may be required to go through**. The good news, as Paul relates it, is that the cross is the "very power of God" (I Cor. 1:18 NLT). Jesus submitted to the cross, but he ultimately succeeded in all that the crucifixion was intended to take from him—his life and mission.

We can see this "lesson of the grass" and its long-run victories throughout modern history. Jews endured centuries, millennia really, of steady discrimination and a diaspora that scattered them around the world in colonies. Yet the very effort to totally exterminate them in the early to mid-twentieth century ultimated in the formation of a Jewish homeland. The citizens of Eastern Europe were suppressed by communist rule for over forty years, but have largely risen up from that period of suppression, which most experts believed would continue for far longer than it did. The irony of the "lesson of the grass" is that **going down can be a pre-requisite for going up**. An ex-offender friend of the author puts it this way: **"Every setback is a set-up for a comeback."** Grass is crushed to the earth for a time, but it springs back into vitality.

---

14. Peel, *Years of Authority,* 84.

Mortals ask, "Why can't we just go straight up?" The answer is that sometimes we can. Then there are times, sometimes brief, sometimes extended, when people throughout history have had to experience dark times, but that submission in "going down" has led to a latter-day liberation.

> *The grass beneath our feet silently exclaims, 'The meek shall inherit the earth.'*
> Science and Health, 516

What and where is the Babylon of today?

Much has changed since the early years of the Christian Science movement, and today Christian Scientists are forced to adapt to what seems to them to be a foreign experience, as the Jews were forced to adapt to the Babylonian captivity. **Can Christian Scientists adapt their practice to the demands and needs of the present age without being co-opted by their society and subsequently losing their moral and spiritual bearings?**

This message is stated throughout these pages: **Christian Scientists may need to experience a collective humbling leading to a return more closely to their Christian roots that would show them how to communally advance, and which allows them to then help their world**. Jeremiah warned that the Jews who failed to follow Jeremiah's guidance from the Lord, and resisted going into captivity in Babylon were **"rotten figs"** (Jeremiah 24:2 ERV). Does his advice seem counterintuitive? Shouldn't the Jews have struggled against their Babylonian captors? From Jeremiah's inspired intuition, the prophet saw the long-run design of things—a necessary period of collective chastisement and humiliation followed by a return to the Jewish homeland.

The religious law as a bridge

In explaining the function of the Jewish Law, Paul referred to it as a "strict tutor in charge of us until we went to the school of Christ" (Galatians 3:24 J.B. Phillips). To Paul the Law's function was not simply to teach obedience to the Law for its own sake. It served to channel or corral the unruly thought and bring it to a higher sense of self-control by the Spirit embraced in Christ.

Perhaps Christian Scientists can view **the role of medical concessions** in our recent age in a similar vein. Those concessions are not a permanent dispensation for the Christian Scientist but can be **a grace of temporary but needful value**, as the Babylonian captivity had been for the Jewish people. The Christian Scientists' concessions today can possess a purpose that may gradually lead us to a purer and deeper love, a more comprehensive form of spiritual treatment, care, and cure that requires less physical intervention, tinkering, and speculation that are inherent in many material processes.

This book suggests that Christian Scientists have gone wrong in a blithe dismissal of the entire role of medical concessions. We haven't wanted to think about this subject, so we have tended to rule it out of our discussion. Even a bothersome fly can teach patience. A traffic jam can slow down a commuter's ego and will. Medical concessions in the lives of a Christian Scientist can be something to be feared, regretted, and avoided at all costs, or those concessions can sometimes serve not as a rebuke for lack of spiritual sense, but—just as the Law of Moses served Paul—they can become part of a pathway higher and forward.

Part of the Christian building process

The context and motivation behind a concession cannot be treated as if it were some random outlier with no moral or Christian basis. Christians and Christian Scientists have tended to dismiss concessions as disconnected fragments that have no connection to the long-run guidance of the flock. As the daughter of a practitioner said so well:

"Relying on prayer completely is a step-by-step process/journey, not a leap from the bottom to the top."

A result of concealing or downplaying our concessions

From a former Principia student dealing with surgery and relief from chronic pain:

> I had two back operations about two months ago. I just spoke to the doctor who said I was already healed up and that I could go back to work full-time! Thirteen years of pain and suffering no more. No more pain medication! No more crying myself to sleep, if I could sleep at all! Not a Christian Science healing but at least some relief. It was getting harder and harder to fake being normal. I have not quit praying about it, however, and expect a full TRUE healing sooner or later.

Was this individual ever told by another Christian Scientist that the texts of Christian Science do not rule out surgery? While no reputable physician or metaphysician guarantees their patient either a risk-free surgery [and back surgeries can be very risky] or a pain-free future, conscientious Christian Scientists should refrain from discouraging anyone from considering surgery, especially in cases like this where the patient has failed to find relief as a result of their prayerful work.

From a church member, discussing the role of mercy: **"What drives people away from church is feeling they have nowhere to turn in their quandary. They have not yet experienced spiritual healing, yet their fellow church members would criticize them if they went to a doctor."**

Drawing the lines in awkward places

When you draw the lines of religious *do's* and *don'ts* based on random or willful justifications, you leave a trail of convoluted teaching and dogma that is as awkward as it may be hypocritical. Then people turn away from things of the Spirit, and religion is made a sham. Too often when religious people cannot find in their faith's inspired writings statements that justify their believed-in dogma, they twist a word or two, take statements out of context, and soon the resulting new teaching possesses a different character from the original.

Summary:
Concessions in line with the spirit of Christ can be:
- **A bridge, not a leap into the unknown; a banister that does not eliminate the stairs to be climbed, but supports and makes our climb more doable.**
  Example: Allowances for pain relief fall into this category. The "prime object" of Christian Science was **"to prevent suffering, not to produce it"** (S&H 457:10–12). Mrs. Eddy wished to prevent any abuse of what she held most dear—the healing work.
- **Scaffolding in the "construction process" of our lives.**
  Example: Mrs. Eddy suggested in a short article about marriage, that Jesus allowed for John's baptism of him because "the period demanded it" (Mis. 298:18). Our church's provision for free prayer treatment in veterans' hospitals in 1947 was possibly a similar concession. It was a merciful action by the church, and that loving action can be a useful precedent today.
- **A hand up, as Jesus helped Peter out of the waves, Love "support[ing] the struggling heart"** (S&H 57).
  Example: Mrs. Eddy's statement in 1901 allowing for vaccinations where required, for the purpose of reducing the fears of the public. Her statement illustrated where **not to "force consciousness"** (Mis. 288:18) in directions that the public could not understand. Her concern that we not force consciousness, is an echo of Jesus' own statement: "First the blade, then the ear, after that the full corn in the ear" (Mark 4:28). Mrs. Eddy wrote in 1893, **"In non-essentials[15] we have always to consider what the general public can accept."**[16] And what the public can accept usually takes place over time and is an incremental, step-by-step process (see Chapter 19).

  Paul, in justifying his support of the need for Christians to get married, wrote: "It is better to marry than to burn" (I Cor. 7:9). While this may seem to be weak as a theological point, it certainly

---

15. The author recognizes that any number of Christian Scientists will find it very difficult to exactly determine what are essential as opposed to non-essential aspects of our religious teaching.
16. Nenneman, *Persistent Pilgrim*, 225.

addressed what the general public of Christians in his day and ours could grasp and receive from Paul as a rational justification for getting married. Paul no doubt realized he could not "force consciousness" where it was not able or ready to go.

- **An empowerment, not an "enabling"**
"Enabling" is defined as well-intended protection of others from the consequences of their own actions.
Example: See Chapter 19 regarding the relative wisdom of Christian Scientists seeking exemptions from various legal requirements. Individual Christian Scientists must be honest with themselves: Are they relying on Christian Science out of fear of the doctor? Or are they conscientiously at peace with the spiritual method they are pursuing? Taking a legal exemption out of fear does nothing to alleviate that fear, and may only increase it. So each one must privately ask, "Are exemptions enabling or empowering for me?"

If Christian Science was a set of unchanging, humanly-imposed rules or laws with no bend, then it would be only a new, updated set of commandments, with no grace, and therefore no rescuing Christ. Discoveries in quantum physics in the past century have not displaced classical physics, but have given that physical science a qualifying twist, so that the broad, sweeping statements of Isaac Newton are found to not be telling the whole story of our world without the addenda which quantum physicists have provided. Grace and honesty similarly affect the hard and fast rules of organized religion, and we're left with the essential spirit of "mercy and truth…met together" (Psalm 85:10) and a faith practice that endures.

Thanks be to God that, sprinkled through the evolving practice of Christian Science from its early, developing stages, and since Mrs. Eddy's passing in 1910, we see grace **rounding off the hard edges of the letter of teaching and revealing a practical core, the spirit of divine Love.** Without that grace, healing becomes problematic or impossible.

Abiding questions for further discussion:
- If "wisdom in human action begins with what is nearest right under the circumstances" (*Mis.* 288:13), how then do we discover what is that "nearest right?" And what is the "right use of temporary and eternal means?" (*S&H* 444:10)
- In trying to reach a conscientious decision, and praying for God's guidance, can I tell if my decision is being **over-influenced by societal pressure or, on the other hand, culturally channeled by church custom?**
- When is a religious concession practical for the long-range progress of a faith, and when does it lead to weakness and long-range demoralization or decline?
- Given that Christian Scientists are not to "recommend hygiene" (*S&H* 453:30), is there a time when a practitioner can appropriately suggest to a patient that he or she see a doctor? A possible answer might take the form of practitioners merely pointing out to their patients what Mrs. Eddy wrote about surgery, pain relief, temporary means, and so on.
- Mrs. Eddy wrote, "I have never found an hour when He would not deliver me."[17] Did that divine deliverance ever take the form of human or material aid?
- What does a Christian Science nursing facility do when a patient in that facility's care is in unrelieved physical pain or emotional suffering?
- The following stark statement appeared in the *Sentinel* in Mrs. Eddy's time regarding physical exercise: "Christian Scientists believe in cleanliness both in mind and body. They believe in exercise, for it is better to be alive than dead" (Alfred Farlow *C.S. Sentinel* May 16, 1903). On this subject, a Christian Science teacher once rhetorically asked his class students if they could imagine Jesus jogging in a sweatshirt and sweatpants. Perhaps he could have also asked those students if they could imagine Jesus in a tie and suit, sitting all day behind a desk. Clearly in Jesus' day physical exercise

---

17. EOR 10, courtesy Mary Baker Eddy Library.

and some manual labor were daily necessities for nearly everyone wanting to drink or eat, rather than being fitness options.
- Alfred Farlow had a talent for making important distinctions about the practice and beliefs of Christian Scientists. In two separate articles about **vaccination** and (nine years later) **precaution**, he made the following points that are as useful today as they were one hundred years ago:
  - First, regarding **vaccination**: Christian Scientists have no faith in vaccination itself, and they lean on divine protection from contagious disease, yet they are in league with no blanket anti-vaccination campaign.

    Christian Scientists do not consider smallpox or any disease to be merely imagination, but they see disease as "based largely on fear, conscious or unconscious." And lastly, **"it does not lessen the efficiency of prayers to be careful in respect to the spreading of disease; Christian Scientists do not recklessly run into its presence."**[18]
  - Then, regarding **precaution**: Christian Scientists have an obligation in this age to often choose between two evils. "Our present limited degree of trust [in God] demands a cognizance of evil as a serious claim, and the **exercise** of **both faith and discretion** in deciding it as such." We **should avoid taking unnecessary risks, but** "mere precaution does not necessarily depreciate one's faith or confidence in God."[19]

There is a familiar proverb of a man stranded on a roof with floodwaters surrounding him. The man turned away helpful rowboats and others offering assistance, because he was "waiting for God to save him." Christian Scientists have too often turned away appropriate, simple means of salvation that would not necessarily compromise their spiritual integrity but would allow their lives to move forward. It is the author's conviction that salvation often arrives at our doorstep wearing simple, humble clothes.

---

18. "A Protest" *Christian Science Sentinel* 1/31/1901.
19. "Proper precaution, reasonable care, pure food, fresh air..." *C.S. Sentinel* 7/9/1910.

CHAPTER 23

Living with questions about prayer and medicine

We do not know how to pray as we ought, but that very Spirit intercedes with sighs too deep for words.

Romans 8:26 NRSV

HUMAN EXPERIENCE IS full of contradictions. This book is an attempt to make sense of some of the contradictions in the lives of Christian Scientists and to see a workable path forward towards a vital present and future in those lives. How do Christian Scientists chart a course for their lives that allows them to survive in the twenty-first century but also allows them to maintain a sense of spiritual integrity—that they are being true to their faith?

Should we ever be reluctant to pray?

One of the aspects of Christian Science tradition that is most confounding to people not of that faith is that many Christian Scientists are **reluctant to pray for their fellows who are under the treatment of a regular physician**. In a moment we'll examine where that conviction comes from. But this book deals with exceptions to that practice, a practice which seems anomalous to many Christians.

Christians are generally taught to think of doctors and medicine as blessings from God and in no way working in conflict with the divine purposes. It may come as a surprise to Christian Scientists that there is a textual, Scripture-connected source for the divine blessing of doctors, and it's found in the Book of Sirach,[1] a non-canonical part of the Bible's Apocrypha that is read in some Christian churches.[2] The following passages are from Sirach (RSV):

> Honor the physician with the honor due him, according to your need of him, for the Lord created him; for healing comes from the Most High, and he will receive a gift from the king.
>
> The skill of the physician lifts up his head, and in the presence of great men he is admired. The Lord created medicines from the earth, and a sensible man will not despise them.
>
> And he [the Lord] gave skill to men that he might be glorified in his marvelous works. By them he heals and takes away pain; the pharmacist makes of them a compound. There is a time when success lies in the hands of physicians, for they too will pray to the Lord.[3]

Christian Scientists may justifiably point to the non-canonical nature of Sirach as a reason to see that book as a biblical outlier. Healing works cited most often in the New Testament of the Bible are connected to prayer and holy men working without herbs and medicines, though occasionally with a placebo such as the poultice of figs which Isaiah prescribed for Hezekiah (II Kings 20:7).[4]

For the purposes of our discussion here, the verses from Sirach are offered as testimony to the socially widespread attitude that doctors are a blessing.

---

1. Written between 200–175 B.C.E.
2. The Catholic, Eastern Orthodox, and Oriental Orthodox churches include this text in their liturgy. Sirach is also included in The New Oxford Annotated Bible, a non-denominational scholarly text.
3. Sirach 38: 1–4, 6–8, 13, 14 RSV; Jesus, son of Sirach; aka Ecclesiasticus.
4. Other Christians are likely to point out also that Sirach professes little compassion for either women or slaves, and therefore, that its praise for doctors might only stem from a bias toward men of their own culture. Despite this collective objection, Mrs. Eddy herself stated praise for physicians: "Great respect is due the motives and philanthropy of the higher class of physicians" (S&H 151).

Teachings and experience

Christian Scientists will explain that one reason they prefer to withhold spiritual treatment from those under a doctor's care is out of professional courtesy to the physician. However, Christian chaplains see little conflict in their prayers for hospitalized patients. What is the main reason behind the Christian Scientists' reluctance to pray in these cases?

There are experiences which lend support to the custom of Christian Scientists not being willing to mentally treat someone who is under medical care. I have heard from several friends of occasions where a Christian Scientist was given an anesthetic, while at a dentist's office for example, and the anesthetic did not work. The church member believed someone was praying for them at the same time, **and the prayers appeared to have nullified the action of the anesthetic**. Can this happen?

In our first chapter we cited the experience of Michael where the morphine injections he was given in the hospital at one point seemed to have no effect on his pain.[5] I wonder if anything like this nullification of a drug's effect happens to people who are not Christian Scientists. When a Christian prays for a friend in the hospital, do those Christian prayers ever neutralize the intended benefit of a medicine given to that person? I've not heard of that happening to Christians, other than Christian Scientists, but I'm open to the possibility.

Reasoning behind not "mixing" meds and prayer treatment

The Epistle of James cautions against **"double-minded"**[6] **consciousness** as an **unstable** entity. *Science and Health* says: "It is not wise to take a **halting and half-way position** or to expect to work equally with Spirit and matter..." (*S&H* 167). This counsel recommends not just single-minded dedication demanded of those praying, but assumes that those relying on medicine for healing are depriving themselves of the full benefit of the divine healing power.

---

5. The morphine's ineffectiveness could have been due to medical factors.
6 James 1:6–8

A problem that the author has encountered with those involved in medical care is the self-conflicting nature of medical treatment when one med causes side effects that another med is then prescribed to counter. At that point the patient begins to wonder whether the intended cure or aid is worse than the illness. I remember visiting a hospitalized patient who complained to her doctor about diarrhea. The doctor looked at her and in a confident tone said, "Well, that's what I would have expected from the drugs you've been taking."

Side effects in drug treatment illustrate one reason why Christian Scientists tend to avoid medicine, and those ill effects were also noted in Mrs. Eddy's critique of medical care one hundred years ago. When Mrs. Eddy was once asked if modern technology was "too material" for Christian Science, she responded that her prime objection was to **"false science—healing by drugs"** (*My*. 345:12).

Research required

The author believes that there should be more thorough study of what works and what heals and what does not in the experience of Christian Scientists who have received medical treatment and spiritual treatment at the same time. At present we only possess a collection of anecdotal testimonies, but an initial study, as non-anecdotal as possible, could serve as a starting point in bringing clarity to this subject. Too often at present any discussion on this topic relies upon conjecture. Note the following caution from William F. Buckley, Jr.:

"General rules based on individual victims are unwise."

National Review June 29, 2004

Science of any kind requires more than solitary examples in order to arrive at a "general rule." The author is willing to apply that statement to everything in this book. But as the scientific method suggests, outcomes that may begin with the observation of solitary examples can ultimately point towards conclusions applicable in multiple circumstances.

I have heard the following view from Christian Scientists: **"Medicine is intended to help the body physically, while prayer, turned** to for healing, is addressing one's body as a composite of thought." Couldn't that view be interpreted in two ways: (a) as a caution against "riding two horses going in opposite directions" (and therefore an argument *against* combining prayer and meds) or (b) supporting reasoning which asserts that because medicine and prayer work on different paths, therefore they are *not in conflict* with one another when operating at the same time with the same person. **But when medicine and prayer are active concurrently, can the patient have a clear sense of where healing comes from?** Maybe that's a question that would be difficult to answer precisely, whether there was a "mixture" of prayer and medical treatment going on or not. Even the most knowledgeable physician is sometimes unsure about the cause of a patient's recovery.

Is this "mixing" or is this success?

The following is an example of a Christian Scientist who recovered surprisingly from the effects of a stroke while continuing to take medicine for high blood pressure. His experience suggests the possibility that we can receive successful spiritual treatment for one problem while still receiving standard medical help for another physical problem, even when the two problems may have a physiological relation. Let the readers judge for themselves based on their personal experience what is useful or counterproductive in their lives.

Bob's hospital sojourn

Although I was raised in Christian Science and attended Sunday school until I was 20, I regret to say that I, and my loving parents, were poor metaphysicians. When we were sick, which was rare, we called a doctor and rarely turned to Christian Science for any kind of healing. We believed that healing was for those who studied it intently for years. I had one significant and instantaneous healing at sixteen with the help of my Sunday school teacher, for which I have always been grateful. At the time of the following events, I had decided to set Christian Science aside for a while as it applied to physical healing and pick it up later—perhaps when I was ninety! At no time, however, did I or my parents ever doubt the veracity of the teachings of Mary Baker Eddy. I did have a primary care physician at the time of the following events although I rarely needed his services.

Early one summer evening in 2009 in New York City I boarded a subway near my home on 54th Street to meet a friend near 14th Street. Although my legs were inexplicably wobbly, I was not feeling ill as I recall. During the ride, I remember some mental confusion regarding subway stops that had been familiar to me for years. At my stop on 14th Street, I had a difficult time climbing the stairs, and by the time I reached the street I had to hold on to construction rails to stand up. A gentleman asked if he should call an ambulance. I declined his offer, and with great difficulty he helped me to a coffee shop. I telephoned a friend who came immediately with someone else. They both got me into a taxi. I was never fearful for a moment during this episode, nor in the weeks that followed. A dear friend, an actress whom I had known for years, was staying with me and during her stay had a severe case of the flu with weird symptoms. I thought this is what I had. She and the doorman met the taxi. The doorman, who was strong, had to practically carry me to my apartment and my blessed bed. During that evening, he undoubtedly wearied of having to repeatedly come up and pick me up off the floor.

In the morning I called a home health-aide I knew who arrived with a walker that proved a godsend. After two days, he insisted we get into a taxi and see my doctor. Both he and my temporary roommate were adamant, and I relented. After hearing the symptoms, my doctor needed only to take my blood pressure, which was "through the roof," in order to say it was not the flu, but neurological, and he called an ambulance to take me to the hospital. (Note: I had been recently warned of high blood pressure but had without much thought decided I might give Christian Science a try and rejected any medical help. I forgot about Christian Science immediately, and the problem went untreated.) Once again, despite the doctor's diagnosis and a ride in an ambulance, I never felt an iota of fear. On the contrary, I viewed it all as sort of an adventure. I had never had this experience and was not in any real discomfort, and I was flattered by all the attention.

At the hospital, gruesome pictures of my brain showed severe damage.

I was having a stroke and was admitted for what turned out to be a three-week stay. I was at peace, however. I had been diagnosed and was being cared for by professionals. I felt safe. If worse came to worse there was, well, Christian Science to fall back on. **I do think this lack of fear, together with my expectation of a complete recovery, albeit based on a confidence in medical science, was crucial to my eventual recovery.** *I have been told that unless a stroke is treated within hours of its onset, severe consequences usually ensue.* **I didn't know this at the time** *and had gone several days without any type of treatment and without any ill effects.*

So I settled in for several weeks of breakfast-in-bed paid for by Medicare. A practitioner I knew well soon paid me a social visit. I asked him to accept me as a patient. He agreed but asked that I not mention his name to anyone. I have never known why, nor have I ever asked his reason for saying that. He never contacted me, and I soon assumed he had stopped treatment. **About this time, I asked one of the many medical residents that visited my bedside regularly what the medications I was taking were supposed to do. He explained that they were lowering and stabilizing my blood pressure. What is healing the brain damage? I asked. In that case, he replied that the body heals itself. I was stunned. Since I wasn't being treated through medication to heal brain damage, the more serious affliction, perhaps I could seek Christian Science treatment for it and leave the blood pressure problem for later.**

I called another Christian Science practitioner I knew and asked for treatment. She at first balked because of the hospital stay, but I talked her into it. Within days I was showing extraordinary progress. The delighted medical staff began parading me up and down the corridor like a teddy bear to show me off. I was soon discharged, at first with a walker, then a cane, and eventually nothing. It was a complete recovery. And there was no evidence of brain damage, although close friends will sarcastically disagree.

Although I am not necessarily advocating it, I firmly believe that, in my case, the **medical support and the blood pressure meds I received prevented fear from overwhelming me and making my spiritual treatment difficult.** *Looking back, I see clearly that after my discharge, I began a slow but steady progress toward the serious study and practice of the*

Christ Truth. A major illness was healed with Christian Science. It was a significant milestone for me.

Why did the first practitioner in the above account behave as he did?

At the risk of speculating, perhaps the practitioner did not want his prayerful work to be known, not merely for reasons of patient confidentiality and for reasons mentioned above concerning a conflict over his patient's reliance upon God for healing, but because praying for a church member in the hospital might be seen by others in the church as spiritually questionable—guilt by association. Is that anything like the priest in Jesus' parable of the Good Samaritan who walked by the wounded man in the ditch? William Barclay writes about the priest: *He hastened past. No doubt he was remembering that anyone who touched a dead man was unclean for seven days (Numbers 19:11). To touch him would mean losing his turn of duty in the Temple; and he refused to risk that.*[7]

Jesus and Sabbath violations

Is our church's "mixing" problem similar to the Sabbath problem that Jesus encountered when he healed someone on the holy day? "Why do ye that which is not lawful to do on the Sabbath days?" the Pharisees asked Jesus about those healing incidents. In response, Jesus pointed to the occasion when David and his comrades ate the priests' holy unleavened bread in the temple. Then the Master said something that must have seriously offended his rule-bound critics—that "the Son of man is Lord also of the Sabbath" (Luke 6:5).[8] **Christ is predominant over mortal, situational distinctions that God did not make. Christ looks past barriers created by mortals towards what is essentially needful in our experience.** According to Genesis, Chapter 1, the Sabbath is at root a day to appreciate the blessedness of God's creation, as

---

7. Barclay, *The New Daily Study Bible,* "The Gospel of Luke," 165.
8. Jesus also said, "**The Sabbath was made to meet the needs of people,** and not people to meet the requirements of the Sabbath" (Mark 2:27 NLT).

God is described in that chapter as "resting" and beholding the wonderful goodness of the divine creation. Is it primarily dogma collected over time that has attempted in many faith practices to honor the Sabbath by forsaking all work, including deeds which could be considered necessary, life-giving, and inherently blessing in their spirit and substance?

"Motive makes medicine"[9]

It's not so much crucial which protocol a church member or a doctor follows as much as being clear about **what we are trying to accomplish, why we are following a particular method, and what we are learning in the process**. Here is the motivation of a patient who recovered from AIDS:

> We made ten trips to the dialysis doctor. There was a doctor who directly told me, 'You are HIV positive.' My thought in response to that was, 'Whether I lived or died, **I so wanted to clean up my life**. It wasn't about kidneys cleaning up my blood. It was Spirit cleaning me up.' After one month or two or three, I can't recall, I was back on my feet. I am so grateful for the freedom. There is an unconditional Love here to help us.

The following from a patient points out both the problem with a mixture of motives and how we might get past that back-and-forth approach:

> *They gave me heart meds in the hospital, and I took them until I wasn't afraid anymore. The practitioner kept praying for me through all this. My Christian Science teacher said about the subject of 'mixing' that the essence of it all was our motive.* ***If our motive was, 'I want to live right and learn about God,' there's nothing mixed about that.*** *The problem of 'mixing' comes when there's a teeter-tottering back and forth, almost a systematic uncertainty if there can be such a thing, using both the medical and spiritual but with no clear trust in either one.*

---

9. A phrase coined by Dr. John Tutt, CSB, who had been a medical doctor before becoming a Christian Scientist.

This last statement lays out clearly the importance of our motivation, and it points to a very vital distinction that is helpful for both patients and practitioners to consider. Christian Scientists, by glibly using the term "mixing" as condemnation of a fellow church member, have tended to demean **people who are trying to find their way in life. The compassion of Jesus is required to appreciate and help in resolving the spiritual struggles that underlie a patient's back-and-forth faith quandaries**. Beneath the stereotype of someone not following others' straight lines of expectation and getting medical help, lies very thought-provoking territory that invites exploration. In pursuing that exploration we not only find through our own experience what produces the best healing and what does not, but we also discover that there are many types of "mixing" in this world. No one is entirely free of compromise, but **the deeper we ponder the lives and thinking of one another, the less judgmental we tend to become**.

> "The struggle for the recovery of invalids goes on, **not between material methods, but between mortal minds and immortal Mind**."
>
> S&H 145:8

When patients using medicine are not doing well…

The story below describes territory where Christian Scientists might agree more than disagree. If a patient is under medical treatment, in a hospital or not, and the treatment is not working, asking for prayer from anyone who offers it may seem like an appropriate thing to do.

A church member wrote the following question to Mrs. Eddy: "If [Christian] Scientists are called upon to care for a member of the family, or a friend in sickness, who is employing a regular physician, would it be right to treat this patient at all…?" Mrs. Eddy's answer may seem surprising to some church members:

> When patients are under material medical treatment, it is advisable in most cases that [Christian] Scientists do not treat them, or interfere with material medica. **If the patient is in peril**, and you

save him or alleviate his sufferings, although the medical attendant and friends have no faith in your method, **it is humane, and not unchristian, to do him all the good you can**…

Mis. 89:4

The reason that many people under a doctor's care ask for prayer is that they are afraid for their health outcome. If they were confident that the doctors had everything under control, and that there was no question about their recovery, they might not seek any kind of spiritual help or feel it was needed even if they believed in the power of prayer. **Wouldn't it be inhumane to withhold spiritual treatment where an individual is fearful about how they're doing?** In the above-cited circumstance, Mrs. Eddy writes that the humane thing to do is, yes, to join in the spiritual work on the patient's behalf and not worry about any possible metaphysical conflict or criticism aimed at the practitioner for doing this.

When a patient is given up by doctors, but still taking meds

The following incident gives a specific example of how a Christian Scientist might deal with someone cared for by a physician but "in peril." Mrs. Eddy reported her own instance of prayerfully treating a man whom doctors had dosed with a powerful purgative called Croton oil (*Mis.* 69). Though he was medicated this man was apparently given up by the physicians. Mrs. Eddy's treatment of him not only healed his intestinal inflammation, but **"neutralized the bad effects"** of the Croton oil. In this case, the Croton oil wasn't seen as an actual healing agent in itself. It was a popular purgative until the early twentieth century when its powerful toxic qualities led to its general disuse.

By "taking charge" of the situation, Mrs. Eddy was praying to see that the drug (the Croton oil) had no effect on the patient. She probably didn't believe that it was useful either medically or practically. If the man was "left to die," the drug could hardly have aided his morale.

So this situation is almost a gold standard of where prayerfully treating someone on medication can be beneficial because so much was stacked against the prospect of the man recovering that prayerful aid was likely welcomed as a form of potential help.

In a case like this the spiritual treatment would not encounter opposition from either the doctor who had left, or from the patient who was suffering under the medicine. Perhaps we could say this was less "mixing" than **replacing something worse with something that provided hope, and brought healing**.

When a Christian Scientist received prayer, under medical supervision

A *Journal*-listed practitioner, a friend of the author, was praying for his own daughter but was not able to relieve her extreme discomfort, so they both went to the hospital. The daughter was diagnosed with acute appendicitis, and surgery was scheduled for the next day. During the night, the practitioner prayed concertedly for his girl. In the morning the doctors ran more tests but found nothing wrong with the daughter's appendix. This testimony was submitted for publication in our church magazines, but was not accepted, possibly due to the initial medical intervention by the parent.

A Midwestern practitioner, noted for successfully working for years with doctors and her Christian Science patients, said: "We are just beginning to understand how to cooperate with physicians and 'thrive together.'[10] Medicine has thrived. We have not. But we can, and for the benefit of society, we must."

Science and Health suggests something similar about the potential positive influence of metaphysics on medical practice: "Through Christian Science, religion and medicine are inspired with a diviner essence..." (*S&H* 107:10).

---

10. "A genuine Christian Scientist loves Protestant and Catholic, D.D. and M.D.,—loves all who love God, good...It will be found that, instead of opposing, such an individual subserves the interests of both medical faculty and Christianity, and they **thrive together**, learning that Mind-power is good will towards men" (Eddy, *My.* 4:14).

Is there a time and place where spiritual, prayerful help is not useful?

Not really, if we believe that Spirit is ever-present, and that prayer is an expression of the heavenly breath. There is always room for true witnessing to be exercised.

Helping Aunt Bertha in the kitchen

Let's say that we're having Thanksgiving dinner at Aunt Bertha's house. She is famous for her Thanksgiving dinners but is notorious for chasing everyone out of the kitchen during the dinner's preparation. We notice that Aunt Bertha is looking flustered in the kitchen, and the hour is getting late, so we offer to help her. At first we're rebuffed, but later we persist and offer, "Aunt Bertha, can't we just slice the carrots for you while you work on the gravy and the potatoes?" Aunt Bertha relents.

Is this a possible way to view how a Christian Scientist can help a person with prayer who is also getting help for another condition from a doctor? In most cases, it has seemed to the author that dividing our reliance between a doctor's care and that of a Christian Science practitioner tends to be unsuccessful, especially where there is a constant "teetering back and forth" or "systematic uncertainty" in the consciousness of the patient as to what should be reliable and helpful. Why is that? **In situations where there is ongoing uncertainty about the source of reliable help, the patient's confusion tends to undermine their faith in which treatment to lean on**. It also tends to create doubt about whether any help can be found. This teetering can even negate potential placebo effects aiding recoveries.

But in cases of dire need amidst indecision over whether a patient should keep taking medicines, though still wanting prayer, why can't prayer function in some way as an aid? After the crisis is over it's then up to the patient to decide how he or she wants to handle any future health problems.

Compromise to what point?

A friend asks, "After a hospitalization, to what extent should a Christian Scientist compromise in submitting to medical after-care?"

Know thyself. Perhaps the best answer to that question is that the patient should **take into account and mentally sort through what they feel they can prove in the way of spiritual healing, what their family can tolerate or support, and what the medical opinions suggest or would dictate about their condition.**

Christian Scientists may talk about the preceding factors in private but have tended to not discuss them in our church publications though they are considerations that may be important for a number of churchgoers.

Standing in the gap and filling a void

Recommendation for practitioners Don't avoid the needs of your patients just because they have gone to the doctor. You may avoid or not treat spiritually the particular function which the doctor's prescription is aiming to alleviate or improve, especially if your patient feels they are relying on and/or being helped by the doctor's prescription. In other words, "**Don't compete** with what the doctor is trying to treat."

But by all means **pray for what the medicine is not intended to help**—the fears of the patient, the concern of the doctor, the attitudes of family and friends, and so on. There's plenty of prayerful work to be done. **Here's an example of a practitioner praying for someone who was on a painkiller, but the painkiller wasn't alleviating the patient's pain**:

> I have a patient who was on a painkiller in the hospital after knee surgery. The opioid was not alleviating my patient's pain enough, but the nurses were reluctant to recommend a larger dose because of the accompanying risks. When my patient's spouse called me about this problem, we got to work prayerfully.
>
> 'How do I go in here with prayer?' I wondered. I know there is nowhere that Christ will not go. We are grateful for the care in the hospital and the remedial good the painkiller is doing, or as

good as it is able to do, but let's go to that area of thought and fill the void that still seems to be in pain. Christ is going there. Christ is the comforter going to human consciousness that is in need. Twenty to thirty minutes later my patient's husband called in gratitude to tell me that his wife's pain was all gone. The nurses asked why the patient was feeling freer without any extra painkiller. My patient's husband replied that prayer is powerful, and the prayerful work going on from church support had been effective. We are open to witnessing how creatively Truth works.

M.D.W.

Can prayers clash with prayers?

Mrs. Eddy, in searching for causes behind the failure of prayer to restore President McKinley after he was shot, pointed to the **"insufficient faith or spiritual understanding, and a compound of prayers in which one earnest, tender desire works unconsciously against the *modus operandi* of another"** (*My.* 292:15). And further she writes of "the effect of one human desire or belief unwittingly neutralizing another, though both are equally sincere" (*My.* 293:7-12). This **appears to refer to those who were praying for President McKinley but were seeing him as a martyr, or they were fearing the likelihood of the President dying**.

Don't these observations point to the problem of one prayer competing with another, and in a sense **battling over the same ground**, especially if one of those prayers is weighed down by fears of death? Isn't this an example of how **negative competition among those engaged in prayer can work to a bad result**?

"Mixing" and support for soldiers and others

War violates the sixth commandment. However, all those caught up in a war or even those volunteering to enlist to fight, as the lesser of two evils, deserve our prayerful help. Just because a soldier is relying on temporary, lethal means for his protection, such as a gun, does not mean that we cannot pray for that soldier. Do soldiers want us to pray for them to kill many people? Probably not. Soldiers mostly want to survive their dangerous experience in the simplest, safest way possible.

In a similar way Christians and Christian Scientists pray for those undergoing surgery or receiving treatment in a hospital. Those praying are not trying to replace the doctor's treatment with their prayers. They are praying about potential problems that their loved one might encounter, which may not be alleviated by the medical treatment. Calming the fear of patients, nurses, and doctors cannot all be accomplished by a medical prescription.

Treating addictions

From a long-time practitioner friend of the author: "When you are asked to help an alcoholic, a drug addict, or a smoker, don't tell them to discontinue drinking, shooting dope, or stop smoking before you treat them. You help them overcome the desire through your ministrations."

It's a myth that any of us seek totally spiritual means for blessing our lives. Unintentionally we may eat foods that have chemicals in them. We may drive cars that pollute the atmosphere or rely on other less than perfect methods of functioning in today's world. We may make compromises in our search to live in a principled, spiritual manner, though we desire to live as consistently and as spiritually as we feel we can. **There are no hundred-percenters among us, neither total sinners nor total saints**.

Spiritual treatment for veterans

For those new to the practices of Christian Scientists, the following charitable offering was quite unique in the church's history, but it shouldn't have to be. Veterans from World War II had many needs, and perhaps a large number of them made it clear to the church headquarters in Boston that they needed help, but often they could not afford to pay for that help, so the church responded with a generous offer of love. There is no reason why this offer could not stand as a precedent for Christian Scientists performing similar charity to those "interested" while they are recuperating in institutions such as veterans' hospitals and ordinary medical hospitals as well.

From the *Christian Science Sentinel* **November 15, 1947**:

> Christian Science treatment from authorized Christian Science Workers is available, without charge, to veterans in government hospitals who are interested in Christian Science. Relatives and friends may send in the name of a veteran in a hospital to Manager, Camp Welfare Activities, 107 Falmouth Street, Boston 15, Massachusetts, and this information will be promptly sent on to the Worker calling at the specified hospital.

"Christ, Truth, gives mortals temporary food and clothing until the material, transformed with the ideal, disappears, and man is clothed and fed spiritually."

Science and Health, 442:23

Surgery

We have discussed this subject in earlier chapters, but it bears repeating: It is the view of the author that employing means such as surgery when prayer has not relieved suffering is not an unworthy compromise of spiritual values. Surgery in an emergency may be simply the employment of material means after a practitioner's work has not been effective in a particular case. Furthermore, cannot spiritual means or prayer be employed during surgery **when those spiritual means are not attempting to duplicate or compete with what the surgeon is attempting to accomplish?**

For example, a practitioner prayerfully supported a friend of the author during cancer surgery. The practitioner was praying that one Mind would be in full action during the surgery. He was also treating the fear of the patient and the physician; he was not competing with the surgical procedure. So is that "mixing," or is it not rather **performing a** role distinct from, but essentially supportive of and complementary to, the beneficial result of an operation?

What is appropriate "mixing"?

Sometimes Jesus' words regarding the impossibility of worshipping God and mammon simultaneously are used as scriptural endorsement for the rejection of medicine, even though *mammon* in Greek refers to the "god of riches" and has nothing to do with medicine. Christian Scientists can hardly be free of worshipping mammon if they give deference to those with material wealth or harbor dreams of their own accumulation of wealth (see Chapter 11). Herein, is the problem: **Christian Scientists (similar to other religionists) have tended to cherry-pick what constitutes heresy**. They have cherry-picked which human actions are an inappropriate or heretical mixing of the spiritual and material worlds and which actions are tolerable concessions for them.

For example, if we take Jesus' words regarding *mammon* and his estimate of the slight prospects for the rich in his time to enter heaven (Matt. 19:23), and apply them rigorously to Christians, or the Christian Science church membership, that would open up a field of judgment so wide in many Western churches as to extremely reduce the numbers of that congregation. This is especially true in the West today where even lower middle class citizens would be considered "rich" by the standards of Jesus' era. Most Christian churches don't discriminate against their wealthy members of course, because it is traditional in the West to encourage the rich, given that their *mammon* can help fund any number of church activities and building programs. All Christians today tend to pass over certain Gospel injunctions and then enculturate that toleration into their normal practice, but they would never call what they are doing "heresy" or "mixing."

The "sliding scale" that can trend upward

In Christian Science church history there is a noticeable **"sliding scale"** as to what constitutes "mixing." Early Christians mapped out precedents for this sliding scale. **In the evolution from Jewish practice to Christian-Jewish practice to Christian practice, what constituted a violation of kosher laws changed** (see Acts 15). The Apostle Paul encouraged Peter's evolution of thought, and the heavenly vision of a blanket of unclean beasts convinced Peter to step over that cultural line and to receive Gentiles into Christian company (Acts 10:11).

The author believes that **a similar evolution is taking place in our current times among Christian Scientists**, as they increasingly realize the fact that a church member's participation in some kind of medical regimen need not exclude that person either from fellowship or legitimacy as a genuine and full-fledged church member. This transition to acceptance must seem strange, even needless, to those who were not raised in Christian Science, but it is so ingrained in our church's tradition, that the quandary over reliance on medicine in relation to one's faith life remains a very open question among Christian Scientists. Paul's admonitions in Romans 14 suggest that the Christian practice **that offends a believer today may not do so later in that believer's experience**. Contrariwise, a practice that a believer tolerates today may be found outgrown and intolerable to that same person tomorrow.

We present here no argument for moral relativism as a precept for Christians. It is rather an observation that beliefs and practices change over the ages depending on a number of factors. This book is not saying there is some bowl of cherries called modern medicine which Christian Scientists should indulge in and forget their native reliance on prayer and God for healing. This book in no way overlooks the inherent limitations in the ability of medical systems to meet many urgent needs of humankind. The first pages of this book's introduction state that the duty of those devoted to the Christian Science faith is to invest all they can in helping their beliefs and practices grow in a direction that benefits humanity, while not straying from commitment to the essence of what they feel in their heart is an inspired teaching.

Helpful hint from a fellow Christian

When a Christian Scientist tried to explain to an evangelical friend her conflict over taking medicine for a time, that Christian friend said that in her church, when faced with possible conflicts of conscience, her fellow Christians would say, **"God over all."** What my church friend derived from that comment was that she would exercise her best understanding of the all-power of God gradually and ultimately, despite any temporary confusion on her part. She would see God, Spirit as supreme, surpassing all human means and fears, to the best of her ability all along life's journey.

This subject should be studied

It has been the author's experience that prayer by Christian Scientists can aid those under conventional medical care, especially when that prayer includes no attempt to counter or compete with the specific goal of what a medical treatment is trying to accomplish. But we must leave room for others to come to their own conclusions on this important subject. As we have said earlier in this chapter, there needs to be much greater clarity concerning this issue. By the results, successful or not, of our work, what constitutes sound guidance and help can be seen and known, and conclusions drawn.

> After all, **those who will live in peace must agree to disagree** in many things with their fellow-labourers, and not let little things part or disunite them.[11] (Rev. John Wesley quoting the Rev. George Whitefield)

The entry of great grace

If our practice of Christian Science was based on a number of dogmas with no bend, then we would have effectively created a new, updated set of commandments, with no grace and therefore no presence of a

---

11, Whitehead, *The Life of Rev. John Wesley,* 529.

merciful, rescuing Christ. Quantum theory has brought "bend" to the established rules of classical physics. Every development in the sciences influences what has gone before it and adds new dimensions to our understanding of the world. While divine Truth is eternally unchanging in one sense of that word, our understanding of it should grow and affect our religious practice as our perception expands.

Recommendations in brief:
Prayerfully treat, but don't compete. Christian Science is not involved in competition with conventional medical practice.

- Help where fear resides and where hope has been given up.
- Help in emergencies.

Our job as spiritual witnesses is not to pray for the drugs to work for a patient or for a patient not to need drugs. We are praying for Love to be with all on life's journey fully, and for Love to meet us all where we are.

- Be ready to speak truth when it is called for—stepping into the gap.
- Ask hospital chaplains how they pray, and be open to learning from their experiences.

Hospital chaplains have seen patient recoveries that have defied medical prognoses. What if Christian Scientists were curious enough to ask a number of chaplains to share with them some of the anecdotal circumstances whereby surprising healings have come about? Were family members praying? Did the doctors essentially give up, or were they still actively fighting for the patient's recovery?

How to make this subject clear in nonreligious language
The following are commonplace ways of saying what we are saying about the possibilities of treating spiritually what is going untreated in a hospital or in a situation involving medical caregiving.

- **"Hit 'em where they ain't"**—Wee Willie Keeler, American baseball player (i.e. hit the ball where fielders can't catch it or aren't in a position to do so). Prayerfully treat what medical treatment is not treating.

- **"Treat the 'undefended' thought"**—Bruce Klingbeil (see Chapter 26). This is very similar to the previous approach of covering neglected mental ground.

If **Jesus was willing** to put saliva on people's eyes and watch a desperate woman derive healing by touching his robe, **can't we squeeze drops of compassionate mercy out of our bucket of metaphysical teaching and help people** who are suffering and need help very much, no matter what their beliefs and personal situation may be?

Possible nocebo effect for the Christian Scientist
This is an hypothesis from the author: Can the fact that some Christian Scientists have experienced negative reactions when they have attempted concurrently to employ medical and spiritual treatment be a result of the nocebo effect? In other words, has the patient's fear and self-condemnation or the practitioner's fear or unconscious judgment caused a negative reaction? And would that negative side effect not have happened if the patient's or practitioner's thought had been devoid of any expectation of bad results due to the patient turning to medical aid?

CHAPTER 24

Accountability and standards for spiritual healing

...to measure themselves by their own standards or by comparison within their own circle...doesn't make for accurate estimation.
II Cor. 10:12 J. B. Phillips

An error doesn't become a mistake until you refuse to correct it.
Orlando Battista, Canadian-American author

THE SELF-IMPOSED STANDARDS of accountability for Christian Science practitioners are somewhere between too low and nearly non-existent, and that situation has existed for decades. It must change if spiritual healing practice is ever to be taken seriously by modern society. Is it possible to regulate and make accountable a religious practice that strives to be essentially spiritual? The answer is, "Absolutely yes!" *if* you are a religious entity that professes to be both Christian and scientific. If Christian Science were called something else, let's say, the Church of the High-flying Spirit, one could safely assume that it would be quite free of any regulation or accountability.

The author has been a Christian Science practitioner for over thirty-eight years, and has been listed in the *Christian Science Journal* for twenty-four of those years, but during that time-frame no church official or other practitioner has ever examined his record, requested current evidence of healing work, or demanded any advancement in the quality of his practice. Is this lack of professional accountability just an internal problem for Christian Scientists? No. It's a large stumbling block to public acceptance of what we preach. Here's how the problem is presented in a letter to the editor of the *Washington Post*, when the *Post* in 2009 carried an article suggesting that Christian Science practitioners might become eligible for reimbursement under the proposed "Obamacare" or Affordable Care Act:

> Christian Science healers are not licensed by any governmental entity. There is no independent certification test they have to pass; no required number of practice hours they must fulfill. They are licensed only by their church after a two-week course of study. Why would the federal government even begin to contemplate insurance coverage for this kind of service?[1]

So while church members' main concern might be whether a practitioner can heal people through prayer, that's not the first concern of outsiders. People unfamiliar with Christian Science want to know about a practitioner's credentials, professional preparation, and record of safe practice, as did the writer to the *Washington Post*, before they delve into the authenticity or effectiveness of the prayers of a practitioner. Church members must recognize this natural skepticism and the reasoning that underlies it.

Our church's lack of self-regulation may be convenient for the individual practitioner, but it should be shameful to Christian Scientists that we require so little credentialing and accountability for those who represent themselves as healers available to the public. The message that our church presents to the public by this inaction and institutional indifference is that we don't appear to care what others outside our religious sphere think about us. Of course, we should and do care. We have some distance to travel as a church in order to prove the value we place on accountability.

Standards and progress in society

The survival of Flight 1549 in the Hudson River in New York City, January 15, 2009 was no accident. Capt. Chesley Sullenberger and his crew landed their disabled passenger jet and safely evacuated all

---

1. Wan, "'Spiritual health care' raises church-state concerns," *Washington Post*, 11-23-2009.

one hundred fifty-five passengers. That accomplishment was not so much a "miracle on the Hudson," as the media dubbed it, as it was the result of a highly-trained pilot who taught and could practice flight safety, working together with a disciplined crew and with nearly all the passengers acting in a cooperative manner following established escape procedures. High standards are what distinguish advanced societies. Quality building standards prevent earthquakes from killing thousands. Strict maintenance and inspection standards have increased safety in air travel. New manufacturing and safety standards have decreased injury and fatality rates in automobile accidents.

What an immense relief we feel when we put our problems in competent hands. A pilot, a tax advisor, a skilled mechanic, a Great Physician— | **The Pure Food and Drug Act passed the US Congress in 1906.**[2]

someone who understands their field of endeavor and can calmly handle emergencies. When we have put our "burdens" under the supervision of someone who has high standards, we feel confident about our life-prospects.

If there was no accountability in society....

The commonly accepted modern tendency to quickly identify and remedy safety issues in society is called **root cause analysis**. This form of critical assessment breaks down a system or chain of events connected with an incident or disaster, and then, through careful analysis of possible combinations and factors, attempts to identify the cause or causes of the particular failure with the intent of preventing any recurrence. *The Christian Science Monitor* has for years pursued solutions to societal issues by identifying when the problem first appeared, then attempting to isolate factors that led to the emergence of the problem, and lastly searching out possible solutions.

From veteran journalist Bill Moyers:
What would happen if after a plane crash, we said, 'Oh... we don't want

---

2. This act mandated federal inspection of meat products, outlawed adulterated food products, and required the labeling of medicines. Many patent medicines prior to 1906 contained alcohol and cocaine.

to look in the past. We want to be forward looking... we don't want to pass blame.' No, we have a non-partisan, skilled inquiry. We spend a lot of money... get really bright people. And we find out to the best of our ability, what caused every single major plane crash in America. And because of that, aviation has an extraordinarily good safety record.[3]

"Fairly Reliable Bob's Used Cars" Boise, Idaho. Fortunately their reviews are way better than their suspicious-sounding name.

A safety-conscious attitude that cares about people's lives will even **search for potential difficulties before they become accidents.** This is the attitude of a forward-thinking people.

Standards and medical consistency

Let's look first at how standardization influenced Western medical practice in the twentieth century and then how standardization could be and has been applied to the practice of Christian Science.

Conventional medicine has achieved admirable technical improvements and an ability to treat a far larger realm of diseases than it did a century ago. The author suggests that much of the progress in medical practice has derived from societal steps forward in standardization and technological advancement. Nevertheless, there are still serious inconsistencies and inequities in the cost and delivery of medical care[4] in the United States.[5]

---

3. *Bill Moyers Journal, PBS*, 4/3/2011. In this interview with William K. Black, Moyers called for similar accountability in regard to the financial collapse and recession in the U.S. starting in 2007.
4. Examining all of current Western medical regulatory problems lies beyond the scope of this book. While medical technology has produced many benefits for patients, the problem of human errors goes unregulated and often untabulated. Kenneth Sands, the director of health care quality at Beth Israel Deaconess Medical Center in Boston, notes, "There has just been a higher degree of tolerance for variability in [medical] practice than you would see in other industries." This comment was elicited in the context of a recent study, which indicated that medical errors in the United States may cause as many as 250,000 deaths per year. Another problem area in American medicine is cost regulation. For example, there is a ten-fold variance in the comparative costs for hip replacements in different American hospitals. In 2013, you could pay between $11,000 and $120,000 for that procedure, depending on where the operation took place.
5. Cha, *Washington Post*.

Standardization and reform—no easy matter

Root cause analysis in the medical profession led over time to wide-scale standardization. While the movement for reforms in medical practice sporadically emerged throughout the nineteenth century, the first serious steps towards authentic medical accountability can be traced to the **Flexner Report of 1910.**

The Flexner Report

The American Medical Association had been founded in 1847 and was finally incorporated in 1897. In the early 1900s, the AMA's Council on Medical Education recognized a crying need for standardization in medical practice. That council impelled the Carnegie Foundation to hire Abraham Flexner, an educator with medical training, to survey the American and Canadian medical fields.

Prior to 1910, many North American medical schools demanded of applicants only two years of medical study in order to graduate and begin medical practice. Laboratory and dissection work were not required. Doctors were taught in medical schools by ill-trained physicians who lectured their students but left hands-on work to begin only once the schools' graduates entered the profession. To compound the problem, state governments exercised little or no control over the medical licensing process.

Abraham Flexner did not tread lightly. Having done graduate work in Germany, he was aware of the far higher medical standards in Europe, so he felt empowered to shed light on the medical mishmash in America. He singled out the Johns Hopkins School of Medicine, his alma mater in Baltimore, as an institution of model cleanliness and lofty standards. He was less pleased with medical schools in Chicago that he termed "indescribably foul."[6]

---

6. There is some irony in Flexner singling out Johns Hopkins as a model of propriety, given that four decades later Johns Hopkins became, for a time, the epitome of ethics-free medical research in the tragic case of Henrietta Lacks and the exploitation of Ms. Lacks' cells for profit.

Flexner's main recommendations called for:
- **A prerequisite minimum of high school diploma and two years university study in basic science, prior to the student entering medical school.**
- **Four years of medical school training.**
- **All medical schools should be connected to universities and not run for profit by physicians unaffiliated with a university.**
- **Medical schools should appoint full-time clinical professors.**

Flexner's recommendations constituted a serious change in medical protocols in the United States beginning in 1910, though these recommendations were far less than is demanded of physicians in our current time.

The impact of the Flexner Report

The upgrading of American medical training stands as an undeniable outcome of the Flexner Report of 1910. Prior to that year, only sixteen of one hundred fifty-five medical schools in the United States and Canada required two years of basic science instruction from their incoming university graduates.[7] By 1920, over 92% of the same medical schools made this science coursework a pre-requisite for admission.

Because of the revolutionary aspect of Flexner's conclusions, the report faced **predictable opposition from established medical faculty**. We can assume those faculty members felt unfairly judged by the Flexner critique.

Depending on one's point of view, a mixture **of reform and injustice** resulted from the Flexner Report. Some medical colleges closed. Women and minorities were disproportionately driven out of the medical profession because they were generally less able to afford medical school tuitions than their white male counterparts. All but two American medical schools run for African-American students closed.[8]

---

7. Numbers, Ronald L. *Sickness and Health in America*, 201.
8. Sullivan, *Academic Medicine* 85 (2): 246–253. From his own words, it appears that Flexner was biased against African Americans, and it appears that the loss of doctors for black Americans had a lasting negative impact long after 1910.

Alternative medical teaching such as homeopathy lost status.[9]

With new stiffer licensing requirements for MDs, the national supply of doctors declined between 1910 and 1920, from one physician per 578 Americans to one for every 730 citizens. Flexner probably did not regret this temporary decline in numbers. He is quoted, **"It is better to have no doctor at all than a badly trained one."**[10]

Flexner's forthright statement finds a sympathetic echo in the words of Mrs. Eddy: "I should have more faith in an honest drugging-doctor, one who abides by his statements and works upon as high a basis as he understands, healing me, than I could or would have in a smooth-tongued hypocrite or mental malpractitioner" (*Mis.*19:20).

The Flexner Report was merely an opening salvo in the campaign to make Western medicine accountable. While we will not attempt in this book to follow the details of medical reform that succeeded Abraham Flexner's endeavor, those first pioneer steps aiming towards institutional self-correction could serve as a helpful model for any would-be healers, whether orthodox, unorthodox, or spiritual in their approach.

Correction and the Christian

Jesus taught regulation of Christian practice by direct counsel and by parable. When his disciples strayed, he verbally reprimanded them, though we have no record of him "excommunicating" anyone. In his betrayal of Jesus, Judas essentially excommunicated himself. Jesus did not berate his followers for deserting him at the cross, though he later chastised them for not believing the women who reported his rising. **The uplifted standard, by virtue of its own instructive capacity, inspires and encourages others.**

> If I am lifted up from the earth, I will draw all people to myself.
> John 12:32 ISV

---

9. Stahnisch, "The Flexner Report of 1910," *Evidence-Based Complementary and Alternative Medicine*, 2012: 1–10. Advocates of alternative therapies justifiably point to the long-running campaign by the A.M.A. against chiropractic medicine. These advocates see this opposition as stemming from the A.M.A.'s historical monopolistic tendencies, and they point to these tendencies as an unintended by-product of the Flexner Report.
10. *Daedelus,* Winter 1974, 105.

In Jesus' parable of the talents (Matthew 25), those who are given talents are expected to account for their performance and are treated according to their motives and actions. **Stewardship** is spiritual trusteeship. Christians are held accountable for the standard of their spiritual performance on behalf of those placed in their trust. The straying lamb is brought back into the fold as a high priority. Christians are to minister to those strangers wounded along the wayside. Jesus did not see the ministry as a financially beneficial position. To him the "hireling" is one who looks after the sheep only for the money and therefore abandons his watch when the sheep are threatened by predators. According to Jesus, the sheep instead naturally follow those shepherds whose voice is trustworthy and whose purpose is unselfish (John 10).

It is no small task for any religious body to maintain stewardship of their adherents while **meeting both the human needs of the stewards and achieving accountability for the church system**. Jesus apparently tested two means of maintaining the mission work of his disciples (Luke 22:35–38). Today's Christians should also find what system works most satisfactorily, and they should make clear the reasoning behind their choice. Historical abuses of clergy payment, such as the infamous indulgences that Martin Luther condemned, may sprout up in any age, so this is an area of accountability that requires continual monitoring.

How do you regulate a spiritual healing system?

In the medical profession, maintaining high standards of sanitation in hospitals and adding training requirements for doctors have seemed to be obvious needs and workable improvements, as judged from our twenty-first century perspective.

How do you accomplish a parallel reform in a spiritual healing system such as Christian Science, which borrows a founding model from the nineteenth century, and earlier, and does not purport to be conventionally medical at all? Is reform of this metaphysical model necessary at this time? A long-time Christian Scientist told the author, **"We have the semblance of a professional structure, and we use scientific, even medical terminology with words like 'patient' and 'treatment,' but** the application of our theory is mostly ad-hoc."

Christian Scientists tend to avoid other terms associated with medical practice: for example, **tests, standards, assessment, experiments, review, examination, oversight**. In other words, the current Christian Scientists' aspirations to be scientific do not conform to what today's Western society acknowledges as systematic or as evidence of any conventional scientific method.

Hypothesis:
Some provisions for self-regulation in the healing practice (e.g. *Church Manual* "Duty to Patients," 47) as well as an aptitude towards scientific curiosity were present in the original system formulated by Mrs. Eddy, but many crucial "fail-safe" provisions have been ignored, downplayed, or mischaracterized since her time, and this has allowed abuse of the practice of Christian Science to take place. Scientific curiosity is too often not found among today's Christian Scientists. (For example, see Chapter 26).

Absence and presence of self-regulation of Christian Science practice

Is there an effective regulatory office? In order to properly watch over the healing work, the current church office and individuals with oversight capacity require sufficient staffing to more thoroughly regulate the performance of Christian Science practitioners. The church allows practitioners who have submitted verifiable testimonies of healings to advertise in the *Journal*, but after practitioners are accepted to list their contact information in the *Journal*, the church does little to regulate or inspect their practice *unless there are complaints from patients*. There is no proactive regulation, and only some reactive regulation.

Shouldn't the work of regulation be initiated by the church in some form that stresses not the convenience of the practitioners, but is dedicated to the safety of the public who call on those practitioners? Mrs. Eddy uses the term "safe and successful practitioners" (*Mis.* 43:11), "safe" meaning "conferring safety," not dangerous. This wording shows a crucial concern for the public's well-being as a result of Christian Science practitioners being well-instructed and trained.

How to "license" practitioners? The *Washington Post* article in 2009, cited earlier in this chapter concerning possible payment for practitioner services under the Affordable Care Act, elicited a firestorm of hundreds of angry readers mocking the notion that prayer should be compensated by insurance coverage. A Christian Science spokesperson had stated in the original article: "The issue here is insurance coverage and has nothing to do with child-protective laws." So then should the financial security and ease for church members and practitioners hold higher priority than the protection of potentially vulnerable children and the public at large? A reader of the *Post* article challenged the church official's argument in this way:

> Actually, the issue is licensure.[11] Medical insurers cover (to a greater or less extent) treatments by LICENSED [medical] practitioners—people who have been licensed by the government-empowered licensing branch of their particular specialty. In other words, there is a mechanism for professional oversight of the services being provided. Whether it's orthopedic surgery… or therapeutic massage, a practitioner [not a Christian Science practitioner] must be tested and licensed by an oversight body that is responsible to the government. And that practitioner must keep his/her skills and knowledge up to date in order to be relicensed when the licensing expiration date approaches. [And as quoted earlier] Christian Science healers are not licensed by any governmental entity. There is no independent certification test they have to pass; no required number of practice hours they must fulfill. They are licensed only by their church after a two-week course of study. Why would the federal government even begin to contemplate insurance coverage for this kind of service?[12]

---

11. Christian Scientists don't currently use the term "license" or "certify" in relation to practitioners, but only offer advertising privileges to practitioners who have presented evidence of healing work to the church headquarters in Boston.

12. Wan, "'Spiritual health care,'" *Washington Post*. Comments section. 11-24-2009.

This pointed comment in the *Post's* blog of letters was one of the more insightful, yet restrained, rebuttals. A retort like this passes the ball of responsibility into the hands of the Christian Scientists…if they truly desire to obtain public recognition for the validity of their form of prayerful care. Granted, it would be a very large undertaking for the church to attempt to change current practices and to license practitioners in a way that approximated protocols of medical fields of therapy. **A change** of that magnitude **would require a very different mindset in terms of qualifications for healers** than has been traditional among the Christian Scientists who have been more or less content with their own, mostly anecdotal, system of recognition and assurances of evidence of healing. But shouldn't Christian Scientists, if they want to share their teaching and practice more widely, work to keep up with, or stay ahead of, the standards of the world?

If "no" is the answer to that question, then Christian Scientists should not be surprised to be seen as an outlier colony of odd practices which the world around them can safely ignore.

Clear expectations of both healing and "back-up" in church writings:
- **A demand for prompt attention and, if needed, help from others**
  From *Science and Health*: "If students do not readily [promptly] heal themselves, they should early call an experienced Christian Scientist [not necessarily a practitioner, whether church-certified or not] to aid them" (*S&H* 420).
- **The standard of quick healing** "I recommend that each member of this Church shall strive to demonstrate by his or her practice, that Christian Science heals the sick quickly and wholly, thus proving this Science to be all that we claim for it" (*Church Manual*, 92).
- **The "back-up" for failure** "If Christian Scientists ever fail to receive aid from other Scientists—their brethren upon whom they may call—**God will still guide them into the right use of temporary and eternal means**" (*S&H* 444).

The church could and should make plain to the public that Christian Science makes **no excuses for failure to heal but provides merciful aid** and safeguard measures (detailed in Chapter 22) for any initial failure to provide spiritual, healing help. Less than perfect tightrope walkers require **a safety net**.

The passage from *Science and Health* about "the right use of temporary and eternal means" has been debated for years by Christian Scientists. Some believe that Mrs. Eddy could not possibly be suggesting that her people should use material means for care. That question is in part answered by the fact that the author of *Science and Health* equates "temporary" and "temporal" with "material" throughout her teachings (e.g. "Material methods are temporary...." *S&H* 318:26). There is no suggestion in Christian Science writings that material "back-up" is a permanent cure.

A contractor friend of the author compares "the right use of temporary...means" to a builder's use of a **temporary wall** in a construction project. The temporary wall keeps the project from collapsing at a crucial stage in the building process, but it is **not a permanent part of the building**.

- **Prevention of pain and suffering** Clearly Mrs. Eddy expected that the prayerful work of her students would be capable of alleviating most cases of pain. Nevertheless, the death of one of her students, Noyes Whitcomb in 1905, and possibly her own pain from kidney stones, impelled her to provide for the use of material pain relief in the Christian Science textbook (*S&H* 464). While this provision especially addresses discomfort so great that those suffering from pain cannot pray for themselves, does it not cover a crucial area of potential abuse?

The following is an example of blatant ignorance of, or disdain for, this "back-up" provision:

A segment *of 60 Minutes*[13] described a Christian Science nursing facility where music was turned up to help mute the moaning of pain-racked patients. Would Mrs. Eddy have tolerated that abuse? Not on your life. She wrote that her "**prime object,** since entering this field of labor, **had been to prevent suffering, not to produce it**" (*S&H* 457:10). So if ongoing suffering occurs for a Christian Scientist or their patient, and other church members are in part

---

13. "By Faith Alone," March 26, 2000.

responsible for the suffering, **is the problem more systemic than individual?** Is that ongoing suffering not a serious indication of "safety procedures" being overlooked or ignored?

Mrs. Eddy proposed in a 1906 letter to Mary Longyear that Christian Scientists provide a home of recuperation for those ill and financially needy persons who could not afford private nursing care in their own homes. She suggested this home would be staffed by Christian Science nurses, practitioners, and **"skillful surgeons."** It would be purely speculation to determine what Mrs. Eddy had in mind regarding her reference to "skillful surgeons." Here is her original letter to Mary Longyear:[14]

January 11, 1906

My dear one,

You as an eminent Christian Scientist can do much in educating others materially and scholastically. But the want of our Cause now is a supply of beneficiaries in the line of hospitals, alias homes for the sick where skillful surgeons, and good nurses, and Christian Science healers are ready to receive the needy. This is no request of mine but only a suggestion of a great need that has not yet been met namely, trained nurses and skillful surgeons in our ranks.

Lovingly yours, MBE[15]

The Board of Directors did follow up on Mrs. Eddy's suggestion for a "home for the sick" ten years later, but the employment of surgeons in those homes for the sick had never been attempted. Here are more measures of self-regulation:

- **The healer's duty to assess the nature of a problem** Under the heading "Duty to Patients" is a specific provision in the *Church Manual* which specifies that if a Christian Scientist does not heal a case, and cannot "fully diagnose" the trouble, he or she **"may consult with an M.D. on the anatomy involved"** (47).

---
14. L05385 courtesy Mary Baker Eddy Library.
15. L00464 courtesy Mary Baker Eddy Library. Ibid. The date "1905" was originally affixed to the January 11th letter to Mrs. Longyear, but researchers have determined that 1906 was the actual year of that correspondence.

The failure of Christian Scientists to follow this potential protocol more frequently, when needed, has had **serious legal ramifications for the church**. In the only legal case that has reached the United States Supreme Court involving Christian Science parents, punitive damages were sought against the church (including a parent, the practitioner, and the Christian Science nurse on the case) for the church's **"failure to train Christian Science practitioners and nurses to perform medical diagnoses."**[16] (We cover this subject in greater detail in Chapter 25 that deals with diagnosis).

- **Christian Science teachers' monitoring of their students** Mrs. Eddy's writings make clear that Christian Science teachers are to be responsible and accountable for monitoring the success of their students' healing practice (*Mis.* 315:15-19). "Teaching and healing…should be fortified on all sides with **suitable and thorough guardianship and grace**" (*Rud.* 15:16). What is embraced in the concept of "thorough guardianship"? Obviously, by today's public expectations, much more than teaching a two-week class. In an interview in 1901, Mrs. Eddy noted that the function of the church was to be that of **"a monitor more than a master."**[17]

The author is aware of church teachers who do faithfully perform this function of monitoring the progress of their students. But in recent decades, according to a former Mother Church official, teachers have too often confined their work to giving yearly addresses to their students, teaching yearly classes, but not making special attempts to keep attuned to the quality of healing work performed by their students. Instead, this official said, the function of accountability has been left up

---

16. *Lundman v. McKown,* 530 N.W. 2d 807 (1995) Court of Appeals, Minnesota (April 4, 1995); review denied May 31, 1995. The punitive damages in this case were later reversed, and it remains questionable how the Church could train its workers to "perform medical diagnoses" without extensive medical school education. Nevertheless, the faulty informal diagnosis in this case by the practitioner and nurse prior to the death of the child (as presented during the trial) certainly was a prejudicial factor against Christian Science. The lawyers who defended the church workers failed to note the church by-law regarding "confer[ring] with an M.D." on anatomy when a case has not been diagnosed or healed.
17. Interview with Joseph Clarke, *NY Herald,* May 5th, 1901, p. 3, 4th section. A monitor is one who **"warns of faults or informs of duty; one who gives advice and instruction by way of reproof or caution."** *Webster's* (1828).

to the Mother Church's department that deals with practitioners. Is this accountability happening or not? It's not difficult to confirm the observation of this former church official; merely speak with students who have taken class instruction about the nature of their contact with their teacher after class instruction is over.

In looking for ways to free up teachers to devote more time for contact with their students, here are some suggestions:
- limit the number of lectures that teachers can give yearly;
- limit any official church positions held by teachers to five years or less (and provide for alternative forms of monitoring for that teacher's students during the period of church employment for their teacher);[18]
- limit the total numbers of students in an association so that the numbers do not overwhelm the teacher's ability to properly "monitor" their students. How does one person manage to shepherd an association of more than three hundred students, and still pursue the healing work?

No one knows the sheep like the shepherd. As Jesus says in John 10, the duties and care of a shepherd for the sheep are not adequately handed off to a paid substitute shepherd (*Ret.* 90: 4–25). Therefore, should not this **monitoring of students' work by Christian Science teachers be especially emphasized in the teachers' training today?** And should not the teachers of Christian Science themselves need to engage in the self-regulation of their activity?

Charles Braden cited this stewardship problem in 1958, in *Christian Science Today*, the only book in wide circulation that has attempted to impartially assess Christian Science church practices.[19] Braden criticized the fact that the training expected of teachers has **"maximum requirements…[that] seem meager indeed."**[20]

---

18. Christian Science Publishing Society, *We Knew Mary Baker Eddy,* Vol. 1, Expanded Edition, 244. **William McKenzie "gave up his work as a Christian Science teacher" when he joined the Board of Directors**.
19. McNeil, *A Story Untold*, Vol. I, 414–415. Keith McNeil writes that the Braden book, while attempting to be impartial, was heavily influenced by Arthur Corey, a Christian Scientist who was very critical of the Mother Church.
20. Braden, *Christian Science Today*, 118.

Peer review

In the medical field, **peer review** serves as a form of monitoring and correction of physicians. Some means of peer review are **"mortality and morbidity conferences"** that take place in many American hospitals. These conferences review recent hospital cases in order to assess where patient-care might have been improved, or treatment altered, in order to obtain a better result in future cases. M & M's, as they are known, did not begin without resistance aimed at their earliest advocate. Dr. Ernest Codman, who pushed for this type of medical self-assessment in the early 1900s, was expelled from Massachusetts General Hospital by his medical colleagues for his efforts at reform.

However, by 1916, Dr. Codman's idea of a case report system caught on with the American College of Surgeons. While it might surprise Christian Science readers, the *Church Manual* includes a mandate for autopsies in the case of a death with unknown cause. (See later in this chapter for specific ways in which peer review might be conducted among Christian Scientists).

- *Church Manual* **mandate for autopsies** The author has never heard of a Christian Scientist adhering to the *Manual* by-law on pages 49–50. It requires that, if a Christian Scientist shall die suddenly without the cause being known, "an autopsy shall be made by qualified experts" (*Manual* 50:1-2). This is not a "maybe," but a requirement. Under current American law, if authorities do not order an autopsy for the purposes of determining a serious contagion, hazard, or the possibility of foul play, only a next of kin can request an autopsy for the deceased.[21] For reasons of cost, the frequency of autopsies has declined in American hospitals in recent years.

    Has anyone ever known of the Christian Science Church alerting members to the possibility that they may need to request an autopsy for a next of kin in order to comply with church standards? It is not the author's purpose merely to point out

---

21. Melissa Conrad Stoppler, MD [MediaNet.com] 7/10/2011.

another measure of unactivated self-regulation. But if this *Manual* provision was well-known and occasionally acted upon, it would help give credibility to the church's standing as a religious entity which was willing to be held accountable even in the event of tragic circumstances. Why should Christian Scientists wait for a state statute to order a coroner to perform this duty, when the church's own by-laws specify that it be requested?

This *Manual* provision puts forward in essence: **We are actually scientific and want to get to the bottom of problems and mistakes that our own people may have had a hand in.** The foregoing church by-law in a small way parallels the "Mortality and Morbidity" conferences in American hospitals.

- **Training required for practitioners** There is training required for Christian Science nurses in order for candidates to be certified by the Mother Church. These requirements have fluctuated in their respective demands over the years. Why is there no **substantial training period or specified internship**, besides the two-week primary class, for practitioners? In Mrs. Eddy's time when the *Church Manual* was written, the qualifications for becoming an accredited doctor were minimal (see earlier in this chapter), so perhaps the founder of the Christian Science Church felt there was less need to outline a period of training or internship for metaphysicians that exceeded qualifications for their medical counterparts. Nonetheless, Mrs. Eddy points out her expectation of "thorough preparation of the student for practice" (*My.* 245:8).

Exactly **what means did she have in mind as constituting "thorough preparation?"** The Church of Religious Science, which has no official connection with Christian Science but whose founder was influenced by a former student of Christian Science, requires courses that take several years in order for their practitioners to be accredited.

Today, there is absolutely too wide a gap between the years of study and hands-on practice required of physicians and the absence of any parallel requirement for Christian Scientists. This lack of training and practice regimen demanded of the metaphysicians should be up to our church to remedy.

The fruits of self-regulation

"If we searchingly examined ourselves... we should not be judged."
I Cor. 11:31 Amplified Bible

Harvey Cox writes in his foreword to a book by Christian Science historian Robert Peel, that **Christian Scientists "do not think they should be judged for the healing they bring—or for the occasional failures."**[22] Isn't that a view regarding accountability that Christian Scientists should seek to change? If, in fact, our church members believe that Christian Scientists should be free of any critical assessment of their work, that belief neither conforms with what Jesus said on this subject nor with what Mrs. Eddy did in relation to her students who inappropriately excused their failures in the healing work. (See Chapter 17). Daniel told his Babylonian captors, **"As thou seest, deal with thy servants"** (Daniel 1:13). *The Message* renders this: "Make your decision on the basis of what you see." Jesus said, "By their fruits ye shall know them [Christians]" (Matthew 7:20).

A *Journal* article concurred with these latter statements and appears to disagree with Harvey Cox on this subject: **"A method of treatment must be judged by its results** rather than by the *a priori* assumption that one method is inherently superior to another."[23] **But how far is the Christian Science Church willing to go when it comes to testing its own healing method and testing its results to the satisfaction of the rest of the world? That is a crucial question.**

Regulation is inconvenient but crucial

Americans complain about the slight inconveniences of air travel today but don't complain at all about air safety. Better to have your plane delayed for factors of risky weather or from the need to ensure that all

---

22. Peel, *Health and Medicine in the Christian Science Tradition*, viii.
23. *Christian Science Journal*, January 1991 Special Issue, 65.

passengers are law-abiding, than endanger the safety of everyone on a plane. If airlines failed to police their own shop, we can bet there would be fewer passengers and much greater fear about air travel.

Christian Scientists might feel very uncomfortable about some of the possible steps of self-regulation mentioned in this chapter. **The author recognizes what a large shift these steps would require for our church.** What our church members should realize, however, is that taking dutiful steps of self-policing upon themselves could have a profound impact on how the public and our own fellow congregants would then view the practice of Christian Science. We repeat: If Christian Scientists truly want to be taken seriously as a faith practice, they must take seriously the task of self-regulation.

The Christian Science "Hippocratic Oath"

The best-known words from the Hippocratic Oath that doctors aspire to follow are: **"First, do no harm"** (or, more properly from the Greek: "to abstain from doing harm"). There is an approximate form of that oath which Mrs. Eddy inserted into *Science and Health* in her chapter on healing. While earlier versions of the healing chapter dealt with the "how-to's" of spiritual, prayerful treatment, something was found crucially missing, and was significantly added to the 1891 version of the Christian Science textbook.

In the 1891 revision of *Science and Health*, Mrs. Eddy launched into a description of Jesus' dinner at the home of Simon the Pharisee and used it as a prolonged parable. In Luke, Chapter 7, a "strange woman" enters Simon's home and anoints Jesus' feet with expensive oil. How the woman treats Jesus becomes, in Mrs. Eddy's moral lesson, symbolic of how **Christian Scientists must treat those who come to them for help. They should demonstrate the same loving reverence to their patients that the unwelcome woman showed Jesus.** Nothing in those pages that Mrs. Eddy added to her book in 1891 appears to relate directly to spiritual healing. Was she telling would-be healers that without the tenderness, "common sense…common humanity," and caring expressed by the unwanted visitor towards Christ, we might as well not even begin to ponder the beginnings of spiritual treatment? Tender love, patience, and kindness are such crucial and precious starting points, that everything else must take a back seat until our Christian spirit shines clearly. Why give instructions about what to know or how to pray if those who read those instructions do not possess the milk of human sympathy?

Much has been written about those pages in *Science and Health*, but suffice it to say that this significant added section in the church's textbook was a very pointed guide and **prod for Christian Scientists to be** above all **humane, commonsensical, and compassionate**.

Warning over lowered standards

Mrs. Eddy called for "more and better healing" from her students. This call has been repeated by Christian Scientists over the years, but unless there is an accompanying, serious assessment of why *healing is not taking place* or how to improve the situation, the call is lacking something. Would a farmer complain that all he needs is to produce more and better crops unless he was also taking specific steps to improve his harvest by changing irrigation methods, rotating crops, allowing soil in fields to regenerate, tightening bookkeeping, plowing or harvesting earlier or later, opening up alternate markets, improving seed quality and weed control, and so on?

Warning about standards: In Mrs. Eddy's work *Miscellaneous Writings* is a significant warning regarding the standards of healing. "**If the uniform moral and spiritual, as well as physical, effects of divine Science were lacking, the demand would diminish…**" (*Mis.* 365:19).[24] In commerce, if the consistent quality of a product or enterprise is maintained, the demand for that product or enterprise remains steady in the eyes of customers. But if a product's quality declines, so does the customer base, stock value, and public patronage.

Isn't it more important that the overall standard of Christian Science healing be maintained than that there be some spectacular, widely-publicized but isolated and possibly anecdotal healings?

---

24. A nearly identical passage appears in *No and Yes*, on page 19:1-3, with a passage that reads: "The premium would go down."

Would we patronize a restaurant which occasionally produced the world's best hamburgers, if that same restaurant's lack of clean facilities also led to occasional cases of salmonella poisoning for their patrons?

Concern about Christian Science becoming a shallow faith healing

In an article that was published after her passing,[25] Mrs. Eddy expressed deep concern about the possibility of Christian Science devolving into faith healing. She was talking about a shallow faith that rested not on an infinite Presence, a divine Principle, an omnipresent Mind, or God, but a trust in prayerful persons, or even in one's own good human resources. **Prayerful endeavor that is accountable rests on an accountable divine Principle, not on a somewhat mysterious Being which blesses some and leaves others unattended to.**

Our mental state must mature over time and broaden to include universal humanity. When Jesus asked his followers to let his words "sink down into your ears" (Luke 9:44), wasn't he talking about a deep faith that rests less on the person of our Savior than on the divine power and Law that undergirds the universe? This faith is accountable because it knows whereof it springs. It rests on the Rock and stays there through the storm. A faith that depends on a human personality will flee from the cross during times of persecution.

The following passage points out the unhappy results of unaccountable, reduced standards of healing: **"When we lose faith in God's power to heal, we distrust the divine Principle which demonstrates Christian Science, and then we cannot heal the sick"** (S&H 351:2-5). On the other hand, spiritual understanding begets a pure and clear faith that produces signs following, even when some of those "signs following" may be attributed to a placebo effect. The founder of Christian Science was profoundly concerned for general improvement in the spiritual healing work:

---

25. "Principle and Practice" September 1, 1917 *Christian Science Sentinel*.

> "It will never do to be behind the times in things most essential
> …a more perfect and practical Christianity."
>
> Mis. 232: 9-11

So how do we approach "a more perfect and practical Christianity?" And **how do Christian Scientists maintain a consistently high standard of healing, or raise a standard that requires upgrading?**

Acknowledge that we have an accountability problem— emphasize self-knowledge

Self-knowledge isn't a metaphysical nicety. It is as necessary in individual healing as it is in maintaining high standards for a business or organization of any kind. If we are not aware of how we're doing by impartial benchmarks or by some form of peer review, we may never objectively know the quality of our work. Again, Paul warned against Christians "comparing themselves with each other, using themselves as the standard of measurement" (II Corinthians 10:12 NLT).

Anecdotal vs. documentable healing

For years the Christian Science Church has contented itself with too much of what the general public considers to be **"anecdotal" testimonies—that is, reports of healing by Christian Scientists that have little or no third-party validation or clinical confirmation. This is a symptom of assessing our performance by using our own informal standards**. While there have been exceptions to this in the church magazines and in some books about Christian Science, Christian Scientists have never taken up the collective challenge, which is implicitly demanded at this time by the public's low opinion of undocumentable testimonies of healing. There is a need to **maintain and keep updated, accurate records of a *certain number of healings* that can be viewed by serious researchers among the general public.** If Christian Scientists were to face this challenge seriously, they would not have to medically verify all testimonies. They could maintain **a division of church**

work that specialized in quietly certifying and sharing non-anecdotal healing experiences with researchers, public officials, students of religion, or their own church members. (More on this subject will be found in Chapter 26. Near the publication date of this book, the author has learned of a book in the works at our church headquarters that will publish testimonies by Christian Scientists that include medical documentation of healings. This is a very encouraging step.)

The Committee on General Welfare —an early attempt at self-assessment

Any church has a hard time getting outsiders to evaluate its conduct, other than to seek out that evaluation from newcomers or trained observers of religious work. The author does not know of any "inter-denominational church evaluation board" in existence that could perform this function. So **stringent self-evaluation** may be the best instrument for progress. There was a serious attempt at self-analysis by our church ten years after Mrs. Eddy's death. The Board of Directors in Boston commissioned a **Committee on General Welfare** (consisting of seven Christian Science teachers) that reported back to the Board on the state of the church March 3, 1920. This wide-ranging review of church performance covered everything from salary parity at the Mother Church, to practitioner evaluation, to the expansion into the legal arena of the Committee on Publication work, to ethical issues such as segregation in the churches. By looking through the totality of the report, it is evident that few of the recommendations of this committee of Christian Science teachers were accepted.[26]

Many American commissions and review panels have come up with recommendations that are ignored by either the populace at large or by the government, but if any social entity desires progress, it makes sense both to study problems impartially and then to outline and follow through with proposed solutions.

> The single worst thing you can do in organizational relations is to solicit ideas and input, and then, when you get that input, to disregard or ignore it.
> From a United Airlines pilot

---

26. The full report is available through *The Bookmark* in Santa Clarita, California.

Assess overall church performance

In our computer-driven world, to troubleshoot a problem, you can backtrack to when a system was working well, and then ask, "What has changed?" **You locate as accurately as possible the point of divergence** when the system started to malfunction. This is similar to "root cause analysis" discussed earlier in this chapter. Can the Christian Science Church do an honest, historical self-review in the attempt to ascertain for itself and its members why things went awry and membership dropped? What are the "external" as well as "internal" factors? Would exit-polls, i.e. speaking at length with former Christian Scientists, be useful in this undertaking? Isn't this a critical work of spiritual and human self-knowledge?

Point out corrective steps, once problems are identified

"The 1902 Change of Front" (Chapter 17) presented an example of how Mrs. Eddy dealt with failure by her students, and the end-result—her **chastening restriction on the scope and nature of the prayer practice at that time**. Mrs. Eddy's example can serve as an encouraging indicator that the limitation or correction of a faulty practice does not ultimately hinder the progress of that practice. Pruning a perennial plant has the capacity to foster fuller growth, though initially it reduces the plant's size. The Flexner Report's critique of American medical practice initially caused a decrease in the number of doctors, but it helped set a new tone and standard that eventually improved the quality of conventional medical care.

In 1902 Mrs. Eddy "pruned" an entire arm of Christian Science practice for a time. That type of **severe therapy should not be needed today if regular and occasional "in-house" forms of self-regulation are instituted**, such as the peer review of practitioners that could help maintain standards. But those forms of monitoring must have teeth. An observer of the Christian Science Church commented to the author: **"If there are no repercussions from unacceptable action or inaction, you are sowing the seeds of institutional failure."** Notice, especially in the Peel biographies of Mrs. Eddy, the many times our church's founder seriously criticized the performance of some of her students, but she did this while still allowing them to prove themselves. A **watchful, self-critical approach** in any institution **encourages good morale** with a work-force, as opposed to fostering a kind of "one-strike-and-you're-out" work atmosphere where employees fear losing their jobs because of one bad move.

Establish a high standard, and improve it over time

If a standard is raised, others seek to emulate it or at least admire and honor it. If a high standard of Christian conduct and healing is "lifted up," why would Christians not be inspired to work towards and beyond that ideal?

Example: the application process to be listed in the *Journal* as a practitioner

The requirements for *Journal*-listing have varied over the years. At one point a few years ago, no specific healings were required but only the vague benchmark that an applicant had worked with others in prayer. Fortunately, that was a brief nadir of accountability standards. **How can the standards be kept very high without discouraging those who are working successfully with others in prayer?**

Adopt active steps and strategy to expand the scope of the work

Upgraded standards are only a base camp for advancement Dr. Paul Farmer has established pioneering medical clinics in Haiti and other underdeveloped countries. Project Hope ships bring free medical care to African nations that lack primary medical care. There is no reason why Christian Scientists cannot envision far-ranging healing work along these lines. One hundred years ago, individual Christian Scientists engaged in evangelical endeavors in Germany, Norway, and on Native American reservations. Spreading any gospel message does not have to follow traditional patterns of past performance.

Outstanding example of current self-regulation

As of this writing, there is little formal self-regulatory discipline among the Christian Science practitioners as a body, at least of the kind of accountability which the public generally demands in other healing professions. A notable exception to this laxity appeared in testimony before the legislature of the state of Maine, on May 9, 2005. A local *Journal*-listed practitioner who was testifying in regard to possible legislation, offered the following to the lawmakers. This testimony, unusual as it might seem to many practitioners, was received warmly by Maine legislators and helped encourage those representatives to scrap efforts aimed at tightening state laws relevant to Christian Scientists.

The author believes that if every practitioner openly stated the following, and abided by its principles, this act alone would do much towards alleviating judgment against the healing efforts of Christian Scientists, especially those relating to children:

- My practice is never secretive. While the work remains confidential, I always insist that school officials, government authorities, and non-Christian Science parents be notified if needed. I recommend that even worried neighbors have their concerns satisfied.
- I always include a non-Christian Science parent in the decision to turn to Christian Science for a child, seeking ways that are satisfactory to all concerned. I also insist that the parents, not the practitioner, be the decision-makers at all times.[27]
- I always insist on Christian Science nursing care if issues of cleanliness, eating, or resting need attention.
- If possible, I visit the patient. If that's not possible, I ask questions about the surroundings and physical care, and I have even asked someone nearby to visit and appraise the situation. I am in daily if not hourly contact with families as needed, and my private, dedicated

---

27. According to court testimony, the apparent neglect of the wishes of a parent who was not a Christian Scientist, or the possible failure to inform a parent of their child's health crisis, was involved in the Christian Science "children's case" *Lundman v. McKown* which reached the US Supreme Court in 1995.

telephone line or cell phone shares my whereabouts 24-7 if necessary.
- If the case is that of a young child, I will not continue treatment unless one of the parents is willing to remain at home with the child and give full attention to the needs.
- If I don't see quick progress and the illness appears serious or life-threatening, I ask that a physician be consulted. If there is evidence of abuse, I insist that it be reported. In fact, I recently contacted a family member of a Sunday school student, explaining that if she did not report an abusive home situation to Health and Human Services, I would have to. The situation was resolved. In my branch church, all our Sunday school teachers are aware of this responsibility.
- I never pressure parents to use or continue Christian Science treatment. In a professional practitioner's relationship to his or her patient there is no sense of judgmentalism along these lines.
- If my name is listed on emergency forms for children involved in scouting, schools, camps, and so forth, I insist that there are also other names [other practitioners or responsible parties?] for contact, in order that public officials, who may not be familiar with Christian Science healing, can deal with the situation.

The previous statement of practice submitted to the Maine legislature could be a useful template for Christian Science practitioners to work from, and in all probability the standards of the practitioner should apply to care for seniors in need of care as well as for minors.

From a mother: **"One of the best healers I ever knew** [Catherine Ross] **would tell us** [parents], **'If she's** [your daughter's] **not healed within a short span of time, take her to the doctor.'"**

Recommendations for further discussion and action:

"Relicense" Christian Science practitioners Submit recent testimonies of healing every five years. The United Kingdom recently required that all physicians undergo a yearly "competency review" and renew their licenses every five years. The revalidation of these UK physicians would require at least 35 patients and physician colleagues vouching for each physician.

Partake in "spiritual feet-washing" All practitioners would be asked to participate in bi-annual peer conferences, rotating in states within their region. For example, Illinois practitioners could interact with practitioners from Wisconsin one year, and then with those from Michigan in another two years. These workshops could share observations, while maintaining confidentiality, in discussions involving the ministry of healing. The reports from these regional conferences could then be more widely shared with all practitioners and those desiring to enter that ministry, while keeping any comments about individual situations anonymous.

Peer review can also perform the function of **peer support**. Out of fear of embarrassment, and for other reasons, ministers in all faiths can find it difficult to "bear one another's burdens" and open up to peers in a confidential setting about their own faith challenges. Peer review might lead to ways of meeting this ministerial need. The author participates in a monthly luncheon for ministers in his local area. At these luncheon gatherings representatives from various churches and synagogues share their faith journeys, and sometimes host speakers. It has proven to be a source of support and camaraderie for all those attending.

In the event of **plausible complaints about practitioners** from church members or others, there may be mandatory follow-through from the practitioner's teacher or other practitioners skilled in interventions with a Christian spirit. The purpose of these follow-through sessions would be to set up steps for spiritual self-improvement and not discipline. Only if the practitioner who received negative evaluations resisted these interventions, or showed steadfast reluctance to improve their work, would there be a need for disciplinary action. The emphasis would always be on collective growth in grace and spiritual growth for the individual practitioner. In some cases, the steps that are set up might develop into a formalized practitioner mentoring that has been previously encouraged by the Mother Church.

Practitioners "in the trenches" Every five years, practitioners who are physically able to do so would be required to spend two weeks working as an assistant nurse's aide in either a Christian Science nursing facility, or on two or more private duty nursing cases for a similar period of time.[28] "The Son of man came not to be ministered unto, but to minister" (Matthew 20:28).

Regulating fees Work with practitioners to reduce their charges in situations that the *Church Manual* (46:24) points out. There are too many instances of exorbitant fees being asked with practically no communication between the practitioner and the patient. This subject could be dealt with at peer-review conferences and not solely from church headquarters in Boston.

Cut the "unfruitful branch" and prune the fruitful one Mrs. Eddy's correction of Abby Corner in an obstetrics case in 1888 is a good example of this.[29] Mrs. Eddy realized that the Christian Scientists were over their heads in taking charge of obstetric cases, and she was willing to change that realm of prayer practice. There may be parallel situations in the future of the Christian Science ministry that require either a new limitation of the ministry or an expansion of it, such as when the church added organized prison ministry and military chaplaincy after 1910, and developed its first nursing home in 1916.

The charting conundrum in Christian Science nursing homes At present there are some Christian Science nursing facilities that fund their work in part by the Medicare payments received through the accounts of their patients. However, this funding comes at a price—those facilities struggle to conform to the government's demand for charting the physical problems of patients who receive Medicare funds. That charting tends to run up against the desire of Christian Scientists to focus on the spiritual goals and spiritual advancement of their patients as opposed to a concentrated tracking of the status of the patients' bodily condition. This is where the demand for accountability confronts the Christian Scientist's desired ideal to minimize the technical charting demands that are customary in conventional medical care.

---

28. Gottschalk, *Rolling Away the Stone*, 296-7. The author describes some practitioners at Mrs. Eddy's home in New Hampshire who were reluctant to engage in "menial" work while serving the church's cause.
29. Peel, *Years of Trial*, 237.

This book doesn't recommend exactly how Christian Science nursing facilities should deal with this problem though the author is encouraged by the efforts of various church members to develop self-funding that can help to fill some of the funding gap left, if a nursing facility decides to "leave Medicare," and lean on non-governmental sources for income.

The preceding suggestions are an effort to recognize the importance of the following words in our church writings that "Christian Science, more than any other system of religion, morals, or medicine, is subject to abuses. Its infinite nature and uses occasion this" (*Mis.* 284:4). There is a great *promise* and *warning* in these words. The promise is to expand the possibilities of our collective and individual thought and action as Christian Scientists. The warning is that *self-regulation* will be key to ensuring that expansive promises can actually be fulfilled.

Our church needs always to adapt to the needs of the times and not be confined by any habitual absence of high standards. Similarly the American constitution has been modified over the years in order to keep our country's legal practice in step with advancing standards of justice.

"To whom much has been given, much will be required…"

Luke 12:48 NRSV

Confronting the demands of national health requirements: The subject of accountability challenges decades of church custom and practice for Christian Scientists. Have our members assumed that the public should be able to understand our ways and means as we do? The enactment of the Affordable Care Act in the United States (2010) has led some Christian Scientists to hope that the United States government would allow practitioners or Christian Science nursing care, for example, to be paid for by church members through their payments to the ACA. **"It would be nice if we're going to pay into a system that we could receive something from the system,"**[30] a practitioner commented recently to a writer from *USA Today*. Before the American public ever recognizes the legitimacy of Christian Science prayer

---

30. Meyer, Holly, *USA Today*, 9-16-2017. "Christian Scientists use prayer instead of medicine."

practice, Christian Scientists must be willing to afford evidence of their own accountability in a way that comes close to satisfying a skeptical public. The author presents suggestions in this chapter that will be seen as problematic by church members. If others can bring forward better, constructive suggestions different from those included here, all are welcome to contribute to the improvement of what constitutes accountability for Christian Science practice.

How do Christian Scientists assess the individual progress of those needing care if they don't wish to conform to the common medical model of charting? The following chapter examines the subject of diagnosis.

CHAPTER 25

Satisfying Thomas
—how do Christian Scientists view diagnosis?

A physical diagnosis of disease—since mortal mind must be the cause of disease—tends to induce disease.
Science and Health, 370:20

...the oldest and strongest kind of fear is fear of the unknown.
H.P. Lovecraft

THE PUBLIC BELIEVES that ignorance of one's human body and the body's potential problems can subject a person to physical danger. So, what do Christian Scientists think about this? We're going to examine in this short space some of the pros and cons of physical diagnoses not just as those distinctions apply to Christian Scientists, but to others as well. We'll also look at how some Christian Scientists have approached this subject while they are praying for guidance and healing.

Are Christian Scientists stuck?

Critics of Christian Science say to church members: "How do you know when you're ill if you rarely go to doctors? You're in trouble, because you don't know enough about your bodies to protect yourself from illness."

This criticism requires a thoughtful answer. Are Christian Scientists **caught between a rock and a hard place?** On the one hand church members are often familiar with the passage cited above from their church text (*S&H* 370, see above), and discouraged by articles they have read in church magazines and by fellow members from seeking advice or help from a doctor.[1] On the other hand, those members may fear that they don't know what they are praying about or wonder if they know enough about themselves spiritually to be healed. If Christian Scientists are experiencing either of these states of mind, fear is present, which is not helpful for healing.

This doesn't have to be so, and here's why: There is more in Christian Science teaching about getting a diagnosis than the passage cited above from *Science and Health*.

Mental self-knowledge and how do we get there?

Diagnosis or anatomy for a Christian Scientist is at its core mental self-knowledge.[2] Mental self-knowledge encompasses being aware of one's spiritual nature and of the spiritual foundation of all, but it also includes knowing one's spiritual and human capacity to handle life's problems.[3] Prayer, meditation, and our internal and life struggles guide us ultimately to the peaceful mental state that includes self-knowledge. Christian Scientists who value mental cause and effect can ask themselves: **Will a medical diagnosis in certain circumstances help me break down or build up the mental image of disease and empower or hamper my prayerful approach to an illness?** That is the question.

Where a doctor's observation helped burst a bubble of fear

A mother found her young son feeling very ill one morning. Even though she sought out prayerful help for her boy, he wasn't feeling bet-

---

1. "Correct Mental Diagnosis," *Christian Science Sentinel*, 10-11-1958. "Christian Scientists do not seek medical diagnosis because they are not interested in physical anatomy." Note: Our church magazines currently do not print statements like this, but there has been no clear rebuttal of these statements from prior years that blatantly advised Christian Scientists against any medical involvement.
2. Eddy, *S&H*, 462:20. **"Anatomy, when conceived of spiritually, is mental self-knowledge…"**
3. Eddy, *Mis.*, 335:12. "Learn what in thine own mentality is unlike 'the anointed,' and cast it out…etc."

ter, and her fears were getting the best of her, so she decided to take her son to the emergency room. She was grateful that the practitioner she had called wanted to go to the emergency room as support. What the doctor in the ER had to say was interesting.

> *He asked her son, "Do you feel absolutely awful?"*
> Son, "Yeah!"
> *Doctor, "Do you feel so bad that you think you could almost die?"*
> Son, "Yeah!"
> *Doctor, "Well, we've had a lot of people in here lately with those symptoms."*

How did this conversation help the mother? She had not only been feeling her son's pain, but she was also **feeling a sense of isolation** and thought to herself: *My son is maybe the only one with this illness, and I have no idea what it is.* Even though she was praying, her prayer was not able to quiet her feeling of not knowing exactly what to do. The doctor's appraisal did two things: (1) It comforted her, in the "misery-loves-company" department. (2) It popped the bubble of fear that her son's problem was uniquely threatening. The mother then thought, *If the doctor isn't panicked, and others are also dealing with this, why should I panic?*

The doctor wrote them out a prescription, but now the mother felt confident about her prayers and her son's prospects for recovery. She decided to get the prescription filled, but ended up not using it. Her son was very soon feeling fine. Whether a skeptic wants to call this a placebo healing or self-healing, it illustrates one way that a Christian Scientist dealt with fear, physical diagnosis, and prayer.

And if the diagnosis in this case had been frightening, then what?

So what does a Christian Scientist do if the diagnosis they get from a doctor is worse than what they had suspected it would be, and their fear is increased, not decreased? The answer to that question is best answered by looking at all that's written on this subject in the Christian Science text *Science and Health*. Let me state briefly how someone without that book handy could pray. If you're not a Christian Scientist, what follows is a brief exploration of our approach to prayer, since it's difficult to grasp this subject without that explanation:

A Christian Scientist prays about an illness in a way similar to how a lawyer advocates for a client who has been wrongfully accused of a crime. The lawyer and the Christian Scientist are often both **working retroactively**—that is, from a standpoint after a law has apparently been broken or after an illness has been felt or become visible or has been diagnosed by a doctor. While lawyers use knowledge of the law to extricate their clients from a conviction or penalty, the Christian Scientist prays from the basis of the steady power and presence of the rescuing and vitalizing law of God that is Love, and the God-created guiltlessness of creation, in order to free their client. "It is the Spirit that gives life," said Jesus (John 6:63 New Life Version).

The first few phrases of Jesus' prayer, the Lord's Prayer, are a good example of the Christian Science way of praying: "Our Father, which art in heaven. Hallowed be Thy name. Thy kingdom come. Thy will be done in earth, as it is in heaven." Notice that those phrases don't ask the divine for healing. Those phrases recognize the all-might of God, our spiritual Parent and Source, the holiness of the divine "signature" in life, the supremacy of the divine intent, and later, at the prayer's conclusion—"Thine is the kingdom and the power and the glory forever"—the reach and supremacy of the divine governing action.

The Lord's Prayer starts with the divine law as its "fact basis" before delving into the problems of life. Christian Scientists model their prayer along Jesus' line of thought to "build a case" for both the goodness and power of God and therefore the spiritual wholeness of the person being prayed for. While many people believe that prayer implores an invisible holy presence for aid, it is more than that. Prayer can be a blessed assurance, a "look[ing] deep into realism" (*S&H* 129).

Here's an example of putting that kind of prayer into action, though it's the experience of a friend of the author, who is not a Christian Scientist:

> My friend was a pastor in a Congregational church where we lived in southern Illinois, but a few years earlier his family had lived in

Michigan. At that prior time my friend's four-year-old daughter fell down a flight of concrete stairs, appeared listless and unconscious, and her parents drove her immediately to the nearby hospital.

The first X-ray taken indicated the girl had a broken neck, and the hospital flew her to another hospital by helicopter. Before my friend and his wife left the first hospital, they both got down on their knees and prayed. After a time, they felt a sense of Christ's presence with them and their daughter.

It took my friend and his wife an hour to drive to the hospital where their daughter had been taken. When they got to the second hospital, to their amazement, their little girl was conscious, and the only thing visibly wrong with her was her state of panic in not knowing where she was and wanting her parents to be with her. The staff at the second hospital had already taken another scan of the girl's neck, and instead of the spaghetti-bowl picture indicated by the first image at the first hospital, the child's neck looked normal in the second scan. The hospital kept her overnight, gave her a neck brace, but she felt no stiffness in her neck. My friend kept the neck brace as testimony to the healing power of the Almighty.

This prayer outcome may seem miraculous to us, but let's look deeper at how the girl's recovery could be explained.

Do we pray to "fix" the patient?

Did it matter exactly what words my friend and his wife uttered in praying for their daughter? What matters far more than words in a prayer are the spiritual understanding, conviction, and patterns of turning customarily to the divine for guidance, often built up over years, all of which undergirded the prayer of my friend and his wife.

When I was a teenager and would ask someone to pray for me, I remember recoveries I experienced, but I had little idea how those recoveries happened. It was almost as if I saw prayer as spiritual pixie dust which you spread over a problem. As an adult, having seen divine Truth at work over the years, I've come to see the kind of recovery that my friend's daughter went through as a proper restoration of divine order, which is a side effect of spiritual awakening.

When the Bible says, "[God] spake, and it was done" (Psalm 33:9), Christian Scientists see in that verse the Word of Truth acting as **a spiritual order of restorative justice** that seems to change things, as an appeals court might overturn the unjust conviction of a defendant in the criminal justice system. Is the divine order intact prior to an accident? Yes, but **prayer acts as an unveiling of what already exists in the mind of the Infinite.**[4] It is seeing through a mist or apparent injustice in life. It is waking up to the divine reality that has been hidden to us, for whatever reason.

The surprise of what we are seeing

To those unfamiliar with what prayer can accomplish, the after-effect of a spiritual healing experience may appear to be surprising, anomalous, or a "spontaneous remission." Dr. Lewis Thomas wrote about the medical records of the "rare but spectacular phenomenon of spontaneous remission of cancer [that] persists in the annals of medicine, totally inexplicable, but real…no one has the ghost of an idea how it happens."[5] Those who have either experienced a "spontaneous remission" from a threatening disease, or have witnessed it in others, or have studied the subject, may add caveats to Dr. Thomas' conclusion that there are no clues as to the causative factors involved in cases of what is termed *spontaneous remission*.[6] But those familiar with spiritual healing may still be stymied by disease or by a doctor's negative prognosis of their prospect for recovery.

For that reason, I point out here a few statements from the Bible and from *Science and Health* that have helped people in facing a negative forecast for their health. These passages point to the "retroactive" nature of spiritual healing:

---

4. Mark 11:24, NRSV. **"Whatever you ask for in prayer, believe that you have received it, and it will be yours."**
5. Lewis, *The Youngest Science,* 205.
6. Turner, *Radical Remission—surviving cancer against all odds.* Dr. Turner's book details the remissions from cancer of individuals in different world cultures and enumerates factors that those people attribute to their recovery from cancer.

- Ecclesiastes 3:15 in the King James Version may be a mistranslation: "God requireth that which is past." The Hebrew word rendered "requireth" is more accurately translated "searches out, seeks for."[7]
- The New Revised Standard Version of this verse reads: "God seeks out what has gone by."
- Wycliffe translated this passage: "God restoreth that, that is gone." There is a related passage in the Christian Science text: "The eternal Truth destroys what mortals seem to have learned from error, and man's real existence as a child of God comes to light" (S&H 288:31).
- In the New Testament letter to the Hebrews, we read: "Everything about us is bare and wide open to the all-seeing eyes of our living God...." (Hebrews 4:13 TLB). Doesn't this suggest the potential for a divine "scan" that can overrule the authority of material scans which have given the patient a frightening prognosis? This passage is helpful to ponder whether a patient has received an apparently encouraging diagnosis, that may later prove to be misleading, or a discouraging diagnosis. Christian Scientists may be wise to take an encouraging diagnosis from a doctor "with a grain of salt, " given the inconsistent record of diagnostic dependability. That is, they would be wise to discover and value from their prayers or from spiritual inspiration a conviction that has a healing impact no matter what even the most insightful physician has told them about their physical condition.

Let's look at the potential impact of spiritual statements (such as Ecclesiastes 3:15) in another experience from a Christian Scientist friend of the author and her mother who is not a church member:

My mother was 89 or 90 years old at the time of this episode. This was about four years ago. She had been ill and was complaining of difficulty with breathing. I was with her at the doctor's office. Dr. M, her general practitioner, ordered an X-ray and told us that it showed liquid on the lungs as well as worrisome nodules. She ordered further testing, and an

---

7. Strong, *The Exhaustive Concordance of the Bible*, Hebrew Dictionary, 23.

appointment for a CT scan was made for several months in the future. In the meantime, my mother had another appointment with a heart specialist, one we had not met before. When the specialist asked how she was doing, my mother mentioned the nodules that she had been very worried about. The specialist suggested she not even go for the CT scan since my mother was known to have congenital heart failure. The specialist reasoned there was no way they would do anything about the nodules, as it would require surgery.

However, when the time came for the CT scan, my mother decided she would go in for the test. I sat outside in the waiting room. A few days later we went back to see Dr. M for the results. Dr. M was invariably soft-spoken and was known for her calming nature. When she walked into the exam room, she appeared uncharacteristically enthused by the test results. She told us the nodules were completely gone, there was no evidence of them at all, and no more tests would be needed. The doctor was certain that the dramatic healing could only have been effected through prayer. My mother has had no problem with breathing since then.

Christian Scientists take a fearful diagnosis or worrisome bodily symptoms to God in prayer as if they were seeking out a divine "second opinion" about their condition. Using another analogy, they are, in a sense, "appealing their case" to a spiritual court. Only they don't see that divine "second opinion" or spiritual "court judgment" as a human, limited assessment, but as a spiritual, over-arching understanding of who they really are. They see that what they receive in prayer is **diagnostic, analytic, preemptive, therapeutic, and curative all in one**—a kind of multi-dimensional answer to their need.

This gets to the heart of the conviction and prayerful approach of Christian Scientists. We believe, as do other Christians, that the divine has "access" to our innermost problems and needs. What that means practically is that even if a physical problem should go undetected by ourselves, by either the absence of a medical test, or by the presence of a faulty or accurate medical test, that problem can still be healed by spiritual truth.

Much healing in conventional doctoring is **retroactive**. That is, the medical treatment is begun typically after the problem has been detected, although the patient may have exercised, taken supplements, and done other things to maintain their health. The Christian Scientist's primary regimen of prevention involves heart and thought searching through "immersion in the Spirit,"[8] and that same regimen is engaged before or after we feel something is wrong in our bodies.

Source of interest in this subject

My thought on the subject of diagnosis was prompted by hearing of an incident that happened in my family when I was very young.

My mother, who had started studying Christian Science, visited her college roommate who was married to a physician. During the visit my older brother came down with an ear infection. The doctor right there in his home examined my brother's ear and told my mother that, if it was his son, he would have recommended an antibiotic such as penicillin, but my mother wanted just to pray for my brother. My brother was healed quite quickly that night, and when the doctor examined my brother's ear the next morning he saw no inflammation. Decades later he reminded me of my brother's recovery which he considered remarkable.

In this case my mother's prayers were not impeded by the doctor's initial examination of my brother.[9] It's possible that my mother might have even been relieved to have a medical appraisal of what she was praying about. Hearing about this incident, years after it happened, made me wonder about the relationship of a diagnosis and recovery for a Christian Scientist.

To be tested or not?

How do we know whether we should submit to a physical diagnosis or not? In the same way that we arrive at any prayer-guided decision. The last verse of the Gospel of Mark relates how the presence and power of Christ, after Jesus' earthly disappearance, continued working with

---

8. Eddy, *Mis.*, 205:13. "The baptism of Spirit, or…immersion of human consciousness in the infinite ocean of Love…."
9. See Chapter 22.

the disciples and confirmed their word "with signs following" (Mark 16:20). Here's an example of how someone was led by listening to those "signs" to *not* have a medical test.

A friend of the author had been praying his way through various medical treatments for his high anxiety and was doing well and recovering his strong spiritual sense, but the doctors were asking him to come in for another test. He agreed but continued to pray about whether he really needed this additional test at all. The waiting room on that day was full of people in various states of misery, and the television was blasting not only the regular drug commercials but was showing a drama about someone dying in the hospital. Another patient in the waiting room stood up and asked, "Could we please change the channel?"

When finally in the examination room, my friend asked the assistant, who would be administering her exam, if she believed that the test was really necessary and useful. The assistant made sure no one else in the office was listening, and she shook her head "no." The cumulative impact of all those "signs" encouraged my friend to feel safe in bypassing the test. Let's look at some other situations.

Where a consultation with a doctor helped

The experience of a friend illustrates a case in which a doctor's observations relieved fear.

One day not long after I had started receiving prayerful help from a practitioner I was at a very low ebb in the hospital, and the thought crossed my mind, 'This is as good an afternoon to die as any.' I called the AIDS doctor, with whom I had good rapport, to find out if he could see me that day, and even though he had a full schedule, he did come to see me in the afternoon. I told him my woeful thoughts from earlier that morning. He said, 'You're not going to die. Your numbers [blood cell count] *are going up. We don't know why, but you're not going to die.'*

In this case the patient's fear and faulty self-diagnosis not only exaggerated the status of his illness. It had also temporarily blinded the man from recognizing his own ongoing recovery.

Where diagnosis didn't help

The same man with AIDS had a completely different reaction to medical observations and comments about his condition on another occasion.

*After I had been discharged from the hospital and had got back on my feet, I started to go back to the AIDS doctor, until one day it came very clearly to me, '**All this is doing is scaring me to death. Why am I doing this?**' I remember going back home that day, and the answer came, 'Just don't go back.' That simple. No one ever called me about re-starting my participation in the program.*

In this situation the patient who was in remission found that the continued monitoring of his physical condition at the clinic, and medical staff talking to him about it , were not helpful for his physical and spiritual progress. He has remained in good health without medical support for two decades since that time.

The limitations of a physical diagnosis

No matter what one's religious convictions, a physical diagnosis may not constitute a road to health. There are at least four possible problem areas within the field of diagnosis that exist as of this writing. The first two of these areas of concern may be limited to the United States:

- Patients are subject nowadays to a quantity of diagnostic testing, more than is conducive to their health.
- There is a lower threshold of what constitutes disease than has existed in previous generations.
- A nocebo (harmful) effect may result from diagnoses.[10]
- Diagnoses can vary from one doctor to another. Let's remind the reader here that these areas of concern are problems associated with diagnoses that doctors have identified and are not the observations of those critical of medical treatment *per se*.

---

10. Eddy, *Science & Health*, 370. "A physical diagnosis of disease…tends to induce disease."

Over-diagnosis leading to more people labeled as "ill"

Dr. Gilbert Welch is a New Hampshire physician and a critic of the overuse of diagnosis. In a column that he wrote for the *Los Angeles Times* in 2011, he noted the following two-part changes in doctors' behavior that may account for more discouraging diagnoses in the general populace:

> Physicians are now making diagnoses in individuals who wouldn't have been considered sick in the past. **Part of the explanation is technological:** diagnostic tests are able to detect biochemical and anatomic abnormalities that were undetectable in the past. **But part of the explanation is behavioral: We look harder for things to be wrong.** We test more often, **we are more likely to test people who have no symptoms, and we have changed the rules about what degree of abnormality constitutes disease**… Low diagnostic thresholds lead people who feel well to be labeled as unwell. Not surprisingly, some subsequently feel less well… Whether you are a drug company, a hospital or any other player in the system, the easiest way to make more money is to encourage lower thresholds and turn more people into patients.[11]

We are presenting here the observations of only one physician, but similar critiques of the current American medical culture support Dr. Welch's view.[12]

The nocebo effect in diagnosis

A nocebo effect, or the harmful effect of a diagnosis, reinforces fear in the patient that may have been latent prior to any visit to a doctor. Psychologist Ellen Langer points out that a diagnosis "primes the symptoms

---

11. Welch, "Diagnosis as Disease," *Los Angeles Times*, May 6, 2011. Dr. Welch is a practicing physician and professor of medicine at the Dartmouth Institute for Health Policy and Clinical Practice. He is the author of *Overdiagnosed: Making People Sick in the Pursuit of Health*.
12. For example: *Overtreated* (S. Brownlee); *The Treatment Trap* (R. Gibson, J. Singh); *Money-Driven Medicine* (M. Mahar).

[which] the patient expects to feel." Dr. Langer cited a study of cancer survivors. "The survivors who described themselves as 'in remission' were less functional and showed poorer general health and more pain than subjects who considered themselves 'cured.'"[13] A Christian Scientist experienced a form of the nocebo effect in the following way:

> *I was having no breathing difficulty at all in the ER for a while. Those were the symptoms I experienced before I entered the hospital. But seconds before the doctor walked into my room, I started experiencing that breathing difficulty again.*

Norman Cousins (see Chapter 13) was the former editor of the *Saturday Review* magazine and later an adjunct professor at UCLA in the Department of Psychiatry and Biobehavioral Science. Cousins, who is known for having battled fearful medical diagnoses with both large doses of Vitamin C and humor, said in an interview that **the diagnosis of a serious disease "often leads to feelings of helplessness, panic, despair, and depression, which produce physiological changes that impair the workings of the immune system."**[14]

Is my diagnosis accurate?

In a study involving 286 patients ("Extent of diagnostic agreement among medical referrals"), researchers from the Mayo Clinic in Rochester, Minnesota "found that 88% of the time, a patient's original diagnosis changed at least slightly when a second medical professional was consulted."[15] In 66% of the cases, patients found their diagnoses varied slightly, while one-fifth of the patients received a completely different diagnosis from that given to them by the first physician they visited. *Science and Health* points out another challenge to the accuracy of a physical diagnosis: "The...physician gropes among phenomena, which fluctuate every instant under influences not embraced in his diagnosis...." (*S&H* 463:1).

---

13. Grierson, "What if Age Is Nothing but a Mind-Set?" *NY Times: The Magazine*, 10-22-2014.
14. Lavin, "In 'Anatomy of an Illness' Norman Cousins..." *Chicago Tribune*, 1-28-1990.
15. Foley, *Quartz*, 4-4-2017. "Get a second opinion—doctors usually aren't right the first time."

Is there any provision for formal diagnosis for Christian Scientists?

Not exactly, but there's this:

On May 4th, 1903, after a serious bout of pain, Mrs. Eddy received an injection of morphine from a local New Hampshire doctor. She had been diagnosed by two other physicians as suffering from *renal calculi* or kidney stones. One week after this incident, Mrs. Eddy sent to her church's Board of Directors the following recommended by-law for the *Church Manual*:[16]

> **Duty to patients.** If a member of this Church has a patient whom he does not heal, **and whose case he cannot fully diagnose, he may consult with an M.D. on the anatomy involved....**
>
> Church Manual 47:4

A few questions readily come to mind about this by-law:
- Is the by-law only recommending that practitioners engage in the inquiry? Couldn't the word *member* refer to anyone, even in cases where the patient was someone in the family or the church member themselves?
- The use of the word "may" clearly leaves the suggested actions in this by-law up to the judgment of the church member. Does the voluntary nature of the wording in this church by-law also take into account that much spiritual healing takes place without an exact analysis of the bodily dysfunction by either the patient or by the practitioner?
- Is this by-law in any way a cautionary note to church members who may be over-confident that their own mental self-diagnosis or their mental diagnosis of others will always be adequate in order for healing to take place?
- Is a strict application of this provision feasible today for first-person interviews with a doctor, let alone third-person questions? How many doctors in our era would be willing to engage in the kind of third-person analysis that the by-law suggests, without that analysis constituting a potential breach in medical ethics? To

---

16. Peel, *Years of Authority*, 239, 462.

answer a third-party inquiry the doctor would be guessing what the problem was without any direct contact with the patient, and he or she might be subject to a lawsuit if the guess was later found to be incorrect.

Usefulness of "Duty to Patients"

However limited the apparent use of this church by-law has been for Christian Scientists, let's look at two slightly different applications of this guidance for the intention of promoting healing. First, we'll look at a case from a practitioner who was able to reach a doctor whom she knew to help guide her approach in a case.

> *A child I was* [prayerfully] *treating was losing weight while eating normally. So I called a doctor about this situation. He asked if the child had been to summer camp. Apparently several kids whom this physician had treated recently were showing similar symptoms, and he suggested that the problem might be a worm in the child's intestinal system. I then* [prayerfully] *handled the case from that standpoint, and a healing took place.*

The following experience is related from a relative of the author who is a retired pediatrician. Dr. B told of a family of Christian Scientists who consulted with him a few times in regard to their young daughter. When the doctor had given the girl's parents his assessment of the daughter's condition, the mom or dad would say, "Thank you, but I think we can take it from here." Presumably the family then proceeded to pray for the girl, after the initial diagnosis. Maybe this family was familiar with other statements by Mrs. Eddy that parallel the "duty to patients" recommendation.

> To know the supposed bodily belief of the patient and what has claimed to produce it, enables the practitioner to act more understandingly in destroying this belief" (*Mis.* 352:15). And "…the [prayerful] negation must extend to the supposed disease and to whatever decides its type and symptoms" (*S&H* 418:18).

Like the "duty to patients" by-law, these passages suggest that some awareness of physical anatomy may be able to aid mental, spiritual treatment. That awareness may come from a doctor's visit, from direct research by the Christian Scientist, from conversation with friends, or from other channels mentioned here.

Why the objections to "naming" disease?

Despite the inclusion of the above-cited provision in our church by-laws, Christian Scientists in the past century have more or less belittled the usefulness of this by-law. Here are three statements from church publications about the function of diagnosis and anatomy, followed by the author's observations about these statements.

- "It is not normal for Christian Scientists to seek medical diagnosis."[17] Certainly most Christian Scientists don't run to a doctor whenever they feel an ache or pain of a discernible or unknown origin. Prayer is their instinctive response to those eventualities. However, this statement suggests that a church member, by going to a doctor, is acting in an *abnormal* fashion **or is perhaps straying from the faith**.
- "Christian Scientists do not seek medical diagnosis because they are not interested in physical anatomy" [cited earlier in this chapter].[18] This implies that our church members are content without having any awareness of what constitutes normal or abnormal bodily action. Our church's "duty to patients" by-law implies that there may be times when a church member should know something about anatomy. Possibly a better way to frame our view could be: "Christian Scientists place high priority on their spiritual sense and less priority on their anatomy, but they don't believe in ignorance of bodily needs and conditions." Mrs. Eddy once asked for prayerful help from her secretary Adam Dickey for congestion in her throat, but she corrected Dickey when he declared that there was "no such thing" as phlegm in her throat. Mrs. Eddy objected, "Do not say that; there is a natural and

---

17. *Century of Christian Science Healing*, 158.
18. "Correct Mental Diagnosis" *Christian Science Sentinel,* 10-11-1958.

normal secretion of phlegm in the throat..."[19]
- "We don't have to know the names or descriptions that medical belief attaches to disease to help us demonstrate Christian Science."[20] This is true insofar as Christian Science practitioners often don't know the exact physical condition of those who call on them for prayer. However, if Jesus in some cases felt a need to name a disease that he would then cure (Mark 9:25), and Mrs. Eddy, as a Christ-follower, believed that mental diagnosis and, occasionally physical assessment, could be useful to spiritual healing, then the complete rejection of naming a disease does not tell the whole story about the interaction between diagnosis and the Christian Scientist.

Note

If any of the above official church statements do not reflect current church views, shouldn't those views be overtly corrected or at least qualified in the present?

"Getting a name"[21] and lessening fear

In Mark 5 Jesus asks the name of the Gadarene demoniac. Barclay comments: "It was...supposed in those days that if a demon's name could be discovered, it gave a certain power over it... The belief was that if the name was known, the demon's power was broken."[22] Fear recedes in a community when the identity, description, and even possible location of a criminal are determined by law officials. For the public at large, the image of a nameless criminal roaming the city is more threatening than the image of an identified criminal.

For a parallel reason, Christian Scientists may find it useful at times to "get the name" of a disease. But how do we do this if there are 100,000 diseases out there and any number or combination of bodily symptoms? The author believes that an accurate approximation of what

---

19. Dickey, *Memoirs of Mary Baker Eddy*, 47.
20. "Physical Diagnosis? Why?", *Christian Science Sentinel*, 9-20-1975.
21. Eddy, *Science and Health*, 412:18. "To heal by argument, find the type of the ailment, **get its name**, and array your mental plea against the physical."
22. Barclay, *New Daily Study Bible: The Gospel of Mark*, 137.

a patient is facing can be sufficient in order for prayerful work to be effective. What Christian Scientists call the "claim" may come to our consciousness through a wide variety of ways. Here's a small example from a friend of the author:

> *My son had a snoring problem that showed up during our family vacation, and this restricted his breathing, but it was not a cold. When we got back home, I happened to overhear a mom talking about how the removal of her daughter's adenoids helped her snoring problem. That informed me of what I could be praying about for our son, and when I got to work* [i.e. prayer] *on that, we saw healing of the snoring issue.*

In this situation, the mother's prayers resulted in her hearing a random comment that aided the eventual healing.

"Calling out" a disease or not

There are statements in the Christian Science text which are pertinent to diagnosis, and these can appear contradictory. We read on one page: "…understand that every disease is an error, and has no character nor type, except what mortal mind assigns to it" (S&H 400:16). Yet a little later, the chapter says, "My first discovery in the student's practice was this: If the student silently called the disease by name, when he argued against it, as a general rule the body would respond more quickly,—just as a person replies more readily when his name is spoken…" (S&H 411:3).

So in *Science and Health* we are told that disease has no inherent identity, but when praying "by argument" about the disease, we are to address it by name. Seeing the context of these statements, it appears that prayer by argument may not be the highest, most exalted form of spiritual knowing, but it may be a practical necessity, given the circumstances. When the author taught middle school, he found that, especially with difficult students, calling out a student by name for specific class misbehavior brought a more prompt response than a general request for good conduct. But every situation is different.

Diagnoses are not the end of the world

As Norman Cousins concluded about diagnoses, there may be a nocebo effect for the patient from a doctor's diagnosis, but in today's information-glutted world there is a good chance a would-be patient, whether Christian Scientist or not, may already have an idea of what is wrong with their body before they get to the doctor's office. *Science and Health* says this: "The thought of disease is formed before one sees a doctor...." (*S&H* 198:14). It's helpful to read this quotation in the context of the words cited at the beginning of this chapter about a diagnosis "tend[ing]" to induce disease.

Is a Christian Scientist made vulnerable by the labeling of a disease that he or she may hear from a doctor? I have a friend who found it difficult to even utter the word "cancer," so she referred to that disease as "recnac," or *cancer* spelled backwards. Those people raised in animistic or tribal traditions believe that a word itself can possess special powers to help or hurt. Isn't it the power we attach to words that makes a difference, whether we consider those words to be positive or frightening?

Science and Health points out a need to "unsee" a disease (*S&H* 461:29). How does that happen if a mental image has been impressed on our thinking? The author has found the following quoted verse helpful: "Naught is the squire, when the king is nigh; withdraws the star, when dawns the sun's brave light" (*S&H* 144:6). As applied to fearsome mental images, the greater mental entity (the divine) has the power to overshadow or outshine the lesser (the mortal or physical, pictured image). "God…remov[es] our knowledge of what is not" (*No and Yes* 30:13–16).

There's the ancient saying: a watched pot never boils. Does this saying suggest that our concentrated attention focused on a problem or even our positive expectation does little to advance the improvement or worsening of a problem? Jesus said, "The kingdom of God doesn't come by watching for it" (Luke 17:21 J.B. Phillips), nor does a feared danger recede either because of our hopeful gaze, or by our concentrated indifference. If you're not familiar with Christian Science, this approach may seem counterintuitive to how people should consider an illness. When the Christian Science text reads: "Look away from the body into Truth and Love" (*S&H* 261:2), does that statement suggest neglect of the body? We might ask whether Paul's statement to "be absent from the body and present with the Lord" also suggests neglect of the body.

A Christian Scientist might explain that statement about "looking away from the body into Truth and Love" as meaning to look to our divine Source, rather than to the visible effect of that Source. We look to our spiritual "control tower" for guidance. We learn more, and help ourselves prayerfully and help others more, by looking away from, rather than at or into, the physique. Dr. Lewis Thomas's commentary on his sense of his body (see Chapter 13) suggests that even doctors could gain clarity about their own being by this approach. How does anyone confirm the utility of this approach in day-to-day practice?

The different paths of self-knowledge

The author has never taken a full course on physiology, but many times he has felt the divine Mind letting him know what is necessary to know about the body in order to see healing for himself or others. That knowledge may have come from a flash of spiritual insight or even in an apparently random fashion—through reading something in the news, seeing something on the computer or on television, or overhearing a conversation between friends. An insightful thought may come totally "out of the blue," which, to Christian Scientists, can mean that the Spirit is reaching them. That information may be more insightful about a physical condition than anything a physician or a CT scan might tell us.

But isn't that already a contradiction? Christian Scientists aren't supposed to worry about material things, including their bodies. How can inspirations, even diagnoses, "come to" a church member about their situation or their body, when we have tended to think that no physical diagnosis is of use to us?

By explanation, Christian Scientists are constantly **"translating."** It's called in *Science and Health* exchanging "the objects of sense for the ideas of Soul" (*S&H* 269:15). In other words, our prayer is looking beneath the surface of the physical body to the thoughts that we believe govern and highly influence the action of the body. We're paying close attention to those thoughts, and praying to see those thoughts under the government of the one universal Mind. A personnel employer looks beyond the résumé of a candidate to try to identify the character of their potential employee. It's not that the body doesn't matter at all to us, but we think of it as secondary to the thoughts influencing the body, and we see the body as best cared for by focusing on those body-influencing thoughts.

Self-diagnosis: the upside and downside

Over twenty years ago I had an experience that taught me something about prayer-guided "self-diagnosis." The sole of my foot felt painful due to no obvious cause, and I felt that the injury was a prayer opportunity. Within a day I felt totally normal, but several days later, the pain returned in the same place near the front of the sole of my foot. This time, despite my prayers, there was no change after a day or so. I ruminated about whether I had fractured a bone or possibly had some small fragment of glass lodged in my sole. My thinking went back and forth between those two possibilities. Finally I realized that it was foolish to ruminate as I was doing, so I prayed for guidance firstly for what direction my prayer should take. The rational thought came quickly that there was no way that glass could be in my foot because none of my shoes that I had worn during that time had holes in them. So with that possibility out of the way I prayed about the problem as a possible fracture, I focused on my oneness with the divine, and the pain went away quickly.

My experience was an example of what we might call accurate "self-diagnosis," which was kick-started by some spiritual illumination. What if our self-diagnosis is way off track?

A Christian Scientist had trouble with what he thought was varicose veins. When he went to a doctor, the doctor told him that his skin problem was not varicose veins, and then the problem, attended to with prayer, cleared up in two to three weeks without any special treatment, physical or spiritual.

Prevalence of self-diagnosis

Chances are that many people in Western society today do not need to see a doctor in order to have a general sense of what is physically wrong with them. Our "general sense" can be misinformed and incorrect, because warnings about a multitude of disease symptoms circulate so liberally in our media today.[23] American society diagnoses you with the simple "on" switch of the television or computer, so there is little chance that a patient entering a doctor's office hasn't already obsessed over scary potential physical problems which he thinks he may have, regardless of what his doctor tells him.

Is our self-diagnosis reliable?

A Christian Science friend of the author once determined that her daughter's condition was something that did not require medical identification or treatment. After the daughter's condition worsened and medical help was sought, the mother concluded: "If you believe that you require a physical diagnosis, go to a doctor for it."

Christian Scientists should be wise to question a pseudo self-diagnosis of their own problem or that of a fellow church member. If Christian Scientists feel at peace about not seeking a physical diagnosis, they should pray to be thoroughly persuaded that what has "come to them" is really from spiritual clarity rather than from a random human hunch. Christian Science practitioners are not trained to make a physical diagnosis of anyone.

Jesus' goal and that of the Christian Scientists

The goal of Christian Scientists is never just to attain spiritual healing in order to make our physical bodies more harmonious. Jesus commented when his disciples returned from a healing mission with reports of wonderful results, "Rejoice not that the spirits are subject unto you; but

---

23. The U.S. and New Zealand, as of this writing, are the only two developed nations that allow pharmaceutical commercials on television.

rather rejoice, because your names are written in heaven" (Luke 10:20). Paul said something similar: "**We want to know the full cover of the permanent** [the spiritual]. We want our transitory life to be absorbed into the life that is eternal" (II Cor. 5:4 J.B. Phillips). While our chapter here has explored some temporal and spiritual means sometimes needed by Christian Scientists today, it cannot be overlooked that the goal before the thought of the Christian and the Christian Scientist looks beyond the limits and blessings of earthly, temporal life towards the "full cover of the permanent,"—towards what spiritual life is and can be.

SUMMARY
Satisfying Thomas

According to the Gospel of John (John 20:25-28), one of Jesus' disciples Thomas refused to believe that the Master was resurrected unless Thomas could actually touch Jesus' crucifixion wounds. Many people, aside from professional skeptics, are like Thomas. They require visible, tangible proof of something, or they will not believe a fact to be a fact.

When Jesus healed the insane man at Gadara (Luke 8:26), the Gadarenes believed that devils went out of the man and into pigs feeding nearby. The Bible narrative suggests that Jesus allowed this reluctantly. After all, there are other accounts of Jesus casting out demons that did not go into anything animate or inanimate, but the incident at Gadara left a profound impression with onlookers that something both significant and visible had happened. The human mind is better persuaded that special healing has taken place because of tangible evidence.

Michael's recovery (see Chapter 1, "Prayer in a Foreign Land") required the surgical removal of toxin from his liver. Michael told the author: "We may need to see the physical removal of what Christian Scientists term mental error in the form of a visible material fluid or substance of another kind leaving the body, just as animistic by-standers in Jesus' time at Gadara believed that devils **didn't just disappear but needed to depart into something else** (i.e. the pigs)."

As with his own hands and side which Jesus showed to Thomas, in letting him feel the marks of the crucifixion, so **tangible physical evidence may not be the highest form of belief, but it can act as a stepping-stone in the process of attaining faith in the divine**.

Because of the willingness of Jesus to stoop to the level of Thomas's mentality or lack of faith, the resurrection was more believable to successive generations of unbelievers. Yet Jesus affirmed that the truly blessed ones were those who would not need material, tangible evidence in order to confirm spiritual revelation.

The lepers whom Jesus healed (Luke 17:12) did not need to go to the priests to know that they were recovered. But Jesus told them to go through that form of **ritual approval not because it was absolutely or spiritually necessary, but because the custom of the times demanded that concession**. Acceding to that custom allowed the healed lepers to get on with their lives, fully and officially freed from their old social stigma.

Christian Scientists in this age may need to occasionally meet, especially when under public scrutiny, the minimal, commonly held expectations of those around them. These "minimal expectations" might include submitting to a physical examination or vaccination for either their children or for themselves under the threat of a contagion. These concessions to public thought around us may be a form of "satisfying Thomas."

In some circumstances there is a need for Christian Scientists to carry their cross in doing what they have learned for years not to do—expose their bodies to medical inspection and/or treatment. Jesus took up his cross. He said, "If it is possible, let this cup of suffering be taken away from me. Yet I want your [i.e. God's] will to be done, not mine" (Matthew 26:39 NLT). So we have Christly company along the path of our reluctant journey.

This chapter is an examination of a field of thought that has too often been distorted by dogma. That dogma has said, "Christian Scientists don't ever get a physical diagnosis. End of discussion." Once we get past that dogma and discover that there is plenty to examine and ponder when it comes to the subject of diagnosis, the subject becomes interesting. Not only do we then discover nuances and healing possibilities, but we also come up with a whole new set of questions for future generations to consider.

A necessary step or a bridge too far?

There is a big difference between the compromise of complying with a law, as Jesus felt a need to do when he submitted to baptism and to paying taxes, and on the other hand **enshrining a concession and turning it into a protocol set in stone**.

While the reluctance of Christian Scientists to submit to a physical diagnosis has become a kind of dogma since the early twentieth century, there is a polar-opposite danger—that of enshrining a concession which is intended to be only of temporary utility. The value of concessions, some of which are suggested in this chapter, is situational.

"Satisfying mortal mind,"[24] (i.e. **satisfying the general consciousness of those around us**) for the intent of long-range spiritual progress, makes sense. Believing that every physical healing requires medical inspection or confirmation is not only an extreme and impractical measure but could also be a nuisance to the physician and unneeded for both society and the Christian Scientists involved in any healing. **Are we placating society too much** (S&H 238:22) **or satisfying society's minimal, reasonable requirements** in order to be freed to live as much as possible following our "spiritual norm?" It is the author's conviction that Christian Scientists can satisfy the world without indulging all of its demands upon them.

Things to consider in demystifying the subject of diagnosis

- While visiting friends in the hospital, you can learn a lot from that visit. Some Christian Scientists and others say that it scares them. But a hospital visit can demystify religious and non-religious preconceptions about medicine.
- Reading updated versions of books on the care for infants (such as *The Baby Book*, by Dr. William Sears especially its updated version,

---

24. Dickey, *Memoirs*, 37–38. Dickey relates on these pages Mrs. Eddy's recognition that her daily carriage drives were not for her enjoyment. Instead, she believed that they served the purpose of "satisfying mortal mind" that she was still alive and well.

and other books by doctors that can be useful in understanding current views of medicine). Some examples of these books are cited in Chapter 13, "Earth Helping the Woman."
- Notice how *Science and Health* comments that some Christian Scientists have condemned their fellow students for embarking on a "course of (systematic) medical study," but Mrs. Eddy does not share in that condemnation and advocates for freedom of conscience on this subject (S&H 443:8).
- Science and Health reads: "…sometimes explain the symptoms [of an illness] and their cause to the patient" (S&H 421:23). Getting "into the weeds" of a patient's problem in this way, for the purpose of removing the patient's fear, may or may not be useful.

Recommendations:
- There is a well-intentioned and often-repeated common remark "you ought to get that looked at." We should daily "get ourselves looked at." The only question is how and by whom is the "looking" done? I have sat in the presence of a Christian Science practitioner whose spiritual sense was so clear that I felt healing at that moment. That spiritual knowing of the practitioner is what Christians call the Holy Spirit and is described in the Bible as a very divine "search[ing] all things, yes, the deep things of God" (I Cor. 2:10 NKJV) and of creation.
- Instead of chastening our fellow Christian Scientists who want a physical diagnosis, can church members emphasize the importance of self-knowledge in healing and call for church practitioners to properly identify and treat the mental elements of disease? Being fully supportive of our fellow members who may or may not go to a conventional doctor should be the norm under all circumstances. "Not domineering over those in your charge, but being examples to the flock" (I Peter 5:3 ESV).
- Prior to childbirth, should Christian Scientists consider sonograms or not? This seems to the author to be a very individual decision.

Jesus said, 'Thomas, do you have faith because you have seen me? The people who have faith in me without seeing me are the ones who are really blessed!'

John 20:29 Contemporary English Version

A novel way to thank your practitioner

Today's Christian Scientists might be interested that their fellow church members have not always been squeamish about all medical interventions such as physical diagnoses and more. An intriguing example of "less squeamish" is the story of Arthur Buswell, a Christian Science practitioner, who healed a doctor, Otto Anderson, of morphine addiction in about a week and then proceeded to walk the extra mile in helping his patient satisfy his skepticism about the authenticity of the cure.[25] The patient, Dr. Anderson, wasn't totally satisfied with his own recovery from the morphine habit, so he proceeded to hypodermically inject his practitioner Arthur Buswell (with permission, of course) with "one quarter of a grain of morphine" to further determine whether it was provable that the drug had no intrinsic power. When Buswell showed not the "slightest physiological effect" at all, Dr. Anderson's doubt about his own healing was fully removed.

Christian Science practitioners today may be more reluctant than Arthur Buswell to act as "lab rats" for the cause of scientific and spiritual advancement.

In the next chapter we will look at the story, little-known by many church members, of the efforts of two Christian Scientists to find scientific ways to present substantial evidence of the effect of prayer—without hypodermically injecting their fellow church members.

---

25. Eddy, *Mis.* 454-5; and Peel, *Years of Trial*, 110-111.

CHAPTER 26

Considering the lilies…
the Spindrift research and prayer-testing

No one has so courageously probed the impact of prayer research on society as Spindrift… They were far out front in considering what these effects might be.[1]
                                                           Dr. Larry Dossey

Is it possible to "measure" the effects of prayer?

MEDICAL RESEARCHERS TEST the effects of drugs on mice before those drugs are used on humans. **Can the effects of prayer be scientifically tested on plants? And are prayer tests involving human subjects reliable indicators of the usefulness of prayer?**

A friend of the author believes the answer to the first question is "yes." Before we tackle the second question, let's hear my friend's experience:

My next-door neighbor and I planted identical Chinese flowering plum trees (Prunus mume) on the same day a few years back. Initially my tree

Plants are as responsive to thought as children.[2] (attrib.)
Luther Burbank

didn't seem to be doing so well, so I fed it lawn fertilizer, and lovingly watered it, but it seemed to worsen, so I prayed for it. I reasoned that as a lovely creation of the creative Mind, it had all the qualities that a tree should have and that life, health, strength, growth, grace, etc., were all included in this lovely small tree. The tree did turn around, and in fact it outgrew and became stronger than the one my neighbor planted. (Today it stands around twen-

---

1. Sweet, *Journey*, 34–35.
2. Peel, *Years of Authority*, 348.

ty-five feet in height, about seven feet taller than my neighbor's tree). When city workers came to prune it, they couldn't believe it was the same age as the tree next door, and they asked me what I had done to it. I told them, and they thought that the lawn fertilizer and water wouldn't by themselves have made the tree do what it had done, so we all agreed it was the prayer.

The only problem with this account is that it is somewhat **"anecdotal."**[3] The woman whose tree was planted has taken photographs of both trees, the author has seen both trees and the photographs, but skeptics might question the author's credibility or the reliability of city tree pruners, or they might say the pictures were photo-shopped. Here lies a persistent challenge for those who assert the benefits of prayer and spirituality—**testimonies attributing power and influence to divine agency tend to not be packaged in impartial and objective tables of evidence, but are often verbal, even second-hand.**

How to answer the "anecdotal" accusation?

One of the most controversial ways in which spiritually inclined thinkers have attempted to relate to the modern world in the past few decades has been in the field of prayer research. People with a background in both religion and the physical sciences have **attempted to bridge** these **two apparently dissimilar fields** by testing the effects of prayer in ways that have aroused disdain from the scientific community and high anxiety from the religious field. Religious folks have sometimes reacted negatively to what they have seen as an unholy intrusion by physical scientists where they do not belong. Physical scientists have rejected the subject because, for many scientists, religious matters dwell in a mystical realm quite distinct from that of the sciences. Furthermore, a significant minority of scientists doubt that a spiritual entity or power either exists or can impact the physical world.[4]

Is **prayer research** therefore a lose-lose proposition for the advo-

---

3. "Based on or consisting of reports or observations of usually unscientific observers" *(Merriam-Webster)*.
4. According to a 2009 Pew Research Poll, 51% of scientists believed in God or a universal spirit or higher power, while 41% believed in neither.

cates of prayer, or is there potential for scientifically testing the possible effects of prayer?[5]

Curious and wanting evidence

What is wrong with being curious? A recurrent theme among skeptics who are critical of religion is the lack of evidence that religious believers tend to produce **for the basis of their beliefs**. According to the Gospel of John, after his resurrection Jesus allowed the "doubting disciple" Thomas to examine the Master's wounds still evident from the crucifixion. While Jesus submitted to this kind of physical test or examination as tangible evidence of his own "after-death" existence, he nonetheless noted, "You [Thomas] believe because you have seen me. But blessed are those who haven't seen me and believe anyway" (John 20:29 The Living Bible).

Do Christ's words suggest that the most blessed conviction regarding divine power doesn't require physical evidence? Yet there may be a human need for physically sensible evidence that God's power impacts our world. **Jesus submitted to satisfying Thomas's skepticism as a human necessity, not a divine one, while Jesus' compassion for the doubters of the world was divine in its patient mercy.**

In a scientific age, a search for scientific evidence

Some Christian Scientists in the past century were convinced that the **doubting Thomases** of our modern scientific era **deserved to see evidence of the power of the Spirit** just as much as did Jesus' disciple Thomas. From 1969 to 1993, a father and son team from the Chicago area, **Bruce and John Klingbeil**, decided that by conducting various experiments on mung beans, soybeans, mold, rye wheat, and other

---

5. James, *Pragmatism*, Lecture 3. The American philosopher William James argued that faith should mainly be a matter of soul-conviction and not rely for the most part on external proofs. James wrote, **"I myself believe that the evidence for God lies primarily in inner personal experiences."** When Jesus' disciple Peter said to Jesus, "You are the Christ, the Son of the living God," Jesus replied that Peter was blessed because Peter's conclusion did not come from a human source but sprang directly from divine inspiration (Matthew 16:17).

seedlings, and exposing these organisms to stressful conditions, followed by prayer for the organisms, **physically quantifiable indications of spiritual[6] power** could be shown to those open-minded individuals who would not believe more anecdotal testimonies of healing that are normative in Christian Science and other churches.

Over this twenty-year-plus period, the Klingbeils, and their like-minded associates, working under the organizational name **Spindrift Research**, discovered that various types of seedlings, exposed to different approaches of prayer, when compared to control groups of seedlings which did not receive prayer, showed measurably positive results that were statistically significant and beyond the range of any margin of error.[7]

The Klingbeils recognized that those **individuals and churches who already believed in the power of prayer didn't need to see results of a plant's growth in a laboratory** in order to believe that prayer can impact the human scene. As we have suggested, many prayer-believers reject the very possibility that prayer can in any way be assessed by tests under laboratory conditions.

But the Klingbeils knew something that prayer-believers don't always grasp—that their prayer experiments **might be a useful means of communicating with a skeptical public in a way that "anecdotal" healing experiences have failed to do**. A spiritual healing which seems substantial and faith-encouraging to the religious believer is devoid of credibility to many scientifically minded individuals who, like Jesus' disciple Thomas, need to see not just physical outcomes, but preferably **before-and-after lab results**, in order for them to accept something as legitimate.

The problem with people as subjects in prayer tests

Why did the Klingbeils not use people as subjects for their prayer experiments? Bruce and John believed that if they used people as subjects, instead of plants, there would be so many **unquantifiable variables** in-

---

6. The Klingbeils, in explaining their experiments, used the term "non-local" instead of "spiritual."

7. Sweet, *Journey*, 241–296. More details of the Klingbeils' experiments can be found in these pages from *A Journey into Prayer*.

truding on the test results, such as unwanted positive or negative mental interference from unpredictable sources, that any conclusions derived from the experiments would always be exposed to **understandable disbelief and skepticism** from an already dubious public audience. How can prayer researchers who use humans as subjects ever know if one of their subjects has a church-going Aunt Mary who is praying for them, or even a fire-breathing Uncle Mortimer who is cursing the experiments with "negative prayer?" And then there are a multitude of uncontrollable mental fluctuations within the minds of the human test subjects themselves, even without any "outside" interference. **The Klingbeils sought out "simpler" life forms as test subjects in an attempt to minimize the potential contamination that these variable factors could introduce into any prayer experiment.**

Weather reporters on television point out on their radar screens what's called *ground clutter* that gives off a distorted picture of precipitation to the casual viewer. The *ground clutter* can be caused not by actual precipitation but by objects within an urban landscape, by warm air inversion, or other factors. The Klingbeils sought to minimize mental or spiritual *ground clutter* from their test results by **conducting their tests in private** and by focusing their prayer studies on life forms that receive less public attention than people generally receive.

Unwanted at the altar

Bruce and John Klingbeil may not have anticipated the storm of opposition that their efforts encountered from many corners, including from their fellow Christian Scientists. However, one of the positive long-range results of their prayer experiments included the **piquing of scientific interest in prayer research** in the minds of medical professionals such as **Dr. Larry Dossey. Dossey** was impressed by both the Klingbeils' findings and research, and by a separate pioneering study on the effects of prayer for heart patients in San Francisco. Since then the doctor has gone on to write several books about prayer.

Bill Sweet, a Spindrift associate and friend of the Klingbeils, has written a fascinating book, *A Journey into Prayer*, about Bruce and

John's research efforts. Sweet's book points out both the potential future of the Klingbeils' work as well as the problems involved with pursuing prayer research. Bruce and John's story illustrates the kind of emotional upheaval that occurs when the fields of science and religion conjoin and collide—two fields that draw people with strong convictions, great dedication, and often volatile opinions as well.

Opposition, persecution, tragedy

Church opposition to the Klingbeils' work wasn't limited to theoretical or philosophical objections. Just as Galileo was told by the church authorities of his era to stop subscribing to the theory of a helio-centric universe, Bruce and John faced **increasing ostracism** due to their experiments that culminated in Bruce losing his official listing as a Christian Science practitioner. The father and son eventually decided to relocate to the Salem, Oregon area where they hoped they could leave behind their critics and carry on with their work. Though their prayer researches were starting to gain encouraging attention, support wasn't coming from their own church, and they were living in relative isolation. In the second week of May 1993, it came as a total shock to their friends and family that both father and son were discovered in the Oregon woods, having committed suicide.

How does anyone completely understand a friend's suicide? The Klingbeils' supporters and friends attributed Bruce and John's untimely deaths to possible depression from the isolation they were living in and from the judgment levied on them by their fellow Christian Scientists and other Christians. There might have been other factors. One friend of the Klingbeils suggested to me that they were "too close to the noise of their own battle...lost in the lab, too close to the flame of their own study and fascination." Possibly so close were they that when the heat of resistance and push-back turned them inward with foreboding edges, it all outweighed Bruce and John's own prejudice against suicide and against their positive hopes for the future. As another potential factor leading toward their deaths, Bruce left behind a cryptic note about a failed case of healing that he feared might result in a lawsuit. A friend of Bruce and John observed: "Maybe Bruce felt that he was a barrier to the progress of his work."

We're left with no definite answers to this part of the Klingbeils' story, but there is one other element we might want to consider. Larry Dossey later wrote about the suicides, **"Edge runners can get discouraged, because they are always swimming upstream."**[8]

The harshest critics of the Klingbeils saw the tragedy of the suicides as an invalidation of all prayer research work. Many famous people, from authors to artists, who have contributed much to society and culture have taken their lives. Even Mrs. Eddy, in describing the burden of pioneering effort that she felt she must endure, once told her student William Rathvon, **"Many times I would have killed myself, but I knew I could not get away from my cross that way. It would follow me."**[9]

Not the end of the road

Death, even suicide, has not been the end of the career impact of many significant figures throughout history.[10] On the contrary, public appreciation of an individual has often only been kindled after such an untimely death, as happened with the fame of artist Vincent Van Gogh that followed his death. The spiritual impact of Christian martyrs, beginning with Jesus, has hugely succeeded their lives. Interest in prayer research accelerated after the deaths of the Klingbeils though the long-run public acceptance of that research remains in question.

Looking for the Northwest Passage

The Klingbeils, in their **search to identify and quantify what many consider to be unquantifiable**, worked in the historical tradition of other pi-

---

8. Dossey, *Explore*, 350. Along similar lines we read in the 1906 Christian Science Church's Annual Meeting notes how that the first members of the fledgling church "must have felt **a peculiar sense of isolation**" (Eddy, *My*. 50:12) in spite of those individuals' trust in God.
9. Rathvon, *Reminiscences*, Dec. 26, 1908, 44. Courtesy Mary Baker Eddy Library.
10. Authors Ernest Hemingway, Virginia Woolf, explorer Meriwether Lewis, inventor George Eastman, Demosthenes, Socrates are examples of this.

oneers. Explorers have searched for an elusive Northwest Passage across the American continent to the Pacific, physicists have pursued a unified field theory and a so-called "God particle," and paleontologists have been trying for years to piece together "missing links" between apes and hominids. What the Klingbeils sought was perhaps as unreachable a star as scientists have pursued before them or will pursue into the future.

What the Klingbeils' experiments accomplished

The Klingbeils were notably modest in summarizing the results of their prayer experiments, but we can point to at least seven contributions their work has given us:

- They stimulated interest in prayer and inquiry into prayer and its effects. (See Dossey quote at beginning of this chapter.)
- They raised the issue of accountability among those engaged in prayer as a ministerial profession, and very controversially, they put forward the need to develop scientific tests whereby to determine the healing abilities of Christian Science practitioners.
- They illustrated the possibilities of prayer made visible to inquirers, and they built a case for how anyone might attempt to indicate, if not prove,[11] to skeptics some evidence of spiritual causation at work. Their tests began to show the effects of different forms of prayer and that all prayers may not be qualitatively "equal." This discovery could be an application of what St. Paul called "comparing spiritual things with spiritual" (I Cor. 2:13).
- Their experiments indicated that **"prayer works best when** [initial] **physical conditions are worse instead of better."**[12]
  Dr. Dossey also points out that placebos work better in tests on humans when a patient's condition is more critical than not.

---

11. Scientists are cautious in their use of the word *proof* because of its potentially unverifiable implications, so we will sparingly use that word in this chapter, though Christian Scientists have customarily used the word *proof* in relation to spiritual healing.
12. Dossey, *Recovering the Soul*, 56.

- The Klingbeils' plant experiments brought to light a phenomenon called **"associational linkage."**[13] That is, plants or seeds that are prayed for by someone in the same room do better than those that are prayed for by someone at a distance. For prayer practitioners and believers of all sorts this finding may point to the need for a personal visiting approach, whether the one prayed for is in the hospital or at home, rather than parishioners only praying for a list of individuals that is read by a pastor during church services.
- The Klingbeils took up the cross of proof and disproof of scientific possibilities in a laboratory setting that was uniquely different from that of a typical Christian Scientist. Their cross was a singular one—the cross of facing resounding public and personal condemnation and criticism from both the religious and scientific communities. What they did might be compared to a Christian priest offering church sacraments in such a different manner as to offend some of the priest's church superiors, his very own congregation, as well as non-religious wine manufacturers.
- The Klingbeils distinguished the different effects of the quality of prayer, especially of the difference between "goal-oriented" prayer versus "non-goal-oriented" prayer. Goal-oriented prayer would be prayer tinged with the human expectation of certain results—a type of "my will be done" prayer. Non-goal-oriented prayer is illustrated in the Lord's Prayer—"Thy [God's] will be done in earth, as it is in heaven." *Science and Health* identifies the same quality distinction of prayer in this way: **"Deity…outlines, but is not outlined"** (*S&H* 591).

---

13. Sweet, *Journey*, 249. Defined by the Klingbeils as "the conscious or unconscious connection of one's thought to another thought, person, or thing."

The Klingbeils discovered that "goal-oriented" prayer could promote growth in seedlings, but that non-goal-oriented prayer helped move[14] seedlings to a pattern of development that was more natural for the seedlings' identical needs.

Biblical precedents for prayer "tests"

Christians and Jews who are skeptical of prayer tests might note various "tests" of prayer in the Bible. The prophet Elijah challenged the prophets of Baal to a contest to determine whose deity was the authentic one (I Kings 18). Gideon put a "fleece before the Lord" (Judges 6:36) and required more than one sign from God to determine whether divinely-sourced power would truly protect and fortify Gideon's attempt to challenge the Midianites. Moses sought a sign from God and then saw his staff turn into a serpent and back again. Daniel asked the Babylonians to prove that his meager diet could sustain him and his fellow Hebrews as adequately as the unkosher diet that Daniel had been offered. Jesus turned to a fruitless fig tree as a symbol of how spiritual authority can shrivel what appeared to be lively, though lacking in purposeful essence.

On the other hand Jesus pointed out, **"An evil and wanton generation is always wanting signs and wonders"** (Matthew 16:4 *The Message*). Jesus' chosen signs were not like the public prayer contest of Elijah, nor did he demand purely symbolic proofs from God, such as the transformation of Moses' staff. Jesus didn't feel a need to vet God's credentials ("Are you sure you're up for this one, Father?") before he

---

14. We use the term "move" since Spindrift and the Klingbeils did so in describing results of their prayer experiments to a public audience that was unfamiliar with the metaphysical views and terminology of Christian Scientists. Christian Scientists tend to see prayer as an act of revelation brought to light by the action of the Spirit, God, an unveiling of spiritual reality, or an awakening to what the divine has in a way already established (e.g. Mark 11:24 NIV): "Whatever you ask for in prayer, believe that you have received it, and it will be yours." So prayer, according to this verse from the Gospel of Mark, is an act of uncovering the divine reality. Only in a few instances do Christian Science church writings use the word "move" in relation to prayer (see *S&H* 419:14–15: "If disease moves, mind, not matter moves it; therefore be sure that you move it off") possibly to avoid giving the impression that spiritual healing is a manipulative activity of the human mind.

healed someone. Even his prayer before the raising of Lazarus (John 11) expressed an assurance of the divine power rather than a pleading for it to be manifested. When once comparing God to the wind, Jesus suggested that, while the effects of the Spirit (as with the wind) may necessarily be tangible to our physical senses, still the direction and source of the wind and the spiritual creation may be mystically hard to pin down by those physical senses.

Here are a few biblical passages that hint at Jesus' (and Paul's) recognition that visible evidence of spiritual power was a necessity in his age, as it is in ours:

- "He [Jesus after his resurrection] showed himself by **many infallible proofs.**" Acts 1:3
- And from another translation, "During the forty days after his crucifixion he [Jesus] appeared to the apostles from time to time, actually alive, and **proved to them in many ways that it was really he himself** they were seeing." Acts 1:3 The Living Bible
- "Wisdom **stands or falls by her results.**" Matthew 11:19 J. B. Phillips
- "All facts must be established by **the evidence of two or three witnesses.**" II Cor. 13:1 NEB

Historical backdrop

If Mary Baker Eddy had not investigated spiritualism and the nature of homeopathy, we may never have known something called *Christian Science*. Mrs. Eddy wrote that it was her **"life-long task to experiment."**[15] In a fashion similar to that of the Klingbeils, early in her teaching career she used plants as a model which she called **"floral demonstrations"** to illustrate what prayer can accomplish with flowers and trees that had been subjected to stressful conditions.[16] Christian Scientists who criticized the Klingbeils' experiments usually have failed to take into account these instances in the life of their church's founder.

---

15. Peel, *Years of Authority*, 248.
16. Von Fettweis, *Christian Healer*, 191–193.

Why Christian Scientists should still be experimenters

What happens when scientists stop all experiments and declare their science a finished product, not to be tampered with? Physical scientists of today would call that end-state *entropy*—the state of degeneration where a body or organization has lost all of its ability to move or be transformed. The end of experimentation is not metaphysical nirvana. **No science reaches a point of completion. Neither should an ostensibly 'Christian' science cease expansion, nor should its adherents settle into a state of self-satisfaction.** *Science and Health* reads: "God expresses in man the infinite idea forever developing itself, broadening and rising higher and higher from a boundless basis" (*S&H* 258:13).

Mrs. Eddy wrote, **"The author's medical researches and experiments had prepared her thought for the metaphysics of Christian Science. Every material dependence had failed her in her search for truth; and she can now understand why...."** (*Science and Health* 152:21–25). Shouldn't successive generations of Christian Scientists **"understand why"** about life and not merely take religious statements on faith alone?[17] Chemistry students repeat basic experiments performed for years by experts and neophytes alike in order to confirm and better understand the principles of their field. But every science expands from the discoveries and failures of prior generations of scientists. Physical scientists build on the work of their predecessors, but they do not build with an unquestioning acceptance of what has been told them by others. What would be scientific about doing that?

Before we dive deeper into some pros and cons of the Klingbeils' experiments, let's briefly touch on an important question about prayer tests.

---

17. Christian Science Publishing, *A Century of Christian Science Healing*, 168–172. Dr. Ernest Lyons, Jr., using technical language, attempted to persuade a fellow chemist of the veracity of Lyons' recovery from an incident of potassium cyanide poisoning which had occurred in a laboratory.

Are prayer tests inappropriate requests?

The God whom science recognizes must be a God of universal laws exclusively, a God who does a wholesale, not a retail business. He cannot accommodate his processes to the convenience of individuals.[18]

William James

Christians and people of other faith practices can agree with William James that **the Infinite** is **not a cab driver** to be summoned for our personal desires. The satirist Ambrose Bierce mocked prayer as a request, "that the laws of the universe be annulled in behalf of a single petitioner, confessedly unworthy."[19] Christian Scientists flip Bierce's sarcasm in arguing that the laws of the universe are actually divine and good, but the humanly imposed laws, including but not limited to theories about disease, limit progress and creation and should be outmoded by the higher, divine laws not just on behalf of church-going individuals, but for everyone. Let's say that the divine power is similar to an overarching principle like gravity that stands available to the masses as well as to individuals. "Am I a God who is only close at hand?" says the LORD. "No, I am far away at the same time" (Jeremiah 23:23 New Living Translation). The Infinite, the divine, is both near and far, "wholesale" (universal) in concept, essence, and breadth, and "retail" (individual) in application.

Occasionally, the author has heard of testimonies by his fellow Christian Scientists where someone who is praying has been kept safe, but others around that person happened to have been harmed by a storm or accident. Can we not validate the protection which the one individual experienced, while at the same time recognize that this could only be called a "partial demonstration" of the protective possibilities of divine care? Along these lines, Christian Scientists believe that miracles aren't the isolated actions of an anthropomorphic deity favoring those who pray. Rather we see prayer as spiritual vision that reveals the divine presence and order as accessible to all, regardless of one's religious ties

---

18. James, *The Varieties of Religious Experience,* 384.
19. Bierce, *The Unabridged Devil's Dictionary.*

or lack of them. **The wider our vision, the more effective and useful is our prayer.** Christian Scientists would say that what are called 'miracles' are simply manifestations of little-understood universal laws, just as fire was probably considered to be miraculous to pre-historic peoples. Maybe William James is wisely discouraging us from trying to **reduce the universal to the self-centered.** This was a criticism levied on the Klingbeils—that prayer tests with plants were mortal attempts to whistle for God or manipulate nature for personal advantage of some kind.

Answering the accusations

"There is a principle which is a bar against all information, which is proof against all argument, and which cannot fail to keep a man in everlasting ignorance. This principle is, contempt prior to examination."[20]
Rev. William H. Poole

It's healthy and sensible to be skeptical in this world. There are a lot of sharks that we encounter in life pushing their notions and potions on credulous mortals. But there is a large difference between healthy, skeptical shark-alerts and outright disdain for ideas that we have not explored, researched, or known anything about. Christian Scientists (and many others) have faced intense skepticism aimed at their teachings since the early history of their faith practice. Ironically Christian Scientists aimed blasts at the Klingbeils' work without apparent attempts to discover what the Spindrift research was about and why it was being undertaken. The following are some of the main arguments put forward in letters by Christian Scientists who argued against the legitimacy and rightness of the Klingbeils' experiments. We follow those arguments with short counterpoints.

- **"The prayer tests are nothing more than an exercise in human will."** *Rebuttal* So what differentiates the "floral demonstrations" of Mrs. Eddy, (cited earlier in this chapter) done in the sight of some

---

20. Paley, *A View*. William Paley, an 18th-century British Christian apologist, first coined the phrase "contempt prior to examination."

of her students, from those of the Spindrift experimenters? How can the former be entirely spiritual and the latter be merely willful manipulation?

Jesus said: "And if I drive out demons by Beelzebub, by whom do your people drive them out? So then, they will be your judges" (Matthew 12:27 NIV). Obviously, the Master didn't believe in "casting out demons by Beelzebub (the devil)." Jesus was mocking the meme with which he had been maligned, and threw it back at his critics as a challenge for them to show evidence of the practical usefulness and blessing of their own faith.

- **"Christian Science was the product of revelation, not experimentation."**
Rebuttal We would not dispute that religious teachings tend to spring from spiritual inspiration. But this critic's statement overlooks that Mrs. Eddy wrote: **"I won my way to absolute conclusions through *reason*, revelation, and *demonstration*"** (S&H 109). She did not say that her work appeared to her exclusively through revelation. Furthermore, Jesus is quoted: "Believe me that I am in the Father and the Father is in me; but if you do not, then believe me because of the works themselves" (John 14:11 NRSV).

The New English Bible renders this: *"Accept the evidence of the deeds themselves."* In other words, those seeking spiritual truth can reach that truth whether or not they grasp the theological underpinnings of the work. If this were not so, think of the billions of people who would automatically be excluded from spiritual good by virtue of the limits of their education level, religious background, or teaching. Jesus did not shut these people out. Only dogmatic attitudes have done that.

- **"I find no support in *Science and Health* for the idea that [Mrs. Eddy's] use of the term, 'Science,' in Christian Science, was intended to link her discovery to the common use of this term in 'physical science.'"**

Rebuttal   Robert Peel refutes this argument in regard to Mrs. Eddy's **use of the word** *science*:

"Science, as the word was used in the textbooks which had helped to mold her thought, was just that—knowledge or understanding of truth; the tried, tested, systematic, and liberating **knowledge of objective fact. While one could believe anything, one could know only what was rationally and experimentally justifiable, and that must necessarily be coherent with all other proven knowledge, or science**."[21] Some Christian Scientists may not have approached their own faith with a scientific, (as in curious, systematic, or open-minded) approach, but this does not at all exclude Mrs. Eddy's sense of *science* from belonging to her faith practice today.

Notice here that Robert Peel, a scholar who in the twentieth century was as familiar with the entirety of Mrs. Eddy's writings as anyone, concluded that her definition of *science* followed a pattern that is in no way divorced from the current meaning of that word.

What confounded the critics of the Spindrift prayer tests was **the form of evidence-gathering that the Klingbeils engaged in. It did not conform to the conventional norm of the church members' faith practice, and so the tests were reviled in part simply because of the nonconformity of the Klingbeils' method and language**. It was a case of contempt after minimal investigation.

- "We find the proof that divine Love heals, in the laboratory of daily living…Love is not learned of the material senses."
Rebuttal   The Klingbeils would not disagree with these general statements. However, learning about and living the essence of divine Love, our basic Christian pursuit, was never the specific focus of Spindrift and the prayer tests. The prayer tests were intended as messages for scientifically minded inquirers, and were not meant to be embodiments of normal, daily Christian Science practice.

---

21. Peel, *Years of Discovery*, 138.

- "**The human mind is not an agent in the healing process, no matter what quality of thought it claims to hold.**"[22]
  Rebuttal This statement is half-true. (1) Yes, the human mind is not the agent of spiritual healing, but (2) no, the *spiritual quality* of the healer's thought is not only important—it is often critical to healing. The writer of the above criticism of Spindrift overlooked notable statements from *Science and Health* such as the following: "**The human mind acts more powerfully to offset the discords of matter and the ills of flesh, in proportion as it puts less weight into the material or fleshly scale and more weight into the spiritual scale**" (S&H 155:21–25). Prayer allows would-be healers to somewhat let go of their mortal sense, their opinions, fears, expectations, etc., in order to "make room" for Christly consciousness which heals. The Klingbeils attempted to assess changes that happened in seedlings and plants when "more [spiritual] weight" was put into the "spiritual scale," of mentality. While Christian Scientists do not look to human mentality as the agent or driving force behind spiritual healing, many passages in Christian Science writings point to the importance of the human mind being imbued with spiritual and humane qualities in order for healing to take place (e.g. pages 362–367 in *Science and Health*).

- "**It is impossible to measure the effectiveness of the power of the Holy Ghost coming to human consciousness…as it would be to develop a protocol to determine how much a mother loves her children.**"
  Rebuttal In fact, the critic here forgot the "protocol" that King Solomon was inspired to employ to **test the degree of love that two mothers felt for a child, whom each of them claimed as their own** (I Kings 3:16–28).

- "**The physical senses can obtain** [ascquire or gain possession of] **no proof of God**" (S&H 284).
  Rebuttal To use this statement as an argument against the prayer tests runs up against Christian Scientists' use of healing

---

22. Letter from Committee on Publication to Bill Sweet, 11-21-1984.

testimonies as the cornerstone of their mid-week church meetings and as the significant spiritual backbone in their church magazines. Many testimonies in our services refer to results of prayer that are confirmed by the physical senses. Of course, Christian Scientists are taught and believe that their spiritual, non-physical senses are the enduring and most reliable "witnesses" of how they are doing. But we have learned over the years to do as a Christian Science teacher once said, "Think in the divine, and speak so as to be understood by people."

Where a New Zealand tomato field served as a laboratory

The following experience illustrates the potential for extending the Spindrift experiments beyond a laboratory into larger venues.

A church official criticized the Spindrift experiments in the following way: **"As far as I know, seeds don't have minds to prayerfully address."**[23] The critic was probably unfamiliar with the words in *Miscellaneous Writings*: "…whatever is of God, hath life abiding in it…. **all is Mind and its manifestation, from the rolling of the worlds, in the most subtle ether, to a potato patch**" (*Mis.* 26:2–8). In other words, brain cells are not required for anything in the world to respond to prayer. Nor was the critic aware perhaps of a testimony published in the *Sentinel* by a New Zealand farmer whose tomato crop was accidentally poisoned by chemical spray from a neighboring farm.[24] The victimized farmer prayed both to forgive his neighbor, and he also leaned on this passage: "God creates all through Mind, not through matter,—that the plant grows, not because of seed or soil, but because **growth is the eternal mandate of Mind**" (*S&H* 520:23–26). The plants that had been severely withered by the poison spray sprang back to life and then followed a pattern of normal maturity.

---

23. Sweet, *Journey*, 86.
24. *Christian Science Sentinel*, "An Interview on Farming," 5-1-1971.

"Nature is our kindest and best critic in experimental science if we only allow her intimations [hints, signs, whispers] *to fall unbiased on our minds."*

Michael Faraday

Scientific "parables"—a new tongue

There is a demand to speak the language of science if we want to be understood in this age.

Nature is not just a teaching vehicle. It can be an arbiter between the scientific and religious communities. Nature spoke to the famous scientist Michael Faraday, and nature spoke to Jesus and religious mystics throughout the ages. Perhaps by means of the small-scale experiments employed by Spindrift and through larger prayer-centered agricultural "experiments" such as the incident of the New Zealand farmer's poisoned crop, scientists and those of religious persuasion can find common ground.

Contrary to the opinion of critics, the Spindrift experiments in no way tampered with the theology of spiritual healing or its metaphysical premises. Those experiments simply sought to **speak the language of their surrounding culture**, not out of fear, but in order that what the Klingbeils and others deeply believed could be understood by those outside the boundaries of faith communities.

The church critics of the experiments did not appear to grasp both the need and the demand to speak that scientific language, and when the Klingbeils used terminology that was unfamiliar to churchgoers, those strange-sounding tongues exacerbated the opposition to the Spindrift prayer experiments. Perhaps church officials felt that neither plant-based illustrations of metaphysical premises nor modern scientific terminology was necessary in order for people to understand Christian Science.

Didn't Jesus speak in parables so that his deeper messages could be grasped by the public at large? What if Jesus had merely spoken in stark theological terms? He could have quoted the Torah left and right, and hoped that Gentiles would listen. Instead he told stories that both Jews and Gentiles would always remember. If he had not done this, a scant few would have listened, let alone understood him. Isn't this **a communication problem with spiritual healing today**—that a small number of people actually grasp the idea of this healing because **too much of what is written and preached is couched in a language that has failed to reach the scientific inquirer and the public at large?** That is not the only reason for a disconnect between the world of faith and the world of science, but it is one reason for it.

The Klingbeils understood that no one can assume that a spiritual message of any kind will be received by the larger community, no matter what the quality or clarity of the message. They were persuaded, however, that if they only spoke in their church community's religious and quasi-scientific language, that that one failing would guarantee their work would not reach the larger world. Bruce Klingbeil observed, **"Today's culture is more influenced by science than by religion. We who have religious mindsets should learn to speak the scientific language of our culture."**[25] A minority culture often needs to learn to speak the language of the majority culture if they want to progress and connect with the larger society.

….and the prayer research on people?

"Every man's work shall be made manifest for the day shall declare it."

I Corinthians 3:13

If you are interested in prayer research on people, you may well have heard about a large-scale study called STEP (Study of the Therapeutic Effects of Intercessory Prayer), authorized by the Harvard Medical School, the results of which were released in 2006. To the disappointment of many prayer advocates, the study appeared to show that patients who were prayed for had worse health outcomes in some cases than the control group of patients who received no prayer. So what happened?

Larry Dossey wrote a pointed analysis[26] of the problems with the

---

25. Sweet, *Journey,* 296.
26. Dossey, *Explore,* 341.

STEP study. Dr. Dossey pointed out that, while the study was very large (surveying eighteen hundred patients) and was very expensive (costing $2.4 million), still it was poorly constructed and possibly arrived at its conclusions for the following reasons:

- It **lacked** what Dossey calls **"ecological validity."** That is, the praying participants used pre-scripted prayers, unlike how those individuals normally would have prayed in a typical hospital setting with patients whom they might have known personally.
- The scripted prayer that test participants all had to pray was "for a successful surgery with a quick, healthy recovery and no complications." Fair enough, but they could have hired robots to do that. Where was the inspiration, the divinely natural spirit?
- Two years after the STEP study was released it was revealed that the group of patients who had fared the worst of the three groups had a higher incidence of heart issues to begin with than the other two groups. So the test was not established on a level playing field.
- The STEP study happened over a ten-year period and received a lot of publicity and ensuing pressure on the participants to come up with a good result.
- The STEP study **did not use experienced healers**. As Dr. Dossey points out, democratic representation is a good thing generally, but in circumstances like this study, wouldn't you want to use very qualified people if you desired usable results?

One of the STEP researchers commented after the study was released, "It's possible that we inadvertently **raised the stress levels of these people**." Indeed. If you were going into risky surgery and were told that someone you've never met might be praying for you…or not, how would you react? Positively? You might instead be inclined to wonder, "Am I in such bad shape, that people want to pray for me? And they're telling me these strangers might, or might not, decide to pray for me even if I'm in terrible condition."

Missed steps and lessons from the STEP study

Bruce and John Klingbeil would not have been pleased with the STEP study. It violated protocols that the Klingbeils honored, such as keeping tests insulated from unnecessary public attention, being careful about the quality of prayer, and certainly avoiding goal-directed, formulaic prayer.

Tim Harford's interesting book *Adapt* promotes the need for organizations and individuals to learn from failure by trial and error in order to succeed. Harford outlines what he calls the *Palchinsky principles*, named after a courageous and outspoken Russian engineer Peter Palchinsky, whose recommendations were rebuffed by both the Tsarist and Communist governments. Ultimately Palchinsky was validated by the failure of enormous, ill-considered projects that he had tried to prevent his Russian superiors from pursuing.

The *Palchinsky principles* outlined by Harford are: (1) **seek and test new ideas;** (2) **keep the trials of ideas modest enough as "pilot programs" so that their potential failure will not be disastrous;** (3) **require "exit polls," the results of any tests, and learn from the feedback received.**[27] Notice how these principles parallel steps in the scientific method.

The STEP prayer tests are a good example of a violation of the *Palchinsky principles*. STEP attempted a **large-scale effort** while disdaining protocols of previous, smaller-scale prayer tests. The large-scale publicity which STEP's results received overshadowed a significant prayer study (Achterberg MRI, 2005) which was conducted using traditional healers in Hawaii who had significant experience in healing work. The Achterberg study showed a statistically significant positive impact of prayer, but few gave those results much notice.

---

27. Harford, *Adapt*, 23–29. Have Christian Scientists sufficiently exit-polled those who have left their faith practice? Have we collected for study and public dissemination sufficient examples of healing which exceed the norm of anecdotal "proof?" We cited earlier that a book of healing testimonies by Christian Scientists showing scientific before and after analysis is in the works. That is very good news.

What can Christian Scientists learn from the STEP study's mistakes?

In a February, 1908 *Christian Science Journal* interview with Clara Barton, the founder of the American Red Cross, Ms. Barton is quoted: "Christian Scientists…impress me that their belief comes **after careful and scientific investigation and conviction**, rather than from hysterical evangelism." The founder of the Christian Science Church continually experimented, tested, refined, and rejected various approaches. Isn't it logical that there be **a continuity of this spirit of trial and error** in Mrs. Eddy's church today? She wrote: "What is the Principle and rule of Christian Science? Infinite Query!" (*Mis.* 337:7) *Query* means searching, seeking, inquiring, questioning.

Trying things out on a small scale

Tim Harford calls the second Palchinsky principle a "survivability" step. It suggests that by testing methods on a small scale, an individual or organization can avoid catastrophe by finding out, without over-investing in a new approach, whether or not success or failure of that approach is likely. Jesus tested one of these Palchinsky "survivability" steps by sending out his disciples, first without much in the way of resources, provision, or protection, and then doing the opposite later by allowing for those disciples to be supplied with extra provisions and bodily protection. Mrs. Eddy writes that he did this in order to **"test the effect of both methods on mankind"** (*My.* 215).

Some of the recommendations in this book could be pre-tested as pilot possibilities for a similar purpose: to determine whether they would accomplish their stated goals effectively or not. Let's look at an example of this test-and-see precursor of the scientific method at work during the Apostle Paul's visit to Berea…

How to adopt new ways and concepts? Model the Bereans.

In Acts 17 is described Paul's ministry to the Jews at Berea, a city of Macedonia. As the Bereans listened to Paul speaking about Jesus and the resurrection, they didn't reject outright the message they were hearing. Instead, they considered Paul's words in reference to what they already believed. Shouldn't that kind of openness be what thoughtful people should seek to emulate? (1) Begin with an established core of values, as did the Bereans; (2) be open to ideas and forms that relate to progress for one's self and for others; and (3) stay alert to what clashes with what has been found to be tried and true in one's experience.

> *"Test everything; hold fast to what is good."*
>
> I Thessalonians 5:21 NRSV

> *"The logic [of Christian Science] can and does satisfy the intellect which is humble enough to **examine and follow unfamiliar evidence** wherever that evidence leads."*[28]
>
> Peter Henniker-Heaton

A potential future area of prayer research

Bruce Klingbeil advocated the exploration of prayer paths of "less resistance." What did this entail? Bruce's daughter Deborah prayed on a regular basis for local farmers near her home in Wisconsin. Her prayers related to milk production for cows, crop growth problems, etc. Deborah was fond of what she and her father called **"praying for the undefended thought,"** which is essentially prayer related to aspects of a problem that others are not focusing mental attention on, or paths of "less (mental) resistance." Often this meant praying about things that others were ignoring in their prayers or their human efforts.

Example: Years ago, Deborah and her brother John worked on a service mission in Haiti. The service mission helped in transporting milk from one village to another needy location. A problem came up that along

---

28. *Christian Science Journal*, July 1960.

the hot trails the milk they were carrying in open buckets would spoil. With the advice of Bruce Klingbeil back in the U.S., Deborah and John started praying for the milk as opposed to just praying to support the hungry children. At that point, the milk began surviving in unspoiled condition throughout the village-to-village journey. Deborah's conclusion was that most people would in their natural sympathy have been thinking about the needy children there in Haiti, but few were praying for the milk. Compare this concept to a basketball player covering a defensive position left open by a teammate running elsewhere.

Example from *Science and Health*: Mrs. Eddy wrote about praying for a "nobler race for legislation" (*S&H* 63), as distinct from praying for politicians, fairer laws, and positive election results.

If you wish to upset the law that all crows are black…it is enough if you prove one single crow to be white. — William James, MD

Recommendations
- That Christian Scientists pursue the continuing study and application of experiments focusing on the effects of prayer on small organisms. These studies and their results (which follow the precedent set by the Klingbeils' studies) would be shared both with the public and interested physical scientists. It may not be necessary to follow the exact methodology that the Klingbeils employed in order to in some way maintain an arm of communication with a scientific and skeptical world.
- That our church maintain files on all prayer studies involving people, but not make efforts to replicate or expand these studies due to the multiple variables and problems in prayer research that uses human subjects.
- That Christian Scientists follow the lead of the Klingbeils' experiments and conclusions pointing to the virtue of letting the "lesser demonstration…prove the greater" (*S&H* 108:14), and learning by **induction** ("We admit the whole, because a part is proved and that part illustrates and prove the entire Principle" *S&H* 461:5–7.) Church members in the author's experience have tended to push to the fore "greater" demonstrations of healing as evidence of spiritual healing, whereas the fields of biology and medicine customarily have begun

their experiments in test tubes, petri dishes, and in the testing of small numbers of mice or rats as precursors to broader applications of a method or treatment.

Christ, doubt, and facts

"No man can go around facts. Christ said, 'Behold my hands and my feet.' The great god of science at the present time is a fact. It works with facts. Its cry is, 'Give me facts. Found anything you like upon facts and we will believe it.' The spirit of Christ was the scientific spirit. He founded his religion upon facts; and he asked all men to found their religion upon facts."

Henry Drummond—"Doubt"

Questions and quandaries resulting from the Spindrift tests

- When Spindrift researchers tested the effects of prayer on wheat and rye and a genetically-altered plant, called *triticale*, which combined characteristics of both wheat and rye, they found that prayer enhanced the growth of the wheat and rye seeds, but prayer inhibited the growth of humanly engineered triticale seeds. Are there implications from this finding that might shed light on our view of genetically modified organisms as well as the potential impact of prayer related to other humanly contrived ventures?
- The Klingbeils essentially tried to disentangle important elements in what most people indiscriminately lump into the general category called *prayer*. Christian Scientists and others have often distinguished between the approaches to prayers based on different theological constructs. They have distinguished between petitionary prayer and prayers of acknowledgment of the divine presence and power. The Klingbeils looked for distinctions between willful versus non-willful forms of prayer. Their conclusions about the value of "Thy will be done" forms of prayer are thought-provoking.
- Even if those who are skeptical of the Klingbeils' research disagree with their methods and purpose, it still is incumbent upon

those critics to come up with their own standards for increasing accountability among spiritual healers, given the demand for standards in modern society.
- **There are no foolproof means whereby to convince all scientific thinkers of the utility of prayer, no matter how exacting is our methodology.** Oscar Wilde wrote: "You can say 'boo' to a goose, but you don't know what he hears." Are the Klingbeils' methods the best ones out there so far by which to encourage inquiry from a reluctant scientific world?
- Is there a way to make the scientific method more "moral" in relation to plant experiments? In other words, is there a way to conduct tests without artificially causing plants stress, or is the stress caused by those tests a needful compromise in order to facilitate prayer-test results?
- Why do so many books on healing fail to mention Christian Science? May one reason be that we Christian Scientists have **reaped the harvest of facile rejection of something new**, just as we have too often rejected the unconventional works of others? And sometimes those "others" have been our own people.

Conclusions

Whether or not Christian Scientists approve the idea of prayer tests with plants, the author submits this chapter as an example of the kind of possible expansive applications of the principles behind Christian Science. Should Christian Scientists *in an organized fashion* be praying about peacekeeping, peacemaking, agriculture, biodiversity and threats of extinction for all species, protection of the environment, governmental and business ethics, economic justice and stability, planetary weather? If individuals and groups believe they are called to do this, is there a limit to what can be attempted, tested, envisioned, or accomplished?

CHAPTER 27

When the coroner gave a testimony
—light at the darkest hour

Many of life's failures are people who did not realize how close they were to success when they gave up.   Thomas Edison

WHAT ARE THE MOST IRREFUTABLE testifiers to the power of prayer? Dead people. One Wednesday night in the early 1970s a California coroner attended the testimony meeting at 9th Church of Christ, Scientist, in Los Angeles. After the readings and hymns, the coroner was the first one on his feet, and he had a surprising message for the congregation.

He related how that in his profession performing autopsies, there were various protocols to follow in determining the cause of death of the deceased. Forms had to be filled out which demanded personal data, apparent cause of death, family relations, and even religious affiliation.

> You have need of endurance, so that after you have done the will of God, you may receive the promise.
> Hebrews 10:36 NKJV

The coroner noted that in the case of some Christian Scientists, he had seen shocking evidence—whole new organs growing in to replace diseased ones, and tissue and skin renewed where there had been decay and loss of flesh. These Christian Scientists' bodies were in the process not just of remission or healing but of transformation, yet the individuals had given up the will to live and died. **"Tell your people not to quit so soon,"** the coroner told the startled Los Angeles Christian Scientists.

This incident would be just another intriguing urban legend, were it not that the "legend" has been validated and its substance echoed in at least **nine other American cities**.

> Not taking the divine "yes" for an answer.

The author has shared the Los Angeles coroner's account with various audiences in the past twenty years, and has collected the accounts of various similar incidents, besides the ones mentioned elsewhere in this chapter. These incidents occurred in the following cities or counties in the United States: San Francisco and Castro Valley, California; Baltimore, Maryland; McHenry County, Illinois; St. Louis; and Indianapolis.[1] A direct confirmation of the Los Angeles coroner's testimony came several years after the initial testimony. A Christian Scientist had gone to a Mission Viejo, California, physician for an insurance-related exam, and his doctor proved to be the coroner in question. Realizing the significance of this man's testimony, the Christian Scientist took down the physician's name and testimony and sent it all to the Mother Church in Boston, where it may still be sitting in a difficult-to-categorize file folder.

In the mid-1980s Lona Ingwerson, a practitioner living then in Kentucky, shared the coroner's testimony mentioned above in First Church, Louisville. After the service, a visitor introduced himself to Mrs. Ingwerson and said: "I'm a coroner here in this county. Why do you think I'm at this meeting?"[2]

In the 1970s a Christian Science nurse in Newton, Massachusetts reported that she heard from a local coroner that he saw tumors fall away from the body of a Christian Scientist who had died.

Robert Peel, in his definitive three-part biography of Mrs. Eddy, presents the report of the undertakers who described the condition of Mrs. Eddy's body after her death. Peel cites these details as of "evidential value."[3]

To Whom it may Concern: December 6, 1910

...The tissues were remarkably normal; the skin was well preserved, soft, pliable, smooth, and healthy. I do not remember

---

1. The author apologizes for the apparent anonymity of some sources in this chapter and elsewhere in this text. He is satisfied with the reliability of the sources and all anecdotes here cited, and is happy to answer any questions regarding more details of the experiences shared and their origins.
2. The author has interviewed this former coroner.
3. *Peel, Years of Authority*, 513.

having found the body of a person of such advanced age in so good a physical condition. The walls of the arteries were unusually firm and in as healthy a state as might be expected in the body of a young person. The usual accompaniments of age were lacking, and no outward appearance of any disease, no lesion or other conditions common to one having died at such an advanced age were noticeable.... In the process of embalming we found the body at sixty hours after death, in as good condition of preservation as we always find at twelve to twenty-four hours after death.... This is our voluntary statement made without solicitation or influence of any kind.

Frank S. Waterman   George A. Pierce   Katharine M. Foote[4]

Saved but don't know it

A friend of the author was called into the office of his boss one day and was asked a pointed, uncomfortable question: **"Bruce, are you saved?"** Maybe typical of many church members who, when faced with a question so blunt, Bruce hemmed and hawed a bit, whereupon his exasperated boss sharply remarked, "That's the trouble with you Christian Scientists. You're saved, but you don't know it."

At times of great danger, surrounded by fear and perplexity, Christian Scientists believe that all are indeed saved, and they need to know and actively accept that present possibility. The patriarch Abraham was saved from having to sacrifice his only son, and the Lord, through an angel, showed our spiritual forefather a way to escape his deadly predicament. Look for angels and listen to them. Listen carefully to how the Lord is speaking to you and showing you the way.

A very important warning here for Christian Scientists

Eager Christian Scientists might be tempted to pounce on the testimonies of the coroners and what they discovered and then think: "This is

---

4. Ibid, 360, 513.

the very evidence that will convince a disbelieving public of the power of spiritual healing. These testimonies are not anecdotal. They are anatomical, physiological, and they don't come from our church members but from those trained in physiology and pathology."

Christian Scientists should think twice about that conclusion. The **Christ must come to each of us on our own terms** and not necessarily through some apparently undebatable, hard to refute, "solid" evidence—an empty tomb that is difficult to deny.

The main beneficiaries of the coroners' testimonies will be those who already believe such things to be possible but who need encouragement and confirmation in their lives. Our hearts have to be prepared to accept deeper things of the Spirit. Otherwise we might just walk by Christ's empty sepulcher without noticing it. Christian Scientists and other believers in spiritual healing might find the coroners' testimonies to be encouraging, exciting, and totally credible, but they should not be dismayed if their friends react differently.

Example A Christian Scientist who later became a practitioner endured to no avail several surgeries to remedy his blindness. Then after working with a church practitioner for a year to the complete healing of his blindness, he told a close friend (not a church member) about his full healing. This friend responded, "Well, what else is new today?"

The disciples of Jesus disbelieved the news of his resurrection, even though they had spent three years in his presence. To them Jesus' rising from the dead was, until they saw Jesus for themselves, an "idle tale." Disbelievers in all ages will **not move easily from their rock-bound convictions** that what seems to be accomplished by action outside their belief system cannot be true.

From Edward Gibbon's widely-known *Decline and Fall of the Roman Empire*:

"…in the days of Irenaeus, about the end of the second century, *the resurrection of the dead was very far from being esteemed an uncommon event;* … the miracle was frequently performed on necessary occasions by great fasting and the joint supplication of the church of the place;

and…the persons thus restored to their prayers had lived afterwards among them many years."[5]

One would be hard-pressed to find most of today's historians, when chronicling Christian history, discussing resurrection of the dead. It's a subject that is not on the table.

Cognitive Dissonance

When new information clashes with ingrained education, culture, or belief, the new information often loses out, and is rejected. **Cognitive dissonance** is the modern description of this form of age-old resistance.

> **If I tell you, you will not believe.** (Christ speaking to his accusers)
> Luke 22:67 NKJV

"Seeing ye shall see, and shall not perceive" (Isa. 6:9). Jesus' parable of the rich man and the beggar Lazarus concludes that the hardened sinner will not be converted "even if somebody were to rise from the dead" (Luke 16:31 J. B.

> **You have seen many things, but you pay no attention; your ears are open, but you do not listen.**
> Isaiah 42:20 NIV

Phillips). Can we infer from this parable that **attempts to convert others by sharing amazing testimonies should begin by sharing something more mundane, and therefore believable, for persons who are unfamiliar with all God can do?**

For example, if the concept of the coroners' reports or Jesus' resurrection seems too far-fetched, someone might believe what happened to the man with the cancer that had been held in check (see Chapter 1, "Prayer in a Foreign Land"), or the experience of David and Mary Ogg whose baby was revived, having been declared dead by Australian doctors.[6]

Two studies completed in 2005 and 2006 at the University of Michigan explore in depth the problem of cognitive dissonance. The conclusions of these studies point out that introducing a novel message or facts to people who are already persuaded or prejudiced against that

---

5. Vol. 2, Chapter XV, 311, emphasis added. This statement from Gibbon is echoed in modern times by Elaine Pagels' *Beyond Belief*, 7; *Pagels' source is Irenaeus, Libros Quinque Adversus Haereses 2.32.4,ed.* W.W. Harvey [Cambridge, 1851].
6. Mail Foreign Service, 8/27/2010. "Miracle mum brings premature baby son back to life with two hours of loving cuddles after doctors pronounce him dead."

information is a **futile exercise** and only causes the receivers of the new information to be all the more reluctant to change their views.[7] The flip-side of cognitive dissonance is called **confirmation bias**, the human tendency to actively seek out opinions or information that align with one's present beliefs or belief system. *Confirmation bias* is the comforting place where those fleeing cognitive dissonance seek to land.

Sharing just the same

While we may warn ourselves and others about various mental barriers to the acceptance of surprising spiritual happenings, obstacles to understanding should not make anyone hide testimonies such as the coroners' from believing Christians or Christian Scientists. To do so would be a form of quenching the Spirit. What if the Gospel writers had concealed the resurrection of Jesus Christ because they were convinced that the message would not be believed and probably scorned by the spiritually unready people of that age? The sower in Jesus' parable (Matthew 13) spread his seed on both rocky and rich soil.

Lessons for believers from the coroners' narratives

If a person seeking healing has lost hope or faith, there may be no positive function in a well-meaning friend saying, "You've just got to keep going." The Bible says, **"Where there is no vision, the people perish"** (Prov. 29:18). A very important ingredient of spiritual vision is the mature understanding gained from experience that **the darkest hours of human life can precede breakthroughs** into progress and healing. This is such an important spiritual concept that Mrs. Eddy presents it in several ways on pages 96 and 97 of *Science and Health*. "The higher Truth lifts its voice, the louder will error scream…the more material the belief, the more obvious its error…the more destructive matter becomes, the more its nothingness will appear, etc." And the

> **Don't throw away your bold faith.**
> Hebrews 10:35 NIRV

---

7. "How facts backfire," *Boston Globe*, July 11, 2010.

marginal heading on page 97, **"dangerous resemblances,"** points to the deceptive, dismaying fleshly appearance that **may discourage patients** from moving forward when their conditions seem very bleak indeed.[8] The prophet Elijah's great discouragement prior to his ascension (I Kings 19) accents our need to not lose sight of the central purpose of our lives while in the heat of struggle.

Suffering people *require a reason* to get better and be healed. An encouraging vision can take the form of a goal or dream that is very basic. A friend of mine defeated cancer with a prime goal being only a desire to rehab a house he owned.

Persistence and patience are necessary in any endeavor of life, but those qualities are more like the fuel in the fire of healing than the igniting flame. And, of course, willful persistence with no vision is headed for a brick wall.

Here's an important question for prayer and discussion: A friend's dad passed on the other day. He was 101, and he had lived a very blessed, fruitful life. While we are taught in the Bible and Christian Science that death is "an enemy," if someone's life is a very full story, do we still fight the thought of passing with our prayers?

"Smallness" of faith can be fruitful soil

The Reverend Peter Marshall, in describing his ministry, wrote: "The greatest answers to prayer in our family came at times when **our faith was so small as almost to expect the worst.**"[9] The Bible calls this *mustard seed faith*—very small and beaten down by life's trials but resilient. A writer in the *Sentinel* noted: "The mustard seed is one of the smallest of seeds, yet it grows abundantly and produces profusely under the *least favorable conditions.*"[10] Though most Christians and Christian Scientists probably desire more faith, they should consider what Jesus said along these lines.

---

8. Eddy, *S&H,* 266. "The opposite persecutions...aiding evil with evil, would deceive the very elect."
9. Marshall, *A Man Called Peter,* 198.
10. *C.S. Sentinel*, Vol. 47, 1446.

When asked by his disciples to "increase [their] faith," Jesus answered that it was not the quantity that mattered. The mustard seed faith was what he pointed to. So should we be hopeless if our faith in the divine is very small and our circumstances appear dire? Not **if our "smallness" of faith and vision has the spark of liveliness in it.**

Anita Moorjani, in describing her healing from cancer that resulted from a near-death experience, takes this thought even further and maintains that her healing arose from "an absence of belief," a yielding to being, and a releasing of all doctrine and dogma.[11]

What may be missing besides persistence? The Christian Scientists, whose bodies the coroners examined, might have had a mustard seed faith, but a **faith that needed reinforcement, perhaps a richer surrounding soil of understanding and vision, or tender support while the healing was going on**. Sufferers need to know they are not alone in their struggle (see Chapter 6, "Sitting at the end of the pew"). It is a huge blessing to have helpers who are attentive, competent, and working for both healing and the support of the patient during recuperation. Whether in illness or wellness, it is encouraging to work out from universal principles and not from a limited denominational belief system.

Countering the phenomenon called "the runner's wall"

In the two pages of *Science and Health* cited above (*S&H* 96–97) are reiterated in several ways the truism that "the darkest hour precedes the dawn." Awareness of this phenomenon is as important in healing as it is for long-distance runners. Marathoners realize that near the end of their race a "runner's wall" of mental inertia may slacken their will to continue and make those runners think that they cannot take another step. The need then for those facing a "runner's wall" of life's apparent impossibilities is to challenge that mental inertia with the **understanding that the screaming from the body of its total inability to continue has been met and mastered by others who ran through that "wall" before them.**

---

11. Moorjani, 137.

What this author finds particularly surprising and inspiring is that **even those who have lost faith can still be healed**. See the experiences in Chapter 1 where those in danger had apparently given up hope, and the credit for recovery might point towards other factors than the action of the patient's frame of mind.

You may ask, **doesn't a loss of faith rule us "out of the kingdom?"** No. For some reason, faith or spiritual understanding had produced in the individuals studied by the coroners, **a healing momentum that appeared to continue even after their personal faith had ended its fight**.[12]

These latter-day Lazaruses showed in death the wonder-working power of God, though they left the gift of good news to be opened not by themselves. It was a gift of physical regeneration found at the doorstep of a few puzzled medical practitioners.

| My feet were almost gone; my steps had well nigh slipped. Psalms 73:2 |

Lesson from the coroners' testimonies for everyone

Do the phenomena of the coroners' testimonies have an application for society at large, including for those who use conventional medicine? The author believes so. A Christian Scientist who worked in a medical lab before he became interested in spiritual healing told the following experience to the author.

> *There was a four year-old boy with leukemia whom we ran lab tests on. The boy was under treatment for three years. His attending physician was convinced the boy would die no matter what treatment he was given. The doctor didn't have much hope, and he didn't want to get the family's hopes up. The longer I worked with this boy, the more undefined the disease became. It got to a point where the pattern of lab results didn't follow any of the guidelines for the progression of that disease.*

---

12. Physical scientist Neil DeGrasse Tyson has said: **"The good thing about science is that it's true whether or not you believe in it."** If belief is not necessary for physical science to be true, is it crucial for spiritual "scientists?"

Were the parents or others praying for this boy? My friend was not positive about that possibility, but the parents' love for their child was quite obvious. The author asked this former lab worker what the parents' reaction was when they heard of fluctuations in the lab tests. He replied, "**They never found out.** The doctor withheld the results." The lab worker speculated that, had the parents been shown clinical signs of their son's improvement, unattributable to any change in medical treatment, it might have called into question the doctor's diagnosis. But, of course, that information would also have encouraged the parents' hopes and/or prayers.

Did professional pride or fear of accusations of quackery interfere with healing in this child's case? Eventually the boy died, though the parents were never aware that their boy's symptoms had at times disappeared. In a legal context, this incident would be comparable to a prosecuting attorney withholding state's evidence that might have exonerated the defendant.

The author asked a physician with wide experience in our country whether it was likely that other recoveries or positive fluctuations in patients' health might be going on with other patients today, similar to the boy with leukemia, and the doctor replied in the affirmative. Does this suggest that there are testimonies out there that have been smothered, positive test results which urgently deserve to see the light of day?

Whether you're a Christian Scientist or not, what do you need when you're tired of running the race of hard recovery?

Lessons from a pilot: "walking by faith, not sight"

Pilots call it learning to "fly by instruments." Christians call it "walking by faith, not by sight" (II Corinthians 5:7). When a pilot peers through the cockpit windshield and sees cloud formations ahead that are disorienting, at that point the pilot's physical senses fail to give an accurate picture of location and elevation. Then the plane's instrument panel is crucial to determine whether the plane is climbing or descending at a proper angle and speed.

The "instrument panel" which Christians need to watch closely is their faith connection. If Christians judge their state of well-being only by signals which their bodies are telling them, they can be seriously misled. **To go into the prayer closet and be very still is to discover how the spiritual senses tell us we are doing.**

Jesus cautioned his disciples away from rejoicing over temporal victories but instead to "rejoice that [their] names [were] written in heaven" (Luke 10:20). Are not our temporal victories,

> Happy will be those in the future who will not need to see in order to believe.

even remarkable healings, a less secure basis of faith than grasping our ongoing oneness with our heavenly reality? Jesus had urged his followers: **"Let these sayings sink down into your ears"** (Luke 9:44). That is, "sink down into your ears" in order to protect Christ's blessed message from the storms of doubt, to protect his truth during the dark times of our lives. If we hope to endure both our brief and prolonged life-storms, defeats, and declines, we require a long-run, hard-scrabble approach to life. If we have imbibed a faith-strength that steadily moves us forward, regardless of the presence or absence of encouraging temporal symptoms or signs, fewer coroners will be needed to share those stories.

> *"Every great work, every great accomplishment, has been brought into manifestation through holding to the vision, and often just before the big achievement comes apparent failure and discouragement."*
>
> Florence Scovel Shenn

Remaining question: Is it feasible for our church to have on record testimonies from retired physicians who have witnessed remarkable patient "remissions?" Obviously, we would not want to embarrass practicing physicians whose reputations might be subject to criticism if they were seen as sympathetic to spiritual healing.

CHAPTER 28

"The drums of dawn"[1]
—the demand for rebirth and evolution in religious practice

Codes must change under the prompting of an everlasting Law.[2]
Interpreter's Bible

Even if you're on the right track, you'll get run over if you just sit there.[3]
Will Rogers

IN 1999, MY FAMILY drove out West. One of our most memorable stops was the small town of DeSmet, South Dakota (pop. 1,089). DeSmet was where Laura Ingalls Wilder lived as a child and was the setting for some of her best-known stories. For such a small locale, we found it curious that there were two, somewhat competing, Laura Ingalls Wilder enterprises. The older one focused on the downtown where the Ingalls family lived at different times. There were several buildings in downtown DeSmet associated with the famous pioneer family including a museum that preserved Ingalls family artifacts, but there were parts of the museum that were off-limits.

The newer Ingalls site is called the Homestead. To call it "newer" is to miss the point. It's actually the very location where Pa Ingalls first farmed and where Laura Ingalls lived for a number of years. The spirit of the Homestead gives you the feeling that you've moved back in time and are not viewing the past from a disengaged distance.

At the Homestead our kids fed the farm animals, rode in and drove

---

1. Dylan, "Lay Down Your Weary Tune, Lay Down."
2. Laymon, *Interpreter's Bible*, Vol. 7, 438.
3. Rogers, *The Wit and Wisdom of Will Rogers in His Own Voice*.

a horse-drawn buggy, visited and participated in an old schoolhouse, and dressed up in old-fashioned clothes. They loved the Homestead. It was a welcoming, hands-on experience. While our family spent less than two hours in the town of DeSmet, we spent over a day out at the Homestead, camping under the stars near the cottonwood trees that Pa Ingalls had planted for his girls. That outdoor experience and engagement connected our family with the land Laura Ingalls called home on the prairie.

Too many churches, not just in our denomination, **come across to their visitors as museums, more than living, breathing homesteads**. When you step in those church doors, you have walked into the time capsule of a prior generation. Church experience too often struggles to recapture the spirit of its founding. **How does any of us bottle and spread the fresh breeze of a spiritual discovery?**

Too many churches try to preserve the shell or external form of the founding vision. A church marquee in our town promised: "Want to experience early Christianity? Come here Sunday at 9am." I couldn't help but wonder if I would find there the spirit of Jesus, or toga-clad Christians battling their fellow Christians over the correct meaning of the Apostles' Creed.

The original wine of the Spirit will always require new bottles, expansive vocabulary, and fresh forms. Otherwise, as Jesus predicted, the containers or outmoded forms and their familiar, but arcane, language will crack, and the original inspiration will flow away.

Where will the new wine flow?

Where will the wine flow to, if it breaks the old wineskins? The Gospel of Matthew gives a hint of the destination of the flowing wine in Jesus' parable of the talents. Those who were given two talents and five talents actively expanded the original investment entrusted to them, while the one person receiving a single talent secreted his gift away. The one talent remained stagnant, inert in its buried condition. Then the lord in the parable took that talent away and *gave it to the one who had done the most expansive job with the original investment.*

Jesus' parable nearly parallels the fable of the tortoise and the hare which teaches its readers that it's not overly important what potential or possibilities we start with in the course of life.

Mark Twain roundly parodied Christian Science. Twain characterized Mrs. Eddy's teaching as "the Standard Oil of religion,"[4] which was probably a back-handed compliment. Does it matter if our church's cause or any movement is the newest, hottest, or most profitable idea of any kind but does not continue to evolve and innovate? Corporations that start with a successful product must continually prove themselves with ongoing new development.

The long-time CEO of Amazon, Jeff Bezos, made this interesting observation: **"What really matters is that companies that don't continue to experiment—companies that don't embrace failure—eventually get into a desperate position, where the only thing they can do is make a 'Hail, Mary!' bet at the very end of their corporate existence."**[5]

Religions, unlike corporations, may not be expected to frequently crank out a novel product-line as a company might, but the demand to develop creative thought-models and to progress in practical ways is just as urgent for them as it is for companies.

Jesus' "innovations" challenged the Mosaic Law

Spiritual living is interactive and expansive. Jesus said, "Now Moses told you such and such, but I say unto you…" and then he elaborated. He didn't reject all of the law which Moses was associated with, but he directly **contravened parts of that law.**[6] **Jesus' thoughts built out from the old religious law, but parted company with some cruel, judgmental conventions of his era. He came to "fulfill" the law**, ("complete the law" Matthew 5:17 J.B. Phillips). Don't Jesus' thoughts about the Mosaic Law, as we find them in the four Gospels, suggest that spiritual teachings through the ages tend to evolve? Jesus began the Christian work, while

---

4. *Chicago Tribune*, "Christian Scientists Entering a New Age," November 11, 1994.
5. Gibbs, "Jeff Bezos," *The Guardian*, 12-3-2014.
6. For example, Jesus forgave the adulterous woman who had been set up for execution "under the law" (John 8).

he expected his followers to proceed to do "greater works" (John 14:12).

All advancement in religious practice springs from the roots of prophetic voices that preceded that advancement. In truth there is nothing totally new under the sun. But age-old truths are recovered, reborn, and given fresh application in order to meet the needs of changing times.

Evolving religious forms

The world's religions and religious practices throughout human history paint a path of spiritual evolution. Buddhism evolved from Hinduism and responded to the excesses and limitations that Hindu practice imposed on people at the time of Siddhartha. Judaism pioneered the worship of one God in an age of polytheism. Christianity sprang from Judaism and maintained Jewish roots, but Jesus' teaching sometimes subtly and sometimes bluntly branched off from Mosaic teaching. Islam was established at a time of relative corruption in both Christian and Jewish practice. Protestant Christianity sprang from and responded to the excesses and mistakes of previous Christian practice. Centuries after the Protestant Reformation, Catholics initiated their own reforming of practices, and at this writing we have a Catholic pope who inspires change and reform within his own church and among many other faiths.

This trend will continue. It's called progress. This logical extension and expansion of religious thought and practice is a spiritual demand. **When religious practice falls into a quiescent pool of entropy with few angels ruffling the waters of its habitual practice, that practice and the religious forms connected to it die away**. Die away stale practice should, so that it may be replaced by something more uplifting and satisfying to the needs of people.

Start-ups are one thing
—continuing progression another

"Every founder is confounded by the graven image" (Jeremiah 10:14). Every discoverer starts the process but does not finish it. No science stops at the point of its discovery. No invention should remain fro-

zen upon the passing of its discoverer. But look at the religious energy in many sects that is continually poured into the commemoration of and celebration of founding years and moments.

Irshad Manji writes about those who cling to the rehearsal of early stages of the development of Islam: **"Who cares how closely we approximate the founding moment?"**[7]

The progress of gravity theory didn't end with Isaac Newton's death. Electrical lighting didn't stop advancing after the life of Thomas Edison. And the development of Christian Science didn't grind to a halt in 1910 at the passing of Mary Baker Eddy. But some elements of church teaching, custom, and practices detailed in this book have **taken on a life of their own**, have become self-serving dogma, and therefore have ceased to nourish those who come looking for spiritual sustenance.

Now over a century after the formative years of the Christian Science Church, too much of the attention of our church magazines and recently published books has focused on the church's early years and especially on Mrs. Eddy's story rather than looking forward and examining how our religious practice can better relate to the current age. Our church writings too often have done exactly what Mrs. Eddy worked against—to "return to positions outgrown" (S&H 74:30). Too often what we write for the public reflects patterns of language, thought, and mental development that might have suited the social climate of the early twentieth century but do not necessarily suit a different time. Much has changed since then, and Christian Scientists need to adapt to that change.

Charles Braden wrote over half a century ago, and his commentary is still relevant: "Mrs. Eddy never ceased to advance in theory and practice, and...in the true spirit of the Founder, Christian Science must always continue to evolve....The present hierarchical insistence on maintaining Christian Science at the precise level at which Mrs. Eddy left it represents a **fundamental betrayal of the very spirit of the woman they** [her students] **think to honor.**"[8] Yes, there have been changes in style, tone, and inclusion in Christian Science churches since Mrs. Eddy's time and since the 1950s when Charles Braden wrote, but it is

---

7. Manji, *The Trouble with Islam Today*, 155.
8. Braden, *Christian Science Today*, 29.

the conviction of the author that far greater changes will be necessary in order to keep our church's spiritual progress in tune with or "abreast of the times,"[9] and able to meet the increasing needs of humanity.

What nature teaches us about renewed forms

The butterfly is not an improved caterpillar. The butterfly emerges from a soup-like mix of the old caterpillar. It's a near-totally transformed caterpillar, so that hardly any of the old creature remains to resemble its earlier version. If Jesus had wanted to illustrate his command to be born again, the caterpillar-to-butterfly transformation would have been a worthy example. In the natural world static perfection is an impossible ideal.

Just as astronomers depict the universe and constellations as an ever-evolving and expanding entity, so here on earth could not the cosmic model be our earthly model—a model of ever-expanding and ever-evolving entities whether that may happen in the field of law, the sciences, or any field of endeavor? The notion of a static state called *entropy* could hardly be termed perfect by physicists, because that state is devoid of energy and therefore very imperfect and non-functional. When Jesus demanded that we be "perfect," he was not referring to a static state of physical perfection but to very active, self-sacrificing love. And self-sacrificing love is the ultimate in expanding beyond self-centeredness, and adapting one's life to the demands and needs of the world.

Is there a danger in excess experimentation?

Is there a danger in expanding beyond the borders of practicality? Not if the Infinite "holds our soul in life" (Psalms 66:9 KJV 2000). Mrs. Eddy writes that the blending of species "urged to its limits, results in a return to the original species" (*S&H* 552). So if we go too far in experimentation, may not Soul's spiritual gravitational power have a way of bringing us back home to an enduring basis of operation?

---

9. Eddy, *Church Manual*, 44.

"No religion or other organization can survive without progressing beyond the confines staked out by its founder[s], and Christian Science is no exception."[10]

"Religions may waste away, but the fittest survives...."

My. 166

The fittest are **the most adapted**, not the strongest or the most populous, but the ones who **adjust to changes in a culture or environment and develop accordingly in order to function as useful contributors in a changing environment or spiritual 'ecosystem.'** The "fittest" aren't a species that replaces or devours those around it while standing alone on a peak of survival.[11]

Didn't the work and teaching of Jesus "fit," in the sense that he adapted himself to the great needs of those around him? Prophets had predicted a conquering Messiah, but that wasn't what the world needed. Like all of the world's greatest leaders, Jesus not only performed his task in the world remarkably well, he looked beyond what he could personally accomplish during his short time on earth.

Looking forward

As Jesus walked on the water, even in a storm, "He intended to pass them [the disciples in a boat] *by."* Mark 6:48, NRSV

On the walk to Emmaus after the resurrection, after encountering some of his followers, "He [Jesus] *seemed to be going farther."*

Luke 24:28, Common English Bible

Do we notice a theme here? The Christ would have us not be content with our present level of understanding and practice.

---

10. Swensen, "The 'Seekers of the Light,'" *The International Journal of Religion*, 143.
11. Darwin didn't actually coin the phrase "survival of the fittest." Herbert Spencer did, after he read Darwin's treatise on the natural selection of species, and later Darwin took up the phrase.

"There is so much more I [Jesus] *want to tell you, but you can't understand it now."*

John 16:12 The Living Bible

If Christ possesses more that we need to know, something more for us to realize, what makes us think that what we're doing today is good enough for tomorrow? Let's look at specific steps where we may need to travel in the way of Christ's guidance into the future…

CHAPTER 29

If…the future

Go through, go through the gates; prepare the way for the people; build up, build up the highway; clear it of stones; lift up a signal over the peoples.
Isa. 62:10, English Standard Version

Make no small plans, for they have not the power to stir men's souls.[1]

IF YOU'RE FIXING UP a house, it makes no sense to redecorate your kitchen with new counter-tops and cabinets and keep the leaky plumbing. You don't repaint the living room but leave lead-based paint on the floorboards. You don't replace walls and leave hazardous electrical wiring within those walls.

Steps already taken

There have been progressive moves in the organization and thinking of Christian Scientists in the past few decades. These changes should not be minimized. These modest changes, that have met with a mixture of membership support and criticism, include greater tolerance towards unorthodox practices among our members, increased reference to Bibles besides the King James Version (not to mention a large increase in Bible classes taught by Christian Scientists on their own, not sponsored by

> The surest way to predict the future is to invent it.
> Stephen G. Post

---
1. Variously attributed to Daniel Burnham (Chicago architect 1846–1912) and Niccolo Machiavelli (15th century philosopher).

church headquarters), expanded access to church history and records, creative adaptation to the computer age, greater outreach efforts toward young people and those at odds with church policy, more up-to-date music, and fresh style and content in our church magazines, media, and talks. Boston church officials have taken the trouble to travel to many of our churches in the United States and around the world and to listen to what church members have to say.

The problem is that, while change always takes time, especially in organizations, our church-wide efforts for change too often have downplayed or have **overlooked some very large elephants in the room.** This book attempts to raise issues that have received too little attention in our church magazines or are nearly completely ignored, but are **problems which directly affect the survival and viability of Christian Science as a spiritual movement, and the lives of individual Christian Scientists.**

The Big "If"

If we can get it together as a family of Christian Scientists, *if* we can be honest with ourselves about our history and all that has been written and practiced in our name, both the good and the bad, and deal constructively with our history, *if* we can continue the long and necessary task

> **That which is, hath been long ago; and that which is to be hath long ago been: and God seeketh again that which is passed away.** Eccl. 3:15, American Standard Version

of reconciling with church members, former members, and others whom we have for generations marginalized, disappointed, and ostracized from our midst, *if* we can learn compassion and love, not just for people like ourselves or for those from our own social groups, *if* we can go into hospitals to visit, pray for, and build up our own and others…then in another ten or fifteen years when Medicare funds begin to run short, few of the antibiotic defenses work anymore, and the cost of medicine forces rationing or makes some formerly common medical procedures beyond the means of most people, and the Christian Scientists are crucially needed, we will not be so downtrodden and discouraged over the fragments of our church that we can be a substantial blessing, full of grace. Then the words *Christian Science*, including its organizational forms, might have a different ring to the public and be a significant utility to the world.

Resurgence can be uneven

If this book were just a chronicle of a century-old New England religious order, someone else would have had to write it. **History is full of resurgent religious movements**. Christianity, Islam, and Judaism are all movements that have experienced peaks and valleys of progress and decline, dependent on the relative moral and spiritual vitality of their adherents. **Moderns are so enamored with straight-line progress that they are impatient with temporary failure and valleys of despair and disrepair**. "Let me teach you about life," the perennial garden tells us gently, as that garden dies yearly, or appears to do so, and then springs to vitality months later.

Religions, businesses, cultures and relationships slide downhill for reasons. This book describes a number of the factors involved in the movement of Christian Science slowing, and then stalling not long after its founding and then continuing to remain in a holding pattern. Has healing continued among the Christian Scientists even in the middle of organizational dysfunction and unchristian practices? Thankfully, by God's great grace and by the dedication, spiritualization, and the Christian love of many individuals, yes. But not as widely as it should have. Otherwise, the respected Christian Science teacher Bicknell Young would not have written nearly thirty years after Mrs. Eddy's passing, **"Nothing has gone right since 1910."**[2]

There is a Bible account where the young boy Samuel hears the voice of the Lord first calling him and then warning him of the impending judgment of Eli's household where the boy was living. Samuel, in his maturity, rebuked the irreligious misdeeds that he had been surrounded by as a child, even though at a later time Samuel's own sons "were out for what they could get for themselves, taking bribes, corrupting justice" (I Samuel 8:3 *The Message*).

While the voice of Truth speaks to the receptive heart in every age and

---

2. Bicknell Young, letter May 4, 1937.

culture, the hard work of following the directing hand of that divine inspiration in purifying and improving our world always lies before us. In every religious community there is always room for improvement and reform.

Analyzing the causes of a downturn in the forms of a religious practice is only one step, and sometimes is the easiest step. From self-knowledge and constructive self-criticism we must move forward to point out missions that require fulfillment—the crucial work and great possibilities before us, *if* the mistakes of the past are to be learned from, so that higher, better models of Christian action can move Christian Scientists and others forward.

J. B. Phillips renders Luke 9:44 as: **"Store up in your minds what I [Jesus] tell you…."** *If* **Christian Scientists heed the warnings of yesterday's mistakes, they can also fulfill the promises of the past, and harvest present possibilities**. Again, as Santayana wrote, "Those who cannot remember the past are condemned to repeat it."[3] The past includes both neglected wisdom as well as mistakes.

"Confessing our sins one to another" and next steps

Nations and peoples are constantly repeating mistakes. That is one reason Alcoholics Anonymous reminds its members to acknowledge their mortal weaknesses, and that's a reason why Catholics have regular confessionals. We all need to exhale and require safe places in which to do that. But there comes a time to **move on from contrite remorse for past failures to the constructive, active present**, all the while remembering that we can be misled if we believe that inherent goodness lies in our mortal person or in our present established organizational forms.

Paths less taken

The following are opportunities for prayer, generally ignored by Christian Scientists in the past century, that are "ripe for harvest."[4]

---

3. Santayana, *The Life of Reason: Reason in Common Sense* [1905-1906], Vol. 1, 284.
4. John 4:35 NLT.

These paths have been "less taken" because church members have considered them to be "Sabbath-violating" paths. The dogmatic interpretation of church teachings has told church members that. This reading of the letter without the spirit, and the questionable interpretation of church teachings, didn't spring from prohibitions established by Jesus, or even from early Christian Science writings preaching that message. Here are some paths less taken:

More active help for those in hospitals For example, spiritual treatment for those patients in hospitals who are "in peril" (see *Mis.* 89) and either (a) are believing that the medical treatment they are getting is not improving their health or (b) whose doctors have grave concern about these patients' health outcomes.

Spiritual treatment for those of "half-faith" Jesus treated people who lacked faith, but somewhere over the past century Christian Scientists have often decided that healing happens mainly for the hundred-percenters—those with few doubts in the power of the divine to heal. There are far too many who have been falsely led to believe that they are "not good enough" to be real church members.

Spiritual treatment regarding iatrogenic illnesses That is, diseases like MRSA arising from patients' hospitalization and from the patients' or staff's contact with others.

Prayer for fearful relatives of patients in the ICU and emergency room waiting rooms, for nurses, doctors, and staff There is a large need for ministers to be praying for these dear people as the need becomes clear to the practitioner present on the scene. Treating the fears of hospital staff relates to the outcome of our loved ones being cared for in those hospitals. **From a practitioner who has done this: "If you're a warrior, you want to be on the front lines. If you're an engineer or mathematician, you want to confront the toughest problem and solve it."**

The future of Christian Science

Here are **reasons that Christian Science has a future**, despite its apparently bleak outlook of near-empty churches full of old folks, stiff customs, and an attitude of disdainful condescension[5] towards conventional medicine.

Reason 1: Society demands its prosperity for spiritual reasons.

Joseph was called out of prison in Egypt by a nation that required prophetic vision to survive famine (Gen. 41). **The practice of Christian Science may be revived less because of our church members' spiritual willingness and the desire of our adherents and more so because modern society demands a lively presence of the principle of spiritual healing.**

Orthodox medicine slowly reformed its own lack of accountability, starting one hundred years ago (see Chapter 24), but it has never outgrown its need for a distinct spiritual element in the healing process. Otherwise, why would so many hospitals have names like Good Shepherd and St. John's Mercy? Why has the author's local hospital promoted itself with a slogan on billboards: **"Feel what a difference faith can make,"**...and our city is not in the Bible Belt. And why do a surprising number of medical schools have courses on spirituality?

The spiritual element is not extinct. Just when a national magazine announces that God is indeed dead, back springs the visibility of and demand for the Spirit.[6] When a pall of disbelief or confusion is bemoaned by some new proponents of a world no longer in need of the divine element, do you think the Spirit just sits there like a terrified opossum?

Faith does "play possum" in our personal histories, lying near-dead for decades in individual lives, and in sects and religious gatherings for centuries, only to break out in fervency when crises drive it to expression. So a scientific, yet spiritual, healing element in medicine can never be obliterated. What will bring it to the surface of renewed expression is need and then demand.

---

5. For an example, see John and Laura Lathrop's remarks to the court in Chapter 17.
6. TIME Magazine ran a controversial cover story "Is God Dead?" (April 8, 1966), followed three years later by a different message on the cover—"Is God coming back to life?" (December 26, 1969).

Reason 2: The overuse of antibiotics

Conventional medical treatment will soon be staring at a brick wall caused by the overuse and over-prescription of antibiotics. Health authorities from the U.S. Center for Disease Control and the World Health Organization have been warning about the consequences of overuse of antibiotics for over half a century, but with the days of reckoning approaching, the warnings have grown sterner, and there is still no obvious solution on the horizon besides less use of them.

Christian Scientists, and Christians in general, have given little attention to what Jesus taught which touches upon **infection and immunity:**

Nothing outside a person can defile them by going into them. Rather, it is what comes out of a person that defiles them. (Mark 7:15 NIV)

Jesus said that it was the corrupt thought whether murderous, lustful, and so on, which defiles the person. That teaching ran directly up against religious teachings of his time, and today it contravenes general teaching about infection and germ theory, but it is **foundational to Christian Scientists in their work of preventing the spread of infection and contagion**. The EMTs, cited in "Earth Helping the Woman," Chapter 13, discovered that fact, and led them to notice that Christian Science could help medical technicians fight infection.

Reason 3: Drug-resistant disease strains

Many of these diseases are by-products of globalization and excessive antibiotic usage and are proving to be resistant to conventional treatment. If Western society gets to a point where no available antibiotics can treat diseases like malaria and diseases found more commonly in the West, or vaccines cannot be developed quickly enough to combat viral epidemics and their varied disease strains, what is the alternative?

Reason 4: Society demands the prosperity of spiritual healing for **financial and health reasons.**

Orthodox medicine is steadily pricing itself out of practical use for all. All economic models current in the United States, as of this writing, indicate that major funding mechanisms such as Medicare, Medicaid, and the Affordable Care Act, which have partially covered the inflated price of medical care in the United States and have shielded patients from direct awareness of medical costs, may hit empty or nearly empty in two decades.

Before society faces the critical reality of an inadequate medicine cabinet, **there will be a more urgent public-wide search for ways to control costs, rediscover, and use alternative treatments**. While holistic options are available, many of them are placebos that can fill the gap of medical needs just so far before faith in them is overtaxed.

The world's current medical model may be compelled to change for its own internal reasons. **The question for this author is not so much whether there will be societal demand for change, because that will happen. The question is whether there will be a willingness among Christian Scientists to make themselves available to help meet the various quandaries of the societies in which they live**.

A punch-list for Christian Scientists

- **Honestly confront our history,** with its failings and shortcomings that have directly led to the steady decline of our organized church to date. Again, sober self-assessment is what Alcoholics Anonymous demands of its members. The demand for self-knowledge and humility extends beyond the needs of recovering alcoholics. What Winston Churchill is reputed to have said about a political opponent could also be said about our church today: "[They] are humble because [they] have much to be humble about."
- **Be reconciled** We need to embrace a real, not limited, magnanimity, with a searching purpose to reconcile with disenfranchised Christian Scientists and to embrace them in full fellowship.
- **Establish unity** Not a narrow base with a narrow list of acceptable teachers and preferred doctrinal emphases, but a **"big tent" approach** (see Isa. 54:2). Much more of the "big tent" existed prior to the passing of Mrs. Eddy (see "The Great Inclusion" Chapter 14). Our "big tent" should, of course, include a renewed appreciation of all that is good in other faiths and traditions.

- **Come to terms with the society in which we live…and adapt foremost our attitudes, then our practices and forms, and even our limited vocabulary, not from fear but out of love.** This includes an awareness of the standardization and modernization of medicine that has changed society, and a reasonable, compassionate approach not just toward church members who have worked with physicians, but an honest assessment of all that Mrs. Eddy has to say on the subject of healing practice relative to orthodox medical care. Truth and love, self-knowledge and mercy, embrace each other, and this compels us to embrace all of God's creation.
- *If…*the preceding can be accomplished, it is conceivable that Christian Science can play an important role in the development of medical practice in the future. If not, the moral of history is that those who refuse to adapt are displaced by those who do. This displacing has already happened somewhat if we take into account various spiritual healing movements that have occurred within Apostolic, Pentecostal, "mainline" and independent Christian churches and elsewhere over the past century

"Things don't go extinct. They just go underground until we are ready for them."[7]

No extinction of spiritual healing needs to happen, but an approximation of Christian Science at its best may find channels other than the present organizational forms. Let's note here Paul's analogy of the pruned and grafted branch (Romans 11:17) that hints at the demand for those of faith to not rest on their laurels, lest others take their place. This warning applies daily to the business world.

"Slouching towards Bethlehem"[8] **—greater works, not because we necessarily want to, but because we have to, fulfill the undivided Body of Christ.**

---

7. Linda K. Hogan, author and poet.
8. Didion, Joan. Didion's book by this title borrows a phrase from the poem "The Seconed Comming" by W. B. Yeats.

Christian Scientists in the next few decades may be reluctant volunteers for progress, pushed forward by a demand not our own. Like the reluctant prophet Jonah, we may ultimately be motivated less by our own unselfish desires but more by the forces of society's need for what we can offer and by the divine impulse to satisfy that human demand.

Progress is not optional for the Christian. Christians vaguely imagine what Jesus had in mind when he forecast that his followers would engage in "greater works." Does this prophecy embody not merely greater quantity of Christian performance, but greater quality of action, with a consistency that has not yet been seen by society?

It always seems impossible until it's done.

Nelson Mandela[9]

Conclusion

This book extends a spiritual challenge to all Christian Scientists and not merely to those engaged in our church's healing ministry and our church leadership. Tomorrow for all of us begins with the modest steps of renewal that we take today.

---

9. Widely attributed to the former president of South Africa.

Epilogue

THE PURPOSE OF THIS BOOK is to inspire discussion and action within the Christian Science Church as well as with other religious bodies. The author's recommendations are not exact paradigms. Rather they are encouragement for rebirth, renewal, and subsequent change. It is the author's desire that any discussion arising from this book will work towards progress in the field of spiritual healing and its useful application.

"Count it as a thing not having his full shape...even as a thing begun rather than finished."
The Epilogue of William Tyndale's translation of the English Bible[1]

---

1. Bobrick, 104

Appendix

Time-line of "Change of Front" in 1902-3

August 1902 *CS Sentinel* "Los Angeles Case"— death of Reed girl in Los Angeles area (Vol. 5, p. 248). Trial is held the last week of November 1902.

September 18th 1902 *CS Sentinel* prints healings of children from contagious diseases.

October 18th 1902 *Boston Times* publishes positive article about Mrs. Eddy.

October 23th 1902 *New York Times* reports coroner's inquest into death of New York girl, Esther Quinby. The practitioner had incorrectly diagnosed problem as tonsillitis.

October 24th 1902 *Boston Herald*: Practitioner John Lathrop and Quinby parents are charged with manslaughter. Lathrop testifies at length before the coroner. Laura Lathrop comments to the court, indicating confidence in her son's exoneration and gratitude for the prosecution.

October 26th 1902 Rev. Charles Parkhurst in his pulpit accuses Mrs. Eddy of lying; another speaker at the same service attacks the "humbuggery" of Christian Science.

October 30th 1902 *Boston Post* reports the coroner's desire to indict Mrs. Eddy as a "principal" in the *Quinby* case.

November 4th 1902 The postscript of letter of Calvin Frye, Mrs. Eddy's secretary, to Alfred Farlow: "I see the great harm JC Lathrop is doing with his tongue and telephoned McC [probably W. McCracken, the Committee on Publication for New York] to caution him." Letter of same date from Mrs. Eddy to Archibald McClellan: "I agree with you that silence on all questions of the court is wise and I deeply regret the absence of this wisdom" (Courtesy of the Mary Baker Eddy Library).

November 5th 1902 "Christian Science and Medicine" by Alfred Farlow (*Boston Times*).

November 6th 1902 *CS Sentinel* "Rights and Duties": An editorial by Archibald McClellan in the *CS Sentinel* concludes with the following statement: "Mrs. Eddy advises, until the public thought becomes better acquainted with Christian Science, that Christian Scientists decline to doctor infectious or contagious diseases" (*My.* 226:27).

November 7th 1902 *Boston Globe* ties Mrs. Eddy's "advice" (known in some of the press as an "edict") to the White Plains case.

November 14th 1902 *New York Times* headlines: "Christian Scientists' Change of Front—'Healers' will not hereafter treat contagious diseases."

November 14th 1902 *New York Times*: Reaction to the Lathrops' testimony appears in a letter to the *Times*' editor: "Do law-abiding citizens carry on a murderous trade for money, and snap their fingers at the idea of punishment, as Mrs. Lathrop did when she was arraigned [sic] before Coroner Banning and found instrumental in causing the death of the Quimby [sic] child? H.E.C."

November 15th 1902 Was there a rebellion against Mrs. Eddy's "advice"? Newspapers portrayed it as such. "Revolt against 'Mother' Eddy—Christian Scientists Resent Order Regarding Infection" (*Boston Post*). *Signs of revolt among the advanced Christians Scientists...Her writings, up to the present time, they cite, have been that their belief could cure all maladies, and that to eliminate contagious diseases while under fire is a retrogression. They will not come out in the open and defy the leader, but among themselves it is taken as a disagreeable command to relinquish the treatment of the infectious.* Former Judge and current church lecturer William Ewing rides in a special car with about sixty fellow Scientists to White Plains, New York, where Judge Ewing pleads on behalf of the unconditional rights of freedom of worship for Christian Scientists.

November 17th 1902 Sarcastic editorial in *New York Times* suggests that a practitioner might need an accompanying regular physician with him in order to know what he is treating.

November 25th 1902 Letter from Mrs. Eddy (to W.D. McCracken LO2611) in regard to Christian Scientists speaking "too metaphysically to others than Christian Scientists. I have often told them of this and shown them the advantage it gives those who sneer at an absolute Science," (quite possibly in reference to J. Lathrop's October 24th testimony).

Novovember 25th–28th 1902 Conclusion of the trial of the "Los Angeles Case" which had similar cause and subject matter as the Quinby-Lathrop case, but had dozens of Christian Scientists testifying to the beneficial effects of Christian Science, reported in the press. (*CS Sentinel* Vol. 5, No. 16, p.248).

November 27th 1902 *CS Sentinel* publishes "Wherefore?" in which Mrs. Eddy elaborates on and explains her advice, including cautions regarding Christian Scientists knowing better their abilities, to the end of preserving themselves and their cause of healing. (Her article was discussed in *Boston Post* of same date; "Wherefore?" is republished in December, 1902 *CSJ*).

December 18th 1902 Editorial from the *Chicago Public* supportive of Mrs. Eddy's advice printed in *CS Sentinel*: *Why is it that so many educated men are so feeble at distinguishing differences? An example occurs to us in connection with the recent proclamation of Mrs. Eddy...in which she advises her followers to bow before hostile public sentiment to the extent of allowing the employment of physicians in the treatment of infectious and contagious diseases...*[Eddy's advice] *is a manifest mark of respect for the rights of others...Her conduct in this matter should command respect...*

December 18th 1902 *CS Sentinel* cites "not guilty" verdict reached in Los Angeles case (see above in timeline August, 1902); this verdict was reached in the last week of Nov. 1902. This edition also cites the exoneration of a Christian Scientist occurring on December 13, in the state of Georgia.

December 25th 1902 *CS Sentinel* "Suffer it to be so Now" by Alfred Farlow (previously published in the *Boston Times*) further elaborates on Mrs. Eddy's themes in "Wherefore?"—citing self-knowledge, allowing for concessions to common customs at certain times, "safe" conduct of the healers, etc.

January 8th 1903 Charles Skinner writing for the Christian Scientists to a Michigan newspaper summarizes Mrs. Eddy's November 1902 action: **"(U)ntil the general thought of the public is more willing to accept the efficacy of Christian Science healing in contagious diseases, it will be wiser to leave such cases to the care of systems from which there will be less fear awakened among the masses"** (p. 292, *CS Sentinel*, Vol. V., No. 19).

January 22nd 1903 Alfred Farlow (in *Journal of Medicine and Science*) is quoted by the *CS Sentinel*: "One critic asserts that a Christian Scientist stated, 'We do not believe in infectious diseases, and a person, if a Christian Scientist, could not contract such diseases.' If a Christian Scientist made such an assertion, he was certainly unwise, to say the least. **Christian Scientists do believe in infectious diseases, though they may differ from others in their interpretation of their nature**, and why? Because they have not yet attained to a sufficient realization of what Christian Science teaches to enable them to unbelieve altogether in disease." [Note: Farlow is clearly doing "damage control" required by the kind of casual church member's comment similar to the testimony of John Lathrop and the comments of his mother in the White Plains case in New York.]

February 5th 1903 *CS Sentinel* reports the spontaneous rejection of anti-Christian Science legislation in the New Hampshire legislature. The opposition formed without any Christian Scientists needing to participate in rallying against the proposal. This victory for the church, together with a similar one reported the following month (March 28, 1903 *CS Sentinel*) having occurred in North Carolina, and yet another one in Texas (*CS Sentinel* April 11, 1903) may possibly be positive aftereffects of Mrs. Eddy's "edict."

[Note: The reader is cautioned here regarding the logical fallacy called *post hoc ergo propter hoc*. This translates from the Latin: "after this, therefore because of this." In other words, it is incorrect to assume that just because an event or events happened after other "neighboring" events, that the latter necessarily caused the former. So, in this case, the fact that some states supported the legal rights of Christian Scientists shortly after the time of Mrs. Eddy's "advice" does not prove that legislators in those states were positively influenced by her "advice." It doesn't rule that possibility out, but, without the transcripts of the legal discussions, we have no way of proving that possibility.]

April 25th 1903 *CS Sentinel* quotes Alfred Farlow writing to *Boston Ideas* perhaps in continuing rebuttal of the Lathrop testimony of October 24th: **"A death or failure under Christian Science treatment is not a true demonstration, but a false one…"** (p. 537).

Selected Bibliography

Adler, Mortimer. *Intellect: Mind over Matter*. New York: Macmillan, 1990.

Aminov, Rustam. "A Brief History of the Antibiotic Era: Lessons Learned and Challenges for the Future." *Frontiers in Microbiology*. Published online 2010 December 8. PMCID: PMC3109405. PMID: 21687759.

Answer to Bill in Equity. Boston: Christian Science Publishing Society, 1920.

Arrington, Leonard. *The Mormon Experience*. Champaign, IL: University of Illinois Press, 1992.

Association of American Medical Colleges. Washington, D.C.: IHS Markit, Ltd., April 23, 2019.

Baker, Anna White. *Reminiscences*. Boston: Mary Baker Eddy Library.

Baker, Heidi. *Compelled by Love*. Lake Mary, FL: Charisma House Book Group, 2008.

Banner, The. Spring, 1988. Zanesville, OH: Self-published, 1988.

Barclay, William. *The Gospel of Luke*. Louisville, KY: Westminster John Knox Press, 2001.

Barclay, William. *The Gospel of Mark*. Louisville, KY: Westminster John Knox Press, 2001.

Barnes, Rev. Jan. "I Refuse to Be a Member of a Dying Church." Sermon given at Trinity United Church of Christ, St. Louis, MO.

Battle Creek Enquirer. 11-29-1993.

Bent, Samuel Arthur. *Familiar Short Sayings of Great Men*, (6th ed.) Boston: Ticknor and Co., 1887.

Berlin, Adele and Marc Brettler (ed.) *Jewish Study Bible*. New York: Oxford Univ. Press, 2004.

Bierce, Ambrose. *The Unabridged Devil's Dictionary*. Athens, GA: The University of Georgia Press. 2017.

Black, Matthew, H.H. Rowley (ed.) *Peake's Commentary on the Bible*. London: Routledge, 1999.

Blake, Aaron. "Here's How Many Americans Are Actually Anti-vaxxers." *Washington Post* 2-9-2015.

Book of Mormon. Church of Jesus Christ of Latter-day Saints: Salt Lake City, UT, 2000.

Boston Globe. "How Facts Backfire." July 11, 2010.

Boston Post. (In print 1831-1956; at one time the Post was one of the largest newspapers in the country) Boston, MA: Post Publishing Co., 1902.

Bowler, Kate. "On Dying and Reckoning with the Prosperity Gospel." *Christianity Today*. Carol Stream, Illinois: Christianity Today International, February 23, 2012.

Braden, Charles. *Christian Science Today: Power, Policy, Practice*. London: George Allen Publishing, 1959.

Brownlee, Shannon. *Overtreated: Why Too Much Medicine Is Making Us Sicker and Poorer*. New York: Bloomsbury, USA. 2007.

Burke, Edmund. "Conciliation with America." Great Books Online: https://www.bartleby.com/library/prose/1026.html Warner, Charles Dudley, et al. *Library of World's Best Literature*. New York: Warner Library Co., 1917; Bartleby.com, 2015.

Cahill, Thomas. *How the Irish Saved Civilization*. New York: Anchor Books, 1995.

Cambridge Advanced Learner's Dictionary. Walter, Elizabeth (ed. et al) Cambridge, England: Cambridge University Press, 2008.

Campolo, Rev. Tony. *Revolution and Renewal*. Louisville, KY: Westminster John Knox Press, 2000.

Cappon, Lester J. (ed.) *The Adams-Jefferson Letters*. Chapel Hill, N.C.: University of North Carolina Press, 1987.

Carlyle, Thomas. *The Works of Thomas Carlyle*, Vol. 5, 143. New York: John B. Alden, 1885.

Carter, Prof. Stephen. "The Power of Prayer Denied" *Christian Science Monitor*. Boston: Christian Science Publishing Society, February, 7, 1996.

Cassill, Kay. "Stress Has Hit Roseto, Pa., Once The Town Heart Disease Passed By." *People*. June 16, 1980.

Catton, Bruce. *U. S. Grant and the American Military Tradition*. New York: Little, Brown & Co., 1954.

A Century of Christian Science Healing. Boston: Christian Science Publishing Society. 1966.

Cha, Ariana. "Medical Errors Now Third Leading Cause of Death in U. S." *Washington Post*. Washington, D. C.: Nash Holdings. May 3, 2016.

Channing, Carol. *Just Lucky, I Guess*. New York: Simon & Schuster, 2002.

Channing, George. "No Concessions to Matter." *Christian Science Sentinel*. Boston: Christian Science Publishing Society, 1949.

"Christian Science Church Adopts Jim Crow." *The Crisis Magazine*. Baltimore, MD: The Crisis Publishing Company. December, 1938.

Christian Science Journal. "Questions and Answers." Boston: Christian Science Publishing Society, August 2012.

"The Christian Science Standard of Healing." *Christian Science Journal*, November 1957.

Churchill, Winston. *Never Give In! The Best of Winston Churchill's Speeches*. Lebanon, IN: Hachette Book Group, 2004.

Clark, J.C.D. Clark. *English Society, 1660-1832: Religion, Ideology and Politics during the Ancien Regime*. Cambridge, England: Cambridge University Press, 2000.

Clarke, Adam. *Commentary on the Bible*. Burlington, ON: Wesleyan Heritage Publications, 1998.

Clarke, Joseph. "Mrs. Eddy outlines basis of her religion" *New York Herald*, May 5, 1901.

CNN 4-12-2017. (see Gilbert, Allison)

Congressional Record Online through the Government Publishing Office [www.gpo.gov], S5455, May 21, 1996.

Corey, Arthur. *Behind the Scenes with the Metaphysicians*. DeVorss: Camarillo, CA, 1968.

Cousins, Norman. *Anatomy of an Illness: As Perceived by the Patient*. New York: W. W. Norton, 2005.

Cyprian, S. Caecilius. *The Treatises of S. Caecilius Cyprian, Bishop of Carthage and Martyr*. Vol. 3. Treatise VI. London: J. G. and F. Rivington, 1839.

Daedelus, Winter 1974. Cambridge, MA: MIT Press for the American Academy of Arts and Sciences, 1974.

https://www.dailymail.co.uk/health/article-1306283/Miracle-premature-baby-declared-dead-doctors-revived-mothers-touch.html.

Dickey, Adam. *Memoirs of Mary Baker Eddy*. Santa Clarita, CA: The Bookmark, 2002.

Didion, Joan. *Slouching towards Bethlehem*. New York: Farras, Straus and Giroux, 1968.

Dossey, Larry. *Explore: The Journal of Science and Healing*. Philadelphia: Elsevier, November/December 2008, Vol. 4, No. 6 (341).

Dossey, Larry. *Recovering the Soul: A Scientific and Spiritual Search*. New York: Bantam Books. 1989.

Drummond, Henry. *The Greatest Thing in the World*. Grand Rapids, MI: Spire Books, 2006.

Dummelow, J. R., editor. *The One Volume Bible Commentary*. New York: Macmillan Publishing Co., Inc., 1974.

Dunn, John R. "Some Thoughts on 'Obtrusive Mental Healing.'" *Christian Science Sentinel*. Boston: Christian Science Publishing Society, June 21, 1947.

Eddy, Mary Baker. *Church Manual of The First Church of Christ, Scientist in Boston, Massachusetts*. Boston: The Christian Science Publishing Society, 1936.

Eddy, Mary Baker. *In My True Light and Life*. Boston: The Writings of Mary Baker Eddy, 2002.

Eddy, Mary Baker. *Prose Works other than Science and Health*. "No and Yes." Boston: The Christian Science Publishing Society, 1925.

Eddy, Mary Baker. *Prose Works other than Science and Health*. "Miscellaneous Writings." Boston: The Christian Science Publishing Society, 1925.

Eddy, Mary Baker. *Prose Works other than Science and Health*. "Miscellany." Boston: The Christian Science Publishing Society, 1925.

Eddy, Mary Baker. *Prose Works other than Science and Health*. "Retrospection and Introspection." Boston: The Christian Science Publishing Society, 1925.

Eddy, Mary Baker. *Science & Health with Key to the Scriptures*. Boston: The First Church of Christ, Scientist, 1971.

Engardio, Joel P. "Jehovah's Witnesses' Untold Story of Resistance to Nazis." *Christian Science Monitor*. Boston: The Christian Science Publishing Society, November 6, 1996.

Enstron, James E. and L. Breslow. "Lifestyle and reduced mortality among active California Mormons," 1980-2004. UCLA School of Public Health and Jonsson Comprehensive Cancer Center. Berkeley, CA: Elsevier, 2008.

Epperly, Bruce. "Abraham Lincoln and the Quest for Religious and Political Stature." Englewood, CO: Patheos, 2-17-2012.

Eustace, Herbert. *Christian Science: Its 'Clear Correct Teaching'*. Berkeley, CA: Trustees for the Complete Writings of Herbert W. Eustace, 1999.

Farlow, Alfred. "The Bible and Medicine". *Christian Science Sentinel*. Boston: The Christian Science Publishing Society, October 2, 1902.

Foley, Katherine E. "Get a Second Opinion—Doctors Usually Aren't Right the First Time." Quartz. New York: 4-4-2017.

Fox, Robin Lane. *Pagans and Christians*. New York: Alfred A. Knopf, 1987.

Francona, Terry. *Francona*. Chicago: Houghton Mifflin, 2013.

Fraser, Caroline. *God's Perfect Child*. New York: Metropolitan Books, 1999.

Friedersdorf, Conor. "The Audacity of Talking about Race with the Ku Klux Klan." *The Atlantic*. Washington, D.C.: Atlantic Media Company, March 27, 2015.

Getzen, Thomas E. "The Growth of Health Spending in the U.S.A.: 1776 to 2026." Philadelphia, PA: 12-12-2017. Https://www.soa.org/globalassets/assets/Files/Research/research-growth-health-spending.pdf.

Gibbon, Edward; Peter Eckler. *History of Christianity: Comprising All That Relates to the Progress of the Christian Religion in "The History of the Decline and Fall of the Roman Empire."* New York: Peter Eckler Publishing Co., 1916.

Gibbon, Edward. *The Decline and Fall of the Roman Empire*. Paris: A. & W. Gaglignani & Co., 1840.

Gibbs, Samuel. "Jeff Bezos: I've made billions of dollars of failures at Amazon." *The Guardian*. London: Guardian Media Group, 12-3-2014.

Gibson, Rosemary and Janardan Prasad Singh *The Treatment Trap: How the Overuse of Medical Care Is Wrecking Your Health and What You Can Do to Prevent It*. Chicago: Ivan R. Dee, Publisher, 2011.

Gilbert, Allison. *Passed and Present: Keeping Memories of Loved Ones Alive*. Berkeley, CA: Seal Press, 2016.

Gladwell, *The Outliers*. New York: Little, Brown and Co., 2008.

Gordon, "Social Class in American Society," 262. https://www.jstor.org/stable/2771137?seq=1#page_scan_tab_contents.

Gottschalk, Stephen. *Rolling Away the Stone: Mary Baker Eddy's Challenge to Materialism*. Bloomington, IN: Indiana University Press, 2006.

Grady, Denise. "In One Country Chronic Whiplash is Uncompensated (and Unknown)." *New York Times*. May 7, 1996.

Greenhouse, Lucia. *fathermothergod*. New York: Crown Publishers, 2011.

Grierson, Bruce. "What if Age Is Nothing but a Mind-Set?" *The New York Times Magazine*. New York City: The New York Times Company. 10-22-2014.

BIBLIOGRAPHY

Halberstam, David. *The Christian Science Monitor.* Boston: Christian Science Publishing Society. November 8, 2001.

Hales, Robert D. "The Eternal Family." Sermon at Quorum of the Twelve Apostles. Salt Lake City UT: October, 1996.

Hamilton, James, D.D. *Our Christian Classics: Readings from the Best Divines.* London: James Nisbet & Co., 1858.

Harris, Stephen. *The New Testament: A Student's Introduction.* New York: McGraw-Hill Higher Education. 2011.

Henig, Robin Marantz. "The Reminiscence Bump—People Looking Back on Life Remember Their Twenties Best." *Psychology Today,* 10-24-2012.

Houpt, Charles Theodore. *Bliss Knapp, Christian Scientist.* Brentwood, MO: Clark-Sprague, Inc., 1976.

http://www.newenglandhistoricalsociety.com/the-1918-flu-epidemic-kills-thousands-in-new-england/.

Hurst, Charles E. and David L. McConnell. *An Amish Paradox: Diversity and Change in the World's Largest Amish Community.* Baltimore: Johns Hopkins University Press, 2010.

James, William. *Pragmatism and the Meaning of Truth.* Cambridge, MA: Harvard University Press, 1978.

James, William. *The Varieties of Religious Experience: A Study in Human Nature.* New York: Penguin Books. 1985.

John, DeWitt. "Love and Church Renewal." *The Christian Science Journal.* Boston: The Christian Science Publishing Society. December, 1981.

Johnson-Coleman, Lorraine. *Just Plain Folks: Original Tales of Living, Loving, Longing and Learning as Told by a Perfectly Ordinary, Quite Commonly Sensible, and Absolutely Awe-Inspiring, Colored Woman.* Boston: Little, Brown and Co., 1998.

Jordan, Clarence. *The Cotton Patch Version of Luke* and Acts. Clinton, N.J.: New Win Publishing, Inc., 1969.

Keohane, Joe. "How Facts Backfire." *Boston Globe,* 7-11-2010.

King, Martin Luther. "Remaining Awake through a Great Revolution." Speech, March 31, 1968.

Kissinger, Henry. "Nature of Diplomacy in the Contemporary Period." Lecture at Principia College, Elsah, IL. April 8, 1999.

Kolata, Gina. "Vast Study Casts Doubt on the Value of Mammograms." *New York Times* February 20, 2014.

Kostenberger, Andreas. *Encountering John: The Gospel in Historical, Literary, and Theological Perspective.* Grand Rapids, MI: Baker Academic, 1999.

Laan, Ray Vander. *Prophets and Kings.* Grand Rapids, MI: Zondervan, 1999.

Lamott, Anne. Help, Thanks, Wow: *The Three Essential Prayers.* New York: Penguin Group, 2012.

Lamott, Anne. *Traveling Mercies: Some Thoughts on Faith.* New York: Pantheon Books, 1999.

Larry King Live, May 4, 2001.

Lavin, Cheryl. "In 'Anatomy of an Illness' Norman Cousins…" *The Chicago Tribune*. Chicago: Tribune Publishing. 1-28-1990.

Laymon, Charles M., Ed. *The Interpreter's One-Volume Commentary on the Bible*. Nashville: Abingdon Press, 1980.

Lee, Harper. *Go Set a Watchman*. New York City: Harper Collins, 2015.

Leedom, Joanne Shriver. "An Enlarged View of Radical Reliance." *Christian Science Journal*, Vol. 92, 1974. Boston: The Christian Science Publishing Society.

Letter to Bill Sweet from Committee on Publication [Chapter 26].

"Let Us Follow Our Beliefs in Caring for Children." *New York Times*. New York City: The New York Times Company, March 11, 2015.

Li, Ming and Paul Vitanyi. *An Introduction to Kolmogorov Complexity and Its Applications*. New York: Springer Science & Business, 1993.

Lifeway Research and the North American Mission Board, 2009. Nashville, TN: B&H Publishing Group, 2009.

Low, David M. *Edward Gibbon: 1737-1794*. London: Chatto and Windus, 1937.

Mahar, Maggie. *Money-Driven Medicine*. New York: Collins. 2006.

Manchester, William. *A World Lit Only by Fire*. New York: Little, Brown and Company, 1993.

Manji, Irshad. *The Trouble with Islam: A Muslim's Call for Reform in Her Faith*. New York: St. Martin's Press. 2004.

Marshall, Catherine. *A Man Called Peter*. Wheaton, IL: Gilead Publishing, LLC. 2013.

McLellan, Archibald. "Consistency," *Christian Science Sentinel*, Vol. 11, No. 14. Boston: Christian Science Publishing Society, 12-5-1908.

McNeil, Keith. *A Story Untold: A History of the Quimby-Eddy Debate*. Carmel, IN: Hawthorne Publishing, 2020. Three Volumns.

Meyer, Holly. "Christian Scientists use prayer instead of medicine." Tysons Corner, VA: Gannett, 9-16-2017.

Moorjani, Anita. *Dying to Be Me*. Carlsbad, CA: Hay House, Inc., 2012.

Nenneman, Richard A. *Persistent Pilgrim: The Life of Mary Baker Eddy*. Etna, NH: Nebbadoon Press, 1997.

Newman, Morris. "Meditation and Yoga Heading for Former Christian Science Building." *Los Angeles Times* April 11, 2010.

Nicolson, Adam. *God's Secretaries*. New York: HarperCollins, 2003.

Niebhur, Reinhold and Andrew J. Bacevich. "Happiness, Prosperity, and Virtue," from *The Irony of American History*. Chicago: The University of Chicago Press, 1952.

Nightingale, Florence, and Lynn McDonald, (ed.) *Florence Nightingale on Women, Medicine, Midwifery and Prostitution*. Waterloo, ON: Wilfrid Laurier University Press, 2005.

Nouwen, Henri. *Discernment*. New York: Harper Collins Publishers, 2013.

Numbers, Ronald L. *Sickness and Health in America: Readings in the History of Medicine and Public Health*. Madison, WI: University of Wisconsin Press, 1985.

Ostling, Richard and Joan. *Mormon America*. New York: Harper One, 2007.

Pagels, Elaine. *Beyond Belief: The Secret Gospel of Thomas*. New York: Vintage Books, 2003.

Paley, William. A *View of the Evidences of Christianity in Three Parts*. Hansebooks, 2015.

Pavlovitz, Rev. John. www.johnpavolovitz.com.

Peel, Robert. *Health and Medicine in the Christian Science Tradition*. New York: Crossroad Publishing, 1988.

Peel, Robert. *The Years of Discovery*. New York: Holt, Rinehart and Winston, 1966.

Peel, Robert. *The Years of Trial*. New York: Holt, Rinehart and Winston, 1971.

Peel, Robert. *The Years of Authority*. New York: Holt, Rinehart and Winston, 1977.

Peloubet, F.N. and Alice Adams (ed.) *Peloubet's Bible Dictionary*. New York: Holt, Rinehart & Winston, 1947.

Pew Forum. "U.S. Religious Landscape Survey: Religious Affiliation," by Pew Forum on Religion and Public Life, Feb. 25, 2008.

Powell, Lyman. *Mary Baker Eddy*: A Life Size Portrait. Boston: Christian Science Publishing Society, 1950.

Rader, Dotson. "Ellen DeGeneres Talks Feelings, Fun and Finding Dory," *Parade Magazine*, 6-10-2016.

Rainer, Thom and Sam. *Essential Church: Reclaiming a Generation of Dropouts*. Nashville, TN: B&H Publishing Group, 2008.

Rathvon, William. *Reminiscences*. Boston: Mary Baker Eddy Library.

Reid, T. R. *The Healing of America*. New York: The Penguin Group Publishing, 2009.

"Relationships improve your odds of survival by 50 percent, research finds." Rockville, MD: ScienceDaily, July 28, 2010.

Religion News Service. "Christian Scientists Entering the New Age." *Chicago Tribune*.

Rogers, Will. *The Wit and Wisdom of Will Rogers in His Own Voice*. New York: Caedmon Audio, 1991.

Rosten, Leo, (ed.) *Religions of America*. New York: Simon and Schuster, 1975.

Rubenstein, Richard E. *When Jesus Became God: The Struggle to Define Christianity during the Last Days of Rome*. New York: Houghton Mifflin Harcourt Publishing Company, 1999.

Santayana, George. *Reason in Common Sense: The Life of Reason*, Vol. 1. New York: Scribner, 1905.

Seal, Frances Thurber. *Christian Science in Germany*. Plainfield, NJ: Plainfield Christian Science Church, 1977.

Segen, J.C. (ed.) T*he Dictionary of Modern Medicine*. Boca Raton, FL: CRC Press, 1992.

Shublak, Linda. "Covered with the Word" *Guideposts* Magazine, September, 1996.

60 *Minutes*, "Killing Cancer," New York: CBS, March 29, 2015.

Skinner, Charles. "Christian Scientists Take the Whole Promise of Immunity...." *Christian Science Sentinel*. Boston: Christian Science Publishing Society, May 28, 1904.

Smith, Huston. T*he Religions of Man*. New York: Harper & Row, 1958.

Snow, Lorenzo. "Discourse," *Millennial Star*, vol. 61, no. 34, 1899-08-24. Liverpool, England: 1840-1970. (In 1970 the Millenial Star was replaced by The Ensign.)

Spirituality.com. Live Chat on May 9, 2006.

Stahnisch, Frank W. and Maria Verhoef. "The Flexner Report of 1910 and Its Impact on Complementary and Alternative Medicine and Psychiatry in North America in the 20th Century." *Evidence-Based Complementary and Alternative Medicine*. 2012: 1-10.

Stark, Rodney. *The Rise of Christianity: How the Obscure, Marginal Jesus Movement Became the Dominant Religious Force in the Western World in a Few Centuries*. Princeton, NJ: Princeton University Press, 1996.

Stark, Rodney. "The Rise and Fall of Christian Science," *Journal of Contemporary Religion*. 13 (2) (1998) 189-214. Philadelphia, PA: Routledge, 1998.

Stedman's Medical Dictionary. Baltimore, MD: Lippincott Williams & Wilkins, 2006.

Strong, James. *The Exhaustive Concordance of the Bible*. New York: Abingdon Press, 1967.

Stephen, Sir Leslie. *Hours in a Library*. Cambridge, UK: Cambridge University Press, 2012.

Stevenson, Robert Louis. *Across the Plains and Other Memories*. McLean, VA: IndyPublish, 2002.

Studdert-Kennedy. *Christian Science and Organized Religion*. Los Gatos, CA: Farallon Press, 1931.

Student's Reference Dictionary (an abridged version of Noah Webster's American Dictionary of the English Language 1828). Macdoel, CA: Keystone Publishers, 1993.

Sullivan, Louis. W. and Ilana Suez Mittman. "The State of Diversity in the Health Professions a Century after Flexner." *Academic Medicine,* 85 (2) 246-253, February 2010. DOI:1o.1097/ACM.ob013E3181C88145, PMID: 20107349.

Swan, Carolyn B. "Radical Reliance and the Church Member," *Christian Science Sentinel*. April 11, 1983.

Sweet, Bill. *A Journey into Prayer*. Bloomington, IN: XLibris, 2007.

Swensen, Rolf. *Pilgrims at the Golden Gate: Christian Scientists on the Pacific Coast, 1880-1915. Pacific Historical Review*, Vol. 72 No. 2. Berkeley, CA: University of California Press, May 2003.

Thom, Helen Hopkins. *Johns Hopkins: A Silhouette*. Baltimore: The Johns Hopkins Press, 1929.

Thomas, Dr. Lewis. *The Youngest Science*. New York: Penguin Books, 1995.

Thomas, Dr. Lewis. "The Uncertainty of Science." *The Key Reporte*r 6:1. Phi Beta Kappa address delivered at Harvard University, 1980. http://www.keyreporter.org/PbkNews/EditorsCut/ Washington, D.C.: Phi Beta Kappa Society, 1980.

Tippett, Krista. *Becoming Wise, an Inquiry into the Mystery and Art of Living*. New York: Penguin, 2017.

Tolle, Eckhart. *A New Earth*. London: Plume, 2006.

Tomlinson, Irving. "A Brief Account." *Christian Science Sentinel*. Boston: Christian Science Publishing Society, Feb. 5, 1903.

Trenchard, Warren C. *Ben Sira's View of Women*. Brown Judaic Studies, No. 38. Chico, CA: Scholars Press, 1982.

Turner, John G. "Why Race Is Still a Problem for Mormons." *New York Times*. New York City: New York Times Company. August 18, 2012.

Turner, Dr. Kelly A. *Radical Remission: Surviving Cancer against All Odds*. New York: HarperCollins, 2015.

Tutt, John M. "A Recompense of Profit." *Christian Science Journal*. Boston: Christian Science Publishing Society. Dec., 1960.

Tuttle, Robert W. "Faith Healing and the Law." Pew Research Center Forum. Washington, D.C.: Pew Research Center, August 31, 2009.

"Vaccination: What did Eddy say?" Mary Baker Eddy Library 12-20-2020.

Verhoeven, Paul. *Jesus of Nazareth*. New York: Seven Stories Press, 2010.

Vitello, Paul. "Christian Science Church Seeks Truce with Modern Medicine." *New York Times*. 3-23-2010.

Von Fettweis, Yvonne and Robert Townsend Warneck. *Mary Baker Eddy: Christian Healer, Amplified Edition*. Boston: The Christian Science Publishing Society, 2009.

Wallis, Lucy. "How to Live Beyond 100." BBC News, July 2, 2012.

Wan, William. "'Spiritual health care' raises church-state concerns." *Washington Post*, 11-23-2009.

We Knew Mary Baker Eddy: Expanded Edition. Boston: Christian Science Publishing Society, 2011.

Welch, H. Gilbert. "Diagnosis as Disease." *Los Angeles Times*, May 6, 2011. Los Angeles: Soon-Shiong, Dr. Patrick, 2011.

Weygandt, Minnie. Extracts from *Reminiscences of Minnie Weygandt*. Boston: Mary Baker Eddy Library.

Whitehead, John. *The Life of Rev. John Wesley*. London: Stephen Couchman, 1793, p. 529.

Widmer, Ted. "Lincoln and the Mormons." *New York Times*. New York City: The New York Times Company, 2011.

Williams, Peter. *America's Religions: From Their Origins to the Twenty-first Century*. Champaign, IL: University of Illinois Press, 2008.

Wilson, Bryan. *The Social Dimensions of Sectarianism*. New York City: Oxford University Press, 1990.

Wilson, Bryan. *Religious Sects*. New York City: McGraw-Hill, 1970.

Willson, Meredith. *The Music Man*.

Wise, Michael, Martin Abegg, Jr., and Edward Cook. *The Dead Sea Scrolls: A New Translation*. New York: HarperCollins Publishers, 1996.

Wolfe, Linden. *Captivated by Christ*. Maitland, FL: Xulon Press, 2008.

Yaconelli, Michael. *Messy Spirituality: God's Annoying Love for Imperfect People*. Grand Rapids, MI: Zondervan, 2002.

Yeats, W. B. *The Collected Poems of W. B. Yeats*. London: Bibliophile Books, 1994.

Index

A Note from the Author: Due to space considerations, this index is not comprehensive. It should function well together with the Table of Contents in locating topics and names with the exception of very significant names, topics, and books of the Bible that are repeated so frequently in the text as to make their listing here unwieldy for the reader. (See page 528 for the omissions.)

A

Adams, Dr. Patch 237
Adams, John 167
Adler, Mortimer 243
Adventure Unlimited 226
Affordable Care Act 388, 396, 416, 502
Amish 92, 259, 515
Analgesic 353
Anderson, Dr. Otto 445
"Anecdotal" testimonies 408
Animal magnetism 109, 257
Anti-Bigamy Act of 1862 319
"Anti-vaxxers" 315
Antonio de Dominis, Marco 91
Approximation 435, 503
Aquinas, St. Thomas 196
Aratus, Greek poet 247
Arbogast, Winifred 99
Armstrong, Mary 24
Arnica 25
Aspirin 17
Associational linkage 455
Augustine (of Hippo) 44, 91
Autopsies 402, 475

B

Babylonian captivity 280, 319, 344, 357, 358
Baha'is 103, 260
Baker, Anna White 24
Baker, Heidi 189
Baptists 259
Barnes, Rev. Jan 135, 223
Barton, Clara 469
"Basic kosher" 89
Bates, Isabel 43
Bell, Rev. Rob 237
Benevolence 167, 344
Bereans 470
Bezos, Jeff 489, 514
Billboards 65
Blame and guilt 161
Board of Directors 72, 92, 93, 94, 95, 201, 204, 296, 305, 399, 401, 409, 432
Board of Trustees 27, 69, 93, 94, 95
"Both-and" Christianity 144
Bowling Alone 116
Braden, Charles 401, 491
Brand/branding 27, 91, 249
Brands 257

Bravado 49, 53
Buckley, William F. Jr. 233, 368
Buddha 245
Buddhists 260
Burden of the Lord 61, 62
Burke, Edmund 344
Burnham, Daniel 495
Buswell, Arthur 445
Buswell, Ezra 195

C

Cahill, Thomas 191, 266
Camel 27
Campolo, Rev. Tony 185
Cancers 242
Candles Behind the Wall 240
Carlyle, Thomas 210, 245, 512
Carpenter, Gilbert, Jr. 29, 159
Carter, Stephen 316
Catholics 92, 101, 259, 262, 490, 498
Caution 36, 60, 62, 70, 119, 136, 356, 368, 369, 400, 507
Channing, Carol 350
Channing, George 350, 351, 352
Chemotherapy 255
Children's cases 323
Christian affection 141
Christian Science associations 123, 337
Churchill, Sir Winston 53, 237, 502, 512
Church mission 125
Clarke, Joseph 512
Codman, Dr. Ernest 402
Cognitive dissonance 295, 479, 480
Columbanus 191
Committee on General Welfare 409
Compassion for the bereaved 177
Compromise 68, 70, 89, 95, 273, 287, 294, 319, 344, 345, 346, 351, 352, 353, 354, 363, 374, 378, 381, 443, 473
Condescension 289
Confessionals 498
Confirmation bias 480

Consent 322
Consistency 43, 45, 326, 352, 390, 504
Contagion of fear 168
Context 6, 40, 44, 45, 49, 54, 58, 59, 68, 98, 112, 114, 118, 166, 167, 216, 271, 277, 349, 350, 358, 359, 390, 436, 437, 484
Contextomy 44
Copyright 255
Corey, Arthur 57, 401
Cousins, Norman 237, 431, 437, 516
Cox, Harvey 404
Crisis Magazine 201, 512
Crosby, Fanny 161
Cross 66, 76, 169, 194, 199, 217, 249, 272, 294, 356, 393, 407, 442, 453, 455
Croton oil 375
Cult 158, 182
Culture 18, 34, 35, 56, 117, 118, 119, 158, 201, 205, 234, 256, 268, 280, 284, 351, 366, 430, 453, 465, 466, 479, 493, 498
Curiosity 163, 247, 248, 395
Cushing, Dr. Alvin 25
Cyprian of Carthage 90

D

Dakin, Edwin 295
Davis, Daryl 99
Davy, Humphrey 23, 282
Dead Sea Scrolls 269, 519
Death-rates 163
DeGeneres, Ellen 172, 173, 517
Democratic Republic of Congo 197
Departures from Christian Science 29, 71
DeSmet, South Dakota 487
DeVita, Dr. Vince 237
DeWitt, John 141
Dickey, Adam 30, 51, 128, 434
Didion, Joan 503, 513
Dispensationalism 285

Divorce 209, 210
Doctors Without Borders 238
Dogged denial 43
Dogma 33, 34, 58, 158
Doorly, John 101
Dossey, Dr. Larry 238, 447, 451
Drummond, Henry 117, 120, 238, 472
Dummelow, J. R. 253
"Duty to patients" 432
Dying To Be Me 239, 280

E

Ecological validity 467
Edison, Thomas 475, 491
Einstein, Albert 119
Eisenhower, Dwight 246
Elijah 60, 85, 126, 127, 148, 169, 180, 221, 233, 252, 256, 269, 301, 456, 481
Elisha 180, 221, 233, 234, 252, 332
Emerson, Brian 21
EMTs 37
Entropy 458, 490, 492
Epigones 51
Episcopalians 259
Eustace, Herbert 27, 69
Eutychus 124, 219, 230, 231
Ewing, William 292, 508
Exemptions 299, 308, 310, 311, 312, 315, 316, 317, 318, 319, 323, 327, 361
Exercise 115, 174, 189, 210, 285, 319, 347, 362, 384, 460, 480

F

Fail-safe measures 348
Faith without follow-through 190
Falling apple 25
Fambul Tok 238
Fanaticism 50
Faraday, Michael 465
Farlow, Alfred 291
Farmer, Dr. Paul 239, 411
Figs 319, 357, 366
Fig tree 253, 456

Fleming, Alexander 331
Flexner, Abraham 391, 393
Flexner Report 391, 392, 393, 410, 518
"Floral demonstrations" 457, 460
Fluctuation 283
Fluctuations 51, 282, 451, 484
Follow-through 109, 110, 111, 112, 190, 414
Food 118, 123, 137, 144, 146, 197, 220, 289, 381, 389
Forbid 71, 167, 194, 313
Forbidden 56, 59, 304, 350
Fox, Robin Lane 164, 238
Francona, Terry 63
Franklin, Benjamin 80
Frantic affirmation 42
Fraser, Caroline 295, 332
Frye, Calvin 290, 507
Fundamentalism 9

G

Gamaliel 84, 85, 214, 221, 234
German Autobahn 246
Gibbon, Edward 125, 238, 478, 516
Gilbert, Allison 176
Gladden, Washington 114
Gladwell, Malcolm 114
Golden Rule 35, 36, 38, 55, 97, 165, 175
"Gold standard" 22
Good Samaritan 110, 141, 144, 338, 372
Gottschalk, Stephen 294, 352
Grace 21, 191, 240, 273, 361
Graham, Rev. Billy 122, 223
Grant, Ulysses 49
"Great Litigation" 93, 95
Gromeier, Dr. Matthias 242

H

Habitat for Humanity 143, 228
Halberstam, David 175
Harford, Tim 468, 469

Harris, David 222
Harvey, Paul i
Health Wagon 238
Henniker-Heaton, Peter 45, 470
Hippocratic Oath 14, 405
Hiscock, Dr. Maybelle 339
Hobson, Harold 77, 340
Holland, Rev. Henry Scott 180
Homestead 487, 488
Hope Ships 239
Hopkins, Johns 241, 391, 515, 518
Hospital chaplains 385
Hubbell, Jack 222
Humor 99, 182, 212, 222, 431

I
"Iceman" 133, 134
Ilibaghiza, Immaculee 239
Immaculate conception 92
Incremental changes 34, 39, 62, 115, 132, 297, 306, 313, 327, 430, 431, 463, 491, 492, 493, 495
Inductive reasoning 245
Ingwerson, Lona 476
Innocent IV, Pope 196
Inquisition 44, 284
Intermediate steps 30
Intolerance 27, 222
Inverted 215, 216
Irenaeus 478, 479
Irish 191, 200, 266, 344, 512
Ironic process theory 54

J
James, William 449, 459, 460, 471
Janes, Loren 48, 49
Jehovah jireh 32, 265, 273, 300
Jehovah's Witnesses 108, 206, 223, 513
Jensen, Daniel 99, 221, 222
Jesting self-defense 212
Jews 126, 153, 206, 213, 214, 246, 249, 259, 260, 262, 280, 319, 324, 344, 356, 357, 456, 465, 470

"Jim Crow" laws 201
John the Baptist 85, 258
Joseph of Arimathea 195
Joseph (of Cupertino) 283
Journey into Prayer 450, 451, 518
Jubilee year 103
"Just-world phenomenon" 156

K
Keeler, Wee Willie 385
Keillor, Garrison 129
Keith, Cathryn 333, 335, 336, 339, 341, 342
Kidder, Tracy 239
Kimball, Edward 87
King, Larry 300, 515
King, Martin Luther Jr. 160, 190, 207, 221, 285, 394, 515
Kinter, George 46, 69
Kissinger, Henry 98
Klingbeil, Bruce and John 449, 451, 468
Knapp, Bliss 101, 353, 515
Ku Klux Klan 40, 96, 99, 201, 514
Kushner, Rabbi Harold 162

L
Laboratory 450, 455, 458, 462, 464
Lacks, Henrietta 391
Lamott, Anne 147, 239, 262
Langer, Ellen 430
Lanza, Dr. Robert 239
Laodicea 189
Lathrop, John 288, 289, 290, 507, 510
Lathrop, Laura 290, 500, 507
"Law unto themselves." 324
Left to Tell 239
Lerner, Melvin 156
Lewis, C.S. 109
"License" practitioners 396
Licensure 396
Lincoln, Abraham 97, 102, 213, 321, 514

INDEX

Lipton, Dr. Bruce 239
Listening sessions 101
Lithuania 279
Logic 30, 38, 44, 48, 167, 243, 244, 245, 470
Longevity 163, 164, 165
Longyear, Mary 198, 399
Lutherans 259
Luther, Martin 160, 190, 207, 221, 285, 394, 515
Lydiard, Robert 222
Lyons, Dr. Ernest 458

M

Magnanimity 502
Maine legislature 299, 413
Manji, Irshad 491
Marshall, Rev. Peter 481
Massachusetts legislature 323
Mastemah 269
Matters, Margaret Glenn 12
Matthew 19:12 208, 209, 210
"Matthew code" 98
Mayo Clinic 241, 431
Mayo, Dr. Charles 241
Mayo, Dr. William 241
McClellan, Archibald 136, 291, 507, 508
McGonigal, Kelly 239
McKenzie, Daisette 356
McKenzie, William 207, 356, 401
McKinley, William 164, 171, 379
McKown case 400
Medical entanglement 18
Memorial services 164, 175, 178, 179, 180, 233
Mennonites 259
Mental self-knowledge 420
Mentoring 124
Methodists 259
Milmine, Georgine 295
Mission Year 227, 229, 230
"Mixing" 61, 338, 367, 369, 372, 374, 376, 381, 382

Moorjani, Anita 239, 280, 482
Mormons 88, 97, 98, 122, 166, 200, 207, 223, 224, 228, 259, 319, 320, 321, 322, 324, 514, 519
Morphine 8, 14, 25, 46, 159, 160, 304, 313, 351, 352, 353, 367, 432, 445
Morrill, Dr. Ezekiel 46
Mortality and Morbidity 402, 403
Mount Moriah 265, 266, 270, 271, 272
Moyers, Bill 389, 390
Music 179, 228, 398, 496
Mustard seed 178, 245, 317, 481, 482

N

"Naming" disease 434
National Leadership Council 226
NDEs 168, 239
Newman, Emma 99
Niebuhr, Reinhold 50, 114
Nightingale, Florence 150, 260, 516
Nocebo effect 386, 430, 431, 437
Numbers 73, 126, 182, 279, 291, 331, 382, 393, 401, 428, 472
Nurses 8, 15, 60, 66, 96, 117, 170, 199, 228, 238, 240, 255, 299, 306, 335, 336, 340, 341, 362, 378, 379, 380, 398, 399, 400, 403, 412, 414, 415, 416, 499

O

Obtrusive Mental Healing 36
Ogg, David and Mary 479
Oliver, Mary 181
"On the Lapsed" 90
Overtreated 80, 430, 512

P

"Pagan court" 94
Palchinsky, Peter 468
Palchinsky principles 468
Palliative 354, 355
Parables 251, 346, 465
Partiality 86, 87
Partisanship 251
Peel, Robert 76, 277, 294, 322, 404,

462, 476
Peer review 402, 408, 410
Pentecostals 259
Perfectionism 67
Peterson, Eugene 160, 162, 325
Pew Foundation 256
Pilate, Pontius 311, 322, 324
Placebo effect 16, 240, 407
"Plowing around" 97, 101
Polygamy 97, 292, 308, 319, 320, 321, 322, 324
Poole, Rev. William H. 460
Powell, Lyman 294
Practitioner fees 415
Pradervand, Pierre 240
"Prayer in Church" 34
Prayer research 447, 448, 451, 452, 453, 466, 470, 471
Premature death 168
Primitive Christianity 117, 118
Principle of consultation 103
Public apology 62
Putnam, Robert 116

Q

Quakers 88, 259
Quantum physics 361
Quinby, Esther 288, 291, 507

R

Racial segregation 200
Radical reliance 13, 39, 42, 43, 45, 49, 50, 55, 57, 60, 62, 112
Rankin, Dr. Lissa 240
Reader's Digest 85, 86
Reading Rooms 137
Reconciled 84, 502
Relation of prayer and medicine 8
Religions in America 28, 72, 73, 304, 314
"Reminiscence bump" 223
"Repaid Pages" 70
Resurgence 1, 308, 497
Reynolds, George 319

Reynolds v. United States (1879) 319
Riley, Gregory 252
Rogers, Will 99, 487, 517
Root cause analysis 389, 410
"Roseto effect" 114
Rotation in office 87, 103, 246
Rugged individualism 111, 142
Runner's wall 482

S

Sabbath violations 372
Safety net 398
Sagan, Dr. Leonard 166, 237, 240
Santayana, George 50
Schrader, Dr. Harald 279
Screwtape Letters 109
Sears, Dr. Bill 335
Secrecy 142
Seeley, Paul S. 220
Self-critical 411
Self-diagnosis 439
Self-healing 3, 120, 421
Self-knowledge 52
Self-limiting conditions 3
Self-regulation 388, 395, 401, 403, 404, 405, 410, 412, 416
Seymour, Winifred 222
Shenn, Florence Scovel 485
Shepherding 229, 303, 305, 306
Shideler, Byron 222
Showing up 4, 145
Shublak, David 20
Shublak, Linda 20
Sinek, Simon 305
Sirach, Book of 366
Skillful surgeons 399
Slippery slopes 27
"Slip-slide away" 355
Smith, Joseph F. 321
Spanish Flu 95, 96
Spindrift Research 450
Spiritual intimacy 130
Spock, Dr. Benjamin 335
Spontaneous remission 37, 424

Stark, Rodney 117, 331
Stephen, Apostle 52, 278
STEP study 467, 468, 469
Stetson, Augusta 92, 99
Stevenson, Robert Louis 83
Strict and Particular Baptist Church 88
Study of the Therapeutic Effects of Intercessory Prayer 466
Suicides 453
Sullenberger, Capt. Chesley 388
Summer camps 226
Swank, Robert 29
Swan, Rita and Doug 329
Sweet, Bill 451, 463, 516
Swensen, Rolf 195
Systematic uncertainty 373, 377

T

Talbert, Sara 219, 220
Tale of two churches 187
Thomas, disciple of Jesus 3, 4, 79, 114, 191, 196, 210, 235, 236, 245, 266, 292, 346, 419, 424, 438, 441, 442, 445, 449, 450, 475, 491, 512, 514, 517, 518
Thomas, Dr. Lewis 114, 235, 424, 438
Tippett, Krista 247
Tolle, Eckhart 240, 256
Tomato field 464
Treatment Trap 80, 430, 514
Triticale 472
Tutt, Dr. John 373
Twain, Mark 54, 281, 489
Tyndale, William 505

U

"Understanding" 261

V

Vaccination 286, 312, 313, 314, 316, 318, 322, 354, 442
Van Buren, Abigail 167, 335
Veterans in hospitals 381

Village, responsibility of 302
Voltaire 67, 282
Von der Heydt, Barbara 240
Vox populi 322

W

Warren, Rick 223
Welch, Dr. Gilbert 430
Welz, Carl J. 208
Wheatley, Margaret 240
Whiplash 279, 280
Whitcomb, Noyes 170
White, Anna 24
White Plains case 288, 291, 293, 294, 295, 296, 297, 508, 510
Wilbur, Sibyl 294
Wilde, Oscar 473
Williams, Peter 59
Wilson, Prof. Bryan 105
Wolf, Dr. Stewart 115
Woodbury, Josephine 92
Woodruff, Wilford 320

Y

Yancey, Philip 240
Yeats, W. B. 503, 519
Young, Bicknell 200, 497
Yun, Brother 237

Z

Zacchaeus 195
Zeus 247

Names and Topics not included:
Jesus Christ
Apostle Paul
Isaiah
Jeremiah
Psalms
Matthew
Mark
Luke
John
Mary Baker Eddy
Christian Science
Healing
Medicine
Surgery
Community
Diagnosis

About the Author and Illustrator

George Wadleigh has worked as a Christian Science practitioner for over forty years. He graduated from Stanford University in 1974 with a degree in journalism, and a minor in religious studies. After college he served as a VISTA volunteer running a youth center in southern Illinois, and then taught middle school in Alton, Illinois, prior to entering the ministry of his church. He has served for over fifteen years as a volunteer chaplain in mental health centers in Alton and Chicago, and has been active in ministerial alliances since 1980. George and his wife Bonniesue have three grown children and currently live in Lake Villa, Illinois.

GeorgeWadleigh@TheRamInAThicket.com
www.TheRamInAThicket.com

Anne Farley Gaines produced the illustration used on the cover and throughout this book. She worked with many challenging suggestions from the author until arriving at the expression on the ram's face. She envisioned the illustration as an ancient ceramic shard of terra cotta clay, perhaps originally part of a vessel on which the ram in Genesis 22 could have been depicted. A 6"x 6" stoneware tile was used as the figure's substrate. Anne's husband, sculptor Geoffrey Novelli, cut out the shape that Anne had drawn on the tile. He used a ring saw so that it appeared like a graceful piece of broken clay. The ram, the background and frontal area of brambles and dry, dusty earth were painted in terra cotta ceramic glaze using very small brushes. Then the shard was fired in a ceramic kiln. Afterwards, Anne intensified the terra cotta effect with acrylic paint of similar brownish-red and orange hues.

The illustrator holds a BA in Studio Art from Principia College, Elsah, IL and an MFA in Painting from Bowling Green State University. Anne is a painter, ceramist, and muralist. She has incorporated ceramic plaques into recent large collaborative works she has designed for Wichita Falls, TX, Carol Stream, IL, and Chicago, her home city.